AF501630

Accustomed to Her Face

ALSO BY AXEL NISSEN

Actresses of a Certain Character:
Forty Familiar Hollywood Faces from the Thirties to the Fifties
(McFarland, 2006; paperback 2011)

Mothers, Mammies and Old Maids:
Twenty-Five Character Actresses of Golden Age Hollywood
(McFarland, 2012)

Accustomed to Her Face

Thirty-Five Character Actresses of Golden Age Hollywood

Axel Nissen

McFarland & Company, Inc., Publishers
Jefferson, North Carolina

Library of Congress Cataloguing-in-Publication Data

Names: Nissen, Axel, author.
Title: Accustomed to her face : thirty-five character actresses
of golden age Hollywood / Axel Nissen.
Description: Jefferson, North Carolina : McFarland & Company, Inc.,
Publishers, 2016 | Includes bibliographical references and index.
Identifiers: LCCN 2016031816 | ISBN 9780786497324
(softcover : acid free paper) ♾
Subjects: LCSH: Motion picture actors and actresses—
California—Los Angeles—Biography. | Actresses—
California—Los Angeles—Biography. | Character actors and actresses—
California—Los Angeles—Biography.
Classification: LCC PN1998.2 .N56 2016 | DDC 791.4302/80922 [B]—dc23
LC record available at https://lccn.loc.gov/2016031816

British Library cataloguing data are available

ISBN (print) 978-0-7864-9732-4
ISBN (ebook) 978-1-4766-2606-2

© 2016 Axel Nissen. All rights reserved

No part of this book may be reproduced or transmitted in any form or by any means, electronic or mechanical, including photocopying or recording, or by any information storage and retrieval system, without permission in writing from the publisher.

Front cover: Ona Munson in *Gone with the Wind*

Manufactured in the United States of America

McFarland & Company, Inc., Publishers
Box 611, Jefferson, North Carolina 28640
www.mcfarlandpub.com

To Miss, Viola, Elzio and Ynde,
and in memory of Minx and Mango

Table of Contents

Introduction

I was a late bloomer as an old movie buff. I can't lay claim to having forged my identity as a gay man on an early diet of Bette Davis and Joan Crawford pictures. I have no memories of being allowed to stay up to watch late night movies with my parents, though classic TV drama series like *I, Claudius* and *The Duchess of Duke Street* on PBS were certainly a formative experience and are fondly remembered. The only classic Hollywood film I can recall having seen before I was in my mid–30s was *Gone with the Wind*. Even today, I've hardly seen any pre–1970s Hollywood films on the big screen.

It was rather unexpected, then, even to myself, that I would end up writing three books devoted to Hollywood character actresses and ultimately chronicle the lives and careers of no less than 100 of them. How did it all begin? Well, there is a simple answer to that: in 2003, I discovered Turner Classic Movies. The channel was part of my cable TV package here in Oslo. Without it I would never have become a film historian. I went on to amass what was probably the largest private collection of videos of old Hollywood films in Norway. I spent thousands of dollars on films in a format that was fast becoming obsolete. I have no regrets.

One of my fondest memories from my early days as a movie buff was watching the video of *Night After Night* starring George Raft and Constance Cummings, but better known as Mae West's Hollywood debut. Rather than focusing on West, though, I found myself being mesmerized by the antics of that gorgeous old wreck Alison Skipworth. It was Skipworth who first sparked my interest in studying and documenting the contributions of older actresses to the American film industry. She is still one of my all-time favorites.

Even though the character women of Hollywood played no role in my childhood, there was one older woman who did. As I write these words, it is 25 years since my maternal grandmother Ingrid Schjelderup Bernt Glad passed away and I suffered my greatest personal loss to date. My grandmother was a vibrant, intelligent, learned, and loving woman, who raised five children who all became foreign language majors like herself. She introduced me to the world of art and literature and set me off down a path that would lead to a fulfilling career as a literature professor, though she would not live to see it. I can see now that she also fueled my interest in the lives and experiences of older women, an interest that indirectly has led to my work on older actresses in film.

In the years after my grandmother's death from cancer in 1990, I tried to write about her, but failed to find a form that might make my private memories available and relevant to a larger audience outside my family. In writing about these 100 screen character actresses, though, some of them her contemporaries, it seems to me I have written about my grandmother after all.

I would like to remind readers who may be perplexed by the selection of names in this volume and miss many of their favorites that I have published two previous collections of profiles of Hollywood character actresses. *Actresses of a Certain Character: Forty Familiar Hollywood Faces from the Thirties to the Fifties* was published in hardback by McFarland in 2006, followed by a paperback edition in 2011, and contained articles on Sara Allgood, Judith Anderson, Fay Bainter, Ethel Barrymore, Florence Bates, Louise Beavers, Mary Boland, Beulah Bondi, Alice Brady, Billie Burke, Spring Byington, Gladys Cooper, Laura Hope Crews, Jane Darwell, Mildred Dunnock, Gladys George, Elsa Lanchester, Jessie Royce Landis, Hattie McDaniel, Butterfly McQueen, Marjorie Main, Agnes Moorehead, Mildred Natwick, Una O'Connor, Edna May Oliver, Maria Ouspenskaya, Lee Patrick, Elizabeth Patterson, Alice Pearce, Jessie Ralph, Anne Revere, Elisabeth Risdon, Thelma Ritter, Flora Robson, May Robson, Alison Skipworth, Gale Sondergaard, Lucile Watson, May Whitty, and Cora Witherspoon. This first book was followed in 2012 by *Mothers, Mammies and Old Maids: Twenty-Five Character Actresses of Golden Age Hollywood*, also published by McFarland, in which I profiled Clara Blandick, Helen Broderick, Constance Collier, Jane Cowl, Henrietta Crosman, Cecil Cunningham, Esther Dale, Marie Dressler, Isobel Elsom, Hope Emerson, Mary Forbes, Marjorie Gateson, Louise Closser Hale, Esther Howard, Josephine Hull, Patsy Kelly, Alma Kruger, Aline MacMahon, Beryl Mercer, Juanita Moore, Marjorie Rambeau, Evelyn Varden, Queenie Vassar, Ethel Waters, and Helen Westley.

Accustomed to Her Face retains the alphabetical structure of the two first volumes, making it possible to dip into the book or read it straight through. As in the former books, too, each actress's profile is meant to be a "partial portrait" in which I attempt to capture the essence of the subject's on-screen persona, unique talents, and popular appeal. But the present study needed its own individual identity as a book, separate from *Actresses of a Certain Character* and *Mothers, Mammies and Old Maids*. While clearly a complementary volume, it differs from its predecessors (beyond dealing with a new selection of players) by treating more in depth the lives and loves of the actresses in question. In most cases, I have done extensive genealogical research, particularly using the U.S. census, to find out about the actress's family background and her own domestic life.

The librarians of the Billy Rose Theatre Division of the New York Public Library for the Performing Arts helped me access their multifarious and fascinating clipping files. I enjoyed my e-mail discussions with Gail Powers about Grace George's family background. I would like to thank Angeline Ferris for sharing memories of her paternal grandfather Walter Ferris and family documents relating to his life and that of his second wife, Violet Kemble-Cooper. My thanks also go to Michael D. Sheehan, General Manager of the St. Michael Cemetery Corp., Boston, for promptly sending me photographs of Rafaela Ottiano's grave. I've dedicated this book to our "fur children," as Kaye Ballard calls them. Nothing is more important to my husband Storm and I than those felines.

What a Joy! Jessie Busley (1871–1950)

If you had happened to be walking down W. 10th St. in New York in the wee hours of Saturday, March 21, 1908, you would have been witness to a man of about 30, tall, of medium build with blue eyes and brown hair, standing outside no. 60, a fairly recent, seven-story, brick and stone apartment building, and yelling at the top of his not inconsiderable voice, "Oh, Jess!" repeatedly and with much variation of intonation and inflection. The man was able to gain admittance to the building without the cognizance of Arthur the elevator boy or Joe the telephone operator, where he continued his characteristic yelling, now accompanied by vigorous pounding on the door of an apartment on the seventh floor. While many of the neighbors were roused from their sleep, the much desired Jess never put in an appearance. The importunate young man was later forcibly ejected from the building, taken into custody by a patrolman, and locked up in the Mercer St. police station until his case could be heard by Magistrate Whale in the Jefferson Market Court.[1]

You will probably already have guessed that the "Jess" in question was our very own heroine, Jessie Busley. As for her not so gentlemanly caller, he was none other than her husband, Ernest C. Joy. Ernest and Jessie had met in the cast of Miss Busley's biggest hit to date, in fact the biggest personal success of her career, a long forgotten melodrama by Channing Pollock called *In the Bishop's Carriage* based on a novel by Miriam Michelson. It told the story of a "girl-thief's reformation," according to the *Washington Post*, and afforded "Jessie Busley an excellent opportunity to display her unquestionable ability" in the role of Nance Olden.[2] Nance "knows no other life than that of the criminal, and yet she is awakened to the abnormality of the life she is leading by sudden and unexpected contact with a gentleman."[3] The *San Antonio Light* remarked, "Not in many years probably has there been upon the stage a more pronounced instance of the actress fitting the part than is exemplified this season in the engagement of Jessie Busley in *In the Bishop's Carriage*."[4] Prophetic words, indeed, when we consider the events to follow.

Ernest Joy played a reporter, Harry Van Ness Star, in *In the Bishop's Carriage* and also acted as stage manager. He, too, was singled out for praise by the critic from the *Washington Post*, for giving only "the second portrayal of a newspaper man, not a caricature, that Washington has seen during the past ten years, or more." A relative newcomer to the acting field, Joy was said by another newspaper to have "created a sensation as the reporter."[5]

They had been on tour for a year, when the star and her supporting player decided to get hitched in Moorhead, Minnesota, on November 8, 1907, much to the surprise of the management

MISS JESSIE BUSLEY
AS NANCE OLDEN IN
"IN THE BISHOP'S CARRIAGE"
LIEBLER & CO., MANAGERS.

Jessie Busley, age 36 in 1907, when she met and married her second husband, fellow actor Ernest R. Joy, while starring in *In the Bishop's Carriage*. The marriage was an unmitigated disaster. Busley never tried matrimony again.

and the public.[6] Busley was 36 at the time of her second marriage. The groom was seven years younger, though he probably wasn't aware of the fact. Ernest C. Joy had been born in Mitchell County, Iowa, on January 20, 1878.[7] He started life in St. Ansgar, Iowa, and from about 1881 he and his family lived in Minneapolis, Minnesota. In 1900, the Joy family was living at 22 Oak St. in Minneapolis and Ernest was working as a day laborer.[8] He appears to have made his New York stage debut as a replacement in the role of a head waiter in the long-running Augustus Thomas comedy *The Earl of Pawtucket* at the Princess Theatre in September 1903 and also acted as stage manager.[9]

Everything was set, then, in 1907, for a fruitful partnership both on and off the stage between Busley and her new, handsome husband. Only it didn't quite work out that way. It was front page news on December 19, 1907, when Joy tried to kill Harry Elmer with a pistol at the stage door of the Forth Worth Opera house, "because he thought the 'press agent' was trying to alienate the affections of his wife of six weeks." Busley and Joy had played a one night stand in *In the Bishop's Carriage* at the opera house the preceding evening. Apparently, Elmer had been "a thorn continuously rankling in Joy's breast."[10]

Then in March 1908, with the *In the Bishop's Carriage* tour finally over, came the episode of Joy being locked out of his home in the Criterion apartment hotel at 60 W. 10th St. in New York. It will surprise no one that the marriage was over as well. Joy eventually managed to get himself back into the apartment and was apparently living alone when Busley showed up there with two men on July 31, 1908, ostensibly to remove her things. To Joy's evident surprise, Busley incited the men, who were strangers to her husband, to attack him and one of them beat him over the head with an iron bar wrapped in a newspaper. He suffered a dozen cuts on the head and face. When the police found him, Joy claimed that Busley had "tried to do the same thing some time ago." Joy was removed to St. Vincent's Hospital, close by in the West Village, ironically enough the same hospital where Jessie Busley would die 42 years later. Joy's physicians declared that, though he had suffered a severe beating, the injuries were not serious and he would be all right in a day or two. According to the injured party, his wife was "preparing to divorce him." Her husband also stated that Busley "had been preparing to sail for Europe and may have gone."[11] We do not have her side of the story.

Apparently, Joy did not press charges against his wife and her henchmen. The couple divorced in 1912. Busley wisely never married again. Joy married actress Mabel Brown Southard (aka Mabel Van Buren) in 1919 in Wayne County, Indiana, and the couple settled in Los Angeles, where they both worked as actors in films in a modest way.[12] Joy died of peritonitis on February 12, 1924, while his ex-wife was still living in retirement in Italy.[13] He was buried in the foyer of the Abbey of the Psalms in Hollywood Forever Cemetery in a crypt he may be sharing with Mabel Van Buren's third and last husband, actor James Gordon (1871–1941).[14]

John Parker often appears to take the actors' own word for their date of birth, which leads to many inaccuracies in his voluminous series of reference books *Who's Who in the Theatre*. Jessie Busley, though, is the only entry I have come across that Parker makes out to be *older* than she actually was. He writes that she was born in 1869,[15] whereas I am quite certain she was born in 1871. When an individual appears in the U.S. census as a child, long before any subterfuge about age is thought necessary, we usually get one reliable indicator of when they were actually born. The census doesn't give the exact date of birth, of course, only the person's age at their last birthday and sometimes, as in the case of the 1900 U.S. census, the month and year of birth. Again, in the case of Jessie Busley, even the census may not always be relied on when she herself is the informant. Thus in the 1900 U.S. census, she appears to have been born in March 1873.[16] The word "actress" under "occupation, trade, or profession" should alert us to the potential for unreliability. I have found Busley in the 1875 New York State census, though, enumerated on June 6, 1875, and it states that Jessie Busley is four years old. If we imagine then that the most frequently given birth date of March 10th is correct, we can be fairly certain that she was born on March 10, 1871.[17]

There is no question that Busley was born in Albany, New York. In 1875, then, we find her living in a $9,500 brick home with her father, James R. Busley (41), her mother, Sara Busley (38), no less than five siblings between the ages of one and a half and 14, and a servant.[18] Busley's father James was a boot and shoe manufacturer born in Monroe, New York, in January 1836 of parents who were both from New York. Sara Busley's maiden name was Shoemaker and she was born in Albany, New York, in June 1836 of parents from New York. We know from the 1900 census, that she gave birth to eight children. Six survived and all had left home by the turn of the last century. At this time, we find shoemaker James Busley and his wife Sara, both 64, living at 1683 Washington Ave. in the Bronx. According to the record, they have been married 40 years.[19] This dates their wedding to 1860 and fits quite neatly with the fact that their eldest child, Clarinda Busley, was born in about 1861.

Jessie Busley herself next shows up in public record in 1892, when she is 21 and still young enough to give her age accurately. On September 12th this year, Busley married fellow actor John McFedries in Boston, Massachusetts. The groom was 30, born in Ireland, and had been brought to the United States as a child by his parents James and Margaret McFedries. Both parties give New York as their place of residence.[20] From the fact that Jessie in the 1900 U.S. census gives her marital status as "single," we can assume that the Busley-McFedries union was not of long duration. John McFedries, who later changed his name to John M. Fedris, is referred to in two 1907 news articles as "long a member of Charles Frohman's business staff" and as "Jack Ferris [sic] the well-known manager."[21] In 1905, we find him in New York City, working as a "manager," and married to Alice Fedris.[22]

By the time of her first marriage, Busley had already made her stage debut. That took place in 1888 with Robert B. Mantell's company.[23] She "made her earliest success in New York," according to John Parker, as Mary Northcote in *The Bells of Haslemere* at the Windsor Theatre in December 1889.[24] In 1892, she began a long association with producer Charles Frohman.[25] Under his aegis, she made her New York debut as the ingénue Ada Delahay in the original production of Brandon Thomas's famous farce *Charley's Aunt* at the Standard Theatre, a part she described years later as "wishy-washy."[26] Her follow-up show in New York, another farce called *The New Boy*, gave her more to chew on. The *New York Times*'s review is worth quoting for its description of Busley in what was described then as "the hit of her life": "Miss Jessie Busley ... made every moment of her presence on the stage enjoyable. Her pertness did not irritate, her forwardness [sic] was not offensive, and her childishness was not ridiculous—which is to say that she is the pearl of ingénues, able to teach all the rest of them how such a part should be played."[27] Busley was only five feet tall and once said she had become a comedienne due to her lack of stature.[28]

For the next 25 years, Busley worked steadily on Broadway and elsewhere in the popular and now long forgotten plays of the day. Every now and then we find a title we still recognize among her many credits: Clyde Fitch's hit play *The Girl with the Green Eyes* in 1903; the original production of *Pollyanna* with Patricia Collinge in the title role in 1916, where Busley played the "Irish serving maid" Nancy[29]; and Shakespeare, of course. Busley played Charmian in *Antony and Cleopatra* at the opening of the New Theatre in New York on November 8, 1909, and appeared in productions of *A Winter's Tale* and *Twelfth Night* at the same Shubert-operated theater in the teens.[30] Her last show in this phase of her career was the flop *A Young Man's Fancy* with Jeanne Eagels at the Playhouse Theatre in October 1919.[31] She was 48, a difficult age for an actress, and decided to retire. She bought a villa in Sorrento, Italy in the early 1920s and moved there permanently. She explained in an interview in 1935, "You couldn't want any nicer place to settle down for the rest of your life" than Sorrento. The trouble was that she simply couldn't settle down: "I kept counting the minutes till curtain time, and wondering what shows George Tyler and the Erlangers were doing. So I came back to America, and George Kelly wrote 'Daisy Mayme' for me after I went to the coast and played the mother in 'The Show-Off' out there."[32]

In Kelly's latest play, the fortyish and irrepressible Daisy Mayme Plunkett, who Brooks Atkinson described as "the maddeningly good-natured spinster from Harrisburg,"[33] is determined to introduce confirmed bachelor Cliff Mettinger (Carlton Brickert) to the joys of matrimony, despite the violent opposition of Cliff's married sisters Mrs. Olly Kipax (Josephine Hull) and Mrs. Laura Fenner (Alma Kruger). They and their two young daughters are used to benefiting from their bachelor brother and uncle's largesse and fear that if he marries, this source of income will dry up. *Daisy Mayme* opened at the Playhouse Theatre on October 25, 1926, and played 112 performances. Atkinson described it in his characteristic style as "a remorseless and unpleasant drama of the suburbs and middle-class life, brittle, searching and drab."[34] I don't think he liked it.

With *Daisy Mayme*, a new and productive phase of Busley's stage career began, which was only interrupted by the few years in the late 1930s when she worked in films. She never starred again, but played a series of choice supporting roles in some of the biggest and brightest Broadway hits of the day. She had always wanted to be a character actress. As early as 1900, when she was a youthful 29 and was still playing girls on stage, Busley said: "I like character parts. I think the audiences like them, and character actors are generally in demand."[35] In demand, indeed. *Daisy Mayme* was followed by Dion Boucicault's *The Streets of New York* starring Dorothy Gish and Ibsen's *Pillars of Society* (both 1931). The opportunities got even better further on in the 1930s, with a series of hits starting with *Alien Corn* via *First Lady* and culminating with *The Women*.

In Sidney Howard's *Alien Corn* (no play was ever better named), Busley's role was modest, as a sympathetic professor's wife in a small Midwestern college town. Katharine Cornell starred as the temperamental but talented, expatriate German "pianiste," Elsa Brandt, who is being slowly worn down by the need to make a living and the materialism and lack of culture of quotidian American life. Playwright Howard had envisioned his Mrs. Skeats as being 40.[36] Busley was still youthful at 62. Charles Waldron played her husband, a pompous professor.

Katharine Dayton and George S. Kaufman's *First Lady*, a delicious satire on what a less politically correct age would have called "petticoat politics" in Washington, D.C., was eminently successful at the Music Box Theatre in 1935–36. Jane Cowl starred in one of her signature roles as Lucy Chase Wayne, the granddaughter of a president and the wife of the Secretary of State, while Jessie Busley played seasoned senator's wife Belle Hardwick, "an ample woman somewhere in her fifties," as the playwrights envisioned her and "an old

Washington warhorse minding her protocol and precedence" in her own description.[37] Belle has an explanatory function in the play and is just the kind of warm, matronly, outwardly sedate, yet quick-witted role Busley excelled at. Marjorie Rambeau played Mrs. Hardwick in the film version from 1937 and Kay Francis played Lucy Chase Wayne.

Clare Boothe's *The Women,* of course, is much better known today than *First Lady,* with its all-woman cast, jungle red nails slashing right and left both figuratively and literally, and a better known film version from MGM in 1939. Jessie Busley originated the central role of the somewhat naïve and overly idealistic heroine Mary Haines's worldly wise and pragmatic mother Mrs. Morehead on Broadway, but Lucile Watson got the plum film assignment. Outwardly the two women resembled each other somewhat, but Watson had more edge to her, inside and out. "Peppery" is a word often used to describe Watson, which you wouldn't use about Busley, however much pepper we've seen she could exude in her private life.

At any rate, *The Women* ran for 657 performances in its original production at the Ethel Barrymore Theatre. Busley did not stay till the end, as by the time the show closed in July 1938 she was in Hollywood and had already done *King of the Underworld* (L. Seiler, 1939) at Warner Bros. There she played "lady doctor" Kay Francis's naysaying Aunt Josephine, who goes with her to the Midwestern town Wayne Center, where Francis sets up practice and tries to prove to the medical board that she did not know her husband and fellow doctor was working for crime boss Humphrey Bogart. Bogart, who is the only star billed above the title (his first such billing),[38] plays the truly stupid gangster Joe Gurney, who has taken Napoleon as his idol and is seen reading *The Sayings and Doings of Napoleon.*

Busley had only the briefest of film careers during the years 1938–40, but she acted in at least one film that is worthy of the vast and varied talents she so ably demonstrated through more than six decades on the stage. *It All Came True* (L. Seiler, 1940) is one of the wonderful ensemble films from Warner Bros. that were more common in the early 1930s, but were still being made as the decade neared its end. Humphrey Bogart and Ann Sheridan are billed above the title, but this is truly a group effort with a plethora of talented supporting players doing what they do best. Here is Una O'Connor being fractious and folksy Irish, as only she could be. Here is Grant Mitchell being avuncular and the fussy male old maid only he could be (though he gets some competition from an equally queeny Brandon Tynan). Here is Zasu Pitts with both the anatomy and the attitude of the spinster and a lively imagination to boot. Here is an equally characteristic Felix Bressart as a played out magician, "The Great Boldoni," who suffers the indignity of being upstaged by his "stooge," the black poodle Fanto. Bogart is Bogart, of course, still stuck in his gangster mode, though not for much longer, and Sheridan is still the good bad girl and man's best friend. Jeffrey Lynn is here, too, doing his thing, whatever that was.

Based on a short story by Louis Bromfield published in *Cosmopolitan* in January 1936 called "And It All Came True," the film predates both the stage and cinematic versions of *Arsenic and Old Lace* (written in 1939) with which it has several things in common. According to one newspaper: "The story is a quaint mixture of a 'Gay Nineties' atmosphere in a modern setting; a theme that only Louis Bromfield could handle so realistically."[39] According to the reviewer for the *New York Times,* the film had "a number of conspicuous although strictly unclassifiable merits, both of a gangsterish and of a comical nature."[40] The plot hinges on the coincidence of the gangster Bogart is playing, Chips Maguire, having been involved both with Sheridan, who worked at his Little Paradise Club as a singer, and Jeffrey Lynn. When

You'd never guess from her meek and mild demeanor in the arms of her screen son Jeffrey Lynn (right) that Jessie Busley had been quite the femme fatale in her youth. Humphrey Bogart is subjected to her tender loving care in *It All Came True* (Warner Bros., 1940).

the film opens, Lynn is working as a pianist at the Cairo Club and tries to quit, but is implicated when Bogart shoots a police informer from his gang, Monks, with a gun registered in Lynn's name. In the wake of his inciting incident, Bogart blackmails Lynn into hiding him in his mother's boarding house, pretending he is "Mr. Grinelli" who is recovering from a nervous breakdown and wants to stay in his room and take all his meals there.

Busley plays one half of a female couple with Una O'Connor, with Busley being the mother of Lynn and O'Connor the mother of Sheridan. They are struggling to keep a boarding house they inherited from "Aunt Minnie" afloat (including paying $1,182.64 in back taxes) and are helped out when incognito gangster Bogart suggests they open a night club there called the "Roaring '90s." The film incorporates an entire "show within the show," including Sheridan singing to Lynn's accompaniment and a delightful number by a group of "real" little old ladies known as the "Elderbloom Chorus," that begins as a spiritual and ends with the old women dancing riotously in the then modern manner. The night club is a big success and the house is saved. Bogart finally goes to jail, allowing the lovers Lynn and Sheridan to marry and the world is saved for heterosexuality once again.

Busley said, no doubt tongue-in-cheek, in an interview in 1941: "I'm a lovely old lady in the movies—and they say the movies get your true character."[41] Busley has a rich, warm voice, which suits the warm, nurturing role she is playing to a "t." Her character, Nora Taylor, is given to making up stories about things and is an eternal optimist. She has lived for 40 years with her more realistic, hard-headed partner Maggie Ryan (O'Connor), who plays "bad cop" to her "good cop" and "downstairs" to her "upstairs." According to O'Connor: "You don't think, you imagine…"

Busley provides one of the emotional "through lines" of the film in her undying faith in the gangster's goodness and her gratitude for what he has done for her and the other residents by helping them save the boarding house. Her emotional thank you speech on the opening night of the new club, which ends in her kissing Bogart's hand, is supposedly what makes him decide to do the right thing and take the rap for Monks's murder, rather than pointing the finger at Lynn. According to the *New York Times,* Busley "by liberal application of maternal sentiment, causes the first cracks ever seen by man to appear in the volcanic crust of Bogart, a mugg who has an alibi, but declines to use it, in the name of decency, of sentiment, and of trusting motherhood."[42]

Busley is concerned that Bogart has never known a mother's love and becomes a foster mother to him, as a variation on the "gangsters and their mothers" theme prevalent in crime dramas from the beginning and epitomized by Beryl Mercer as Ma Powers in *The Public Enemy* (1931). Gangster mothers in this mold believe unfailingly in their sons' basic goodness, but are for the most part passive bystanders, powerless to intervene and alter the course of events, as their boys live by the sword and die by the sword. Busley's character does her redemptive work without even knowing it. Or does she? On some level, Busley must realize who she's dealing with, especially as she finds a heap of weapons in his suitcase early on in the film, but she never reveals any insight about the reality of their situation. Maybe Ma Taylor is a better "player" than Chips Maguire is….

Busley loved all the creatures comforts of movie-making compared to the rough, Spartan life of the stage.[43] For whatever reason, though, she returned to New York and her long-term home at 18 E. 60th St. after completing work on her fifth and final feature film, *Escape to Glory* (J. Brahm, Columbia, 1940), in September 1940.[44] Her only hit on Broadway in the 1940s was Ruth Gordon's *Over 21* (1944), which like *First Lady* was staged at the Music Box Theatre by George S. Kaufman.

Busley's last show on Broadway was a new comedy called *The Happiest Years,* which only lasted eight performances at the Lyceum Theatre in late April 1949. In July 1949, she gave what was probably her last performance in Rachel Crothers's comedy *Let Us Be Gay* at the Berkshire Playhouse in Stockbridge, Massachusetts, where she was reunited with Kay Francis.[45]

Jessie Busley died on Thursday, April 20, 1950, at St. Vincent's Hospital, which was located at 7th Ave. and 11th St. in the West Village and has now been converted into apartments.[46] After a funeral service in Walter B. Cooke Chapel at 117 W. 72nd St., she was buried in Kensico Cemetery.[47] Busley had said in an interview in 1900: "I believe that if a woman has brains and is willing to work hard she can accomplish anything, not only on the stage, but anywhere."[48] Then she went on to prove it.

Raising Caine: Georgia Caine (1876–1964)

I can actually remember the first time I noticed Georgia Caine in a film. She had a small, uncredited role as a guest in a birthday party scene in *Nora Prentiss* (V. Sherman, Warner Bros., 1947), starring Ann Sheridan. If you didn't know better, you might have mistaken her for Bess Flowers, "Queen of the Dress Extras." Only Caine had a little dialogue, I think, and Flowers seldom did. All I remember is that she looked distinguished and elegant with her thick, salt and pepper hair done up in a fancy chignon. Funny what one remembers.

Not every character actress can say she's done six pictures with Bette Davis. Even fewer can say in addition that they acted in eight Preston Sturges pictures. But how many of these films can you name without checking and what parts did Caine play in them? Got you stumped, haven't I?

Caine's parts in the six Bette Davis pictures between 1937 and 1944 were typical of the "low-key" casting she experienced in Hollywood. The first was the comedy *It's Love I'm After* (A. Mayo, Warner Bros., 1937), where she played Bonita Granville's mother and one of the weekend guests at Olivia de Havilland's home, when the matinee idol played by Leslie Howard comes down uninvited for the weekend to make de Havilland fall out of love with him. Caine's character was called Mrs. Kane ("My friends call me Sugar") and she was credited as Georgia *Craine*. In *Jezebel* (W. Wyler, Warner Bros., 1938), Caine appears six minutes into the film as Mrs. Petion, a Francophone guest at Davis's party, who speaks briefly with a newly arrived Spring Byington about their hostess being late to her own party and then reacts negatively to Davis not having changed out of her riding habit before greeting her guests. Caine only has a brief scene as a lady in waiting who brings a bowl of soup to Davis's increasingly crazy Empress Carlota in *Juarez* (W. Dieterle, Warner Bros., 1939), but was given screen credit. Her bits in *All This, and Heaven Too* (A. Litvak, Warner Bros., 1940), *The Great Lie* (E. Goulding, Warner Bros., 1941), and *Mr. Skeffington* (V. Sherman, Warner Bros., 1944) were uncredited.

The only Hollywood hotshot willing to give Caine a real chance was writer and director Preston Sturges. In the 1940s, she belonged to his informal stock company with other veteran actresses like Elizabeth Patterson and Esther Howard. In his autobiography, Sturges reflected on why he liked to use the same character actors again and again: "My bosses could never understand why I kept using practically the same small-salaried players in picture after picture. They said, 'Why don't you get some new faces?' I always replied that these little players who had contributed so much to my first hits had a moral right to work in my subsequent pictures."[1]

For Caine, it all started with *Remember the Night* (Paramount, 1940), where Sturges wrote the screenplay and Mitchell Leisen directed, followed by seven films where Sturges was both writer and director: *Christmas in July* (Paramount, 1940), *Hail the Conquering Hero* (Paramount, 1944), *The Miracle of Morgan's Creek* (Paramount, 1944), *The Great Moment* (Paramount, 1944), *The Sin of Harold Diddlebock* (California Pictures, 1947), *Unfaithfully Yours* (Twentieth Century–Fox, 1948), and *The Beautiful Blonde from Bashful Bend* (Twentieth Century–Fox, 1949), Sturges's final film, which was practically Caine's last film as well.

Caine does an impressive job as Barbara Stanwyck's forbidding and judgmental mother in *Remember the Night*. She has one powerful scene 45 minutes into the film, where she lambasts her daughter in Fred MacMurray's hearing, which decides him on taking Stanwyck to his family for Christmas. It turns out Stanwyck started on her life of crime by "borrowing" her mother's missionary money and her mother shamed her before the whole community. Dressed in black with her hair center-parted in a bun, Caine is almost unrecognizable, differing so much from her customary elegant dowager look in films. Her scene has especially effective use of lighting, as Caine comes to the door with a paraffin lamp in the otherwise dark and somber house. As Stanwyck and MacMurray stand before the house after she has shut the door on them, we see Caine first peering out the window and then passing to the back, as darkness again descends on the house.

Caine's big opportunity, though, came with her third film for Sturges. Comparatively speaking, *Hail the Conquering Hero* was her *Gone with the Wind*, her *The Grapes of Wrath*, and her *How Green Was My Valley* rolled into one. As Mrs. Truesmith, she is the root cause of all her anti-hero son's troubles. Woodrow Truesmith, in a classic performance by Eddie Bracken, is afraid to disappoint her by coming home on a medical discharge for hay fever after only a month in the marines, rather than being a war hero like his father, who was killed in World War I. He has been working in a factory for a year and pretending to be overseas. His fear of disappointing mom engenders the whole plot of imposture, where some marines he encounters in a bar in San Francisco engineer a hare-brained scheme whereby he can return home a decorated hero from Guadalcanal.

Though clearly a film about the war hero phenomenon and a satire of small town life, this is also a satire on "Momism." Bugsy (Freddie Steele), one of the marines, is an orphan, and mother-fixated to such an extent that Woodrow at one point in exasperation exclaims: "You and your mother complex!" To make things perfectly clear, the film opens with the song "Home to the Arms of Mother," written especially by Preston Sturges and performed by a blonde singer and a waiter quartet at the Dog Watch club, where Woodrow is drowning his sorrows in beer.

Caine has one good scene showing the marines the small shrine she has constructed in her husband's memory and another serving them pancakes for breakfast, but she is ever present from the moment Woodrow returns to his hometown until the finale at the train station, when Woodrow ends up staying to run for mayor and the marines going, their mission accomplished. In truth, Caine's part, however visible in one sense, consists mostly of being part of the background for her son, as she sends him loving looks and exclaims "Oh, my boy!" and the like.

Caine's role in *The Sin of Harold Diddlebock* was considerably more unconventional. In what is basically a walk-on, she appears 55 minutes into the film with a very full beard, as one of many circus employees, including a trained seal, presenting their new owner Harold

Diddlebock with their demands. "When someone asked how she could show her face in a beard, she replied that she would do *anything* Preston Sturges asked her to do."[2] She was quite a different actress then from the young woman who had captivated New York audiences with her dark, exotic beauty in the late 19th and early 20th century.

Considering that Georgia Caine is one of only two actresses in this volume who was a stage beauty in her younger years, it is surprising that she is also one of the few profiled here who never lied about her age. Her birth is well documented and took place on October 30, 1876, in San Francisco, California.[3] Like Laura Hope Crews, who was born in San Francisco three years later, Caine was born into a theatrical family, or, as she put it herself, she was "practically born on the stage": "My people were stage people and I was a stage child in every sense of the word. I was put to bed in a trunk in a dressing room, got lost in the scenery, and did all the things that stage children do."[4]

Caine's father was George Redfearn Caine and her mother Jane Darragh Caine. Her parents are described in an 1897 article as "an actor of the old school," who "went to California in the [Gold Rush] excitement of '49," and "a New York actress, long better known as a leading woman in Salt Lake City and the stock theaters of the west than in the east."[5] George R. Caine was born in 1846 in either Virginia or Wisconsin of parents born either in Virginia or, more likely, in England.[6] Jane Darragh Caine was born in New York on December 12, 1853, of parents born in Ireland and also grew up in Aurora, Illinois, as the eldest of the three children of an ironsmith.[7] In addition to her parents, little Georgiana Caine, as she was originally named, spent her earliest years living with maternal grandparents John H. Darragh (b. 1829) and Margaret McEvoy Darragh (b. c. 1822). In 1880, the extended Caine-Darragh family was living at 558 Bryant St. in San Francisco, an address which still exists "South of Market" between 3rd and 4th St., directly adjacent to Highway 80, but their home is long gone.[8]

We may learn something more about Caine's background from a feature article in the *Fort Wayne Sentinel*, which appeared when she was on a flying visit to Fort Wayne in September 1896, en route from New York to join her company in St. Louis. The not yet 20-year-old "brilliant and charming actress" was described as being accompanied by her husband, Charles Winters. Caine herself was "too fatigued from her journey to submit to a reporter's interview, but her husband, a pleasant gentleman, vouchsafed some information." Caine is described as having "within the past two years attained an enviable position in the comic opera," "inherits her histrionic talents from clever parents," and "made her debut as a child actress in San Francisco." Her parents did not want stage work to interfere with her education, though, so while attending school at Notre Dame, "she was only allowed to fill engagements during vacations." Caine joined the Denver stock company after graduating from Wolf Hall in the same city. She came east three years ago and got her big chance when, as understudy for Jennie Goldthwaite in *Lost, Strayed or Stolen* in Chicago, she had to take over the lead on short notice.[9]

Caine's marriage to Charles Winters appears to have been a brief, as I have found no public record of it beyond this news article. Six years after it appeared, Caine married again. Her second husband was a real estate broker 17 years her senior. Alphonzo Bell Hudson was born on December 5, 1859,[10] as the seventh child and fifth son among the 11 children of James D. Hudson (1818–84) and Mary Bell Hudson (1824–84). He was born and grew up in Greenfield, Ohio, a village right up in the northeast corner of Highland County with Cincinnati as the nearest major city.[11] Fast forward to 1900 and we find 40-year-old "A.B. Hudson," now a widower, living with his daughter Mary B. Hudson (b. 1882), his son Ernest R. Hudson (b. 1886), and a servant on Pine St. in Chicago, Illinois. The children are at school and Alphonzo Hudson is working as a broker.[12] From the 1930 U.S. census, we know he married for the first time at age 23, that is in 1882.[13] Caine was only six at the time and her and Alphonzo's marriage was more than 20 years in the future.

Georgia Caine and Alphonzo Bell Hudson married in about 1903, when she was 27 and he was 44. Despite the age difference, they were able to spend 30 years together. During most of the years of their marriage, the Hudsons made their home in Elmhurst, Long Island, in the New York borough of Queens. For many years, they lived at 101 Whitney Ave. In 1930, they are recorded as living in a $53,000 owned home at 40–57 Case St.[14] Judging from the fact that 101 Whitney Ave. no longer exists and that 40–57 Case St. is in the immediate vicinity, these two addresses may refer to the same property. Elmhurst, according to Wikipedia, was "an almost exclusively Jewish and Italian neighborhood" prior to World War II.[15]

It made no difference to her career that Caine married in 1903. Indeed, her major years on Broadway were still ahead. Naturally, she gained the economic security that followed with being married to a wealthy businessman, as was the case with other actresses in this volume, such as Ruth Donnelly, Minna Gombell, and Patricia Collinge. During the decade leading up to World War I, Caine was known as a "queen of Broadway musical comedy."[16] From 1899 till 1915, there was hardly a New York theatrical season without her gracing at least one show on the Great White Way.

It all started with *A Reign of Error*, which was the first show at Hammerstein's new Victoria Theatre on 42nd St. and 7th Ave. when it opened on March 2, 1899. The *New York Times* wrote, "Georgia Caine frisks, in her languid way of frisking, through its mazes."[17]

There was trouble in the air by the time she got to her sixth show on Broadway, though, when she had to leave the cast of *Peggy from Paris* at Wallack's Theatre in November 1901, "her voice gone, perhaps beyond recovery." *The New York Times* reported, "Every day the singer goes to one of the most eminent throat specialists in New York City": "It is said that the trouble with the vocal chords is almost incurable."[18]

It turned out the trouble was curable and Caine went on to star in numerous now long-forgotten musical comedies in the years that followed. *The Sho-Gun* (1904–05), "a Korean comic opera," was one of them: "Miss Georgia Caine, as the widow of the former Sho Gun, attractive to the American eye, though destined for the funeral pyre, is one of the best singers in the cast."[19] In 1905, when she was starring in one of her biggest hits, *The Earl and the Girl*, produced by Sam S. and Lee Shubert, she was described as "the prima donna of the organization," "one of the best known in her line in this country," and as "a remarkably beautiful girl, with an exceptionally good voice, and a clever actress."[20] Twenty-nine-year-old Caine played Elphin Haye, "a little school girl," and one of her numbers was the "delightful solo" "I Would Like to Marry You."[21] The show, which was the first at the Casino when it reopened after a devastating fire, was described as a "veritable frolic from start to finish, light, tuneful, and full of color, and engaging a company of exceptionally clever people."[22]

In the "musical farce" *The Rich Mr. Hoggenheimer*, "Georgia Caine, as Flora Fair, an actress, had some of the prettiest songs in the production and received many encores."[23] The press did not always sing her praises, though. In *Miss Hook of Holland* ("a Dutch musical incident in 2 acts"), "One of the best songs in the score, 'The Flying Dutchman,' went for little last night, for Miss Georgia Caine tried to do lyric embroidery all over it, with the result that the words got lost in her top notes, and the fun of the song went astray."[24] On August 31, 1908, Caine appeared as the sixth Sonia in the first two years of the original New York production of *The Merry Widow* at the New Amsterdam Theatre.[25] She also starred in the show in London in 1914.[26]

It was as she was gearing up for *Adele*, which opened at the Longacre Theatre on August 28, 1913, that she tried to dissuade young people from going into the acting profession. She pointed out in an interview, "Ninety out of every hundred who come to New York to go on the stage fail. Some go back home. A few stay in New York and find some other work. There are many who go—into the maelstrom."[27] And we all know what that means.... In December 1913, she was advising "the women of America" to design their own clothes: "Parisian fashions are all right—for Parisians!" Caine added that she was "strong for American designs and fashions." "Miss Caine," reported the *Syracuse Herald*, "has designed all the striking gowns that she wears in 'Adele,' several of which have caused a sensation among New York designers of feminine apparel."[28] Indeed, the reviewer for the *New York Times* thought "Miss Georgia Caine, looking remarkably handsome, has seldom if ever done anything quite so well as the widow in this piece."[29] She also did *Adele* at the Gaiety Theatre in London.[30]

In the 1920s, Caine was often associated with the producer and show man George M. Cohan and appeared in no less than five of his shows on Broadway: *Mary* (1920–21), *The O'Brien Girl* (1921–22), *The Home Towners* (1926), *Little Nellie Kelly* (1922–23), and *The Baby Cyclone* (1927–28). She also did others on tour, like *Whispering Friends* in 1928, where she played Spencer Tracy's wife.[31] He was 24 years younger than her. Their only common film credit was the drama *Dante's Inferno* (H. Lachman, Fox, 1935), which despite the title was not an adaptation of the Italian classic. Tracy starred with Claire Trevor and Caine played an uncredited role as a fortune teller.

In *Hooray for Love* (RKO Radio Pictures, 1935), starring Ann Sothern and Gene Raymond, Georgia Caine plays a wealthy dowager conned into backing a Broadway musical in return for the dubious romantic interest of Thurston Hall. Caine, who was nearly 60 and a rare example of an actress who never lied about her age, had sparked no small degree of genuine romantic interest in her youth, as one of Broadway's great beauties during the first decade of the 20th century.

One of Caine's distinguishing features was her love of animals. In a 1928 feature article in the *New York Star*, it was reported that her three Pekingese Cyclone, Sunshine, and Rainbow lived in the lap of luxury and traveled with their owner in a drawing-room car, where they had their own "silk-lined sleeping and traveling basket": "Hotel chefs are asked to prepare their favored foods and hotel waiters bring it to their room."[32] The dogs appeared with Caine in her 1927–28 hit show *Baby Cyclone* with Grant Mitchell, Natalie Moorhead, and Spencer Tracy at Henry Miller's Theatre followed by a tour and were "very much a part of the show."[33] The production was even named after one of them. According to the reviewer for the *Boston Herald*: "George Cohan has it in for silly women who waste their maternal affection on toy dogs and treats of this situation in satirical vein in his latest farce."[34] Let's hope Caine didn't take the play personally....

This wasn't the first time Caine appeared with her canines. She had performed with her own fox terrier in *The Earl and the Girl* in 1905–06.[35] One time going home in a taxi from the studio after a day's work on *The Beautiful Blonde from Bashful Bend*, she saw an injured cat on the road: "Miss Caine, trying to attract her driver's attention so that she could order him to stop, rapped on the cab window so hard she broke two fingers."[36]

Caine listed her profession as "Actress Motion pic." in the census taken on April 8, 1930,[37] despite the fact that she still had two shows to go on Broadway and her debut film, the crime drama *Good Intentions* (W.K. Howard, Fox, 1930), had not yet premiered. Clearly she was looking ahead and redefining herself as a film actress, even at this early stage of her screen career. It may well have been that the Hudsons were adversely affected by the stock market crash, like so many others. That may explain both the move to California and Caine's eagerness to take most any kind of film role that was on offer. By the end of her 20-year film career, in which she acted in 83 feature films, the tally shows that over half her roles were uncredited.

With such strong Broadway credentials, it seems surprising that she got so few real chances in Hollywood. As I discuss more in detail in my profile of Zeffie Tilbury, there is no real logic to the shape of many prominent stage actresses' film careers and no easy way to explain why some lucked out and landed the really juicy roles and others had to take the left-overs. Caine's background in musical comedy rather than straight plays may have counted against her; she'd never done a dramatic role on Broadway. I'm guessing, though, that by being willing to take so many uncredited roles at the beginning of her film career, she more or less unwittingly sabotaged her own chances for better parts in the future. As I've already suggested, she may no longer have had the luxury of being able to pick and choose.

A more specific indicator of Caine's financial condition is the 1940 U.S. census, which shows that after ten years in Hollywood she had no income beyond her own wages. She earned $4,192 for 12 weeks' work in 1939 and had been unemployed for 15 weeks up until March 31, 1940. Her 86-year-old, widowed mother, who had no income from any source, was living with her in a home rented for $75 a month at 2118 Las Palmas Ave. in Los Angeles. Caine also had a lodger, a 29-year-old male clerk in an antique shop. On the other hand, Caine could afford to have a maid, the 50-year-old, German-born widow Augusta H. Jefferson, who lived in and was paid $480 a year.[38]

Caine's father had died on August 25, 1924, as she was gearing up for a new musical comedy, *Be Yourself*, at the Sam H. Harris Theatre, where she played a grandmother. George R. Caine was 79 and was buried in Fresh Pond Crematory and Columbarium in Queens, New York.[39] Caine lost the other male mainstay of her life ten years later in Los Angeles, when Alphonzo Bell Hudson died at the age of 75 and was buried in Hollywood Forever Cemetery.[40] Her mother, Jenny Darragh Caine, lived to the vast age of 95 and died on February 1, 1949.[41] She was buried in Forest Lawn Memorial Park in Glendale.[42] Caine continued to work in films for 16 years after her husband's death, so she clearly needed the income. And then acting was all she knew. In an interview in 1920, she had said: "The whole life of an actress must center in the theater.... I do not mean she shouldn't have any outside friends, but so far as is possible she should live in the stage atmosphere."[43]

Caine finally retired the year after her mother's death, when she turned 74. Her last screen appearance was in the James Cagney film noir *Kiss Tomorrow Goodbye* (G. Douglas,

William Cagney Prod., 1950), where she had a small, uncredited role. She never worked in television or, as far as I know, returned to the stage during the last 14 years of her life. Georgia Caine Hudson died in Los Angeles on April 4, 1964, and was buried in Pierce Brothers Valhalla Memorial Park in North Hollywood.[44] As fate would have it, Caine, her husband, and her mother found their final resting place in three different Los Angeles cemeteries.

Mr. and Mrs. Smith: Patricia Collinge (1892–1974)

If Connie Gilchrist represented the "Shanty Irish" on the silver screen, one might say that Patricia Collinge represented the "Lace Curtain Irish," which is the same as saying that she didn't appear as particularly Irish in films at all. The two women's backgrounds were very different, of course. Gilchrist was a second-generation Irish immigrant born into a solidly working-class family in Brooklyn, while Patricia Collinge was born in Ireland into a solidly middle-class, Anglo-Irish family and came to the United States when she was 16. Gilchrist married a not particularly successful playwright and had to help support her family, while Collinge married an affluent executive in the insurance business and didn't strictly need to work at all. As Collinge herself explained in 1924: "That's why I appear comparatively seldom. Jim and I are so honest-to-goodness happy every minute of the time that I don't like to leave New York for any long stay."[1] It's all right for some....

You can read about several happy marriages in this volume, usually between an actress and a "non-professional," such as Ruth Donnelly and Basil de Guichard or Georgia Caine and Alphonzo Bell Hudson. Here comes another one. In private life, the Broadway leading lady and sometimes Hollywood character actress Patricia Collinge was, in the usage of her day, "Mrs. James Nichols Smith." But before we get to that happy day in June 1921 when Patricia Collinge and Jim Smith became Mr. and Mrs. Smith, let us go back to the beginning to see how it all started for Miss Collinge.

Patricia Collinge was born Eileen Cecilia Collinge in Dublin on September 20, 1892.[2] During her own lifetime, she was commonly believed to have been born in 1894.[3] She was known both at home and on the stage as Patricia Collinge, though I've never come across an explanation of when and why she started calling herself Patricia. Her father, Frederick Channon Collinge, was born in England of English parents in 1867 and worked as a composer of choral and church music and a musical director.[4] Her mother, Emma Cecilia Mary Russell, was born in Dublin of Irish parents in 1869 and was a homemaker.[5] The Collinge family counted three children, as Collinge had two younger brothers, Norbert J. Collinge and Frederick R. Collinge, born in Ireland in about 1898 and 1904.[6] The family immigrated to the United States from Rathmines, a southerly suburb of Dublin, in stages. First came Mr. Collinge in 1905, next Patricia Collinge and her mother in 1908, then Norbert in 1913, and finally Frederick and Collinge's maternal grandmother, Cecilia Russell, in 1914.[7]

We have a record of Collinge and her mother's first arrival in New York aboard the *Philadelphia* from Southampton on September 19, 1908, the day before Collinge's 16th birthday.[8]

Less than three months later, on December 7, 1908, she made her New York debut as a flower girl in the musical comedy *The Queen of the Moulin Rouge*, which ran for 160 performances at the Circle Theatre.[9] Collinge had already made her London debut on December 21, 1904, at the Garrick Theatre in a show whose title indicates that at least some progress has been made since then in the struggle for racial equality: *Little Black Sambo and Little White Barbara*. It was a Christmas pantomime in which Collinge played neither Sambo nor Barbara, but a Chinese doll called "Ching-a-Ling," which indicates an ethnic variety in this show beyond the ordinary.[10]

When you think of it, it is quite remarkable that an immigrant daughter should have made both her London and New York debut by the age of 16. Collinge herself, or one or both of her parents, must have had a steely determination to see her on the major stages of the English-speaking world. Actually, we get a hint at who was at the back of it from the following statement Collinge made in an interview in 1926. She said that her mother "Emmie" had "histrionic ability": "I suppose I am her suppressed desire burst forth upon an unsuspecting world." She added, though, that she had "always wanted to be an actress."[11]

It seems remarkable, too, that the no doubt eminently respectable, middle-class, Anglo-Irish Collinges should allow their 16-year-old daughter to make her Broadway debut in what the critic for the *New York Times* described as "a girl show, which exhibits her in various types and in various stages of dress and undress."[12] They must have felt great confidence in Patricia's impermeable innocence and virtue.

Maybe to balance things out, Collinge appeared in 1911–12 as "Youth" in *Everywoman*, which was subtitled "a modern morality play in five canticles."[13] The author, Walter Browne, had managed the ultimate public relations stunt by dying of pneumonia on the evening of his play's out of town premiere.[14] The *New York Times* found *Everywoman*, which was a play with music, "more nearly like a musical comedy (without the comedy) than anything else" and "a rather tedious affair." Collinge was "noticed" for the first time by the *Times* and must have thrilled to the words: "The exquisite beauty of Patricia Collinge, occupied with maidenly sweetness, makes a most ingratiating figure of youth."[15] She played the same role in the London production at the Drury Lane Theatre in September 1912.[16]

In a revised and updated version of Bronson Howard's old chestnut of a comedy *The New Henrietta*, Collinge next played the bride-to-be of matinee idol Douglas Fairbanks at the Knickerbocker Theatre, starting just before Christmas in 1913. The *New York Times* thought her "a really adorable-looking little Agnes."[17] Fairbanks was also starred in her next Broadway show, the new comedy *He Comes Up Smiling* (1914), and Collinge was again his love interest, this time named "Billy" Bartlett, a role she played "sweetly, with just the right ingenuousness of manner and just the right use of a voice that is hauntingly reminiscent of Elsie Janis's."[18] *The Show Shop* (aka *In the Limelight*), "a play of stage people," came next. It premiered at the Hudson Theatre on December 31, 1914, and ran for 156 performances followed by a tour.[19] This was Collinge's third and final show with Fairbanks, who went into the movies after that and never returned to the Broadway stage.

Fairbanks would have a more lasting effect on Collinge's life, albeit indirectly, than his presence in three of her early Broadway shows. It was on his recommendation that she went to a summer resort in 1915 where she met her future husband. Collinge relates: "I met a charming husband and wife by the name of Smith. One day I was on the beach talking to them when a very thin, very wet, young man came out of the water who was introduced to me as their son. That was Jim and five years later I married him."[20] On their marriage in 1921, the *New York Times* recorded a different version of their first meeting. The newspaper of record claimed that they had met ten years before when Collinge was appearing in a stock company in Hartford.[21]

It is true, at any rate, that James Nichols Smith grew up in Hartford, Connecticut. He was born in New York on October 2, 1891, as the first of the three children of Harry Alexander Smith (1869–1928) and Helen Christine Nichols Smith (1870–1943).[22] Harry A. Smith was a wealthy businessman from Massachusetts, who by the time of his son's marriage in 1921 was President of the National Fire Insurance Company and had no less than three live-in Irish servants.[23] Jim would follow in his father's footsteps in the insurance business. In 1920, he was living in Chicago and working as a clerk in an insurance company.[24] His future wife was living with her parents, two younger brothers, and maternal grandmother at 98 Central Park West in New York City.[25] On June 10, 1921, James Nichols Smith and Patricia Collinge were married by Father Daly of St. Patrick's Cathedral in the Collinge home "with only the immediate families of the couple in attendance."[26] The *New York Times* reported that they would spend their honeymoon in Bermuda and "make their home in Chicago, where Mr. Smith has insurance interests." Miss Collinge would continue on the stage.[27]

By the time of her marriage, Collinge was a star. If we backtrack a little, we find that her breakthrough role came in 1915 as the titular heroine of the hit play *Pollyanna*, based on the novel by Eleanor H. Porter and the sequel *Pollyanna Grows Up*, as dramatized by Catherine Chisholm Cushing. Collinge, then, had the dubious distinction of being the original stage Pollyanna. You will recall that Pollyanna was that decidedly irritating, pig-tailed child-saint, who has lent her name to an entire philosophy of being glad. Collinge, who was 24 at the time, played 12-year-old Pollyanna Whittier first at the Blackstone Theatre in Chicago in August 1915, then for 112 performances at the Hudson Theatre in New York in the second half of 1916, and finally took the show on a lengthy tour in 1917–18.[28] She described Pollyanna years later as "a dreadful little girl with a pernicious philosophy."[29]

As if *Pollyanna* wasn't enough, according to Daniel Blum Collinge "reached stardom in 1919 playing the title role in *Tillie*."[30] This play was a "Mennonite Romance" set in the Pennsylvania Dutch country about Tillie Getz "a Mennonite maid born and bred in the faith," who nevertheless "feels the stirrings of revolt against the tyranny of her man-ridden community, and ultimately she triumphs over it."[31]

I cannot give a detailed account of all Collinge's 28 shows on Broadway between her debut in 1908 and her last hurrah there in 1952. What strikes me, though, is the unusual mix of leading and supporting roles that she played throughout her career. Even after she attained a degree of stardom with *Tillie* in 1919, she did not balk at taking a secondary roles in later productions, such as Sheridan's *The Rivals* (1922), where she played the maid Lucy to Violet Heming's Lydia Languish; *Hedda Gabler* (1926), where she was seen as Thea Elvsted, while Emily Stevens starred as Hedda; *Becky Sharp* (1929), where Mary Ellis played the title role and Collinge was Amelia Sedley; and *The Lady with the Lamp* (1931), where she supported Edith Evans in the leading role as Florence Nightingale.

At the same time, she continued playing ingénues like Linda Lee Stafford in *Just Suppose* (1920–21), an attempt to capitalize on the Prince of Wales's recent trip to America by imagining him falling in love with an American girl while he was there (Collinge was the girl), chiefly distinguished in retrospect by being Leslie Howard's Broadway debut in the role of the Prince's friend; Cecily Cardew in *The Importance of Being Earnest* (1926), when she was almost 34, with Lucile Watson as Lady Bracknell; and Constance Neville in an "all-star" revival of Oliver Goldsmith's *She Stoops to Conquer* (1928) with Fay Bainter, Mrs. Leslie Carter, O.P. Heggie, and Glenn Hunter.[32]

Collinge's final roles as a conventional heroine and leading lady on Broadway were Stella Hallam in a 1933 revival of Rose Franken's *Another Language* when she was 40 and Caroline Allerton in *To See Ourselves* (1935) when she was 42. In 1935, her maternal grandmother, Cecilia Vaughn Russell, who had lived with the family and been a continual presence in Collinge's life died at the tremendous age of 98.[33] The following year, her father passed away at the age of 69.[34] It was a watershed moment for Collinge in her career, too. After *To See Ourselves* failed to please, she went into a temporary retirement from the stage that would last almost four years.[35] In the 1930 U.S. census, she had listed her occupation as "housewife." Jim and Pat Smith, who lived at ten Beekman Place in 1930, had by 1933 found their final home in an apartment at 30 Beekman Place, a narrow, Romanesque style, red brick building between 50th and 51st St. overlooking the East River.[36] They would live there till the end of their lives.

"She had almost abandoned the thought of ever acting again, when Herman Shumlin sent her the script of 'The Little Foxes.'"[37] So the story goes. Collinge's early retirement was suddenly at an end. Columnist Axel Storm called "the faded flower of the Old South who tips the jug," Birdie Hubbard, "The fattest of all roles in recent years."[38] Lillian Hellman's "fearful fable of second-generation carpet-baggers in a small Southern town around 1900"[39] opened on February 15, 1939, and ran for over a year at the National Theatre, which is now the Nederlander, followed by a year-long national tour. Collinge estimated that she had played Aunt Birdie 551 times.[40] Brooks Atkinson wrote of her performance in the play: "Miss Collinge drags the whole truth out of a character, and acts it with extraordinary lightness and grace."[41]

The show no doubt provided a boost both to Collinge's confidence as an actress and to her pocket book, as she reported to the census enumerator in 1940 that she had earned more than $5,000 for 44 weeks' work in 1939. Her husband also earned more than $5,000 as the owner of a re-insurance company. They could now afford to have a live-in maid at Beekman Place, 28-year-old New Yorker Edith Dover, whom they paid $500 a year.[42]

The road company of *The Little Foxes* closed for three months in Philadelphia on April 12, 1941, to allow Collinge, Charles Dingle, Carl Benton Reid, Dan Duryea, and John Marriot to reprise their Broadway roles in the film version.[43] This was Collinge's film debut, as indeed it was for most of the others mentioned. She signed her contract with producer Samuel Goldwyn on April 15, 1941.[44] Two weeks later, under the able direction of William Wyler, production started at Samuel Goldwyn Studios at 7200 Santa Monica Blvd. in West Hollywood. The shoot wrapped on July 3.[45]

As we well know, the production period was marred by the ongoing conflict of director Wyler and star Bette Davis over how Regina Giddens should look and how she should be played.[46] As Birdie Hubbard, Collinge now had to relate to three new actors in the most central roles of the drama: Davis replaced Tallulah Bankhead as her nefarious, self-centered sister-in-law Regina; Herbert Marshall replaced Frank Conroy as her sympathetic brother-in-law Horace Giddens; and Teresa Wright replaced Florence Williams (and later Eugenia Rawls) as her beloved and loving niece Alexandra "Zan" Giddens. Richard Carlson was cast in the role of Zan's love interest, David Hewitt, a character who was not in the play.

Collinge gave the performance of her screen life as the alcoholic, nervous, talkative, and

Patricia Collinge acted in only seven feature films, but she managed to co-star with Teresa Wright in three of them. Here they are seen in the best of the lot, *The Little Foxes* (Samuel Goldwyn Co., 1941), where Collinge played Wright's pathetic, alcoholic Aunt Birdie. Both actresses were Oscar-nominated in the supporting actress category for this film and lost to Mary Astor for *The Great Lie*. In the later *Shadow of a Doubt* and *Casanova Brown*, Collinge played Wright's mother.

patrician Birdie Hubbard, who drinks wine alone in her room and has never had a headache, despite her family saying that that is why she is unwell. Birdie and her aristocratic family represent culture and breeding, as a contrast to the boorish, materialistic Hubbards. She symbolizes old money being forced by circumstances to marry new money, the leisure classes marrying trade to survive. Oscar Hubbard (Carl Benton Reid) married her for her family's cotton fields and she often refers fondly to the family estate Lionette and wishes they could all go and live there. Birdie is physically and emotionally abused by her brutal and uncaring husband ("I'm sorry, Oscar"), but dislikes her loutish, lazy, and stupid son Leo (Dan Duryea) even more. Temperamentally, Birdie gets along best with her brother-in-law, Horace Giddens (Herbert Marshall), and her niece Alexandra (Teresa Wright), whom she teaches piano and performs with (poorly) on the evening of the important dinner party for northern investor William Marshall (Russell Hicks). As usual, she drinks too much and talks too much and ends up getting slapped by her husband for warning Alexandra against Leo. Her fear is "Zan" will end up like her and be forced into an uncongenial marriage.

Birdie's big scene is when she acts as hostess at an informal, impromptu tea party in the garden with Horace, Alexandra, and David Hewitt (Richard Carlson), with the Giddens's African American maid Addie as amanuensis (Jessica Grayson in a wonderful performance). Birdie has a touching monologue about elderberry wine and the first time she saw Oscar Hubbard. As she gets drunker, she also reveals the story of her unhappy marriage and admits to drinking in her room alone. It was when filming this garden scene, Collinge recalled in an hilarious newspaper article, that they surprised cinematographer Gregg Toland on his birthday by having a young Western Union messenger come bounding in hand in hand with Wright and Hewitt, while the camera was rolling, and eventually leading the cast in a rendition of "Happy birthday." Toland sat behind the camera "watching with the baffled wariness of a man who thinks he sees a Western Union boy but isn't going to commit himself."[47]

Collinge was nominated as Best Actress in a Supporting Role at the Academy Awards in 1942. She did not win, but then neither did Sara Allgood, Margaret Wycherly, or Collinge's *Little Foxes* co-star Teresa Wright. Mary Astor did. The nominees illustrate the variability, incommensurability, and basic incoherence of the "Supporting Actress" category, which consisted that year of one former movie star giving a star performance, three traditional character actresses doing what character actresses do best, and an ingénue doing what ingénues do best, which is as little as possible.

Despite Collinge's admiration and liking for Alfred Hitchcock, her part as Teresa Wright's dowdy, frazzled mother and Joseph Cotten's sister in *Shadow of a Doubt* (Skirball Prod./Universal, 1943) was one she could have done in her sleep. With the relentless bad hair day she is having, she looks like she just got out of bed too. Collinge has a good moment, though, at the party after Cotten's talk at the woman's club, when he surprises her with the news that he has to leave in the morning and she breaks down and cries to everyone's embarrassment. She admits she has felt more like herself with him there, rather than just being someone's wife or mother. "You sort of forget you're you," she says. Teresa Wright is so annoying I wanted to throw her off that train myself. In retrospect, Collinge said she "never had such a good time in her life, nor laughed so much."[48]

In *Tender Comrade* (E. Dmytryk, RKO, 1943) (there's a title for HUAAC), Collinge plays one of four married women working together at a defense plant and sharing a house in what is a typical home front film. Collinge is the oldest by far and has both a husband and son in the service. Despite her WASP credentials, her character favors turbans and bandanas, like some parody of an African American mammy. She is soft-spoken and sensible, a peace-maker and voice of reason in the group, and she knits. Ginger Rogers is togged out in a series of juvenile, "cute" outfits that make her look like Heidi (not to mention the braids). The "now" of this terminally dull film is punctuated with flashback scenes from Rogers and Robert Ryan's tumultuous life together prior to the war. We don't get a similar background on the other four women. Again, Collinge has her moment when she receives a letter from her husband to say that their 23-year-old son is being promoted to major. Rogers has to take over reading it aloud, though, putting herself literally front and center in the image and relegating Collinge to the background. At the end, Rogers receives word her husband has been killed and has a rousing, patriotic monologue of interminable length to her baby son in his crib. Surprisingly, it doesn't put him to sleep!

As if two films with Teresa Wright weren't enough, Collinge managed to squeeze in a third with *Casanova Brown* (S. Wood, International Pictures/Christie Corp., 1944), playing

Wright's astrologically-oriented mother, Mrs. Drury, who adamantly opposes her daughter's marriage to Gary Cooper, because the stars say it will be a disaster. "Let us not waste our time in idle speculation, let us go straight to the stars for our facts," she intones. The Drurys' palatial, $750,000 mansion burns to the ground after a hilariously botched attempt on Cooper's part to hide from his new mother-in-law that he has been smoking. Mrs. Drury avers that she "would sooner associate with a time bomb" and is not seen again. Collinge thought the role as the eccentric Mrs. Drury suited her, as "I think there's always been a rather demented look about me on the screen."[49]

By her late 40s, Patricia Collinge was seen as a viable replacement for Josephine Hull, eight years older and considerably plumper, as Abby Brewster in the long-running comedy *Arsenic and Old Lace*, while Hull spent eight weeks in Hollywood in the latter part of 1941 reprising her role in the screen version.[50] The final hit of Collinge's stage career came with *The Heiress*, a 1947 dramatization by Ruth and Augustus Goetz of Henry James's short novel *Washington Square*. Wendy Hiller (and later Beatrice Straight) played the heiress of the title, Catherine Sloper, Basil Rathbone was her autocratic father, and Collinge played her romantically inclined, live-in aunt, Lavinia Penniman, who proffers unsound advice and lives vicariously through her niece's on-again-off-again romance with Morris Townsend (Peter Cookson). You may recall that in Paramount's 1949 film version, Aunt Lavinia was wonderfully well played by Miriam Hopkins and the same goes for Olivia de Havilland as Catherine Sloper.

In 1951, Collinge was billed third in *Teresa* (F. Zinnemann, MGM), a "home from the war" drama starring Pier Angeli in her American screen debut and John Ericson in his screen debut, where Collinge played Ericson's possessive mother in the best "silver cord" tradition. One wonders if she ever saw her screen son's January 1974 photo spread for *Playgirl*.... Collinge's last two shows on Broadway, a revival of James M. Barrie's *Mary Rose* (1951) at the ANTA Playhouse and John Van Druten's *I've Got Sixpence* (1952), both flopped. This may have contributed to her decision to retire from the stage at the relatively early age of 60. That same year, she had a small part in *Washington Story* (R. Pirosh, MGM, 1952) and made her television debut. Last but not least among the many important events of 1952 was the death of Collinge's mother Emmie at the age of 83.[51] Symbolically, Collinge's stage career died with her mother, who had always spurred her on.

Collinge was last seen on the big screen in 1959 in a modest role in *A Nun's Story* (Warner Bros.), helmed by *Teresa* director Fred Zinnemann and starring Audrey Hepburn. That year she published a collection of her stories entitled *The Small Mosaics of Mr. and Mrs. Engel*. This volume consisted mainly of eight semi-autobiographical sketches about an American middle-class married couple's trip to Rome. You can learn much about Collinge, her husband, and her marriage from this whimsical and wise book. Collinge continued to take occasional roles in television till 1967, appearing several times on *Alfred Hitchcock Presents* (1955–61) and *The Alfred Hitchcock Hour* (1962–64).

Patricia Collinge died in New York on April 10, 1974, at the age of 81 and was buried with her parents and maternal grandmother in St. Mary's Cemetery in Nantucket.[52] Her family had long had a summer home in Siasconset.[53] Her husband died ten months after her.[54] After five years of marriage, Collinge had said in 1926: "I haven't any theories about matrimony. I don't know anything about Jim's business. He doesn't know anything about the theatre. We don't interfere with each other."[55] Mr. and Mrs. Smith were married for 53 years.

The Trophy Wife: Ruth Donnelly (1896–1982)

The row house at 10 West End Ave., just off W. State St. in Trenton, New Jersey, presents a melancholy aspect today, abandoned and derelict, with boarded up windows. It sits in the middle of a row of similarly modest, three-story, brick and stucco houses, each with a covered porch on the ground floor and a mansard roof. Out back, there is a long, narrow garden that leads down to the Delaware and Raritan Canal. Once upon a time, about a hundred years ago, there was a large and no doubt lively, middle-class family living here. They were the Donnellys, father and mother and five children and they lived in the house, which they rented, from at least 1900 till 1910 and probably longer.[1] In 1900, when their daughter Ruth was four, the address was ten Philemon St., but by 1910, the street had changed names to West End Ave.

Ruth Donnelly may well have been born in this house. We know she was born in Trenton on May 17, 1896, as the third of the five surviving children of Harry A. and Bessie B. Donnelly.[2] Harry Augustus Donnelly was born in Philadelphia in June 1860, the son of Richard Grant Augustus Donnelly (1841–1905) and Susie Isabel Gould Donnelly (1856–1907).[3] Ruth's paternal grandparents made their home on the other side of town, at 523 E. State St., which today is the site of a parking garage.[4] They both died when Ruth was a child and were buried in Trenton's Greenwood Cemetery, where she herself would be laid to rest many years later. Her grandfather fought in the Union army in the Civil War, was captured by the Confederates in the Battle of Gaines Mill and imprisoned in the notorious Libby Prison. He and his wife owned a clothing store in Trenton. Richard Donnelly had been mayor of Trenton in the mid-1880s and his younger son, Ruth's uncle Frederick W. Donnelly (1866–1935), was also mayor of Trenton and much longer, from 1911 till 1932.[5] In her younger days, the local newspapers often referred to her as "Mayor Donnelly's niece."

As for Ruth's father, possibly the black sheep of the family, in 1900 he was 40 years old and working in a humble capacity as a clerk in the Quarter Master General's Office. The Quarter Master General for New Jersey at that time was his own father, Richard Donnelly, who had been brevetted as a Major General in 1899.[6] Ten years later, at 50, Harry Donnelly was working as a reporter on a newspaper.[7] He died suddenly in June 1919 at the age of 59 and was buried beside his parents in Greenwood Cemetery.[8]

Ruth's mother Bessie was a local girl and was born Elizabeth D. Weart in April 1861, the daughter of hotelkeeper John A. Weart and Margaret Weart.[9] She was a homemaker and had five children who lived to maturity: Richard Jr. (b. 1883), Bessie (b. 1892), Ruth, Margaret

(b. 1898), and Dorothy (b. 1903).[10] The Donnellys' first born, named Richard A. Donnelly, Jr., only lived a day, from October 3 to October 4, 1882.[11] Bessie B. Donnelly died in 1922.[12] According to Ruth Donnelly's *New York Times* obituary, only her younger sister Dorothy (Hegeman) survived her among her siblings.[13]

Ruth Donnelly's life may be divided into three parts: before, during, and after her marriage to Basil de Guichard. The first part, spent growing up in Trenton, New Jersey, and working as an actress in New York, lasted till 1931. The second part, consisting of 26 years of her marriage with de Guichard, also corresponds with the years of her film career in Hollywood, which resulted in 84 feature films between 1931 and 1957. The final part, her life as a widow in semi-retirement in New York City, lasted for 24 years, from de Guichard's death in 1958 till her own death in 1982.

Donnelly got her start as a chorus girl in the touring show of *The Quaker Girl* when she was 17.[14] The *Trenton Evening Times* announced proudly on August 23, 1917, that because Donnelly "had scored a personal success" in a previous play, producer A.H. Woods had engaged her for his new production, *The Scrap of Paper*, "in the ingénue role ... said to fit her to perfection."[15] As it happens, Donnelly made her New York stage debut in this "sometimes entertaining but never very hardy melodrama" by Owen Davis about "an attempt to corner the resources of the country," which the *New York Times* thought "lacked reality" and suspense. It also appears from this review that her hometown newspaper had rather inflated Donnelly's importance to the production. It was Carroll McComas who played the heroine of the piece and Donnelly, as Miss Small, was not even mentioned in the review.[16] *The Scrap of Paper* did not run and closed after 40 performances at the Criterion Theatre in November 1917.[17]

Donnelly's next show, *Going Up*, was significant for being her first musical comedy. Between 1917 and 1922, Donnelly did four shows for the legendary showman and producer George M. Cohan. *Going Up* was the first of them and opened at the Liberty Theatre on Christmas Day 1917. Her other Cohan shows were *A Prince There Was* (1918–19), *The Meanest Man in the World* (1920–21), and *Madeleine and the Movies* (1922). Even though Donnelly did several dramas on Broadway, she would be more closely identified with musicals and comedies, just as in the movies. *Going Up* was a light, frothy piece about a successful author, played by Frank Craven, who has to fly an airplane to win his girl (Edith Day). Again Donnelly's efforts did not rate a mention the *New York Times* review, which found this "musical farce" as a whole "full of comedy and tuneful airs."[18] Donnelly played a telephone operator. As Miss Zonne, she was in the opening number "Paging Mr. Street" with the ensemble, but did not have any other songs. *Going Up* was a big hit and ran for almost a year.

In early 1920, as the musical revue *As You Were* was about to open at the Central Theatre, we find Donnelly living in an apartment at 120 W. 70th St. between Columbus Ave. and Broadway.[19] In September 1927, when she returned from a trip to Europe, she was residing in a handsome apartment building at 14 E. 60th St., just off 5th Ave.[20] In April 1930, she was living at the fabled Sutton Hotel at 330 E. 56th St.[21]

New York character actresses usually made their way to Hollywood in the 1930s either on the crest of a wave of success to reprise on film some role from a hit Broadway show or they came as the result of dwindling opportunities or repeated flops on the Great White Way. Donnelly belonged to the second category. Though she had some good opportunities and performed in several hit shows, my feeling is that as a stage actress Donnelly never hit the big time.

Donnelly's last show in New York for more than 30 years, *She Means Business*, closed after only eight performances at the Ritz Theatre in February 1931. In April that same year, she was before the cameras at Fox Film Corporation in Hollywood. The maritime crime drama *Transatlantic* (W.K. Howard, Fox, 1931) was to have been her sound film debut, but her role was deleted and she debuted instead in the mystery *The Spider* (K. MacKenna, W.C. Menzies, Fox, 1931) on September 27, 1931.[22] Exactly nine months later, Donnelly could call herself Mrs. Basil de Guichard, almost as if she'd become one of her own nouveau riche screen characters.

I think Ruth Donnelly and Basil de Guichard would rate pretty high on the "Most Unlikely Couple" list, which makes their story all the more romantic and unusual. She was an old maid character actress from Trenton, New Jersey; he was a two-times divorced industrialist from Denver, Paris, and London via Flint, Michigan. They met and married in Los Angeles, California. What are the chances?

Basil Winter de Guichard was often referred to as a Frenchman, but he was actually born in Denver, Colorado on December 18, 1885, and was an American citizen.[23] His was a cosmopolitan family, as both his parents, Arthur H. de Guichard and Gertrude Baines de Guichard, were born in England and Basil grew up in London (1890–97) and Paris (1897–1900).[24] In his late teens, he was a record-breaking, champion cyclist and motorcyclist, who competed on both sides of the Atlantic. He made his American cycling debut in Boston on May 30, 1902, against his friend and fellow Frenchman Albert Champion and American Harry Elkes.[25] He competed till 1906 and then went to work for Champion.[26]

Albert Champion, who was born in Paris in 1878, was a pioneer of the American auto industry, as the inventor and developer of his own brand of widely used spark plugs and the founder and owner of the A.C. Spark Plug Company in Flint, Michigan, from 1908. De Guichard moved with him to Flint and became his "right-hand man and expert at quality control."[27] "Even tempered and tactful," he played "good cop" to his "impatient and demanding" boss's "bad cop," according to Champion's biographer Peter Joffre Nye.[28] In 1910, de Guichard was an assistant manager; by 1918, he was the assistant general manager; and in 1920, he was the manager of the company and lived with Albert Champion and his wife Ips and a chauffeur-housekeeper couple at 423 E. Kearsley St. in Flint, according to the census taken January 12, 1920.[29]

Less than two months later, de Guichard married Mae Nash Miller, the daughter of another "gründer" in the American auto industry, Charles William Nash (1864–1948), and "heiress to the Nash motor car fortune."[30] Mae was 34, divorced, and had a nine-year-old son from her first marriage. It was the second marriage for de Guichard as well. He had married for the first time in 1911, when he was 26 and was already living in Flint.[31] He was divorced by the time he registered for the draft in 1918, as he gave his sister in England as next of kin, and he appears as divorced in the 1920 U.S. census .[32] After marrying Mae Nash, writes Nye, "De Guichard ranked among the auto industry's nobility."[33]

On Albert Champion's death under mysterious circumstances in Paris in 1927, leaving a fortune estimated at $15 million, de Guichard was the executor of Champion's will and assumed the presidency of the AC Spark Plug Company.[34] He resigned at the end of 1929 "because of ill health." At that time, it was "one of the largest automobile accessory companies in the world" and employed 5,000 people.[35] In 1930, Basil and Mae were living in style in a home at 1603 Crescent Dr. valued at $45,000, but the marriage was nearing its end.[36] Basil and Mae divorced in 1931.[37] The stage was set for de Guichard's third and final matrimonial venture.

So what did Basil de Guichard look like? An account of a bicycle race in Boston in 1904, refers to Donnelly's future husband as "little Basil De Guichard." Another article from the same year describes him as "the stocky-built French lad."[38] De Guichard is described in his 1918 draft registration as being of medium height and build with blue eyes and brown hair.[39] In his 1924 passport application, we get a more detailed description and a black-and-white photograph showing him at age 38 as a handsome man with a square-cut, manly face, dark hair graying at the temples and neatly parted on the left side, and a pensive expression in his light-colored eyes. De Guichard is described as being 5'5" tall (Donnelly was 5'7½"[40]), having brown hair, and a round face with a low forehead, blue eyes, a medium nose, a medium mouth, a square chin, and a dark complexion. He had no distinguishing marks.[41]

One might have expected an attractive, recently divorced millionaire and potential "Sugar Daddy" of 46, who has just moved to Tinseltown from Flint, Michigan, to fall for some blonde starlet. Basil de Guichard, though, chose as his wife a 36-year-old spinster character actress who had never been a vision of beauty at any age. Clearly he was old enough and wise enough to know that looks aren't everything and you can get much further in a marriage with someone you can laugh with than with someone who only has her appearance to recommend her.

Playing Edward G. Robinson's upwardly mobile and socially ambitious wife in *A Slight Case of Murder* (Warner Bros., 1938) was arguably the best screen assignment Ruth Donnelly ever got. Robinson plays a reformed gangster who goes "legit" after the repeal of Prohibition, but the beer his company produces is murderously bad.

Basil de Guichard and Ruth Donnelly were married by the minister of the Presbyterian Church of Beverly Hills, Arthur Lee Odell, on June 27, 1932. It may have been a small wedding, as the pastor's wife was one of the witnesses.[42] Basil and Ruth lived a comfortable, if not luxurious life in Los Angeles and New York. Their first recorded address is a romantic-looking apartment building at 1338 N. Harper Ave. in West Hollywood.[43] In 1940, they paid $90 a month for their rented home at 948½ Hilgard Ave. in Westwood. Donnelly reported to the census enumerator that she had earned in excess of $5,000 in 1939 for 52 weeks' work. Her husband was listed with no profession and no salaried income, but was said to have income from other sources.[44] They were living at the same address in Westwood in 1944.[45] When they returned home from a trip to Europe in 1949, they gave their address as 130 E. 61st St. in New York, which is a handsome, five-story townhouse on the south side of the street between Lexington and Park.[46] Three years later, they were living at 66 Park Ave., which stood on the corner of 38th St.[47]

By that time, Donnelly's film career was nearly over. It's important to remember, though, that she was a very busy actress in Hollywood during the first 15 years of their marriage. In

Funnily enough, Ruth Donnelly is wearing almost the same print on her oversized shirt in this photograph from *Autumn Leaves* (William Goetz Prod., 1956) with Joan Crawford as the dress she wore in the still from *A Slight Case of Murder*. She plays the landlady in the bungalow court where Crawford lives her cloistered life as a typist for hire.

her peak year of 1933, no less than 14 of her films were released. It says something both about Donnelly and about her husband, that she wanted to keep on working even when she no longer needed to support herself and that he understood her desire to have a career even when his own was over. Having been so successful himself, I imagine he enjoyed just being along for the ride and having a front row seat to the passing Hollywood parade. As a character actress, Donnelly had all the benefits of being an integral part of the movie industry without the liabilities and pressures of being a star. Generally the press had little or no interest in her, debonair millionaire ex-industrialist husband or not.

Basil de Guichard suffered a fatal heart attack in Los Angeles on Thursday, May 29, 1958.[48] According to Louella Parsons, who was in a position to know, "Theirs had been 27 years of happy marriage."[49] After her husband's death, Donnelly gave up their home in Los Angeles and based herself in New York.[50] There she could be closer to family and still keep her toe in the water. Her film career ended 25 years before her death with *The Way to Gold* (R.D. Webb, Twentieth Century–Fox) in 1957; she was seen in a few TV roles until 1965; and last appeared on the stage as a replacement for Patsy Kelly in the role of the cook Pauline in *No, No, Nanette,* which she had first done on tour.[51] Old timers like Ruby Keeler, Kelly, and Donnelly got a real lift from this nostalgia fest, which ran for over two years at the 46th Street Theatre in 1971–73.

Her final years were spent living in the Wellington Hotel, which is still welcoming guests today at 871 7th Ave. on the corner of 55th St.[52] David Ragan paints a somewhat dreary picture of Donnelly in her dotage, living alone, working on her (never published) autobiography, *Tripping Along,* and writing patriotic and religious songs, "the vulgar trend of today's movies" not to her liking.[53] She sounds a bit like her contemporary and fellow Presbyterian Agnes Moorehead, who spent the last ten years of her life ranting and raving publically against the evils of the age, but was still a lot of fun in private. Moorehead had to keep on working to pay the bills and never retired. Donnelly was no doubt left well provided for and could pick and choose. Mostly, like Melville's Bartleby the Scrivener, she preferred not to. She proudly asserted in 1982 "she wouldn't do a commercial for one million dollars."[54]

Ruth Donnelly died at Roosevelt Hospital in New York City on Wednesday, November 17, 1982, and was buried with her husband, parents, and paternal grandparents in Greenwood Cemetery in her hometown of Trenton, New Jersey.[55]

Falling into Fame: Maude Eburne (1875–1960)

I'd be tempted to call Eburne the Canadian Marie Dressler, if it weren't for the fact that Dressler herself was Canadian. At any rate, Eburne had a mug so mobile it made even Dressler seem stony-faced in comparison. Like Dressler, too, she was prone at times to exaggerated histrionics. A particularly egregious example of this is her sound film debut role as the hysterical maid Lizzie Allen in the 1930 film version of Mary Roberts Rinehart and Avery Hopwood's classic stage thriller *The Bat*, which on this occasion was entitled *The Bat Whispers* (Joseph M. Schenck Prod./Art Cinema Corp.). Director Roland West, who was himself a seasoned actor, had apparently given her no help in trying to tone things down for the camera and the end result is some of the worst over-acting from a 1930s character actress on record. In her defense, Eburne learned fast and delivered a tour de force comic performance in a classic mother-in-law role in her next film, *Lonely Wives* (R. Mack, Pathé Exchange, 1931).

If nothing else, Eburne at least had a rightful claim to being the most famous and popular comic maid of the generation of actresses born in the 1870s. It all started with a new farce by Edward Peple called *A Pair of Sixes*. It premiered on March 20, 1914, at the Longacre Theatre, which had opened in 1913 and is still in operation under the same name at 220 W. 48th St. The headline in the *New York Times*'s ecstatic review read "'A Pair of Sixes' Uproarious Fun" and one of the three subheadings was "And as One of an Exceptionally Good Company Maude Eburne Scores a Big Success." According to the *Times*'s critic, "it seemed too good to be true that playwright and players would keep up the fun all evening at so fast and furious a pace. But it was true": "the people on the stage, shout as they would, could hardly make themselves heard above the howls of laughter that came from the other side of the footlights."[1]

As one news article summarized the plot, "the farce deals with the quarrels of two business partners who, being unable to agree on any plan of dissolution, assent to the proposal of their lawyer that they settle their affairs on a sporting basis." It was agreed that "on the result of a single hand of 'show-down' poker" the loser would have to go to work as a butler in the home of the winner.[2] In the most decisive role of her career, Eburne came on in the second act as Coddles, "the English maid of all work ... much enamored of the new butler and earnest in her pursuit of him."[3] Her key moment came "when told she had better reconcile herself to remaining a maiden..., with a glance of unutterable woe cast to Heaven, she fell like a shot to the floor."[4] "In all the recent history of stage falls," commented the *New York Times*, "there has been none executed that meant so much."[5]

Maude Eburne was nearly 40 years old when she literally fell into fame in March 1914.

She was born Maud Eburne Riggs in 1875 on a farm in Trafalgar, Halton, Ontario, which today is part of Oakville and lies on the shore of Lake Ontario about midway between Toronto and Hamilton.[6] Her father was John Riggs and her mother Mary Riggs and she had at least six older siblings, as indicated by the 1881 census, which shows that all the Riggs children were born in Ontario. Maud's parents were both born in Ireland. The most curious thing about Eburne's family background is that her mother was 48 when she was born and her father 52.[7] Now I suppose this was medically possible even in the 1870s, but we have to consider the possibility that little Maud was adopted.

Maud Riggs was also living in Trafalgar, Ontario in 1891.[8] Ten years later, we find her at age 25 still in Ontario and probably still on the farm with her older brother Joseph Riggs and three other siblings.[9] Her parents are both dead and the time has come to take her life into her own hands. She later indicated in an interview that her father's death at 81, which occurred on February 7, 1901, in Oakville, Ontario, had finally allowed her to pursue a stage career, something he would strongly have disapproved of: "If my father knew I was on the stage he would not rest in peace."[10]

A lengthy feature article on Eburne in the *New York Times* after the sensational premiere of *A Pair of Sixes* was headlined "Coddles Awakes at Last to Find Herself Famous" and started by saying, "One would have to go back several seasons to match the unexpectedness of her sudden rise from the unknown into prominence."[11] Though her rise had been precipitous, the article did not fail to mention that there was more than a dozen years of hard work in the provinces behind Eburne's seemingly overnight success in New York. In fact, the story consisted mostly of a detailed account in Eburne's own words of her painful and painstaking rise to the top of the character woman heap. She told the interviewer how every summer for a dozen years she had come to New York to try to secure a role for the coming season. "It was always difficult for me," Eburne said, "because I do not look any type."[12]

Maude Eburne in the defining role of her career, the comic maid Coddles in the hit farce *A Pair of Sixes*, which opened on Broadway in 1914 and kept her busy for the next couple of years. She would play comic maids for the next 15 years in New York and in Hollywood from 1930.

She had finally got started with the Shubert stock company in Buffalo, New York, "playing the smallest kind of parts," followed by an engagement with a repertoire company. After three years, she found that if she told managers her experience was from stock and repertoire, they refused to consider her for anything else. One of her friends finally convinced her that to get on in New York she needed to "select some 'line.'" Because she "wanted parts that had something queer in them," she decided to become a "character woman." But the New York producers still did not want her. She had almost decided to go home to the family farm in Canada, when her big opportunity presented itself: *A Pair of Sixes*, which she had first done in stock, was picked up by New York producer H.H. Frazee. Eburne was the only remaining cast member from the original stock production. Her famous fall was in fact put in at the Sunday dress rehearsal before the opening at the Longacre.[13]

During her more than dozen years of touring in stock companies, Eburne managed to pick up a husband in addition to a lot of acting experience. She married Eugene J. Hall, known as "Gene," in about 1905 and the couple had their first and only child, a daughter named Marion Birdseye Hall, in Hamilton, Ontario on May 7, 1907.[14]

Hall himself was born in Illinois in November 1874.[15] In 1900, we find him age 25 working as an actor in Chicago and boarding at 281 Dearborn Ave. with his first wife, Lillie Hall, who was 24 and an actress. They had been married a year.[16] What fate befell the first Mrs. Hall is uncertain. There is a "Lillie Hall" who had a few roles on Broadway between 1901 and 1904.[17] Gene Hall never made it to Broadway as an actor and turned to producing after he and Maude Eburne married.

A Pair of Sixes ran for six months in New York, closing in September 1914, and then went on tour, including no less than 22 weeks in Boston.[18] The *Boston Sunday Post* reported after the show had been running for seven weeks at the Wilbur Theatre: "From the opening night the performances of this merry comedy have been attended by large and laughing audiences, and there has not been one dissenting voice in the general verdict that it is the funniest farce that has been seen in Boston in many years."[19] Eburne went on to play a "Scotch housekeeper" in Edward Peple's next play, *The Girl*, which never made it to New York.[20]

Sadly but not atypically, Eburne never again achieved the level of celebrity and acclaim that *A Pair of Sixes* brought her, though she had 35 years left of her acting career, including 20 years on the silver screen. As she had feared, her success as Coddles obliged her to play comic maids, often pining from unrequited love, in forgettable but commercially successful farces and musical comedies for the remaining 15 years of her career on Broadway.[21] At least she was working and where she'd wanted to be for so long.

Her next Broadway show, *A Pair of Queens* (1916), was a "fair-to-middling" attempt to cash in on the success of *A Pair of Sixes* by producer Frazee at the Longacre, though with different authors. Eburne was "at her grotesquely amusing best" as Martha, but the show lasted only 15 performances.[22] In *Here Comes the Bride* (1917), produced by Klaw and Erlanger at George M. Cohan's Theatre, Eburne actually got to play the bride of the title, while Otto Kruger, "hardly happy in a piece of so coarse weave," was the young man who "weds because certain circumstances make it possible for him to earn $100,000 thereby."[23]

Eburne made her musical comedy debut in *The Canary* (1918–19) at the Globe Theatre and sang "You're So Beautiful" with the seasoned star comedian Joseph Cawthorn. Music and lyrics were by Irving Berlin. She played Mary Ellen, "an enamored cook of plain visage and awkward gait, the object of whose attentions and intentions was Mr. Cawthorn."[24] Coddles all over again, in other words. When the show came to the Colonial Theatre in Boston, one reviewer noted: "Maude Eburne was only in one act, but she created a vast amount of hilarity. Her Hibernian 'vamp' was a comic joy to be treasured in memory."[25] The successful comic pairing with Cawthorn was repeated again in *The Half Moon*, but the *New York Times* thought "that excellent awld Lunnon servant, Maude Eburne" was "unfortunately limited to the too short period of the third act."[26] This time, she didn't have any songs. *Love Dreams* (1921) saw her in yet another "burlesque maid's role."[27] As Hildegard, she got to sing "Reputation" with Harry K. Morton. With the exception of 1924 and 1925, Eburne averaged a show a year on Broadway throughout the 1920s.

In 1930, the Halls packed up and moved to the West Coast. Eburne's final show on Broadway was the new comedy *Many a Slip* at the Little Theatre (now the Helen Hayes), starring Douglass Montgomery and Sylvia Sidney, who would soon be going to Hollywood themselves. The show closed in March 1930 after 56 performances.[28] On April 4, 1930, Maude Eburne and her family appear in the U.S. census just as they are about to embark on their new lives in California. Maud Hall [sic], admitting only to 50, gives her profession as "Actress Theatrical"; Gene Hall, 52 on this occasion, though he was 55, gives his profession as "Producer Theatrical"; and the Hall's ostensibly 21-year-old daughter Marion, who is nearing 23, is also an actress. The family is living in a $15,000 owned home at 4137 Richmond Ave. on Staten Island.[29] Gene Hall only lived to be 57. He died in Los Angeles in January 1932 and was buried in Hollywood Forever Cemetery.[30]

Eburne made her sound film debut in *The Bat Whispers* on November 13, 1930. During the next two decades, she racked up well over 100 feature film appearances, though her roles were often uncredited. Despite starting out in a comic maid role very much of a piece with the parts she had been playing on the stage, Eburne was determined not to be typecast in films the way she had been in the theater. She was done with "Maude Eburne types": "servants, slaveys, housekeepers."[31] She discussed her plight with the director Russell Mack and was able to secure "something entirely different" in his next film, *Lonely Wives* (1931).[32]

The role in question was the ultimate mother-in-law, Mrs. Mantel, who sees it as her duty to stop her potential Lothario son-in-law, Edward Everett Horton, from straying while his wife is on holiday. Mrs. Mantel longs for the pitter-patter of little feet and surprises her son-in-law with his wife's sudden return. As was the case in most 1920s sex comedies and bedroom farces, the adultery is revealed at the end not to have taken place, but the endorsement of marriage in the film is anything but strong. Mrs. Mantel has the final word: "Well, thank heaven, all my husbands are dead."

As for so many others, the 1930s was Eburne's heyday. Though the parts were usually small, she finally "reveled in variety."[33] The pre–Code classic woman's prison film *Ladies They Talk About* (H. Bretherton, W. Keighley, Warner Bros., 1933), starring a still brunette Barbara Stanwyck, had a great part for Eburne as Aunt Maggie, a pipe-smoking, rocking-chair-enamored inmate and former madam with her hair in major disorder and a loud cackle. Aunt Maggie likes to refer to her whorehouse as a "beauty parlor" and gets the last line, when she says of Stanwyck: "She'd knock 'em cold in my beauty parlor." She rated a rare mention in a review for this effort, which stated, "Maude Eburne, as a lady of no uncertain past, is pleasing."[34]

One of the films she is best remembered for today is the Leo McCarey comedy *Ruggles of Red Gap* (Paramount, 1935). She has a high visibility role as Ma Pettingill, the mother of Mary Boland and Leota Lorraine, two socially ambitious women. Eburne has bankrolled them and got the latter a socially prominent, Boston Brahmin husband. Ma herself is unspoilt and earthy, favoring slouch hats, bandannas, and bow ties, with a cigarette always hanging from her lower lip. She has a whale of time when Boland's well-laid plans for attaining social prominence in Red Gap, Washington, go awry and is a supporter of both her son-in-law Charles Ruggles's and butler Charles Laughton's emancipation from domesticity and domestic service respectively.

In *Vivacious Lady* (G. Stevens, RKO, 1938), Eburne participates in an hilarious scene in a train compartment with her screen husband Spencer Charters, and stars James Stewart and

Maude Eburne in a bonnet that perfectly complements her timeless beauty is flanked in this still from *Lazy River* (Metro-Goldwyn-Mayer, 1934) by star Jean Parker and Erville Alderson. Eburne played Parker's mother and the owner of a failing shrimping business in a Cajun village in Louisiana.

Ginger Rogers. The two couples fight over the compartment and the marrieds fight with each other. Finally, Rogers and Stewart have to concede defeat. She played a judge presiding at a hearing about two babies switched at birth in *The Town Went Wild* (R. Murphy, Roth-Green-Rouse Prod., 1944), wearing pince-nez, with a distinctive white "Bride of Frankenstein" streak in her wavy hair and a mole on her chin. In *The Suspect* (R. Siodmak, Universal, 1944), another of her later films and a reunion with Charles Laughton almost ten years after *Ruggles of Red Gap*, she is visibly older and thinner as a romantically inclined forewoman at the dress shop in which Ella Raines works.

Despite the greater variety of her roles on film compared to her stage career, Eburne still played plenty of maids on the screen and landladies were another of her specialties. Her parts were mostly so small that she was seldom singled out in movie reviews. The following accolade in the *Syracuse Herald*, after the premiere of *Henry Aldrich, Editor* (H. Bennett, Paramount) in November 1942 with Jimmy Lydon in the title role, is an exception to the rule: "A very minor role—that of a neighbor who comes to the Aldrich home with a bowl of broth—is most delightfully played by that sterling character actress, Maude Eburne. Miss Eburne has been one of the most hilarious bit players on the screen since the days of the Lunts' early talkie 'The Gaurdsman,' and it is to be wished that we might see her more frequently."[35] The opposite turned out to be the case. Eburne's career started falling off after the war. She was last seen in a tiny, uncredited role as "woman companion at stock exchange" in the Western *Belle Le Grand* (A. Dwan, Republic), which opened on January 27, 1951.

Though *Belle Le Grand* marked the end of Eburne's acting career at age 75, including her many and marvelous impersonations of the classic mother-in-law, ironically it marked the beginning of her belated opportunity to be a mother-in-law in real life. For playing a modest role as stock exchange clerk in the same scene of *Belle Le Grand* as Eburne was a 30-year-old actor by the name of Sam Sebby. On April 11, 1953, Sam Sebby became Eburne's son-in-law when he married her daughter Marion. At this point, of course, Marion was no longer in the first blush of youth, in fact she was nearly 46 and thus 13 years older than her husband. Lest this age difference appear too vast, she resorted to a stratagem worthy of one of Eburne's many lovelorn spinsters and shaved off no less than 11 years from her age.[36] One wonders if this was on her mother's recommendation.

The fact that both bride and groom give their address on the marriage license as 1623½ N. Lyman Pl. in Hollywood makes me suspect that young Mr. Sebby may have begun his relationship with Mrs. Hall and her daughter as a lodger in their home. It is all too easy to imagine Eburne meeting a good-looking young man on her last film set and inviting him home for a nice home cooked meal. Or, indeed, in a different scenario, maybe Sam was already living with the family as a lodger and Eburne got him a bit part in her final film.

Prior to *Belle Le Grand*, Sebby had played an uncredited role as a bandit in *Hit Parade of 1951* and a spectator in *The Pride of Maryland* (1951). His film career never came to anything and was over by 1952.

Sam Raymond Sebby, Jr., was born in Arizona on March 4, 1920, as the eldest of the two children of Sam Sebby (1885–1944) and Carmelita Michaels Sebby (1892–1987).[37] In 1940, 13 years before he became Maude Eburne's son-in-law, 20-year-old college student Sam was living with his parents, younger sister Juanita and her husband in a home valued at $1,200 at 4421 Staunton Ave. in the Central Alameda section of South Los Angeles. Sam Sebby, Sr., earned $1,200 in 1939 in a janitorial job at a masonic temple.[38] In comparison, Eburne and her daughter Marion were living in style in a $75 a month rented apartment in the resplendently white, French chateau style Trianon apartment building, which still stands at 1750 N. Serrano Ave. on the corner of Loma Linda Ave., just a block up from Hollywood Blvd.[39] Marion Hall at 32 was still calling herself an actress, though apparently no one was willing to pay her to be one, as she had no wage income in 1939. She had been unemployed for 78 weeks up until March 30, 1940.[40] Her mother had earned in excess of $5,000 for only ten weeks' work in 1939,[41] one of her peak years with ten films released, including the first "Dr. Christian" film *Meet Doctor Christian* (B. Vorhaus, Stephens-Lang Prod.). Eburne played Jean Hersholt's devoted housekeeper Mrs. Hastings in all six films of the series, one of the roles she is best remembered for.

Towards the end of World War II, Sam Sebby, Jr., married a woman called Helen Isabel Richards. She was born in 1907 and was thus 13 years older than him.[42] The couple had two children: Holly Linora Sebby (b. 1944) and Scott Lawrence Sebby (b. 1947).[43] So in addition to getting a husband from a working-class family, whose acting career was more or less at a standstill, Marion Hall Sebby also got two stepchildren aged nine and six. One imagines, though, that her mother was no snob and was probably thrilled that her one and only daughter had finally gotten herself a man.

Alas, Maude Eburne was not able to enjoy being a mother-in-law and step-grandmother for long. Her daughter Marion Birdseye Hall Sebby died in Los Angeles on February 14, 1960, and was buried in Hollywood Forever Cemetery.[44] She was only 52. It is always especially poignant when a mother lives longer than her child. This happened to Grace George. It happened to Sally Munson, Ona Munson's mother. It happened to Molly Moorehead, Agnes Moorehead's mother. And it happened to Maude Eburne. She did not long have to mourn Marion, though. Maude Eburne Hall died in Hollywood on October 15, 1960, only eight months after her daughter.[45] She was 85.

As for "the son-in-law" Sam Sebby, he appears to have had a thing for older women. After Marion Hall's death, he married for the third and final time in 1968. His new wife, Frances Severns Price (1904–97), claimed to be 54 at the time of her marriage, but was actually 64, while Sam was 48.[46] Sam R. Sebby, Jr., died in 2004 and is buried in Forest Lawn Memorial Park, Glendale.[47]

The Show Must Go On: Effie Ellsler (1855–1942)

As the wronged miller's daughter Hazel Kirke, she became a star of the American stage in the 1880s. She created the role of the amateur lady detective Cornelia Van Gorder in the classic thriller *The Bat* on Broadway in 1920. And she was Hildy Johnson's hard-tried and increasingly belligerent, potential mother-in-law Mrs. Grant in the first film version of *The Front Page* in 1931. Beyond that, though, Effie Ellsler deserves to be remembered as the earliest born actress to have had a film career in the sound era.

By a film career, I don't just mean a couple of films. I mean at least a dozen identifiable, credited roles. What about May Robson, you may object. Or Jessie Ralph? Or May Whitty? Well, they certainly had more important film careers than Ellsler, but they were all born later than her: Robson in 1858, Ralph in 1864, and Whitty in 1865. Still, what about Gertrude Norman or Clara T. Bracy, who both appeared as extras with Ellsler and Robson in the "Grandma" segment of *If I Had a Million*? Granted, Norman and Bracy were both born in 1848, but the majority of their roles were in silent films. Norman only had four credited roles in sound films and Bracy had none. Ellsler, on the other hand, appeared in 19 sound features between 1929 and 1936, from *Woman Trap* (W.A. Wellman, Paramount) to *Camille* (G. Dukor, MGM). Twelve of her roles were credited. Before that, she had done three silent films in the mid–1920s.

Euphemia "Effie" Elizabeth Ellsler was born in Philadelphia or Cleveland on September 17, 1855.[1] While most people grow older as the years go by, Ellsler had an unnatural tendency to grow younger. Indeed, she had the most creative attitude to her age of any actress I've written about. I've located her in every U.S. census from 1880 till 1940 and she doesn't give her correct age in any of them. In 1880, she claimed to be 20 when she is in fact 24.[2] In 1900, she pretended to be 36 when she was 44.[3] In 1910, she said she was 42 rather than 54.[4] 1920 really takes the cake, though. Ellsler was 64, but claimed to be 45![5] In 1930, she was 74 when the census enumerator knocked on her door, but only admitted to 64.[6] Finally, in 1940, though retired and living in an old age home, she still isn't ready to come clean, saying she is 72 when she is really 84.[7]

Ellsler's parents were important figures in the American theater in the mid-nineteenth century. John A. Ellsler was born to German parents in Harrisburg, Pennsylvania, in 1822 and went on the stage at an early age. For 21 years, Ellsler was the manager of the Cleveland Theatre (later the Academy of Music) and in 1873–75 he built the Euclid Avenue Opera House in the same city. On his death in New York City in 1903, he was said to have "started in their careers Clara Morris, Joseph Haworth, James O'Neil, his own daughter, Mrs. Effie Ellsler Weston, the original Hazel Kirke, and several other well-known actors and actresses."[8]

Ellsler's mother was born Euphemia Emma Murray in Philadelphia in 1823 and like her daughter was known professionally as Effie Ellsler. She was born into a theatrical family with a father from Scotland and a mother from England. The "First Effie Ellsler," as one newspaper called her on her death in 1918, performed with many famous players of her day, such as Joseph Jefferson, Edwin Forrest, Charlotte Cushman, Clara Morris, and Edward and Charles Keane. She also co-owned and managed the Cleveland Academy of Music and several other theaters with her husband. Ellsler retired in 1874 after playing Portia to Edwin Booth's Shylock in *The Merchant of Venice*. He called her "the best Portia I ever heard." It was a long retirement, as Ellsler lived to be 95. Towards the end of her life, she was referred to in the press as "the oldest living American actress" and "the oldest English speaking actress in the world."[9]

The younger Effie Ellsler was so closely tied to her birth family that she lived with her parents and siblings most of her long life, even as a married woman. Ellsler's younger brother, William Cary Ellsler (1865–1936), was married to Martha B. Chamberlin (b. 1871) in 1898, but did not live with his wife and worked as a theatrical agent and business manager.[10] Younger sister Annie May Ellsler (1859?-1938) supported herself as a typewriter and music teacher and lived all her life with Effie.[11] She made a brief stab at an acting career, when she supported her sister as the maid Clara in *Hazel Kirke* and is listed as an actress in the 1880 U.S. census.[12]

On the stage, Ellsler would be most closely identified with the title role of Steele MacKaye's popular drama *Hazel Kirke*, which she played in a record-breaking run starting February 4, 1880, at the newly reopened Madison Square Theatre in New York.[13] She was then living with her sister Annie and a 30-year-old actor called Frank Weston in the Bell family's small boarding house at 250 W. 21st St. in New York, only a few blocks from the theater.[14] All told, Ellsler played Hazel Kirke for three years and an estimated 1,500 performances.[15] It was thought by some "she might have become a greater actress had not prolonged association with Hazel Kirke stunted her development."[16]

It was at the height of her success with *Hazel Kirke* that Ellsler married Frank Weston in Chicago on May 25, 1881.[17] Weston was born in New York in 1850 and served in the Civil War "when still a boy."[18] Weston was "a leading man with the McVicker stock company in Chicago and also with the Ellsler stock company in Cleveland."[19] He was known for playing Shakespearean roles and had a smattering of credits on Broadway as a character actor in the first dozen years of the 20th century, including supporting his wife who was playing the title role in Clyde Fitch's *Barbara Frietchie* and as the Duke of Venice in *The Merchant of Venice*, both in 1901.[20] Ellsler was carrying on in her mother's tradition by playing Jessica in the latter play at the age of 45, while Nat Goodwin was Shylock and Maxine Elliott was Portia.

After *The Merchant of Venice*, Ellsler went into retirement for the first of several times.[21] Maybe poor reviews had something to do with it. The *New York Times* observed, "Miss Effie Ellsler as Jessica made no particular mark."[22] Producer Arthur Hopkins brought her back to Broadway in 1913 for the farce *We Are Seven* at Maxine Elliott's Theatre and again in 1917 at age 62 for her first "old lady's part," Mrs. Widdimore in *The Gipsy Trail* at the Plymouth Theatre (now the Gerald Schoenfeld).[23] This time the *New York Times* wrote: "Miss Ellsler sounds every note in the part with unerring art."[24] On August 23, 1920, Ellsler opened at the Morosco Theatre in what would prove the biggest hit of her later career: Mary Roberts Rinehart and Avery Hopwood's classic thriller *The Bat*.

Effie Ellsler at about the time she rocketed to stardom in Steele MacKaye's drama about a wronged miller's daughter, *Hazel Kirke*, in the early 1880s. Born in 1855, Ellsler was the earliest born actress to have a film career in the sound era.

Ellsler and Frank Weston had been wed during the long run of *Hazel Kirke* and their 40-year marriage ended during the long run of *The Bat,* when Weston died at their home at 172 W. 79th St. on Saturday, January 28, 1922. Ellsler had to give two performances that day and her husband's death was kept from her till the matinee was over. She also went on in the evening, as she had no understudy to replace her. This "esprit de corps" in the face of the worst loss of her life captured the imagination of the newspapers. "Plucky Effie Essler Goes On With Acting Though Husband Dead" read the front-page headline in the *Helena Independent.*[25] Under the title "Frank Weston Dead as His Wife Plays," the *New York Times* gave an account of Ellsler's domestic tragedy. Weston was first taken ill with pneumonia on Wednesday evening while waiting for his wife behind the scenes of the Morosco Theatre.[26] He had to be taken home in an ambulance and lost consciousness. Christian Science healer Claude M. Spaulding was with him when he died at 9 o'clock Saturday morning, as was his sister-in-law Annie Ellsler, who gave a statement to the press. When his wife came into his room briefly at noon before leaving for the theater, Annie explained, "She thought Frank was still unconscious and would recover all right. We did not tell her to the contrary." "It was a beautiful death," she added. Weston was 72 and had retired "some six years ago."[27] "My husband would tell me to

Florence Vidor (left) as the heroine Gail Grant and Effie Ellsler as her companion Miss Molosey in the silent film *Honeymoon Hate* (Paramount Famous Lasky Corp., 1927). Ellsler's once fashionably retroussé nose is clearly visible here, while her hat could never have been fashionable at any time.

go on with my work," Ellsler explained.[28] This was the last time Ellsler was in the headlines, though she had 20 years left to live. She stayed on for the entire run of *The Bat* until it closed in September 1922, giving 867 performances. It was her last show on Broadway.[29]

Ellsler first went out to Hollywood in 1926, when she, William, and Annie lived at 1825 Ivar Ave., though she did not begin to get steady work in films until the advent of sound.[30] In 1927–28, they lived at 1800 El Cerrito Pl, which was also in Hollywood.[31] In the early 1930s, the three of them were living at 242 N. Western Ave., a large, plain apartment building, which as the seedy-looking San Marco Hotel and Apartments is still standing on the corner of Beverly Blvd. in the Oakwood section of Hollywood.[32] In fact, all the apartment buildings in which Ellsler is known to have lived in Los Angeles are still standing.

During her years in Hollywood, Ellsler was given large roles in "small" films and modest roles in more prestigious pictures. Her credited role as the vengeful, widowed ranch owner and matriarch Granny Dunn in the minor western *Drift Fence* (O. Lovering, Paramount, 1936) is an example of the former and her uncredited role as Robert Taylor's lace-capped grandmother, Madame Duval, in *Camille* (G. Cukor, MGM, 1936) is typical of the latter. Ellsler only had one line in *Camille*—"What a happy day!"—which was the last she would ever utter on stage or screen.

My favorite Ellsler performance apart from Mrs. Grant in *The Front Page* (L. Milestone, Caddo, 1931) is probably Mona in *Song o' My Heart* (F. Borzage, Fox, 1930), an oddly stagey film and a blatant vehicle for the legendary Irish tenor John McCormack (1884–1945), who basically plays himself and naturally breaks into song at regular intervals. Ellsler's exact relation to him is never explained, but she is his friend and confidante and asks him at one point to sing "The Rose of Tralee." The best part of the film, though, is Ellsler's interaction with the arch villainess of the piece, Emily Fitzroy (1860–1954), as tall and thin as Ellsler is small and dumpy. Ellsler's big moment comes when she gives Fitzroy a piece of her mind and tells her she is the kind of woman who should use less time arranging the affairs of others and more on her own. Fitzroy starred in Roland West's 1926 silent film version of *The Bat*. It is an amusing coincidence that the two original Cornelia Van Gorders should be confronted in this way.

In 1936, the year she retired for good, Ellsler was making her home with William and Annie at the Havenhurst, an imposing, five-story, white stucco apartment building on the southwest corner of Whitley Ave. and Franklin Ave. in Hollywood, across from the present-day Hollywood Ardmore Apartments.[33] 1861 Whitley Ave. was a good address in an area favored by supporting actresses of a certain standing in the profession. With the death of her brother William in 1936 and sister Annie in 1938,[34] Ellsler found herself the last surviving member of her family.

Ellsler's final years were spent in the Pacific Old People's Home of the German Methodist Church at 1055 N. Kingsley Dr. near Santa Monica Blvd.[35] Hopefully, it was a cheerier place than "Idylwood" ("A Rest Place for Elderly Women") under Blanche Friderici's draconian regime in the final segment of *If I Had a Million*. Hopefully, Ellsler did not miss her husband quite as much as her character in that film, Mrs. Scott, who talks to a pillow and pretends "James" is still alive. Effie Ellsler Weston died in Los Angeles on October 8, 1942, of hardening of the arteries after a three week illness and was laid to rest with her brother and sister in the "Pineland" section of Hollywood Forever Cemetery.[36]

I Remember Edith: Edith Evanson (1896–1980)

As a Scandinavian author, it is high time I wrote about a Scandinavian American character actress. As the daughter of Swedish immigrants to the United States, I imagine that Edith Evanson's childhood was not unlike that of Katrin, the character played by Barbara Bel Geddes in *I Remember Mama*. Evanson would indeed grow up to play stern, pettish Aunt Sigrid in RKO's sentimental comedy about a Norwegian American family in San Francisco in the early years of the last century. The Carlsons, though, were Swedish American and Edith Carlson, as Edith Evanson was born, grew up on J St. in Tacoma, Washington, and not Larkin St. in San Francisco. Evanson's own "mama," Eva Carlson, would have been about the same age as Irene Dunne's Marta Hansen. Maybe she, too, was glad "ve do not haf to go to de bank."

At any rate, Edith Evanson's mother was born Eva Hokanson in Sweden in September 1856, the daughter of Nels Hokanson and Martha Jacobson.[1] Eva immigrated to the United States in 1880, when she was 24, and became a naturalized American citizen in 1885.[2] Five years later, we find her married to John Carlson and living with him and their one-year-old son Carl in Minneapolis, Minnesota.[3] John Adolph Carlson was born in Sweden in 1858.[4] Between 1884 and 1896, John and Eva had six children: five boys and then, finally, a girl. Edith's five older brothers were Carl Martin Carlson (1884–1971), Edwin H. Carlson (1886–1977), Victor Emanuel Carlson (1888–1923), Iver Adolph Carlson (1890–1982), and John Hugo Carlson (1894–1951). Carl, who never married, was a sheet metal worker in younger years, lived in Alaska during World War II, and was living in Los Angeles at the time of his death. Edwin was working as a welder in an auto shop in Olympia, Washington, in 1920, was back living with his mother in Tacoma at the time of her death in 1930, and finally married a much younger woman late in life, settled down in Los Angeles and worked as a machinist. Victor, who had lived in Vancouver and worked as a stationer in a bindery during World War I, had just graduated from the Palmer School of Chiropractic in Davenport, Iowa, when he died on July 8, 1923, only 34 years old, leaving a widow and two children. Iver (also spelled *Ivar*), who outlived all his siblings and died age 92, worked as a plumber and spent his life in his hometown of Tacoma, Washington, though he met his end in Clark County, Nevada. He never married. Finally, John Hugo, who was known as Hugo, lived in San Francisco with his wife Ellen and son Gordon, worked as the manager of an electrical supply store, and died at the age of 57.[5]

The two eldest Carlson boys were born in Minneapolis, but by 1888 the family had relocated to Tacoma, Washington. It was there that Edith Carlson saw the light of day on April

29, 1896.[6] On October 27, 1898, Edith's father John Carlson died at the age of 40 and was buried in Tacoma Cemetery, where his gravestone is still to be found.[7] Edith was only two and a half years old. Eva Carlson was left to raise six children on her own. She never remarried. In 1900, we find the family living at 3607 S. J St. in a modest one and one half story wooden house, which they own. Carl (16) and Edwin (14) are working as office boys. The other boys are in school. Edith is just four years old.[8] Edith grew up in this two bedroom, one bathroom house from 1890, just a block from Lincoln Park in South Tacoma.[9] In 1910, Eva and her six children were still living there. The four oldest boys were now working. Edith (14) was still at school.[10]

Just a mile away at 4310 S. Sheridan Ave., in the same South Tacoma neighborhood, there lived a 17-year-old boy called Morris Otto Evanson with his widowed mother Oline and four brothers and sisters between the ages of 14 and 27.[11] Morris Evanson, who you will have guessed became Edith's husband, was born on March 2, 1893, in Shell Lake, Wisconsin.[12] He was just a year older than Edith's youngest brother Hugo. Indeed, the two of them may have been friends. Many years later, when Morris registered for the draft during World War II, he listed Hugo Carlson as his next of kin.[13]

In 1910, Morris was working to support his family as a bundle-wrapper in a dry goods store. His mother Oline A. Evanson (*née* Borgin) was born in Norway in 1858 and had eight children with her equally Norwegian-born husband Hans, six of whom were still living.[14] Oline and her family had come to Tacoma from Duluth, Minnesota, in about 1904.[15] Oline died in 1915, by which time the Evanson family was living at 3718 S. M. St, which was just three blocks from the Carlsons' house on J St.[16] Morris was still living there when he registered for the draft on June 5, 1917, the same day as Edith's 26-year-old brother Iver also registered. Morris was described age 24 as tall with a slender build, blue eyes and dark hair. He was working as a mechanic.[17]

By 1920, only Iver and Edith were still living at home with mama Eva. The family had moved to a better house on a corner lot, but they hadn't moved far. 3602 S. Thompson Ave. was just across the back alley from their old house.[18] Edith, who was now 23 years old, was working as a stenographer in a law office and Iver, unmarried at 27, was working as a pipe fitter in a smelting works.[19] Edith had left home by 1930, when we find Eva still living in the Thompson Ave. house with her two unmarried sons Edwin, 44 and a machinist, and Iver, 39 and a plumber.[20] Eva died on April 10, 1930, just eight days after census enumerator Nellie C. Power called at her home. She was 73 years old.[21]

Edith Carlson and Morris Evanson disappear from the public record between the 1920 and the 1940 census. These decades included the early years of their marriage and the beginning of Evanson's acting career. Apparently her greatest claim to fame prior to the beginning of her film career in 1940 was a recurring role as the Swedish maid Helmi on the radio soap opera *Myrt and Marge* (also called *The Story of Myrt and Marge*), which originally starred Myrtle Vail and Donna Damerel and ran on CBS from 1931 till 1942. Radio historian John Dunning describes it as "one of the first important dramatic serials on radio" and Evanson's role as "the faithful maid who has gone through so many of Myrt and Marge's experiences with them" and who has a propensity to sing *Yingle Bells* endlessly at Christmas.[22] During its first six years as a nighttime drama, the serial was broadcast from Chicago,[23] which suggests Evanson must have been living there at the time. We know she and her husband were living in Oakland, California, by 1935.[24]

By April 21, 1940, when census enumerator Norbert J. Valla called on the couple, they were living in a $30 a month rented apartment at 1610 Cosmo St. in Los Angeles. This house number near the corner of Selma Ave. no longer exists, but Cosmo St. is a small street only a block long running between Selma and Hollywood Blvd. in the heart of Hollywood. The Evansons probably had not lived in L.A. long, as Edith Evanson had just started on her film career the previous year. She reported that she was working as an actress in motion pictures and had earned $600 for three weeks' work in 1939, though she also had income from other sources than money wages or salary. Morris Evanson was working as a trimmer of window displays and earned $1,200 for 34 weeks' work in 1939. Edith had two years of college, while Morris only had a high school education.[25]

By the time Morris again did his patriotic duty and registered for the draft on April 26, 1942, he and his wife were living at 1933½ Vista Del Mar Ave., a neighborhood of modest but cozy Craftsman style homes on small lots just above the Hollywood Freeway and Franklin Ave. Morris is described at age 49 as being 5'11" tall, weighing 160 pounds, with blue eyes, gray hair, and a light complexion.[26]

Evanson is different from the vast majority of the Hollywood character actresses I have profiled, because she didn't have extensive stage experience prior to her film career. At least I haven't found evidence of any. She certainly didn't have the imprimatur of Broadway and never performed on the New York stage. Thus she must have found an entrée into the movie industry through a different channel. Though Evanson got a late start in the movies (she was 43 years old when her first feature film was released), her film career spanned 30 years and five decades. She reported for work on the first of her 75 feature films, *The Man Who Wouldn't Talk* (D. Burton), in September 1939 and her final film, *The Seven Minutes* (R. Meyer), was produced in late 1970.[27] As it happened, both films were for Twentieth Century–Fox.

Character actresses are usually either ordinary looking or extraordinary looking. Evanson belongs to the former group. Her appearance was chiefly distinguished by narrow, almost vulpine eyes, often hidden behind severe, steel-rimmed glasses, and a long, sloping, pointy nose. With this physical starting point, Evanson was able to convey quite a remarkable sense of ordinariness on the screen. This may not sound like high praise, but is intended to be. To be able to convey the quality of being a perfectly ordinary woman, usually a working woman, going about her day to day, mundane tasks is much harder than it sounds. Evanson was a gifted portrayer of the "little woman," and for that reason alone I love many of her performances, however modest. Ironically, because she so often fades into the woodwork, I imagine there aren't many, even among avid film fans, who remember her today. Yet, to quote Linda Loman: "attention must be paid" to such a woman. Someone has to play the cleaning ladies, maids, and housekeepers in the movies and there is a craft to that, too, just like everything else in acting.

Though she gave perfect performances in films like *I Remember Mama* (G. Stevens, RKO, 1948), *Caged* (J. Cromwell, Warner Bros., 1950), and *The Big Heat* (F. Lang, Columbia, 1953) and even had a small part as Joseph Cotten's nurse in *Citizen Kane* (O. Welles, Mercury Productions, 1940), there is really only one picture that shows to the full what Edith Evanson was capable of on the big screen and that is Alfred Hitchcock's *Rope* (Transatlantic Pictures, 1948). *Rope* was Hitchcock's "first Technicolor film, his first as an independent producer, his first release by Warner Bros., his first with actor James Stewart, and the first film in which he could experiment with new creative techniques."[28] It was based on a hit play by British playwright

Riding this streetcar named desire in *I Remember Mama* (RKO Radio Pictures, 1948), we find (from left) Edith Evanson as Aunt Sigrid, Hope Landin as Aunt Jenny, Edgar Bergen as Mr. Thorkelson, and Ellen Corby as Aunt Trina. As a Norwegian myself, I have to note that Bergen is the only actor with a genuine Norwegian accent in this film, which may have been because he was the only cast member who was actually Norwegian American. Evanson was Swedish American, Landin had Swedish grandparents on her father's side, and Corby was of Danish descent.

Patrick Hamilton. Evanson plays Mrs. Wilson, a cleaning woman for an effete, upper-class male couple in New York City, Brandon (John Dall) and Philip (Farley Granger). Mrs. Wilson also works part-time as a server at parties and one of those parties is about to take place when the film opens with the murderous and unmotivated, thrill-seeking strangulation by Brandon and Philip of a mutual friend, David Kentley, and the placing of his body in an antique Italian chest in the middle of their living room.

Evanson's Mrs. Wilson is quite a character in every sense of the word. Her hair is frizzled in its usual home permanent, mousy brown style and she also wears her customary steel-rimmed glasses, which make her eyes seem even smaller and narrower. Her two touches of genius are in the wardrobe department, if indeed they were her own creations. Character women frequently had to provide their own wardrobe. The first is the incredible hat with two small white, feathered wings protruding like a kind of grotesque parody of Mercury's helmet and the other is the headpiece of white flowers she dons in the place of a traditional maid's cap when she realizes this is going to be a fancy supper party where champagne will be served.

Mrs. Wilson is clearly in the maladroit maid tradition, that in film can be traced back to the various versions of Lizzie Allen in *The Bat*, Hattie McDaniel's disastrous attempts to lend "tone" to the Adams's dinner party in *Alice Adams* (1935), and less familiarly to Helen Lowell's delightful performance as the family maid Martha in *Big Hearted Herbert* (1934), starring Aline MacMahon and Guy Kibbee. The comedic aspects of Mrs. Wilson are subtle and understated, of course, given the generally somber and suspense-filled mood of *Rope* and mostly consist in the juxtaposition of her folksy, opinionated, and loquacious personality with the urbane, sophisticated, and blasé spirit of most of the guests at the party.

Beyond comic relief, Mrs. Wilson's more important function is to heighten the suspense through her attempt to clear away the supper table and put the old books back in the chest. She also serves as what Henry James once described as a *ficelle*, which is French for thread and indicates a character who provides information needed by another character or characters in the story and, by extension, the reader or audience. Thus, Mrs. Wilson is an important source of information for Rupert Cadell (James Stewart), the two young men's former schoolmaster, in his subtle investigations into the strange goings on in the apartment prior to his arrival. Mrs. Wilson's big scene is when she fills Rupert in on the events of the day leading up to the party: how Brandon was in a rush to have her set up the table and then told her to take her time in shopping, how both he and Philip must have gotten up on the wrong side of the bed that morning ("When I came back he and Mr. Philip were going at it hammer and tongs"), and how they changed the table arrangements in her absence, ruining her lovely table and making more work for her. Philip finally gets fed up with her mixing with the guests and tells her: "Mrs. Wilson, please serve the guests, don't lecture them."

During a long conversation between Rupert and the boys off screen about what might have happened to David, the camera stays resolutely focused on Mrs. Wilson as she begins to clear away the supper things and gets closer and closer to putting the books back in the chest which contains the murder victim David Kentley's body. It is Mrs. Wilson who mistakenly gives Rupert David's hat, which is far too small for him and has the initials DK embossed in gold inside. After getting her keys back so she can come in and finish clearing up in the morning, she says to her employers, "I want both of you to come back in tip top A1 shape" after their trip to the farm and takes herself off.

Rope was filmed during May and June 1948 at Warner Bros. Burbank studios.[29] Farley Granger recalled that there had been 15 days of rehearsals and 21 days of filming.[30] Screenwriter Arthur Laurents made the revealing remark in his autobiography *Original Story By*, "the actress who played [the maid] ... was treated like a maid by the other actors when they sat around the set."[31] The film was released on August 28, 1948. One reviewer took time to note, "Edith Evanson invests her role of the domestic with sharp clarity."[32] Hitchcock probably appreciated the mix of mundanity, myopia, and meddlesomeness Evanson projected so well on the screen. Yet there was also an ever so slightly ghoulish air about her, that made her an apt handmaiden to two murderers. Hitchcock used Evanson again in two episodes of *Alfred Hitchcock Presents* in 1957–58 and in *Marnie* (1964), her last major film, though her role as a hard-of-hearing cleaning lady was tiny.

It's ironic that the only time the press showed any real interest in Evanson was in 1962 after Marilyn Monroe committed suicide. Evanson had been hired on the behest of her "old friend" George Cukor to coach Monroe in the Swedish accent she needed for what was to be her final film role, though never completed, in *Something's Got to Give*, which Cukor was

Part of the excitement of *Rope* (Transatlantic Pictures, 1948) is the impending threat of Edith Evanson's character Mrs. Wilson literally blowing the lid off the murder committed by John Dall (left), while James Stewart looks suspiciously on. Evanson was always good, but she was never better than in this classic thriller.

directing. At this difficult time in Monroe's life, Evanson apparently became as much a confidante as a coach and was "in almost daily contact with Marilyn for most of the last two months of her life." AP Hollywood correspondent James Bacon's interview with Evanson about Monroe was widely reprinted. Under the headline "Film Coach Tells of Marilyn," Evanson related some of her experiences with Monroe during her final days. "I never noticed anything odd about her," she said, "except her too-casual—for a movie star—style of dress. But there appeared to be a gap in her life. She had only two moods. One moment she would be a little girl. The next a serious, matured woman." Monroe had once remarked to Evanson: "Isn't it a terrible thing about life, that there always must be something we have to live up to?"[33]

Between 1953 and 1974, Evanson worked extensively in television with appearances on shows like *The Ford Television Theatre*, *Letter to Loretta*, *The Millionaire*, *General Electric Theatre*, *Wagon Train*, *Gunsmoke*, and *Nanny and the Professor*. By the time of Morris Evanson's death on December 30, 1975, at the age of 82, he and his wife were living in Riverside, California.[34] Edith Evanson died in Riverside on November 29, 1980, at the age of 84.[35] She was cremated and her ashes scattered in the Pacific Ocean.[36]

Gone Too Soon: Blanche Friderici (1873–1933)

In the 1930s, there were three major character actresses who died while still in their prime. The first was Louise Closser Hale, who played the maid Miranda in *Letty Lynton* with Joan Crawford, Powers in *The Barbarian* with Myrna Loy, Mother Hallam in *Another Language*, and Hattie Loomis in *Dinner at Eight* among her many fine, mostly comedic roles during her fours years in Hollywood. Hale died aged 60 on July 26, 1933. The cause of death was given as a heart attack due to heat prostration, but there were rumors of a botched operation. Then there was Beryl Mercer, who specialized in Cockney servants and landladies in films like *Outward Bound, The Miracle Woman*, and *Cavalcade*, and was James Cagney's mother in *The Public Enemy*. Mercer was thought to be 56 when she died on July 28, 1939, following a major operation, but she may have been older.[1] Finally, there was Blanche Friderici.

When Friderici died only five months after Louise Closser Hale, it was front page news in small town newspapers across America. "Heart Attack Fatal to a Noted Actress" read the headline in the Joplin, Missouri *News Herald* on Christmas Day 1933. The newspaper reported that the previous day Friderici had died suddenly of a heart attack near Visalia, California, en route to a Christmas Service in General Grant Memorial Park. With her at the time was her husband, Donald Campbell, "stage manager for the Henry Duffy productions."[2] The *New York Times* reported that Friderici had died in her automobile, while the *New York Herald Tribune*, based on an AP bulletin, claimed her death had taken place at the Giant Forest Lodge on December 23rd.[3] She was buried December 26th in Hollywood.[4]

When Friderici died suddenly and unexpectedly in late 1933, the *New York Times* reported that she was 55 years old.[5] Yet her birth certificate and census data from 1892 and 1900 give us incontrovertible evidence that Friderici was born in 1873, not 1878. Blanche L. Friderici saw the light of day in Brooklyn on September 12, 1873.[6] Nothing has hitherto been known of her family background. I have discovered that Blanche was the only child of William E. Friderici (from Pennsylvania) and Rosetta Elizabeth Freeman Friderici (born in Pennsylvania in 1833).[7] Apart from his name on her birth record, William Friderici has disappeared from the public record. We know only that he died before 1892, when we find Blanche aged 19 and her 58-year-old mother still living in Brooklyn. Blanche is working as a "professional reader."[8] Eight years later, we find the two of them at 131 Quincy St., a small but handsome, three-window-wide, three-story-tall, red brick row house with white stone trim, a classic stoop, and an elaborate Italianate pediment which still stands in the Clinton Hill section of Brooklyn. They are sharing their home with two male boarders and a 16-year-old maid from an orphan asylum. At age 26, Friderici is still unmarried and is working as a teacher.[9] I have not found Blanche or her mother in the U.S. census for 1910 or 1920.

The early years of Friderici's acting career are obscure. She appears to have gotten a relatively late start as an actress. As we have seen, she was working as a teacher in 1900. A feature article from 1922 makes it clear why traces of her early days on the stage are hard to find. The article explains that she "had to change her own name for others according to the whims of different managers." Among her aliases were Katherine Miller, Elizabeth Everett, Harriet Halstead, and Jane Burnett."[10]

An article from 1928 claimed that Friderici "studied voice and drama under Rose Eytinge, Sarah Cowell LeMoyne and May Robson." She was conducting her own concert orchestra and her own dramatic classes at 20, but "a budding promise of greatness was cut short by near-blindness." Her sight improved after a year and she did two roles in *The Darling of the Gods* ("A Drama of Japan") for David Belasco, which played at the Belasco Theatre in New York during the 1902–03 and 1903–04 seasons, though there is no record of Friderici's participation under any of her known stage names. During a 100-week stock engagement in Portland, Maine, a local doctor helped bring back her sight permanently. "In her career of the stage," the newspaper reported, "she has played 600 character parts, from comedy to tragedy, but never an ingénue and not in one love scene." Friderici also performed in vaudeville under the management of Percy Williams.[11] In 1932, we find her being described as a "former Syracuse stock actress."[12]

In 1908, we know Friderici wrote a comedy monologue "Huldy Hoadley" with Charles Barnard for the Southern Illinois State Normal University jubilee afternoon entertainment.[13] The following spring, she is on record as playing an "Irish character part" in a modern farce by Radcliffe College alumna Agnes Bangs Morgan presented at the Berkeley Theatre by the Radcliffe Club of New York to benefit the scholarship fund. Class of '99 Radcliffe graduate Josephine Hull (as Josephine Sherwood) was in the lead.[14] Friderici's earliest known Broadway show under her own name was *Omar, the Tentmaker*, which starred Guy Bates Post in the title role and ran for more than 100 performances at the Lyric Theatre in 1914.[15]

Five years later, Friderici created the classic spinster role of Miss MacMasters in Rachel Crothers's New York boarding house comedy *39 East*. The play opened at the Broadhurst Theatre on March 31, 1919, and starred Constance Binney with Tallulah Bankhead taking over the lead during Binney's summer break.[16] Friderici made her film debut in September 1920, when *39 East* (J.S. Robertson, Realart Pictures) was filmed with the original cast of the play.

One of her more successful but ludicrous stage roles was Mammy Pleasant in the classic thriller *The Cat and the Canary*, which she played in blackface in support of fellow Brooklyner Florence Eldridge and Henry Hull at the National Theatre in New York in the spring of 1922.[17] According to the *New York American*, Friderici managed to "inject a blood-curdling interest into that mystery drama" as a "saturnine old West Indian woman."[18] She reprised her role in the first sound version entitled *The Cat Creeps* (R. Julian, J. Willard, Universal, 1930), while Gale Sondergaard played it in the 1939 remake at Paramount.

Presumably Rosetta Friderici, who would have been 92, was dead by the time her daughter unexpectedly left spinsterhood behind in 1925 and married a man 20 years her junior. Donald Campbell would have realized he was younger than his wife, but how much younger he probably never knew, as by this time Friderici was pretending to be ten years younger than her real age. Despite the commonness of his name, I have been able to find out quite a bit about Mr. Campbell, who was prepared at age 32 to marry a 52-year-old woman. Maybe they had a union of the spirit and many common interests. Maybe Campbell, who is described aged 23 in his draft registration as being of medium height and build with blue eyes and brown hair, was no big looker himself.[19]

At any rate, Donald T. Campbell was born in St. Louis, Missouri, on November 19, 1893, the son of newspaper compositor Malcolm Campbell, who had emigrated from Canada in 1885, and his wife Katie from Michigan. Donald had a younger sister, Katherine, and a younger brother, Malcolm. He grew up at 2618 N. 21st St. and 4331 College Ave. in the working-class St. Louis Place and O'Fallons Park sections of St. Louis, ghostly neighborhoods now, where many of the homes have simply been abandoned or razed.[20] When Campbell registered for the draft at age 23 on June 1, 1917, he was still living in St. Louis and working as a laborer on the railroad.[21] He was a veteran of World War I.[22]

Sometime between the end of the war and about 1925, Campbell and Friderici met and married, probably in New York City, where Friderici was performing regularly on Broadway at this time. The 1930 U.S. census states that Campbell was 32 when they married.[23] In the fall of 1927, Friderici sold her country home on the Cape Shore and her New York apartment.[24] She and Campbell were pulling up stakes to start a new life in California. After two false starts in the early 1920s, Friderici would begin her film career in earnest by reprising her stage role as the minister's wife, Mrs. Davidson, in the 1928 silent screen version of *Rain* called *Sadie Thompson* (R. Walsh, Gloria Swanson Pictures), starring Gloria Swanson as the titular South Sea siren and Lionel Barrymore as Arnold Davidson, the man of God tempted by Sadie's wiles.[25] Donald Campbell, according to one press report, would "be associated with the management of a large hotel."[26]

The Campbells first lived in an apartment in the Ojai, a five-story, white stucco building at 1929 Whitley Ave. on the corner of Padre Terrace, where the palm-lined street rises to Whitley Heights.[27] After living briefly at 1800 N. La Brea Ave. in 1929, by April 1930, they had bought their own home, a modest, two-bedroom, one-bathroom bungalow from 1924 at 8708 Crescent Dr. in Laurel Canyon, which was valued at $7,000 in 1930 and sold in 2014 for $770,000.[28] In September 1930, the syndicated "Screen Gossip" column reported that Friderici's "exceptional work in talking pictures has won her several fine reviews in the past few months."[29] Campbell is registered as a stage actor in the census that year.[30] By 1932, they had moved to their final home together, 8649 Crescent Dr., a 1,168 square foot bungalow from 1926 right across the street from their old house. It sold for $980,000 in 2013.[31]

Friderici spent the final six years of her life living in Los Angeles and working full time as a character actress in the American film industry. During this period, we know she acted in over 50 feature films. Nearly all of her roles were credited (often as Blanche *Frederici*). She often played upper-class mothers-in-law or potential mothers-in-law, termagant wives, or working women like nurses and superintendents. Her roles were nearly always unsympathetic; "pickle-puss, battle-axe roles," according to David Ragan, while she herself was described as "vinegar-visaged," severe, and baleful.[32] My favorite Friderici performances, though, include two films where she was allowed to show more nuanced or unexpected aspects of her acting talent. I want to dwell for a moment on *The Office Wife*, *If I Had a Million*, and *Man of the Forest*.

The Office Wife is a fairly representative, well made, but somewhat stagey, pre–Code Warner Bros. drama from 1930, directed by Lloyd Bacon and starring Lewis Stone as suave, unhappily married publisher Lawrence Fellowes and Dorothy Mackaill as his efficient, attractive, and increasingly enamored secretary and "office wife" Anne Murdock. What is unusual about this film based on a best-selling novel by Faith Baldwin is not the then topical office romance it depicts, but Friderici's remarkable performance as butch author Kate Halsey, who writes a book about the "office wife" on her publisher's suggestion. In what is a kind of prologue in Fellowes's office, he convinces her to write a nine-part serial on the relationship between bosses and secretaries, while Halsey scoffs at men, marriage, and children (the topic of her last book and bestseller). In the second, brief scene, we see Halsey at her typewriter, smoking a cigar, wearing a bow tie and suit jacket, with her hair flattened mannishly, as she works on the book. She is not seen again.

The hard-boiled, cynical, cigar-smoking, behatted, and tailor-suited Halsey with a tie and pocket square makes even Hope Emerson in *Caged* look feminine in comparison! Film historian Richard Barrios observes, "Such characterizations would not be uncommon over the next few years, but his one remains singular and oddly inspiring."[33] There is no such character or narrative frame in Faith Baldwin's original novel, nor despite Barrios' claim is there reason to believe Miss Halsey is a portrait of Baldwin herself.[34] I wonder what director Bacon and screenwriter Charles Kenyon thought they were doing. Bacon is most famous for *42nd Street* (1933), which certainly also has its queer resonances. It seems Friderici was one of his

It was rare to see Blanche Friderici attempting a smile on the silver screen. We can almost sense in this still from *The Way to Love* (Paramount, 1933), with a youthful Maurice Chevalier (center) and a dapper Edward Everett Horton, that smiling didn't come naturally to her.

favorite character actresses, as he also used her in *A Notorious Affair* (First National, 1930), *Honor of the Family* (First National, 1931), and *Miss Pinkerton* (First National, 1932). Kenyon also wrote the screenplay for *Night Nurse* (W.A. Wellman, Warner Bros., 1931) in which Friderici played the housekeeper at a mansion that appears to be serving as a brothel. She is responsible for taking care of two children, who are dying of malnutrition. Ultimately, she repents of her evil ways and tries to do all she can to save the children, including urging nurses Joan Blondell and Barbara Stanwyck to give one of the children a milk bath.

In the popular anthology film *If I Had a Million* (S. Roberts, Paramount, 1932), Friderici's role as a stern nursing home director in mortal combat with belligerent resident May Robson was par for the course, but is still hugely enjoyable. Under the guise of being caring, Friderici's Mrs. Garvey is a martinet who removes what little joy she can from the elderly female residents' lives. They are not allowed to have pets ("cats are disease carriers"), they are not allowed to play cards (it "promotes ill-feeling"), they have to wear uniforms, and they are not allowed to engage in former domestic activities like baking. After Robson receives one million dollars from an anonymous benefactor, she doesn't fire Friderici but keeps her on with her only duty being to rock in a rocking chair for $200 a month.

Man of the Forest (H. Hathaway, Paramount, 1933), starring Randolph Scott and Verna Hillie, provided a surprisingly important role for Friderici in a surprisingly interesting film, considering it's a classic programmer clocking in at under an hour and a crime comedy western that doesn't take itself too seriously. Dressed in black widow's garb with a white lace collar and her usual center-parted, dark hair in a bun, Friderici plays Peg Forney, a woman who for ten years has been housekeeper to arch villain Clint Beasley (Noah Beery). When the young, pretty niece of a local rancher, Alice Gayner (Hillie), comes into Beasley's home after her uncle has been killed, Peg's friend (Tempe Pigott) suggests Alice may be a threat to Peg's position and her hopes someday to become Mrs. Beasley. Friderici shows great subtlety in her scenes, including bringing in a bowl of fruit just at the moment when Beasley is sexually harassing Alice, stopping him dead in his tracks ("I thought you might enjoy some fruit, Miss Alice"). When Alice locks the door on Beasley, Peg laughs out loud. She later tries to stop him from going after Alice when the latter makes her escape, saying she has taken care of him for ten years and Alice doesn't want him, but Beasley merely brushes her aside with a sneer. Peg is later seen in a window raising a rifle and the question is whether she is going to shoot Beasley or the hero, Brett Dale (Scott). She shoots Beasley dead, ending the fight between the two men and concluding the film.

Among other of Friderici's more familiar film roles, we find her playing one of the three eccentric aunts in *Love Me Tonight* (R. Mamoulian, Paramount, 1932) and a stern head nurse in the opening scene of *A Farewell to Arms* (F. Borzage, Paramount, 1932), when Gary Cooper and Helen Hayes first meet in a hospital. On her death, Friderici's "most famous role of both stage and screen," according to one obituary, was Mrs. Davidson in *Rain*.[35] Her most familiar film today was her last, released exactly two months after her death. In *It Happened One Night* (F. Capra, Columbia, 1934), which she finished work on just two days before her fatal Christmas outing,[36] she played the righteously indignant wife of a motel-keeper, who runs "a respectable place." She and her husband Zeke, played by Arthur Hoyt, eject Claudette Colbert from their establishment in the middle of the night when they discover that Clark Gable has gone off with the car and that Colbert is sleeping with a blanket dividing the room, indicating that they are not married.

Grace Come Lately: Grace George (1874–1961)

Though she is completely forgotten today, Grace George was one of the biggest stars on Broadway in the first half of the 20th century. Her acting career spanned seven decades from the 1890s to the 1950s and she was a star for more than half a century. Few Broadway luminaries of her era could compete with the longevity of George's career. One of the wonders of film is that it makes it possible to experience the magic of actresses who spent most of their careers working in the ephemeral medium of the theater. George racked up more than 50 credits on Broadway, but in film she was a "one work wonder." Even that one film was not a very good one, but at least it has preserved the presence of an actress who captivated American stage audiences for most of her adult life.

Little has been known and even less has been recorded of George's family background. Her given name appears to have been Grace, but her real surname was the Irish "Dougherty." Grace Dougherty, then, was born in New York in 1874. She herself claimed to have been born in 1880 (she even swore to that fact when she applied for a passport in 1919), but I'm basing myself on the earliest plausible dating, which is usually the accurate one in these cases. Her surviving relatives chose to inscribe 1874 on her gravestone in Sleep Hollow Cemetery. As for the month and the day, it was either December 25, 26, or 27.[1]

Grace Dougherty's father was George Dougherty, born in New York in March 1842 to Charles J. Dougherty and Mary Driscoll Dougherty, both born in Ireland. He died in New York in 1911. George Dougherty enlisted in the navy when he was 16 and worked as a clerk and a bookmaker.[2] As we can see, his Christian name became Grace Dougherty's stage name. Her mother was Nellie Kenny. Nellie, too, was born in New York and she died sometime before 1900.[3] George and Nellie also had a son, Grace's brother Charles Dougherty. Before he died young in about 1909, he found time to marry Carrie Thomey in 1898 and produce no less than five children.[4] In 1910, we find Charles's eldest daughter, six-year-old Grace Dougherty, no doubt named for her aunt, living with Grace George and her husband, legendary Broadway producer William A. Brady, at 50 Central Park West.[5] Grace and Bill Brady had been married a dozen years by that point and had one son, William A. Brady, Jr., born April 17, 1900.[6] William Brady, Sr., had a daughter from a previous marriage with the French dancer Rose Marie René. In 1910, Bill Brady's 19-year-old daughter was about to embark on an acting career and would be known to the world as Alice Brady.[7]

George herself had made her stage debut in 1894 and first starred on Broadway in *The Princess Chiffon* in 1900, which was described by one contemporary observer as "a complete failure."[8] Undeterred, she went on to fame and fortune in her husband's productions of the hits of the day like *Her Majesty, the Girl Queen of Nordenmark* (1900), *The Two Orphans* (1904), *Divorcons* (1907/1909/1913), *The New York Idea* (1915), and *The Merry Wives of Gotham* (1924); and in older and modern classics like *The School for Scandal* (1909), *Major Barbara* (1915), and *Captain Brassbound's Conversion* (1916). George had talent, of course, and no one could dictate the tastes of the audience, but it didn't hurt to be married to one of the major American stage producers in the first half of the 20th century.

Drama critic Lewis C. Strang described George in 1902 as "an actress of dainty personal beauty, of potent magnetism and of sweet womanliness." He added, "Her versatility and her range of expression will probably never be vastly great, and she will probably always have to be content with combining mild humour, refined but easily understood, with emotion that is prettily pathetic rather than compellingly strong."[9] According to Daniel Blum, writing more than half a century later: "She is considered difficult and temperamental, a reputation achieved probably because she is a perfectionist." "The dominant tone of her personality is daintiness," he added.[10]

Grace George had been a star on Broadway for 40 years when she played her only role on film: Vinnie McLoud in *Johnny Come Lately* (William Cagney Prod., 1943). As an idealistic small-town newspaper proprietor and editor, she gives the charming vagrant and journalist played by James Cagney a job. It would probably have been a shock to George, who was one of the great beauties of the American stage in the early decades of the 20th century, to see how old and dowdy she looked in this film.

Seen from the outside, it must have looked as if Grace George had everything. She was beautiful, talented, and rich. She was one of the biggest stars on Broadway, her husband was a powerful and ingenious producer dedicated to keeping his wife continually before the public and in the best possible light. George had even managed to produce a son amidst all her other accomplishments. As Mrs. William A. Brady and as the star Grace George, the woman who had been born Grace Dougherty into a working-class, Irish American family in Brooklyn lived a life of luxury that the rest of the Dougherty clan and most of America could only dream of.

Starting in the late 1920s, though, dark clouds began to gather on the horizon, that would burst in thunder and lightning, drenching the Bradys in tears. They had no sooner returned from a trip to Europe in October 1929, when they were financially ruined in the disastrous stock market crash.[11] The Bradys were able to retrench and rebuild, largely through the success of Brady's production of Elmer Rice's *Street Scene* and George's smash hit in her next Broadway show *The First Mrs. Frasier* (1929–30), but there was worse to come. A series of domestic tragedies rained over their heads. The first was also the hardest for Grace George: the loss of her only child, William A. Brady, Jr., in a fire on September 26, 1935, at the age of 35. Bill Jr., who was working as an actor and producer, had according to a police detective on the scene "apparently let a cigarette fall into his bedding as he went to sleep" in a summer bungalow he had borrowed in Colt's Neck, New Jersey. "The resulting blaze burned the frame house to its foundation and left only a few charred bones in the bed."[12] Only two weeks before, columnist L.L. Stevenson had concluded an article on the elder Brady with the words: "At seventy-two, William Brady is content with life—and looking forward to further accomplishment."[13]

This catastrophe was followed by the cancer death of William Brady, Sr.'s talented and amusing daughter Alice Brady in 1939, just five days short of her 47th birthday. Alice's son, Donald William Crane, who had been sickly since he had been born prematurely in 1922, died in Los Angeles on January 17, 1942.[14] These sad losses were the background for George's one and only venture into Hollywood film-making in 1943.

She had actually put a foot forward in Hollywood in 1934–35. The Bradys stayed with W.C. Fields at 9950 Toluca Lake Ave. in North Hollywood, while William Brady tried to sell the film rights to some of the 125 plays he controlled and his wife sought "a chance to appear in pictures."[15] But nothing came of it, for George at any rate, and she returned to Broadway and had one of the greatest successes of her later career creating the role of Mary Herries in Edward Chodorov's thriller *Kind Lady* (1935/1940). She was doing this show when her son died. George actually had a clause in her *Kind Lady* contract that gave her first refusal on the role in any screen version,[16] but in the wake of her son's death she was not up to new challenges and the film role went to a considerably younger New York actress, Aline MacMahon. Ethel Barrymore starred in the 1951 remake.

Eight years after her first, brief sojourn in Hollywood, then, George was finally ready to make her film debut. The star of *Johnny Come Lately* (W.K. Howard, William Cagney Prod., 1943), James Cagney, who at 43 did not yet look like Mr. Toad of Toad Hall, was no doubt both charming and persuasive. As it happened, he was the same age as George's own son would have been had he lived. Cagney had just won a Best Actor Oscar for *Yankee Doodle Dandy*.[17] And he and his producer brother William were as Irish as they came. I imagine George trusted and felt comfortable with them.

It was no doubt an added inducement that she was given star billing above the title and second only to Cagney himself ("Introducing to the screen Miss Grace George"). Thus she was credited above such screen veterans as Marjorie Main, Hattie McDaniel, and Margaret Hamilton. Not many Broadway stars could boast of such a prestigious debut, even if it turned out to be a false start. According to Homer Dickens, "The film's important event was the casting of Grace George as Vinnie McLeod."[18] In his analysis of George as a rising star of the American stage back in 1902, Lewis Strang had predicted that she would "be at her best in a character that unites quiet whimsicality and delicate coquettishness with tender pathos and barely perceptible heart-burning."[19] Though she played an elderly widow, 40 years later this was not a bad description of George's first and only role on the big screen.

In *Johnny Come Lately*, she plays Vinnie McLeod, the idealistic and determined owner and editor of the Plattsville *Shield and Banner* ("Banner for the Brave"), that her husband J.E. McLeod founded. He died 30 years ago and his widow still lives in the family mansion, "McLeod's Folly," that her husband built half a century earlier. "The paper is everything to me," she sighs when the pawn shop owner says it is an expensive hobby. Mrs. McLeod comes upon the vagrant ex-newspaperman Tom Richards (Cagney) in the town square reading *The Pickwick Papers* and tells him she actually met Charles Dickens when he was in America in 1867. After Tom's arrest for vagrancy, he is released into her custody for two months and she is to pay him $35 a week to work on her paper. Mrs. McLeod is fond of uttering brave maxims like "Life doesn't matter. It's what you do with it." Funnily enough, the villain of the piece, Mr. Dougherty (Edward McNamara), has the same surname as George's own maiden name. Hattie McDaniel plays Vinnie's faithful cook Aida, who likes to know everything that is going on and when she is kept out of things gets "a 'miz'ry' of the spirit." In the second half of the film, George is eclipsed by the rambunctious, riotous, and raucous Marjorie Main as "Gas-house Mary," a thinly veiled whorehouse madam with powerful connections, who runs a "straight" place, the El Dorado, whatever that means. George comes back for a nicely acted and touching farewell scene with Cagney, before he again hits the road: "Johnny come lately and gone so soon."

Johnny Come Lately is a film with an excellent cast in which, sadly, the whole is *less* than the sum of its parts. It was a period piece in more ways than one and seemed dated even on its initial release. Archer Winston wrote in the *New York Post*, "It is an old-fashioned story told in a very old-fashioned manner.[20] John T. McManus in *PM* was even more scathing: "*Johnny Come Lately* is so palpably amateurish in production and direction, so hopelessly stagey, uneven, and teamless in performance and so utterly pointless that it is bound to cause raised eyebrows wherever it is shown."[21] *Time* chose to emphasize the positive: "Grace George seems effortlessly to have learned what so many transplanted Broadway actors ache over—how to project her touching elegance in a medium new to her."[22] *New York Times* critic Bosley Crowther was not so impressed by the "curiously second-rate film" or by George's performance. "Except for a true touch now and then," he found that she "plays the lace-and-lavender lady with the mannered hush of a theatrical grand-dame."[23]

So why didn't Grace George do more films? At least part of the answer lies in the fact that she was a New Yorker born and bred and had spent her entire career on Broadway. Even with her husband semi-retired from producing by the early 1940s, she probably did not want to move permanently to the West Coast. Beyond that, her first film venture was "a financial and critical disaster,"[24] though she received praise for her own efforts. Finally, I would guess that for George, as for so many former stage beauties, it would have been a shock to see herself on the big screen. She was nearly 70 years old and looked it. All her life, she had been made to look glamorous, beautiful, and ageless on the stage and in *Johnny Come Lately* she just looks look a little old lady in frumpy costumes with hardly any make-up and minimal attention to her hair. She was probably happy and relieved to get back to her New York home in a penthouse at 510 Park Ave.[25] It was there William A. Brady died of a heart attack on January 6, 1950. He was 86.[26]

Among George's closest relatives, only her granddaughter Barbara Alexander Brady (1927–78) was still alive during her final decade. Barbara was the daughter of William A. Brady, Jr., and the actress Katharine Alexander (1897–1977) and lived with her grandparents in the late 1940s.[27] Barbara, too, went into the family business, so to speak, and made her Broadway debut with her grandmother in *The Velvet Glove* at the Booth Theatre on December 26, 1949. This was George's first show on Broadway since the release of *Johnny Come Lately* on September 3, 1943, and would be her second to last. William Brady died just ten days after the opening, but George stayed on till the end of the run in May 1950 and didn't miss a single performance. "Bill would have wanted it that way," she said.[28] Grace George Brady passed away on May 19, 1961, and was laid to rest beside her husband and son in Sleepy Hollow Cemetery.[29]

When Irish Eyes Are Smiling: Connie Gilchrist (1895–1985)

Connie Gilchrist was a Brooklyn-born, Irish American, working-class woman, who played mostly Brooklyn-inflected, Irish American, working-class women. This is not to suggest that her talent was limited, but rather to say that she found her niche in the film industry and Hollywood producers were happy for her to stay in it. Only rarely did Gilchrist get to dress up or play an upper-class character. Even with her ample forms covered in silk evening dresses, though, you could be sure she was "nouveau riche" and just as folksy as when she appeared in cotton print dresses and aprons. Two good examples of this phenomenon are her role as Olive Ransom, the genial, hospitable wife of a cigar-smoking, beer-drinking millionaire in Norma Shearer's penultimate film *We Were Dancing* (R.Z. Leonard, MGM, 1942), and her final scene as Ruby Finney in *A Letter to Three Wives* (J.L. Mankiewicz, Twentieth Century–Fox, 1949), after her daughter Lora Mae (Linda Darnell) has married department store mogul Porter Hollingsway (Paul Douglas) and Ruby has moved up in the world and taken a liking to crème de menthe and betting on the horses. Gilchrist later called *We Were Dancing* one of her favorite "dress ups," because she got to wear a gorgeous black spangled dress.[1]

In American films of the 1940s and '50s, then, there was no character actress more Irish American than Connie Gilchrist. It's worth asking, though, if Gilchrist would have become such an icon of screen Irishness, if she'd been called Gertrude Volmer. As it happens, Connie Gilchrist *was* called Gertrude Volmer. It took some detective work to uncover this fact, but that's part of what makes research of this kind exciting. Sometimes separating fact from fantasy turned out to be as challenging in Gilchrist's case as if she'd been an enigmatic screen star, rather than a very down-to-earth and middle-of-the-road character actress.

Some of the "mysterious issues" surrounding Gilchrist relate to her date of birth, her real name, her mother's background, and her own early show business career.[2] With regard to her year of her birth, there really is no mystery at all, however much the actress herself tried to cloud the issue. Gilchrist was not born in 1900, 1901, or 1906, or in any year starting with 19. She was born in 1895, which means she was 40 when she made her Broadway debut, 45 when she made her film debut, and almost 90 years old when she died. There are two pieces of incontrovertible evidence to prove this. First and foremost, the Social Security Death Index (SSDI) gives her date of birth as July 17, 1895.[3] This is supported by the 1900 U.S. census, which states specifically that she was born in July 1895.[4] Later census data differ, but in these cases it pays to trust the earliest available information about an actress's age.

"Connie Gilchrist" was not our subject's real name. Thus Gilchrist is a relatively rare example of a character actress acting under a stage name. Most character actresses used their own names. Marjorie Main is another exception to the rule. She changed her name from Mary Tomlinson, apparently because of family opposition to her choice of profession. Gilchrist's name wasn't entirely invented, as the surname came from her step-father and Constance may have been one of her (unrecorded) middle names, but Connie Gilchrist was not a name she used in private life. She was born Gertrude Rose Volmer in 1895; she took her stepfather's name and was known as Gertrude Gilchrist by 1910; after her marriage in 1922, she was Gertrude O'Hanlon; and then finally in 1935, she emerged on the Broadway stage as Connie Gilchrist, under which name she would also be known to film audiences from 1940.

According to Parish and Bowers, Gilchrist's mother was "actress Martha Daniels."[5] I've been able to confirm only that her mother's given name, indeed, was Martha. In 1900, she was a widow with two young daughters living at 495 Baltic St. in Boerum Hill near downtown Brooklyn and worked as a "restaurant keeper." She claimed to have been born in Ireland in July 1870 and immigrated to the United States in 1880, but later census information shows that she was probably born in about 1867 and came to America as an adult in 1887.[6] If Martha Volmer, as Gilchrist's mother was then known, had ever been an actress, her career on the stage was over by 1900. Her first husband and Gilchrist's father, Mr. Volmer, who sounds more German than Irish, must have died sometime between the conception of his second daughter, Gilchrist's younger sister Anna (Annie), who was born in New York in June 1897, and the 1900 census, where Martha Volmer appears as a widow.[7]

In 1900, Martha Volmer married the barkeeper John Gilchrist, born in Ireland in about 1866, who emigrated in 1895 and who was the closest thing Connie Gilchrist and her sister would have to a father. In 1910, the family was living at 141 Gold St. in Vinegar Hill, which is also close to downtown Brooklyn and the Brooklyn Navy Yard. The Gilchrists had been married ten years at this point and Martha Volmer Gilchrist was now the proprietor of a "general store," while John Gilchrist worked as a bartender in a saloon.[8]

During the next ten-year period, we have no documentary evidence about Connie Gilchrist. She resurfaces in the public record again in the 1920 U.S. census, where we find "Gertrude R. Gilchrist" living with her once again widowed mother Martha Gilchrist, now 53 and not working, and her younger sister Anna H. Gilchrist at 326 43rd St. in Brooklyn, a very modest three-and-a-half-story, brick and stucco house with a large stoop, which is still standing between the Gowanus Expressway and 4th Ave., not far from Sunset Park and Greenwood Cemetery. The sisters were both working as supervisors at a telegraph company, single, and only admitting to 22 and 20, though they would turn 25 and 23 that year.[9] When Gilchrist 27 years later had a small role as a switchboard operator in the opening scene of *The Hucksters* (J. Conway, MGM, 1947), she was on familiar ground.

Gertrude Gilchrist married the aspiring playwright Edwin O'Hanlon in 1922, when she was 27 and he was 22.[10] He may, indeed, not have been aware that his wife was five years his senior, given her "imprecise" reckoning of her own age. In 1928, when they returned from a trip to Europe, she gave her birth date as June 29, 1900.[11] In the 1930 U.S. census, she claimed to be 29, when in fact she turned 35 that year.[12] At any rate, Connie Gilchrist and Edwin O'Hanlon were married for 61 years, which is impressive by any standard and must have been some kind of record in Hollywood. They had very similar backgrounds, which in addition to their common interest in the theater, may partially explain the longevity of their marriage. Both came from working-class, Irish immigrant families and were born and raised in Brooklyn.

Both lost their fathers at an early age, though Gilchrist gained a stepfather when she was five, while O'Hanlon's mother never remarried.

Edwin A. O'Hanlon was born in Brooklyn on September 16, 1900.[13] Unlike Gilchrist, who grew up in a small nuclear family, Edwin grew up in an extended, matriarchal family with three generations of his mother's family living under the roof of his grandmother, Anna Bridget Gallagher, who was born in Ireland in 1844 and came to the United States in 1875 with her husband Patrick and their two eldest children. Edwin's mother Winifred Gallagher O'Hanlon was the fourth of Bridget and Patrick's ten children, of which seven were still alive in 1910. Grandpa Pat was dead by that time, as was Edwin's father and his only sibling, and grandmother Bridget now headed the household that consisted of her unmarried sons John (40) and Martin (34), her widowed daughters Margaret Santry (37) and Winifred O'Hanlon (35), her unmarried daughter Alice (28), her grandsons Edwin O'Hanlon (9) and Joseph Santry (7), and granddaughter Mary Santry (4). These ten people and a whole other family of four shared a small, wooden-sided, narrow-windowed, and flat-roofed, three-story building, which still stands at 36 Driggs Ave. on the corner of Sutton St. between the Brooklyn Queens Expressway and Msgr. McGolrick Park in Brooklyn's Greenpoint. Edwin's Uncle John worked as a shoe cutter in a factory, his Uncle Martin was a stevedore at the docks, and his Aunt Margaret and his mother Winifred worked as hairdressers.[14]

Ten years later, Edwin was still living at home with his grandmother, mother, Aunt Margaret, and cousin Mary, only their home was now at 671 Lincoln Place, which runs parallel with Eastern Parkway in Crown Heights, not far from the Brooklyn Museum. Edwin was going to college, which may well have been a first in the Gallagher-O'Hanlon clan, while his mother still worked as a hairdresser and his aunt now worked as a laundress in a private family.[15] We know Edwin had a four-year college education and studied archaeology at Columbia University.[16]

In 1922, then, Edwin O'Hanlon and Gertrude Gilchrist were married. They were living in Woodstock, New York, in 1928, where O'Hanlon was manager of the Maverick Theatre for several years, and in Manhattan in 1930.[17] Their final home in New York City before they moved to Los Angeles in 1940 was a $37 a month, rented apartment at 206 W. 69th St., a block that has changed completely since they lived there. In the 1940 U.S. census, Edwin O'Hanlon gave his profession as a writer for the theater and stated that he had earned $810 for 40 weeks' work in 1939, while his wife "Rose G. O'Hanlon," who claimed to be 41, had earned $2,000 for 16 weeks' work as an actress in the theatre. Neither of them had income from other sources than their wages. Their 16-year-old daughter Dorothy was attending high school as a sophomore.[18]

Gilchrist's daughter Dorothy was born on January 6, 1924.[19] In having a child, Gilchrist was different from the average run of character actresses, who were not uncommonly both unmarried and childless or who, even if they married, remained childless. Out of the 35 actresses profiled in this book, for example, 23 are known to have been married, but only seven of these—Eburne, George, Gilchrist, Hamilton, Taylor, Westman, and Wycherly—had children. Only Libby Taylor had more than one child. This is, relatively speaking, a small sample, but it is representative. It was almost as if a career as a character actress in the first half of the 20th-century was so all-consuming it precluded motherhood, if not marriage.

Actually, Gilchrist herself didn't seriously pursue an acting career until Dorothy "reached school age," according to Don Stanke. Before that, the O'Hanlons had run a "comedy theatre" in New York with Edwin writing the scripts and directing and Connie in charge of casting and accounts. They went to Europe in the late 1920s "to gain further experience with English and French stock companies."[20] It was on their return in April 1928, that Edwin took hold of the stock company at the Maverick Theatre in Woodstock. With Dorothy turning six in 1930, Gilchrist "turned her own energies to the acting side of the footlights" and made her Broadway debut in 1935.[21]

You would as little expect to find Gilchrist in a play set on a Southern plantation, as you would Sara Allgood or Una O'Connor. Nevertheless, she made her New York debut in Langton Hughes's melodrama *Mulatto* at the Vanderbilt Theatre on October 24, 1935. Hughes's play about the dire consequences of white plantation owners having children with their slaves was a big hit and ran for 373 performances. Legendary African American actress Rose McClendon had one of the lead roles as Colonel Norwood's slave, housekeeper, and mistress Cora Lewis. It was McClendon's last show, as she was forced to leave the cast due to pleurisy in December 1935 and died of pneumonia on July 12, 1936, while *Mulatto* was still running.[22] Gilchrist, who was 40 years old, played Mary Lowell, a minor character who is not mentioned in Burns Mantle's plot summary in *The Best Plays of 1935–36* and who did not make it into the published version.[23]

Edwin O'Hanlon never had any of his own plays produced on Broadway, but his big project as his wife's run in *Mulatto* was drawing to a close between July and September 1936 was staging two different but equally unsuccessful dramatizations of Oscar Wilde's famous novel *The Picture of Dorian Gray* at the Comedy Theatre. It stood at 110 W. 41st St. and was later known as the Mercury Theatre until it was demolished in 1942.[24]

Gilchrist's next play on Broadway was as different from *Mulatto* as may be imagined. Victor Wolfson's successful comedy *Excursion* was one of the biggest surprises of the 1936–37 season, according to Burns Mantle, and was "a sort of exultant paean to the essential gallantry of the battered human spirit," according to Richard Watts, Jr.[25] The play was set entirely aboard the SS *Happiness*, a Coney Island ferry making what is to be the last journey both for the ship and its captain. Gilchrist played Martha, a "big and blond" employee in the wall paper department at Gimbels. She is making the trip with her friend and fellow worker Lollie (Frances Fuller) and is bubbling over with excitement over her affair with a man from Flatbush, who despite his interest in interior decorating "certainly is no fairy."[26] The play ran for 116 performances at the Vanderbilt Theatre in the spring and summer of 1937. The Vanderbilt, where Gilchrist also did *Mulatto*, stood at 148 W. 48th St. next to the Cort Theatre, until it was replaced by a parking garage, which ironically was "designed by reknowned theatre designer Herbert J. Krapp."[27]

Gilchrist's next Broadway outing, the comedy *Work Is for Horses* in November 1937, lasted only nine performances at the Windsor Theatre, which was later known as the 48th Street Theatre and was razed in 1955.[28] Gilchrist played Millie Prentiss, married to a Rip Van Winkle type, Cornelius Prentiss (Robert Keith), "a genial but useless loafer." The play detailed the various threats to his laidback lifestyle, before the happy ending found him "back in the old armchair."[29]

Gilchrist's next play on the Great White Way, another new comedy called *How to Get Tough About It*, was hardly more successful, despite being produced and staged by Guthrie McClintic. Gilchrist played the café owner Mrs. Clugg, who ends up firing the waitress-heroine Kitty (Katherine Locke) in one of the many trials and tribulations of this young lady's life before a happy ending with a man on a houseboat. The play ran for only 23 performances in February 1938 at the Martin Beck Theatre, which still stands at 302 W. 45th St. and in 2003 was renamed the Al Hirschfeld Theatre. It was at this same theatre, Gilchrist performed in her final Broadway show. *Ladies and Gentleman* was written by the well-known collaborators Charles MacArthur and Ben Hecht and starred the former's wife, Helen Hayes, as Miss Scott, a secretary and juror, who manages to combine a love affair with the jury foreman, Campbell (Philip Merivale), with her duties in defending the innocence, as she perceives it, of a popular novelist who is being tried for the murder of his wife. Gilchrist played Mrs. Rudd, who I assume was either a juror or a witness. The play closed after 103 performances on January 13, 1940, and in late August 1940, Gilchrist reported to work at MGM studios for her first film venture *Hullabaloo* (E.L. Marin, 1940). The O'Hanlons left their rented apartment on W. 69th St. in New York and found a home in Los Angeles at 1118 Hacienda Pl. in West Hollywood.[30]

As we have seen, Gilchrist was a late bloomer on Broadway and was also a late arrival in Hollywood, relatively speaking. In that respect (and probably in that respect only), she resembled her fellow MGM contract player Agnes Moorehead, who made her film debut in 1941 and came to MGM in 1942. Moorehead held on to her contract till *Show Boat* in 1950, while Gilchrist's last film while still under long-term contract with Metro was the 1949 remake of *Little Women* (M. LeRoy).[31] During her close to ten years at MGM, Gilchrist acted in 46 feature films and took on whatever part large or small, usually small, that her home studio demanded of her. She well proved the old adage about there not being any small parts, only small actors. Her co-star in *Sunday Punch* (D. Miller, MGM, 1942), *Born to Sing* (E. Ludwig, MGM, 1942) and *The War Against Mrs. Hadley* (H.S. Bucquet, MGM, 1942), Rags Ragland, once said: "I want one of those Connie Gilchrist parts where everybody works their asses off all week and she comes in on Saturday for one scene and steals the picture."[32]

Some of Gilchrist's more memorable roles from her heyday at MGM in the 1940s were Mrs. Torelli, John Garfield's sex-starved, widowed neighbor in *Tortilla Flat* (V. Fleming, 1942); Frankie, the theater cleaning lady in *Presenting Lily Mars* (N. Taurog, 1943), who sings the poignant "Every Little Movement Has a Meaning of Its Own" to convince Judy Garland to pursue her dreams; and Martha Finney, Janet Leigh's friend and neighbor in *Act of Violence* (F. Zinnemann, 1948). Don Stanke rightly points out that when Gilchrist occasionally "was permitted to move forward from the tail end of the credit line-up; this generally happened on loan-out."[33] It was not uncommon that contract players got better roles on loan-out to other studios. The best example of this, of course, is *A Letter to Three Wives* (1949), which Gilchrist did for Twentieth Century–Fox. In addition to Frankie in *Presenting Lily Mars*, I consider Ruby Feeney to be her signature role. At MGM, Gilchrist was "confidante and mother to half the studio," writes Stanke. Greer Garson dubbed her "the Countess," a nickname that stuck, "because of her noble appearance."[34]

Gilchrist freelanced for the last 20 years of her acting career, but the films became fewer. Two of her best opportunities in her later years came in *Thunder on the Hill* (D. Sirk, Universal, 1951) and *Auntie Mame* (M. DaCosta, Warner Bros., 1958). In the former, Gilchrist plays Sister Josephine, the cook and mother of the lay sisters at a convent hospital. Her most important function in the film, though, is to act as a sidekick and assistant to fellow nun Claudette Colbert in her amateur sleuthing attempt to save Ann Blyth from being hanged for the murder of her dissolute brother Jason. Sister Josephine's motto "Never discard a newspaper or throw

Connie Gilchrist's film career had already reached its peak, while Thelma Ritter's was on the rise, when they played a couple of tough old broads in *A Letter to Three Wives* (Twentieth Century–Fox Film Corp., 1949). They were both born in Brooklyn. Ritter (right) died just before her 67th birthday, and Gilchrist lived to be almost 90.

away a piece of string" becomes an important plot element, when they find newspaper articles about Blyth's trial all over the convent that help them solve the murder mystery and save Blyth from the gallows. Sister Josephine relaxes by peeling potatoes and saying her rosary with the small potatoes. She speaks with a thick Irish brogue and wears a pair of steel-rimmed glasses throughout the film, possibly to make her easier to identify. Gilchrist's role in *Aunt Mame* was less spectacular, but is one people still remember. She plays trusty and conservative Irish maid Norah Muldoon, who brings Mame Dennis's orphaned nephew Patrick from Chicago to Mame's luxurious apartment in 1928 and then, reluctantly at first but later devotedly, begins to work for her.

In the 1960s, Gilchrist's main source of income came from working in television. Her first role on the small screen was an episode of *Letter to Loretta* in 1954 and she was seen on shows like *Leave It to Beaver* (1957), *Wagon Train* (1960), *General Electric Theatre* (1960–61), *Alfred Hitchcock Presents* (1962), *The Twilight Zone* (1963), *Dr. Kildare* (1965), *Perry Mason* (1964–66), and *The Adventures of Long John Silver* (1956–57; during a lengthy sojourn in Australia). An uncredited role in the feature film *Some Kind of Nut* (G. Kanin, 1969) was her final appearance on the screen, large or small.

The O'Hanlons' daughter Dorothy married Joseph F. Sanson (1923–90). The couple had a son, Todd Joseph Sanson, in Los Angeles on December 8, 1948, but the marriage ended in divorce in March 1970.[35] To her parents' regret, Dorothy moved to New York after her divorce.[36] "Pet" and "Gertie," as they called each other, spent their final years in Santa Fe, New Mexico.[37] Edwin O'Hanlon died at home after a lengthy illness on December 13, 1983.[38] On March 3, 1985, his wife of 61 years, Gertrude Rose Volmer Gilchrist O'Hanlon, known to the world as Connie Gilchrist, followed him in death.[39] They lie buried in Santa Fe National Cemetery.[40]

Minna's Modern Marriage: Minna Gombell (1892–1973)

She was as sharp and tacky as a tack. She was as hard and colorful as varnished nails. Among all the hard-bitten, brassy bottle blondes in Hollywood films of the 1930s, no one was more bitter, brassy, and blonde than Minna Gombell. Not Gladys George, Glenda Farrell, Claire Trevor, or Veda Ann Borg. Not even Isabel Jewell or Iris Adrian.

Gombell is almost completely forgotten today, but among film historians she has inspired some lively descriptions of her screen persona. Springer and Hamilton wrote in 1969, while she was still alive: "Always one of our favorite people—at least in the few pictures of the many she made which gave her more to do than react snappishly in the background. Miss Gombell, with her pursed mouth and tight dimples, was one of our best snappers."[1] According to James Robert Parish, she "generally played the smart-mouthed babe who has seen it all."[2] More recently, David Quinlan has observed, "The characters of this flinty, pinch-faced diminutive blonde American actress, who sized up many a taller opponent before cutting her down to size, were always ready with a sharp retort. They had seen it, done it and got the scars to prove it."[3] Watching Gombell on film, it is hard to believe that during her younger days as "the best-loved leading lady who ever played in a Syracuse stock company," a journalist had written, "Minna Gombel [*sic*] radiates the spirit of happiness."[4]

Gombell had been a soft, winsome, almost elfin beauty in her youth with a halo of curly light brown hair. Her looks hardened with the coming of the years and the "arts" of Hollywood into a Kabuki mask of make-up with eyes that could freeze you at a glance below tortured eyebrows and a helmet of often brutally short, peroxide locks. Maybe it was her German ancestry, the Teutonic toughness coming out in her face. Maybe it was the "school of hard knocks." Or maybe Minna Gombell was just a really good actress. To those unfamiliar with her particular talents, I would recommend taking a look at *After Tomorrow* (F. Borzage, Fox, 1932); *Bachelor's Affairs* (A.L. Werker, Fox, 1932), where she has a rare starring role; *Babbitt* (W. Keighley, First National, 1934); or *Make Way for Tomorrow* (L. McCarey, Paramount, 1937). Generally, her roles in the films of the '40s are much less interesting.

Though Gombell was entirely of German origin, she was not known for playing Germans on the big screen. She was born Minna Marie Gombel in Baltimore on May 28, 1892.[5] Her father William Gombel came from Dieburg, a small town in Hesse-Darmstadt just south of Frankfurt, which Gombell once described as "her favorite spot in Europe."[6] He was born in 1854 and immigrated to the United States as a 25-year-old doctor on May 15, 1880, when he arrived in New York City aboard the *Mosel* from Bremen via Southampton.[7] On June 1, 1880, we find him in Baltimore, where he would live and work as a GP for the remainder of his life.[8] William Gombel married Emma M. Debring in 1891, when he was 37 and she 26.[9] Emma, born in Baltimore in 1865,[10] was the daughter of German immigrants from Oldenburg and Cloppenburg near Bremen. Her father, Bernard Debring (1835–1906), worked as a laborer and later as a machinist and he and his wife Helen Brandt Debring (1833–1917) raised six children.[11] Emma worked as a dressmaker from an early age to help support her family.[12]

Minna would have a more sheltered and privileged childhood than her mother and grew up at 835 W. Fayette St. and 1704 Madison Ave. in the Poppleton and Madison Park neighborhoods of Baltimore.[13] The Gombels' substantial, three-story, red brick row house on Madison Ave. is still standing. Emma Gombel stayed on there after her husband's death in 1916. Though she owned her own home, she went back to work as a seamstress in a factory and filled the 6,400 square foot building with five other families (11 people) and a maid.[14] Minna had left home by then; as one newspaper put it many years later: "An attempt to correct awkwardness eventually led her to the stage."[15] She made her stage debut in 1912 and her New York debut the following year as Denise in Charles Frohman's hit production of *Madam President* at the Garrick Theatre.[16] Emma Debring Gombel, who had the audacity to claim she was 38 in the 1920 U.S. census, when she was actually 58, died in 1929.[17] Her daughter was her sole heir.[18]

Both Minna and her mother demonstrated hypergamy in practice: the fine art of "marrying up." While young Emma Debring had no doubt been happy to marry a doctor, her daughter made herself a match in Yuma, Arizona, in May 1933 that upped the marital sweepstakes considerably. There was no single event or relationship that garnered Gombell more press attention than her marriage at age 41 to 52-year-old millionaire banker Joseph W. Sefton, Jr. Beyond the union of fame and fortune they symbolized, the press was fascinated by the unique arrangement the couple had made from day one of their marriage.

Sefton and Gombell had found their own unique solution to the particular challenges of a marriage between an actor and a "civilian" and a long-distance relationship with him based in San Diego and her in Los Angeles. A year and a half after their wedding, entertainment writer Dan Thomas was able to publish the terms of their "Declaration of Trust," which stated: "To Whom It May Concern: In accordance with the authority vested in me, J.W. Sefton, Jr., party of the second part, by Minna Gombell, party of the first part, on May 19, 1933, the said party of the first part is hereby authorized and permitted to dine, dance and 'go places' with any eligible and unattached male of her selection, between the hours of 12:00 noon and 2:00 a. m., without either party incurring those dangers which are supposed to follow such a transgression of the codes conventional."[19] Thomas explained, "Both realized when they were married that they would be separated much of the time by the 25 miles lying between Hollywood and San Diego. Hence the declaration of trust."[20]

According to an *Oakland Tribune* feature article on Gombell: "Lots of people in San Diego felt that because Joseph W. Sefton, Jr., of a long line of bankers, had married an actress, he might not be quite the solid personality that a banker should be. They've got nothing to worry about. Any woman who will knit her husband a sweater—and like it—isn't going to lead him into too many extravagances."[21] Sefton himself weighed in in an interview given after their "pact" had been renewed for a second year: "'All a man has to do,' says the broad-minded banker, 'is to keep a woman in love with him and she will be loyal and the kind of companion all men dream of discovering. You can't hold a wife by placing limitations on her activities.'"[22]

By 1935, the Seftons were known as "the film colony's champion live-aparters."[23] When the census enumerator arrived at the Sefton mansion in San Diego's Point Loma Heights on April 24, 1940, she recorded both husband and wife as living there, but in 1942 we find Mrs. Joseph W. Sefton, Jr., in the Los Angeles telephone directory as "Mrs. Minna Gombell," living at 9255 Doheny Rd., which today is the site of the luxurious Sierra Towers apartment building.[24] Social register types and their spouses were not usually "in the book," but then Gombell was never just a rich man's wife.

Joseph Weller Sefton, Jr., was born September 4, 1881, when his family was still living in Dayton, Ohio.[25] They subsequently moved to San Diego, California, where the elder Joseph Weller Sefton (1851–1908) founded the San Diego Savings Bank (later the San Diego Trust & Savings Bank) in 1889.[26] On April 16, 1909, Joseph W. Sefton, Jr., married Helen Wolcott Thomas (1888–1971), later known as only the third woman in the United States to ride in an airplane. The couple adopted a two month old, orphaned boy from New York City in 1917, who was named Thomas Wolcott Sefton (1917–2006).[27] The marriage ended in divorce.

In 1930, the census shows that Sefton (48) and his son Thomas (12) are living at 3800 La Cresta Drive in San Diego with a dozen servants and laborers on a property valued at $50,000.[28] In 1912, noted local architect William Sterling Hebbard had designed matching houses in the "Mediterranean" style for Sefton and his mother, Harriet Lyle Hollida Sefton-Campbell (1859–1936), on their 15-acre property.[29] Joseph W. Sefton, Sr., who like Gombell was from Baltimore, had died long before she came into the family. For the first three years of her marriage, though, Gombell had to contend with her no doubt formidable mother-in-law, who had remarried but still lived next door.[30] Gombell also got a 16-year-old stepson in the bargain.

This publicity photograph of Minna Gombell was taken in 1925, when she was 33 and a star of sorts on Broadway. During the teens, she was immensely popular as the star of a stock company in Syracuse, New York, and the Syracuse newspapers followed her career closely for years.

By 1933, Gombell was no stranger to marriage. In 1916, when she was 24 and the leading lady of the Knickerbocker Players at the Empire Theatre in Syracuse, she had married the company's manager.[31] Howard Chesham Rumsey was born in Gateshead, England, on August 3, 1884, and immigrated to the United States with his widowed mother and four older brothers in 1888.[32] The Syracuse papers told a touching tale about how the wedding had been put forward so that Gombell's ailing father could witness the happy event at the family home in Baltimore on July 2, 1916, but the fact of the matter was that the couple had already married in New York City on March 9, 1916.[33] The marriage lasted nearly as long as the five year romance that preceded it, but ended in divorce in 1921.[34] Only two weeks after his divorce, 37-year-old Rumsey married his latest protégée, who happened to be 20-year-old Florence Eldridge. Eldridge, as we know, went on to a famous marriage and artistic collaboration with Frederic March in 1927, which lasted until March's death in 1975. By 1940, Rumsey was working as a foreman in an auto shop in Queens, New York, earning $750 a year.[35] He died in obscurity in Orange, Vermont, in 1968.[36]

In 1922, Gombell was married for about a minute to her press agent Ferdinand Eggena. Gombell swiftly sought an annulment when Eggena was jailed for fraud in Albany, New York.[37] We have to assume she got it. While the marriage to Eggena, however brief, has not been documented in modern accounts of Gombell's life and career, she is sometimes recorded as having been wed to a man who couldn't possibly have been her husband.[38] Myron Coureval Fagan (1886–1972) was a playwright, director, and producer, who was active on Broadway between 1923 and 1931 and tried to make a comeback there with the anti-communist play *A Red Rainbow* in 1953. Gombell starred in no less than four of his plays during a two and a half year period; the first of these, *Jimmie's Women* (1927–38), being the most successful; *Nancy's Private Affair* (1930), being her last show on Broadway; and intervening *The Great Power* (1928) giving her her first screen role when it was filmed with the original cast at the Bristolphone factory in Waterbury, Connecticut.[39] The film "earned the dubious record of

Minna Gombell and Roland Young exchange a meaningful gaze in *The Pleasure Cruise* (Fox Film Corp., 1933), their only film together. Gombell arrived in Hollywood when she was 38 and never became a star there, but played a number of interesting supporting roles in the 1930s.

being the shortest run of any movie at the Capitol Theatre, New York," being replaced after one showing.[40] Fagan's and Gombell's collaboration may well have extended beyond the stage and given the impression in some quarters that they were married; they may even have moved to Hollywood together in 1930, where they both started off at Fox Films, but they could never actually have been married for the simple reason that Fagan already had a wife (and a son) at home in Pelham Manor, New York.[41] He and Florence M. Fagan were married for nearly 50 years, until her death in 1966.[42]

It would have been nice to record that the Seftons kept true to their modern marriage for the rest of their lives. They finally separated, though, in 1947 and Gombell obtained a divorce on the grounds of cruelty in 1954.[43] She made no further marital experiments. Joseph Sefton died in Los Angeles on March 3, 1966, and was buried beneath the massive obelisk marking the Sefton family plot in Greenwood Memorial Park, San Diego.[44] Minna Gombell died in Los Angeles on April 14, 1973, and was laid to rest with her parents in Baltimore's Loudon Park Cemetery.[45]

"The World's Oldest Working Actress": Ethel Griffies (1878–1975)

As an actress, Ethel Griffies had more lives than a cat. She was a child actor from the age of three in her parents' company. As a young woman, she toured extensively in the English provinces and also appeared in London. She had lived nearly half her long life by the time she came to the United States in 1924. She did not debut in American films until she was 52 and had been on the stage nearly half a century. She had three separate careers on Broadway and nearly as many film careers. She retired about half a dozen times during a 20-year period, but it didn't stick till she was almost 89. When she was 87, she explained: "I'm not working for the money, but for something to *do*.... That's the thing nobody understands about old people. We get so *bored* doing nothing. And so lonely. Work keeps me going."[1] By the end of her life, she was known variously as "probably the oldest working actress on the English-speaking stage," "the oldest working actress in the English-speaking theater," and even as "the world's oldest working actress."[2]

Griffies lived to be 97 and acted for 86 of those years. She was certainly the actress of her generation with the longest career. We get some idea of her longevity, when we compare her to her contemporaries among Hollywood character actresses born between the mid-1870s and the early 1880s. Blanche Friderici and Beryl Mercer died in the 1930s. The 1940s saw the end of the lives and careers of Laura Hope Crews, Maria Ouspenskaya, and Helen Westley. Sara Allgood, Ethel Barrymore, Nora Cecil, Constance Collier, Josephine Hull, Una O'Connor, and Margaret Wycherly all died in the 1950s. By the end of the 1960s, Clara Blandick, Mary Boland, Georgia Caine, Jane Darwell, Margaret Dumont, Emma Dunn, Maude Eburne, Sara Edwards, Elizabeth Patterson, and Lucile Watson had also passed away.

The only one of Griffies's contemporaries to live to a greater age than her was Mary Carr, who had an important career in silent films, subsided into mostly uncredited roles after the advent of sound and was intermittently active until the mid-1950s. Carr was born in Germantown, Pennsylvania, in 1874 and died in Woodland Hills, California, in 1973 at the age of 99. As it happened, Carr and Griffies had a good scene together in the 1933 Jean Harlow comedy *Bombshell* (V. Fleming, MGM). As representatives of a local orphanage, the two women call on Harlow as movie star Lola Burns at her home to examine what kind of environment she can offer a child. Everything goes wrong, when a mass of people, including Harlow's lush father, ne'er-do-well brother and his dubious girlfriend, a raft of reporters, Harlow's current director and would-be lover, and a thwarted gigolo, Lord Hugo, converge on the house creating chaos.

Griffies attributed her longevity to "good health and good luck": "I don't attribute it to any effort of mine. I have not followed any diets. I have no solution."[3] Her long life began in Sheffield in Yorkshire, where she was born Ethel Woods on April 26, 1878, the daughter of actor-manager Samuel Rupert Woods and actress Lillie Roberts.[4] As for her family background, Griffies once explained: "I'm the third and last generation of an acting family. That is, on one side. The other side was all doctors and ministers. I was brought up on tour until the age when I should be sent to school. I was—sporadically."[5]

Griffies made her stage debut in the arms of her mother at age two years and ten months in Whitehaven, England in 1881, as Willie in *East Lynne*. Her maternal grandmother, Mrs. R. Walters, was also in the cast.[6] As a child, she recalled in 1949, "I wanted to be a small fairy and dance my way through life. Instead, I grew to be five foot, seven—and that was considered enormous in my time."[7]

Griffies's first appearance on the London stage was in a revival of *Uncles and Aunts* at the Great Queen Street Theatre on November 4, 1901, but her real London stage career didn't begin until 15 years later.[8] "I was a leading woman for years in the provinces," she said, "but by the time I got to London I was a character woman. That was all right with me."[9] One of her better roles during her years on the London stage was Lady Marden in the original production of A.A. Milne's *Mr. Pim Passes By* at the New Theatre in 1920.[10]

In December 1900, Griffies married fellow actor Walter Beaumont, who died in 1910.[11] She met her second husband, Edward Cooper, who was also an actor, in a Shakespearean company in Manchester. She was Viola and he was Orsino in *Twelfth Night*.[12] They married on June 20, 1914.[13] They both made their silent film debuts in *The Cost of a Kiss* (A. Brunel, Mirror Films) in 1917, the first of four films together. The three others were in Hollywood: *Torch Singer* (A. Hall, G. Somnes, Paramount, 1933), *Mystery of Edwin Drood* (S. Walker, Universal, 1935), and *Holy Matrimony* (J.M. Stahl, Twentieth Century–Fox, 1943). In the first mentioned film, Cooper played Griffies's butler. He was often cast as manservants and most of his 65 American film roles were no more than walk-ons and nearly always uncredited. Cooper was described in 1949 as "long and lean and tweedy" and was pictured in one "at home" interview "serving as an English-accented Greek chorus" to his more loquacious wife.[14] Griffies once said: "The only lover I ever had besides my husband was the theatre."[15]

After 19 years of marriage, the Coopers decided to try their luck in America. Griffies made her Broadway debut as Alice Derring in the new play *Havoc* at Maxine Elliott's Theatre, a role she had also played at the Haymarket in London with Irene Vanbrugh.[16] Griffies recalled in later life, when she had become a hit on Broadway: "I spent six years in New York once and no one took any notice of me."[17] She did nine shows during this first phase of her Broadway career between 1924 and 1930, including John Galsworthy's *Old English* in which she supported George Arliss for two years at the Ritz Theatre and on tour.

Old English gave Griffies her first opportunity in American films, when she was asked to reprise her role in the film version directed by Alfred E. Green at Warner Bros. in 1930. After six years in New York and as a new decade commenced, the Coopers were ready to begin a new stage of their lives and careers in California. They left their $115 a month, rented apartment at 141 E. 62nd St. in New York and found a home in Los Angeles at 6213 Winans Dr. in the hills above the Hollywood Freeway and Franklin Ave.[18]

By 1940, they were living at 8454 Cole Crest Dr.[19] Cole Crest Dr. is one of many tortuous roads that rise and spread out like capillaries from the central artery of the Laurel Canyon

Road and end up running high along the ridges of the hills over Sunset and West Hollywood. There is no number 8454 any longer, but 8460 Cole Crest Dr., a home from 1968 that sits on or next to the site of the Coopers' former home, is described as having "unobstructed jet liner views from the Ocean to the Santa Anas."[20] It may have been here Griffies added "the making of cement" to her list of hobbies, which already included painting, needlework, and gardening, when she built 35 steps for their house.[21] In 1940, Griffies reported to the census taker that she had earned more than $5,000 the previous year, while Cooper had earned $1,000.[22]

Griffies and Cooper spent the years between 1930 and 1947 in Hollywood with a break between 1935 and 1938, when they returned to live and work in England.[23] Clearly, Griffies felt underappreciated in the American film capital. She once observed, "I never even got feature billing."[24] Out of Griffies's more than 90 feature films, about two thirds of her performances were credited and the remaining one third were not; not a bad average, though she clearly thought she could have done better. When asked in 1949, after she had left Hollywood, what she thought of "the movie capital," she responded with characteristic candor: "I don't. At least, I try not to." She added, "Hollywood's like a piece of discarded scenery. It should be taken down when you've gone to your dressing room."[25]

To make matters worse, Griffies had felt unwelcome in the British expatriate community in Hollywood. "It is a strange and terrifying place Hollywood. It is by far the most stratified society in the world, far more class-conscious than England ever was.... I made the mistake of taking a few small parts, because they were good parts. That made me an untouchable. I suddenly found out that people I'd played with in England no longer knew me." According to Griffies, who clearly saw this interview as an opportunity to even some scores, "[C.] Aubrey Smith was the only one who remembered how to be a gentleman. His was the only English house open to me."[26]

Despite her complaints, Griffies was given many opportunities in Hollywood, however small. She played Grace Poole in both the 1934 and 1943 versions of *Jane Eyre*. She played the landlady in both the 1931 and the 1940 versions of *Waterloo Bridge*. She was given solid spinster aunt and dowager roles in films like *Love Me Tonight* (R. Mamoulian, Paramount, 1932), *We Live Again* (R. Mamoulian, Samuel Goldwyn, 1934), *Irene* (H. Wilcox, Imperadio Pictures, 1940), and *Saratoga Trunk* (S. Wood, Warner Bros., 1945), not to mention playing a dedicated head nurse to great effect in support of Carole Lombard in *Vigil in the Night* (G. Stevens, RKO, 1940). And then, of course, there was Mrs. Bundy in Hitchcock's *The Birds* (A. Hitchcock, Alfred J. Hitchcock Prod., 1963), after she came out of retirement. If I were to recommend three of Griffies's films to someone who didn't know her work, I would choose the original version of *Waterloo Bridge* (J. Whale, Universal, 1931), *Werewolf of London* (S. Walker, Universal, 1935), and *How Green Was My Valley* (J. Ford, Twentieth Century–Fox, 1941).

By 1947, the Coopers felt used up in Hollywood. "They got tired of seeing our faces and we found ourselves back among the wines and spirits," Griffies said in 1965, using a British term for the most inconspicuous, back part of the menu. "So we picked ourselves up and came to New York."[27] Leo G. Carroll, who directed and acted in Griffies's first play on Broadway, *Havoc* in 1924, was instrumental in bringing her back to Broadway after a 17-year absence. Griffies and her husband had been set to take "a real vacation" in England, their first return to their native land in years, when she allowed herself to be tempted into playing Mrs. White, "the old lady with the acid tongue and iron constitution," in John Van Druten's new drama *The Druid Circle*.[28] Griffies found "the joy of being in a play after pictures, is that you have a chance to act. You keep working in a part, growing in it. Screen acting isn't like that. You can't grow in a part. Why, you don't even play the scenes in the right order."[29]

Ironically, fame didn't catch up with Griffies till she was 70. We can attribute the rash of feature articles and interviews with her from the late 1940s onward to the unexpected resurgence of her Broadway career after she and her husband left Hollywood. Griffies went on to score a personal hit in the Irving Berlin musical *Miss Liberty*, which ran for 308 performances at the Imperial Theatre in 1949–50 and where she played the heroine's grandmother, "a flower vendor of Paris."[30] One columnist wrote at the time: "To a man, the critics agreed that the high spot of the show is the raucous, rollicking 'Only for Americans' number in which Griff bellows, prances and skips about the stage with a vigor undiminished by the heat, the years or the heavy load of rags in which she is clothed."[31] It was Griffies's first musical role in 40 years. She had "spent five seasons in musical comedy from 1905 to 1909, in London."[32] "Without that experience behind me," Griffies said, "I wouldn't have dared to step into a musical comedy now."[33]

Griffies found "it's rather a disconcerting business, this being discovered, when you're my age, after a lifetime in the theatre."[34] She celebrated her 70th anniversary as an actress in Philadelphia on February 28, 1951, just before the New York opening of Lillian Hellman's *The Autumn Garden*. She and her husband retired from the stage after this show and moved in with a sister-in-law on the Isle of Man.[35]

Ethel Griffies in a press photograph from 1950, a few years after she and her husband Edward Cooper had left Hollywood for good. Her verdict on America's film capitol after having spent 14 years and making 90 films there was "Hollywood's like a piece of discarded scenery. It should be taken down when you've gone to your dressing room."

Fate dealt her a bitter blow when Edward Cooper died in 1956.[36] Griffies went back to work, explaining, "Retirement by yourself is no use ... if you've lived all your life with one person—absolutely content with each other."[37] She took stage roles both on Broadway and in the West End of London and in both American and British films. For example, she created the role of the grandmother in *Billy Liar* both in London and New York and on film (J. Schlesinger, Vic Films Prod./Waterfall Prod., 1963). Her final Broadway show, indeed her last show of any kind, was Lee Thuna's *The Natural Look* with Brenda Vaccaro, Gene Hackman, Jerry Orbach, and Doris Roberts, which opened and closed at the Longacre Theatre on March 11, 1967.[38]

By virtue of having lived an unusually long and active life, combined with the inner light of a sparkling personality, Griffies became a celebrity in her old age. At the drop of a hat, she was willing to hold forth on most any topic, making her a favorite among journalists and talk show hosts. In the 1960s, she was a regular visitor on the *Merv Griffin Show*, celebrating her 90th birthday there and making "about a dozen appearances" on the show, "where informal conversation allowed her wit full play."[39] "Lavender and old lace have nothing in common with Griff," wrote

Ethel Griffies is here seen age 85 in her penultimate film role as the garrulous grandmother in *Billy Liar* (Vic Films Prod./Water Fall Prod., 1963) with (from left) Mona Washbourne, Wilfred Pickles, and Tom Courtenay. She also created the role on the London and New York stages.

one journalist in 1949. "She's a zesty, pungent old party who might have been conceived by Bernard Shaw. Off stage and on, she delivers her lines with crackling humor."[40]

Griffies once said: "I'm sure if I were on my deathbed and somebody waved a contract at me, I'd get right up, put my clothes on and go see about it."[41] Thus we must attribute her death in London on Tuesday, September 9, 1975, not primarily to a stroke, but to the untimely absence of a producer with a contract in his hand.[42]

"Old Frozenface": Sara Haden (1898–1981)

There's a limit to how excited I can get about Sara Haden, I must admit, but for her sheer ubiquity in the mainstream Hollywood films of the 1930s and '40s, she deserves a place at the cutting room table and not just on the floor. Haden may have been relegated to modest roles throughout her 24-year film career, but the fact of the matter is: out of more than 70 feature films, only three of her roles were uncredited. Not many character actresses of similar (lack of) stature can say the same. The three films in which Haden did not get a credit were all for MGM while she was a contract player there and had to do as she was asked or risk being put on suspension.

Sara Haden was born Catherine Haden in Center Point, Texas, on November 17, 1898. While some sources claim it was in 1897 and others says 1899, the 1900 U.S. census and the California Death Index both make it perfectly clear that the year was 1898.[1] As for the date, even Haden's mother was uncertain about it, according to columnist Robin Coons. He wrote in 1936, that Sara Haden was born in Center Point, Texas, and that her mother, the actress Charlotte Walker, could not remember if it was on November 17, 18, 27 or 28! Both Haden's father and the doctor who delivered her were dead at this point, so there was no one to provide corroborating evidence.[2] Center Point is a small community in Kerr County in what is known as the "Hill Country," just south of Kerrville and 45 miles northwest of San Antonio. Thus it is quite some distance inland from Galveston, where Haden would grow up, in fact more than 300 miles.

We find Catherine Haden (1) living with her father, John B. Haden (28), mother Charlotte W. Haden (22), older sister Beatrice S. Haden (2), and an African American cook called Della Brown (24) at 2321 Ave. O in Galveston when the U.S. census was taken on June 14, 1900.[3] As it happens, Haden's mother had also lived on Ave. O. as a child.[4] Charlotte Walker was soon to become one of the celebrated beauties of the American stage, but for the first couple of years of Sara Haden's life, she was "just" a mother to Catherine, as she was called then, and her older sister Beatrice, born in New York in November 1897, and a wife to the young doctor John B. Haden. Walker had made her stage debut in London when she was 17 and became a member of the company of the star Richard Mansfield on her return to the United States, but left the stage when she married John Haden in 1896.[5] The marriage only lasted till 1902,[6] so Haden would hardly have remembered her parents together. We've been told "Sara as a child was a model of good behavior, and all because she didn't want anybody to say, 'What can you expect of the girl—her mother was an actress!'"[7]

Sara Haden's father John was born in Texas in August 1872, the son of a wealthy doctor, John Miller Haden, and Sarah Brannum Haden. In 1880, we find eight-year-old John living with his parents John M. Haden (50) and Sarah B. Haden (36), sister Bessie (11), brother Harry C. (6), maternal grandmother Elizabeth Hughes (60), and four African American servants between the ages of ten and 30 at 270 E. Broadway in Galveston, Texas.[8] Bessie, the aunt Sara Haden never knew, passed away in 1884.[9] Haden's paternal grandmother Sarah died four years later, when her son John was only 16.[10] Grandpa Haden died in 1892,[11] so Haden's father was parentless at 20. Haden's paternal uncle Harry Haden, on the other hand, who was a dentist, lived to be 82 and died in 1956.[12] All the Hadens are buried in Old City Cemetery in Galveston. Twenty-five years after her uncle's death, Sara Haden would also find her final resting place there.[13]

Haden had strong ties all her life to her family in Texas and returned there often, particularly while her mother was alive, so it is well worth saying something of her ancestry on the distaff side too. Haden's maternal grandmother Charlisa, born in Georgia in 1855, was the daughter of the wealthy Kerr County landowner, doctor, and Confederate Army Civil War veteran Charles F. (de) Ganahl (c. 1829–1883), who was one of the earliest settlers in Center Point, Texas, and his wife Virginia "Jennie" Wright Ganahl (1834–95).[14] Charlisa Ganahl married Edwin Anderson Walker, born in South Carolina in 1849, "the son of the British Consul" there,[15] and they had three children: Sara Haden's mother Charlotte Walker, born in Galveston in 1877; Charles Ganahl Walker, born in 1881; and George Pinckney Walker, born about 1883.[16] Haden's maternal grandfather, Edwin Walker, who had a cotton brokerage business, died in an accident in 1889 at the age of 40 and was buried in Galveston's Evergreen Cemetery.[17] Charlisa Ganahl Walker, the only grandparent Sara Haden knew, was a widow for 45 years and died in 1934, the year her granddaughter made her film debut.[18]

When Haden's mother Charlotte Walker left her doctor husband, she set her sights on New York City.[19] Between 1900 and her final show there in 1934, the Internet Broadway Database (IBDb) records no less than 30 shows that Walker either starred or played a supporting role in. One of her biggest hits was William C. deMille's *The Warrens of Virginia* (1907–08), where William's brother Cecil B. DeMille was in the cast and a young actress, who also had a big future in film, was making her Broadway debut: Mary Pickford.

Walker was even more identified with *The Trail of the Lonesome Pine*, Eugene Walter's dramatization of a novel by John Fox, Jr., in which she starred at the New Amsterdam Theatre in early 1912. Readers may know this story from the 1936 film version starring Sylvia Sidney, Fred MacMurray, and Henry Fonda. There were several silent versions as well, including one from 1916 directed by Cecil B. DeMille in which Walker reprised her starring stage role. De Mille had also directed Walker's film debut in *Kindling* (1915), based on another Broadway play of the period. Walker was active in silent films in the teens and did some character roles in the 1920s, but with the coming of the sound era, her film career ended, just as her daughter's was about to begin.

The author of the play version of *The Trail of the Lonesome Pine*, Eugene Walter, just happened to be Charlotte Walker's second husband. He was born in Cleveland, Ohio, in 1874. He and Walker married in Hamilton, Ohio, on December 1, 1908.[20] In 1910, we find them living in fine style in the famous Dorilton apartment building at 171 W. 71st. St. on the corner of Broadway with a 29-year-old Japanese valet, William Oishi.[21] The census records that Walker is the mother of two children, but they are clearly not living with her at this time, nor have I been able to locate them or their father, Walker's ex-husband, in the 1910 census.

Charlotte Walker and Eugene Walter divorced in 1930 and he died in Los Angeles in 1941.[22] After failing to reignite her film career in the early 1940s, Walker retired from acting and moved back to Center Point, Texas. Haden and her sister Beatrice visited her there many times up until her death at Sid Peterson Memorial Hospital in Kerrville on March 23, 1958, at the age of 80. Walker was buried in Old City Cemetery in Galveston.[23]

Back in 1940, the census enumerator Flora W. Bateman found Walker in Los Angeles, admitting to 60 and living at 1107 S. Doheny Dr., a pleasant but fairly modest, two-story, Spanish-inspired house on a narrow lot, with a Kathryn Vandenburg and a Seamon Vandenburg, both 40 and listed as the owner/manager of an auto court.[24] So who are these "furriners" old Miz Walker is living with?

Well, to answer that question, we have to backtrack a bit. After all, the last we heard of Sara Haden, she wasn't Sara Haden at all, but Catherine Haden and she and sister Beatrice had gone missing, at least in census terms. In fact, we don't have much specific information about Haden between the 1900 census and 1921, that is, the years of her schooling and training for the theater. We do know, though, that she went to kindergarten at "Miss Aves' school" and attended the Dominican Convent in Galveston, which was a boarding school, and later "eastern schools." She spent her vacations with her father in Galveston or on her Grandmother Walker's ranch.[25] One news article about her claims she made her stage debut as a child "in a stock company in Washington, D.C., where her mother was a leading lady."[26] This seems doubtful for several reasons, not least of all because we know Charlotte Walker was originally opposed to her daughter going on the stage.[27] According to a 1934 news item, "Miss Haden played for a while in stock companies, playing many of the feminine leads in plays given by the James Hayden Players."[28] That was in Galveston, but another paper insisted she had played character roles and "showed up as possibly the best character woman in the long and painful annals of dramatic stock in Dallas."[29] She was also a "dog impersonator for her own stories on the radio," according to another source.[30]

In 1921, Catherine Haden debuts on Broadway as "Sara Haden" in Shakespeare's *Macbeth*. And what part was the 22-year-old Haden playing? Macduff's son! Walter Hampden, who was directing and producing and playing the lead, must really have wanted her in the play. We notice, too, in the cast list, playing the modest role of "Ross, a nobleman," an actor called Richard Abbott. Abbott was Sara Haden's one and only husband and they were married for 27 years. He had made his debut on Broadway in 1918 in a new play called *Success*, which had only been a moderate one.[31] He had done a few things since then, but nothing major, and then he and Sara met in Walter Hampden's production of *Macbeth* at the Broadhurst Theatre and were married that same year.

The man who became Richard Abbott on the American stage was actually born Seamon (Simon) Vandenberg in Antwerp, Belgium on May 22, 1899.[32] That solves the mystery of who Charlotte Walker was living with in 1940, her very own daughter and son-in-law, though not why they chose to identify themselves as the owners and operators of an auto court rather than as film actors. When Simon was about three years old, his parents brought him to the United States,[33] where he by due stages grew into the actor Richard Abbott who won and wed Sara Haden in 1921.[34]

Haden and Abbott worked regularly on Broadway throughout the 1920s and Abbott

In this glamour shot from 1936, Sara Haden looks about as glamorous as Ellen Corby. Haden was the daughter of the legendary stage beauty Charlotte Walker. Let's venture a guess that Haden took after her father.

into the early 1930s. Haden was in nine shows in New York between 1921 and 1929. Her biggest commercial hit was Samuel Shipman's comedy *Lawful Larceny* at the Theatre Republic in the first half of 1922. The play that was most important to her career, though, was *Trigger* by Lula Vollmer. Vollmer was already famous as the author of the successful play *Sun-Up* in which veteran actress Lucille La Verne scored a big hit as the "good hater" and matriarch of her rustic North Carolina mountain home, Widow Cagle. Apparently, Haden played the role of Emmy in a London production of *Sun-Up* a year or so after her New York debut.[35]

In *Trigger*, she played the somewhat intellectually challenged Etta Dawson, who is the fair-weather friend of the eponymous heroine, Trigger Hicks, played by Claiborne Foster. Natalie Schafer was also in the cast, making her Broadway debut as a big city siren, a staple character in Vollmer's paeans to the joys and ideals of rustic mountain life. *Trigger* ran for 47 performances at the Little Theatre (now the Helen Hayes Theatre) in late 1927 and early 1928 and was directed by a young, pre–Hollywood George Cukor, who many years later would direct Haden again in the film *A Life of Her Own* (MGM, 1950).[36]

As he had been in her first Broadway show, Richard Abbott was also cast in her last before they moved to Hollywood. This was Louis Weitzenkorn's new drama about suburban "ennui" in New Jersey, *First Mortgage*, starring Walter Abel and staged by Mary Nash's ex-husband José Ruben, where Haden and Abbott actually played a married couple. That is, they didn't for long. The play unfortunately opened on "Black Tuesday," October 29, 1929, and only lasted four performances at the Broadhurst Theatre.

In 1930, we find Haden and Abbott, both claiming to be 29, living in a $120 a month, rented apartment at 159 W. 85th St. in New York.[37] Haden's older sister Beatrice had also moved to New York by this time. She was working as a librarian and lodging at 410 W. 115th St.[38] The 1930 U.S. census also reveals the whereabouts of Sara's and Beatrice's father. He was 57 and a patient at the U.S. Government Hospital No. 78 in Pulaski, Arkansas. John B. Haden died before 1936.[39]

Haden and Abbott went to Hollywood in late 1933. The opportunity came for Haden to reprise her role in *Trigger*, which was being filmed at RKO with Katharine Hepburn as the rough-and-ready yet spiritual heroine with a special connection to the Almighty. Trigger Hicks in *Spitfire* (J. Cromwell, 1934) is in heavy competition with the title role in *Sylvia Scarlett* and Jade Tan in *Dragon Seed* as Hepburn's most ludicrous film role. Her distinctive voice quality and idiolect limited the range of roles she could realistically portray, but it took a while for the studios to catch on. *Spitfire* was early days for Hepburn, too, not just Haden. It was Hepburn's fifth film to be released; after *Little Women* and before *The Little Minister*.

In the summer of 1934, the now 35-year-old Abbott also got a film role at RKO, albeit a modest one, playing Allard von Leyden, the son of a baron in pro–Nazi Holland during World War I. *The Fountain* (J. Cromwell, 1934) starred Ann Harding and Brian Aherne, with Jean Hersholt and Violet Kemble-Cooper playing Abbott's parents, the Baron and Baroness von Leyden, Paul Lukas as his brother, and Betty Alden as his wife. Haden was also in the film playing a jealous stepsister. It was her fifth film to be released.

During her first years in Hollywood, Haden was kept very busy at RKO and Fox. In a feature article by Paul Harrison from 1936 entitled "The Gals You Love to Hate," she was discussed at length in a motley company of screen villainesses that included Gale Sondergaard, Priscilla Dean, Myrna Loy, Betty Furness, Benita Hume, and even Bette Davis. In a statement that years later would crop up in her UPI obituary, Harrison pointed out, "Within two years she has glared and grouched herself through more than 15 pictures" and been "more rigidly typed as a heavy than any other woman in Hollywood." The writer put this down to her appearance: "With very little effort she can look acidly austere."[40]

From 1938 till 1946, Haden was a minor yet integral member of the MGM "stock company." During these years, she was kept so busy that she wasn't loaned out a single time. Haden's long-term contract at MGM gave her a secure and regular income, but it also meant that she had to take the parts the studio told her to play. This may be why she had a tendency to get cast in the least important of the credited supporting roles, such as in her most popular film today, *The Shop Around the Corner* (E. Lubitsch, MGM, 1940). In the original version, Flora, the spinster shop assistant in Frank Morgan's luggage store, is the least important and interesting character among the six employees, also when compared to the roughly equivalent role played by Spring Byington in *In the Good Old Summertime* (1949) and Jean Stapleton in *You've Got Mail* (1998). Stapleton has a romantic past, as Spanish dictator Franco's mistress, and Byington has a future, as S.Z. Sakall's wife. In the 14 "Andy Hardy" films in which Haden portrayed the irrepressible hero's prim and proper, maiden aunt Milly Forrest, she was considered "the least essential of the Carvel family regulars"[41]; Carvel being the Midwestern town where the films are set.

Here we see Sara Haden (far left) as Aunt Milly Forrest with the rest of the Hardy family in a still from the final film in the series, *Andy Hardy Comes Home* (Metro-Goldwyn-Mayer, 1958), which was Haden's last feature. The other cast members are (from left) Fay Holden, Gina Gillespie, Patricia Breslin, Mickey Rooney, Teddy Rooney, Cecilia Parker, and Johnny Weissmuller, Jr.

I would suggest that Haden's best opportunity came just after she left her secure berth at MGM. *She-Wolf of London* (J. Yarbrough, 1946) is a playful and delightful, low budget, late horror film from Universal, starring Don Porter and June Lockhart and with Haden billed third for once as a classic dyed-in-the-wool villainess. Haden's character, Martha Winthrop, concocts a plot to be able to stay on in the house where she was originally a housekeeper and where she now pretends to be the aunt of the real owner, Phyllis Allenby (Lockhart), though she is no blood relation at all. She frames Phyllis to make it look as if she is a she-wolf, while the plot also contains a twist where it seems for a while that Martha's own daughter Carol Winthrop (Jan Wiley), might be the she-wolf. In truth, there is no she-wolf and Martha herself has murdered a little boy and a police inspector and attacked her daughter's impoverished boyfriend Dwight Severn (Martin Kosleck), whom she heartily disapproves of.

When Haden finally gets a really juicy role with scenery-chewing potential, when she finally has the chance to shine and be the center of attention, naturally you want her to be really good. And then she isn't. Given the tortured, melodramatic motivations of her character, though, and the patent implausibility of the plot, it's worth asking if anyone could have been convincing in circumstances so alien to verisimilitude. Opinions may differ, too, on Haden's performance here. No less an authority than Theresa Loeb, film critic for the *Oakland Tribune*, thought that while Lockhart was "a trifle wooden as the young Allenby heiress who fears she is 'cursed' and therefore the mutilating werewolf," Haden was "excellent in her role as a sinister 'aunt' who tries to drive the girl insane by instilling the werewolf belief in her." She found the film as a whole "decidedly above the run-of-the-mill horror films."[42] It was shot in just two weeks before Christmas in 1945. Sara Haden was paid $2,167 a week and was the most highly paid cast member, while June Lockhart got only $1,000 a week.[43] Lockhart remembered Haden as "a wonderful actress" and thought the scene where she "went cuckoo" was "very much Mrs. Danvers in *Rebecca*."[44]

After *The Fountain* in 1934, nothing more had happened for Richard Abbott in films except a few uncredited bit parts. By the late 1930s, he is described in articles about his wife as a "Los Angeles businessman."[45] On the occasion of their 18th wedding anniversary in 1939, Haden was given the opportunity to expound her views on marriage in Alexander Kahn's United Press column. "Most people don't realize," says Haden, "that marriage is a profession, much like law or medicine. A doctor will take great pride of accomplishment in curing a patient, but married people don't realize there should be the same pride of accomplishment in saving a marriage." "Marriage can't endure in cases where drunkenness or brutality are present," she adds, "but in most cases, if people realize marriage is a profession and must be regarded in that light, the problems will solve themselves if analyzed."[46]

Sad to say, the Vandenbergs' problems ultimately did not solve themselves, even when analyzed, and the couple divorced after 27 years of marriage in 1948.[47] Haden explained in an interview in 1955, "Abbott didn't click in Hollywood ... and the marriage was dissolved when he returned to his first love—the New York stage."[48] Richard Abbott died in New York City in 1986 and was buried in Kensico Cemetery at the expense of the Actors' Benevolent Fund.[49]

Catherine Haden Vandenberg, known to the world as Sara Haden, died in the Motion Picture Country House and Hospital in Woodland Hills, California, on Tuesday, September 15, 1981.[50] Upon her death at the age of 82, she had not been seen on the stage or screen for 16 years.

From Euclid Avenue to the Yellow Brick Road: Margaret Hamilton (1902–85)

With the possible exception of supporting players who appeared in *Gone with the Wind*, there are few character actresses whose long and varied careers were more dominated by a single role than Margaret Hamilton. She said herself that the Wicked Witch of the West was "the most spectacular thing I've done," though she did not consider it "the only thing I've done that's important."[1] She was grateful for the celebrity and recognition the dual part in *The Wizard of Oz* had given her, but it was clear she would also like to be remembered for other roles both on stage and screen; in television, where she worked frequently between 1950 and 1982; and in radio. She said several times, "'Playing the Witch was not great shakes of acting.'"[2] Her second most famous role, as Cora the genial storekeeper who would only sell Maxwell House Coffee in the 1970s TV commercials, was no more challenging. In her own words: "I rarely turn anything down. I'll act in anything."[3]

One prophetic soul wrote back in 1934, when Hamilton was 32 and just starting out on her belated professional acting career, "Margaret Hamilton may never play Juliet, but she'll have an interesting career."[4] She was a serious, hard-working, and versatile actress, whose opportunities on the big screen were limited by her characteristic physiognomy and the lack of imagination of Hollywood producers. As one particularly unkind observer put it, she had "a face that would not only stop a clock but probably demolish it."[5] "In the movie colony, they call her 'Great Stone Face,'" wrote Karl Kohrs in 1951, the year Hamilton moved back to New York after 15 years in Hollywood.[6] Hamilton herself insisted, "'*I'm glad I'm homely*'": "'My face has given me lots of work.'"[7]

Fortunately, stage producers were more willing to let her move beyond the scold, gossip, and landlady segment of the character spectrum. Maybe for that reason, live theater was Hamilton's first and greatest love. There she was able to play roles she would never have gotten on film. What film producer would have cast her as Madame Armfeldt in *A Little Night Music* or Mrs. Bramson in *Night Must Fall*, roles created by Hermione Gingold and Dame May Whitty?

Indeed, Hamilton owed her acting career not to *The Wizard of Oz* (V. Fleming, MGM, 1939), which represented the apex of her fame and fortune, but to a role in a now forgotten hit play by Rose Franken called *Another Language*, which opened at the Booth Theatre in New York on April 21, 1932, and ran for 344 performances.[8] Hamilton played the heroine's only sympathetic in-law, Helen Hallam, in this drama of a dysfunctional, emotionally stifled,

The distinctive profiles of Margaret Hamilton and W.C. Fields are evident in this still from *My Little Chickadee* (Universal Pictures, 1940). This riotous comedy also starred Mae West and gave Hamilton one of her best comedy roles as West's straight-laced, inquisitive, and interfering antagonist Mrs. Gideon.

and materialistic, lower middle-class New York family ruled by the "silver cord" of the subtly domineering matriarch Mrs. Hallam, played by Margaret Wycherly. *Another Language* gave Hamilton not only her debut on Broadway, but her screen debut as well, when MGM filmed the play starting May 24, 1933, with Edward H. Griffith directing and Helen Hayes in the lead.[9] Helen Hallam spent most of her scenes nibbling on grapes. Hamilton recalled in 1963, "I was identified as the one who eats grapes, until the witch came along."[10] She got "mightily sick" of eating grapes.[11] Till the end of her life, though, if anyone ever said they remembered her in *Another Language*, she was "ready to kiss them."[12]

So what more can I tell you about Margaret Hamilton? That she started her professional life as a kindergarten teacher? You know that, of course. That she and landscape architect Paul Meserve had a son, Hamilton Wadsworth Meserve, the day before their fifth wedding anniversary in 1936, and divorced two years later?[13] You know that, too, no doubt. Do you know, though, that Margaret's father offered to pay for a nose job when she was a child?[14] That her older sister Dorothy was a pioneer in the birth control movement? What about the fact that by the time she was 75, Hamilton had lost four inches in height through slipped disks? "Maybe I'm melting," she suggested tongue in cheek.[15]

Margaret Brainard Hamilton was born at home at 64 Tilden Ave. in Cleveland, Ohio, on November 2, 1902.[16] Brainard was her paternal great-grandmother Salinda Hamilton's maiden name.[17] Margaret's father was a prosperous lawyer, Walter Jones Hamilton, who was born in Cleveland on April 14, 1865, and educated at the University of Michigan and Cornell.[18] Her mother, Mary Jane Adams Hamilton (known as "Jennie"), was born in Cleveland on August 28, 1865, or possibly two years earlier.[19] Walter and Jennie were married in about 1893 and had three children before Margaret was born: Dorothy Adams Hamilton (b. March 14, 1894), Gladys E. Hamilton (b. September 13, 1895), and Edwin Timothy Hamilton (b. in September 1898).[20]

When Margaret was about five, the family moved to the house at 2058 E. 96th St., just south of fashionable Euclid Ave., that she would call home until she married and moved away from Cleveland for good in 1931.[21] Margaret grew up surrounded by the extended Hamilton and Adams families. Her maternal grandfather Edgar Adams, born in England in 1836, who had been a gilder and art dealer with his own his shop at 47 Euclid Ave., where he also sold painting materials and picture frames, had died of pneumonia in 1889, but her maternal grandmother, Mary Jane Elliott Adams, born in England in 1838, lived nearby at 10075 Keemar Ct.[22] Margaret's paternal grandfather, who had been a lawyer like her father and was usually referred to as "Judge E.T. Hamilton" (b. 1830), died of apoplexy in 1905, but his widow, Margaret's grandmother Mary E. Jones Hamilton (b. 1839), still lived in the family home at 2028 E. 89th St. with her unmarried daughter Florence Hamilton (b. 1867).[23] Grandma Adams died in 1916, but Grandma Hamilton held on until 1929, when she died at home of myocarditis and chronic nephritis at the age of 90.[24]

Walter Hamilton only had the one sibling, Margaret's Aunt Florence, who lived until 1960, but Jennie Adams Hamilton had two brothers: Charles E. Adams (1859–1933), who was the president of a hardware company and married to Jennie Bowley Adams (1859–1931); and Edgar Elliott Adams (1870–1937), who was also in the hardware business and was married to Elizabeth Carlton Adams (1872–1950).[25] The Hamiltons lived roughly midway between Uncle Charles and Aunt Jennie to the east in Cleveland Heights and Uncle Edgar and Aunt Elizabeth to the west in Lakewood.[26] Margaret had three cousins in all: Charles and Jennie's daughter, Bessie Jennie Adams (b. 1885), who had left home by 1910, probably to get married[27]; and Edgar and Elizabeth's daughters Martha R. Adams (1908–82) and Mary Jane E. Adams (1910–96), who never got married.[28]

As for Margaret's older siblings, Dorothy was the first to leave home when she married Charles F. Brush, Jr., in 1917, the year she graduated from Smith College.[29] Charles Brush was an electrical engineer and the son of Charles Francis Brush, the millionaire industrialist and inventor of the arc lamp, who lived in an elaborate 17-room "Italianized Romanesque" mansion at 3725 Euclid Ave., which had been designed by George H. Smith outside and Herter Bros. and Louis Tiffany inside and built in 1887–88.[30] Dorothy and Charlie settled on more modest quarters, though; first in an apartment at 2753 Euclid Blvd. in Cleveland Heights and later in a house at 2262 Tudor Dr. in the same neighborhood.[31]

In 1922, Margaret's then 27-year-old sister Gladys married the salesman John Giles Mohler and moved to his hometown of Columbus, Ohio, where she would live for the rest of her life. Gladys was a housewife, she and her husband would be childless and lived for many years at 224 Woodland Ave. in a large, vertically divided wooden house with John's mother Lillian R. Chappelear Mohler occupying the other half until her death in 1950.[32] Both parts of the house, virtually unchanged since the Mohlers lived there, were sold together for

$150,300 in 2014.[33] John G. Mohler died in Columbus in 1971 followed by Gladys Hamilton Mohler in 1977 and both lie buried in Green Lawn Cemetery.[34]

In 1921, it was Margaret's turn to go off to school, which in her case meant spending two years at the Wheelock Kindergarten Training School (now Wheelock College) in Boston.[35] She had already been bitten by the acting bug in high school, but did the sensible thing and trained for a profession that was more dependable than the stage. In one version of the story, her father "refused to accept her desire to act," so "she was sent to a sensible school to learn a sensible career" and spent two years in Rye, New York, and four years in Cleveland as a kindergarten teacher.[36] In a slightly different version, it was her mother who insisted that she stick to her original plan and go to Wheelock; "then when you're out earning your living, you can fool around with the theatre all you want to," she told her daughter.[37]

At any rate, Hamilton returned to her home town from Rye in about 1927, and joined the Cleveland Play House, in her own words, "when no one was looking."[38] She would spend three years there and performed 25 different roles, including Prossy in *Candida* and Miss Prism in *The Importance of Being Earnest*.[39] She is not recorded with any profession in the 1930 U.S. census or on her marriage license, so she was probably devoting herself full time to caring for her widowed father in addition to her acting.

These were difficult years in the Hamilton family. Jennie Adams Hamilton was diagnosed and underwent an operation for colon cancer in September 1925 and finally died of a recurrence of the disease on July 1, 1926, at the age of 60.[40] An even more cruel tragedy struck the family in the spring of 1927, when Dorothy Brush's little daughter Jane fell gravely ill with pleural empyema on her right lung (a form of pneumonia). In an effort to save her life, she was given a blood transfusion by her then 33-year-old father, but she died nevertheless on May 23, 1927, at the age of six years, nine months, and 28 days.[41] Six days later, Charles F. Brush, Jr., also died, of blood poisoning from an infection in his left arm caused by the transfusion.[42]

In 1927, then, Dorothy Brush found herself alone with her four-year-old son Charles F. Brush III (1923–2006). Margaret's oldest sister dedicated the remainder of her life to fighting for women's rights and the birth control movement, becoming one of Margaret Sanger's closest friends and collaborators.[43] She married a wealthy South Carolina attorney, Alexander Colclough Dick, Jr. (1893–1991), in 1929 and moved with him to Riverdale in the Bronx, New York. The couple had a daughter, Sylvia Dick (Karas), in 1930 and divorced in 1947.[44] During the last six years of her life, Dorothy was married to Dr. Lewis C. Walmsley.[45] Dorothy Adams Hamilton Brush Dick Walmsley died on June 21, 1968, and her ashes were scattered over the ocean from a plane above her home at Bridgehampton, New York, by her son Charles.[46]

We can imagine the surprise in the Hamilton and Adams families when homely school teacher Maggie didn't end up a spinster like her aunt Florence Hamilton and her two younger cousins Mary Jane and Martha Adams. I don't know how Hamilton met her husband. When the U.S. census was taken in the spring of 1930, just a little over a year before they were married, Hamilton was living at home with her father on E. 96th St. in Cleveland and her future husband was living at 2 Park Ave. in Eastchester, New York, and working as a landscape architect.[47] Paul Boynton Meserve was born in Framingham, Massachusetts, on November 2, 1902, making him and his future wife nearly exactly the same age.[48] His father Frank was an electrician in a machine shop and his mother Alice was at home. When Paul was 7, the Meserve household, which included his four older siblings, a maid, and a lodger, were living in a simple two-and-a-half-story wooden house, which still stands at 28 Gilbert St. in Framingham.[49]

More than any single role on stage or screen, one might claim that Hamilton owed her career to the fact that she got married and moved to New York in 1931. If nothing else, her brief marriage saved her from spending four more years as her father's unpaid housekeeper and caregiver and got her out of Cleveland for good. It reignited the commitment to pursuing a life on the stage, that had been sparked by seeing Gertrude Lawrence in George and Ira Gershwin's musical *Oh, Kay!* in New York in 1926 or '27 and put her in the one place in the world where she could really make her acting dreams come true.[50] Walter J. Hamilton died at Lakeside Hospital in Cleveland on August 22, 1935, of acute intestinal obstruction, bronchopneumonia, and paralytic ulcers with coronary disease and myocardial fibrosis as contributory causes.[51] He was buried with his wife and parents in Lake View Cemetery.[52]

After being married in Cleveland on June 13, 1931, by the same minister, Adelbert P. Higley, who had married her sister Gladys and John Mohler, Margaret Hamilton Meserve left the city of her birth for good. Today little remains of the Cleveland she knew as a child

In the romantic comedy *Texas, Brooklyn & Heaven* (Robert S. Golden Prod., 1948) starring Guy Madison and Diana Lynn, Margaret Hamilton (center left) played one of three eccentric sisters living in a mansion on Flatbush Ave. in Brooklyn, who rent their stable to Florence Bates (left) and Lynn. The other two sisters were played by Angela Lansbury's mother, Moyna MacGill (right), and Irene Ryan (center right) of *Beverly Hillbillies* fame.

and young woman. The decimation of the city's architectural heritage is most vividly illustrated by the demolition of practically all the stately mansions that once lined fashionable Euclid Ave., including the elaborate Brush mansion, which the owner decreed should be pulled down after his death in 1929.[53] Anyone, then, seeking out specific places associated with Margaret Hamilton's life in Cleveland is going to have their work cut out for them. The house she was born in, the house she grew up in, her grandparents' homes, her aunt and uncle's house in Lakewood, her elementary school, and the schools where she taught herself are all gone. One exception is the Cleveland Play House building from 1927, which still sits with its characteristic front squatly facing Euclid Ave. at 86th St. Uncle Charles and Aunt Jennie's capacious, mock Tudor home at 2700 E. Overlook Rd. in leafy Cleveland Heights, where they lived for more than 30 years, is also still standing, as is Dorothy's home on Tudor Dr. where Charles Brush, Jr., died in 1927.

If we turn to look for traces of Hamilton in Los Angeles, the situation is not much better. Only one of the three homes she is known to have occupied for any length of time still exists. 1087 Courtney Ave. is a small apartment complex from 1926 in Nichols Canyon, just above Hollywood Blvd.[54] Hamilton was living there during the years 1936–38, before she moved to a more prestigious address in the "Flats" of Beverly Hills. The house she owned at 611 N. Canon Dr. was valued at $42,000 in 1940. She reported to have earned in excess of $5,000 in 1939, one of her better years, and paid her live-in cook Kathryn Curse $1,200.[55] Fellow actor Ralph Bellamy and his wife Catherine lived next door at no. 609; the producer and studio head Hal Roach, his wife Marguerite, and their two grown children lived across the street in a French Provincial house at no. 610, while producer Jack S. Cummings (son of Ida Mayer Cummings and nephew of L.B. Mayer), his wife Marjorie, and their daughter Julie Ann lived at no. 603. Hamilton's house was razed in the early 1980s, while 505 N. Elm Dr., where she lived during her final years in Hollywood, was demolished in the early 1990s.[56]

Hamilton moved back to New York in 1951, though she would continue to act in films intermittently until the early 1970s. The home most fans and friends associate her with was her apartment in what has been called New York's first cooperative apartment building, the Gramercy at 34 Gramercy Park East.[57] This towering, eclectic building in warm red brick and rough grey stone stands on the corner of E. 20th St. Hamilton made her home here from about 1958, when fellow resident Mildred Dunnock helped her find an apartment in the building, until shortly before her death, when her increasing senility made it necessary for her to move to the Noble Horizons nursing home in Salisbury, Connecticut.[58] She died there of an apparent heart attack on Thursday, May 16, 1985.[59]

Margaret Brainard Hamilton was not buried with all the Hamiltons and Adamses in Cleveland's Lake View Cemetery. Her ashes were scattered over her property in Dutchess County, New York.[60] She had once said in an interview that, rather than being buried in a place like Forest Lawn, she'd "'just as soon be cremated and left in an alley.'"[61]

"Ivan the Terrible": Rosalind Ivan (1880–1959)

Sometimes the right role comes at just the right time for an actress. Such was the case for Rosalind Ivan. When the census enumerator visited her in her room at the New Weston Hotel at 34 E. 50th St. in New York City on April 9, 1940, Ivan reported that she had been out of work for 55 weeks, that is for more than a year. She claimed to be 50 years old, when she was in fact 60, was born in England, was single, had only eight years of schooling, was an "alien" and worked as an actress in radio. She had earned $786 for nine weeks' work in 1939. Even though Ivan had "income of $30 or more from sources other than money wages or salary," she was probably much concerned at this point with how she would stay afloat in the coming year.[1] By the end of the 1940, she would be playing in one of the biggest hits of the season on Broadway, described by Burns Mantle as "the most distinguished and absorbing of the season's importations."[2]

The role that would get her out of a tight spot and lead to a film career on the third attempt was that of Mrs. Watty in *The Corn Is Green*, Emlyn Williams's classic drama about an independent, progressive, and unpartnered "female M.A.,"[3] Lily Christabel Moffat, who decides to open a school in the Welsh coal mining village of Glansarno, where she has inherited a house. Or as one reviewer put it, *The Corn Is Green* "tells the story of a high-spirited Englishwoman's struggle to raise the educational level of the impoverished miners of Wales at the turn of the century."[4]

The Corn Is Green was a big hit at the National Theatre (now the Nederlander), later transferring to the Royale (now the Bernard B. Jacobs), and ran for 477 performances between November 26, 1940, and January 17, 1942, followed by a tour lasting more than two years.[5] Ethel Barrymore, in her early 60s at the time, created the role of Miss Moffat on Broadway and had the longest run of her career in the part.[6] Rosalind Ivan, who was just a year and a half younger than Barrymore, supported her as her housekeeper Mrs. Watty, Thelma Schnee played her daughter Bessie Watty, and Richard Waring played Morgan Evans, a coal miner who shows promise as a writer. Mildred Dunnock created the role of the virginal Miss Ronberry, who is recruited by Miss Moffat to teach at the school.

Warner Bros. bought the film rights for $135,000 and production took place between June 20 and September 13, 1944.[7] Before she reported to the Warner Bros. set, Ivan had time to do a small role at RKO, as the owner of a fish and chip shop who tells Cary Grant he needs to settle down in *None But the Lonely Heart* (C. Odets, RKO, 1944). There she was reunited with Barrymore, who was embarking on a film career. Barrymore was not fated to play Miss

Bette Davis (left) met her match in Rosalind Ivan, who played her devoted, ex-pickpocket housekeeper in *The Corn Is Green* (Warner Bros., 1945). Here they have both just arrived in the Welsh mining village of Glansarno. Unfortunately, this was their only film together.

Moffat on film, though, as her role was given to Warner Bros. number one star Bette Davis. Davis at 36 was actually much closer to Miss Moffat of "about forty,"[8] as Emlyn Williams had conceived her. Out of the original Broadway cast, only Ivan, Dunnock; Rhys Williams, who played the teacher Mr. Jones; and Gwyneth Hughes, who played the village postmistress, reprised their roles in the film. Richard Waring had to be replaced by John Dall when he was drafted.[9]

As her Dickensian name suggests, Mrs. Watty is "a woman of the people," an illiterate London Cockney and a reformed shoplifter, whom Miss Moffat has set to work as a housekeeper as an alternative to her going to jail. Mrs. Watty has also found religion and goes around trilling, "I am saved, I am, I am saved, I am." During the course of the film, she is elevated to the heights of "Sergeant-Major" of the local chapter of the "Militant Righteous Corpse," which Watty pronounces "corpse" and which is a thinly veiled parody of the Salvation Army. Unlike the local country squire, played with suitably self-satisfied bluster by Nigel Bruce, who must be won over by stages to Miss Moffat's unusually self-assertive and, by the standards of the day, masculine charm, and Miss Ronberry, who also needs time to adjust to her new friend and employer's idiosyncrasies; Mrs. Watty is all for Miss Moffat from the start, as signaled by her signature question: "Ain't she a clinker?"

The story centers on the relationship between Miss Moffat and a gifted, young coal miner, Morgan Evans, whom Miss Moffat gets out of the mines and dedicates herself to preparing for Oxford. While Mrs. Watty is excited about her new life in Wales; her nefarious, manipulative daughter Bessie is decidedly not. Out of boredom and sheer devilment, Bessie does her level best to scotch Miss Moffat's dearly held plans and to nab Morgan for herself. At a low point in Moffat's and Morgan's relationship, Bessie is able to seduce Morgan, resulting in a child or, as Bessie calls it, "a little stranger." The fear is that Morgan will throw up his unique opportunity to go to Oxford and live a life of the mind to do the honorable thing and make Bessie a respectable woman. Mrs. Watty, who thinks "a drop o' tea" will solve most of life's problems, has a more practical solution to this particular conundrum, which is that Miss Moffat adopt the baby. Symbolically, then, Moffat and Morgan have a spiritual child born out of the loins of Bessie Watty. A kind of surrogacy "avant la lettre"!

In his *New York Sun* review, Robert Lockridge wrote: "to hear Rosalind Ivan announce that she couldn't quite take to her daughter is an experience not to be missed."[10] Bosley Crowther wrote, "Rosalind Ivan is a clown as Bessie's ma."[11] Doug McClelland considered this one of three of Ivan's performances that "still bristle in memory."[12] That was in 1968. Writing in 2015, I have to agree, though I think Ivan is even better in *The Suspect* and *Scarlet Street.*

The Corn Is Green was not Rosalind Ivan's first excursion into movie-making. Apart from a single silent film from 1916, *Arms and the Woman* (G. Fitzmaurice, Astra Film/Pathé Exchange), which happened to be Edward G. Robinson's film debut as well, she had made two previous attempts to break into the movies. Her sound film debut was in 1935 in a "Philo Vance" mystery starring Edmund Lowe and Virginia Bruce called *The Garden Murder Case* (E.L. Marin, MGM) in which she played the uncredited role of Gene Lockhart's housekeeper. On her first jaunt to California in 1935, she gamely claimed to be 40, when she was in fact 55.[13] Then in the summer of 1941, in the middle of the Broadway run of *The Corn Is Green,* she did two films for Universal: *It Started with Eve* (H. Koster, 1941) and *Paris Calling* (E.L. Marin, 1942). Her parts were small and uncredited and led to nothing more until her final and decisive call to Hollywood came in 1944.

The actress known as Rosalind Ivan was born Rosalind Muriel Johnson in London on November 27, 1880.[14] There is a record of a Rosalind Muriel Johnson being baptized at St. Martin's in the Fields in 1885, who is probably her, though being baptized age four or five is unusual; and a girl of ten called Rosalind M. Johnson living in Hampstead in 1891 with her chartered accountant father Charles, her mother Annie, and a nursemaid.[15] Little information has come down to us about Ivan's early life. Doug McClelland gathered some of it in an article in *Film Fan Monthly* in 1968, where he insisted somewhat disconcertingly but consistently on referring to his subject as "*Rosiland* Ivan." We must hope he's got the rest of his facts straight when he writes: "The actress did not come from a theatrical family. Her father had his own firm of chartered accountants, an uncle was British Consul-General in China, a cousin was master at Harrow, another a Don at Cambridge. Still others held commissions in the Army and Navy. Although she had always wanted to act, she was raised to be a musician and at ten gave a piano recital in London. At 16, in boarding school in Germany to continue her music studies, her father died and financial reverses forced her out on her own. She became an actress."[16]

Ivan made her stage debut with Sir George Alexander's company in a comedy entitled *Too Happy By Half*.[17] A piece about Ivan in *London Mainly About People* in 1901, states that she "has been on the stage for a very short time" and that she "made her first appearance in public as a child pianiste, and won the silver and gold medals at the Royal Academy before she was sixteen."[18] She appears to have made her first trip to America in the company of Sir Henry Irving, no less, playing Queen Marie in *Louis XI* in 1901.[19] There would be several more trips to the States, before she settled there permanently. She became a naturalized alien in 1948.[20]

Two of the highlights of Ivan's younger years on the London stage were being handpicked by George Bernard Shaw to play in his *Candida* and by John Masefield to play the lead in *The Tragedy of Nan*.[21] Appearing in character roles from the beginning of her career, Ivan racked up an impressive list of credits on both sides of the Atlantic. She played Mrs. Linde in *A Doll's House* both in London and in New York, supporting Alla Nazimova in the role of Nora at the Bijou Theatre in New York in late 1907.[22] Just before, she had supported Nazimova in *The Master Builder* and the *New York Times* had found her Kaia Fosli "a vibrantly appealing bit."[23] Warner Oland was in both these Ibsen productions at the Bijou. This was long before his "Charlie Chan" days. He and Ivan also did *The Father* by another path-breaking Scandinavian dramatist, August Strindberg. That was in 1912.

Ivan, then, was clearly identified with serious European drama in her earliest years on Broadway, which also included appearances in Maxim Gorky's *Night Lodging* (1919–20) with Edward G. Robinson and playing Queen Margaret to John Barrymore's Richard III at the Plymouth Theatre in March 1920. During the early "teens," she was for several years a member of Ben Greet's stock company both in England and in America.[24] She joined the Henry Jewett Players at the Copley Theatre in Boston in 1917 and soon became "quite a favorite with the patrons of the house."[25]

Ivan was off the stage for most of the 1920s, supporting herself mainly by writing, including reviews for the *New York Times* of "biographies of historical figures and books of travel and exploration."[26] She was well versed in foreign languages and was responsible for English adaptations on Broadway of the Russian and French plays *Nju* (1917) and *The Brothers Karamazov* (1927), in which the stellar cast included Alfred Lunt and Lynn Fontanne, Morris

Carnovsky, Cheryl Crawford, Dudley Digges, Clare Eames, Henry Travers, and Edward G. Robinson. When she returned to New York from a trip to England in 1929, she gave her name as Rosalind M. Johnson and listed her occupation as "writer."[27]

Ivan returned to Broadway as an actress in 1930 and "actress theatrical" was the occupation she listed in the U.S. census that year. She was then living at the Hotel Wolcott, which is still in operation at 4 W. 31st St.[28] Her shows in New York in the 1930s were considerably "lighter" fare than the heavy drama of her early career there. She supported Katharine Hepburn, for example, in the infamous production of *The Lake* at the Martin Beck Theatre in 1933–34 (you know, "the calla lilies are in bloom again"). Another of her plays of the period, *Don't Throw Glass Houses,* was dismissed as follows in *The Best Plays of 1938–39*: "Chet Smith, Nita Marx, and Burke Morgan are the editors of a Communist magazine. Mrs. Wilson Pratt Honifeather, Jean Wilson and Murray Tserk represent the tiresome rich. The rich are deposited at the door of the Communists by a motor car accident. For three acts the two forces play upon each other, the Communists trying to wangle supper money, the rich trying to keep it. Nothing much happens."[29] In this case, Ivan played one of the rich, Mrs. Wilson Pratt Honifeather. The show only lasted 15 performances at the Vanderbilt Theatre and was Ivan's last before she struck gold in *The Corn Is Green.*

In later life, Ivan looked younger than her years; "ageless" would be a good word for her. This meant she could realistically be cast as the mother of Joan Lorring, who was 46 years her junior, and as the wife of Edward G. Robinson, who was 13 years younger, and Charles Laughton, who was almost 20 years younger. Usually it's the other way around: older male actors end up being paired with increasingly younger actresses. Yet Robinson and Laughton were hardly "toy boy" material anyhow and were pretty ageless themselves in their unrelenting ugliness.

Besides *The Corn Is Green,* her films with Robinson and Laughton gave Ivan her best screen opportunities. In *The Suspect* (R. Siodmak, 1944), which was produced at Universal right after *The Corn Is Green,* but released before it, Ivan played Cora Marshall, the wife of a meek and mild manager of a tobacconist's shop, Philip Marshal (Laughton); a woman so terrible no degree of feminist criticism could probably entirely redeem or explain her. "Married people's lives is everybody's business," says Cora. She is so unbearable in spying on, browbeating, emotionally blackmailing, and threatening her husband, she actually drives him to beat her to death 30 minutes into the film, though we don't see the murder directly and it is all the more effective for it. It is to screenwriter Dudley Nichols's credit that he makes this killing understandable, if not defensible. What is not understandable, though, is that Ella Raines would have any kind of romantic interest in the extremely ordinary and extraordinarily unattractive nobody portrayed by Laughton. It is as if we were invited to believe that Rock Hudson was earnestly and unselfishly in love with Florence Bates.

Scarlet Street (F. Lang, Fritz Lang Prod./Universal, 1945) was an even better opportunity for Ivan, as her character wasn't killed off early on, but remained persistently alive to make her regulation henpecked husband's life a living hell from start to finish. The husband was Edward G. Robinson in one of his classic portrayals of the "little man," in this case the New York cashier Chris Cross. The cross one, if you'll forgive the pun, is his wife Adele (Ivan). She worships the memory of her first husband, Det. Sgt. Homer Higgins (Charles Kemper), whose vast portrait dominates the parlor; holds it against Chris that he can't afford to buy her a radio, so she has to go downstairs to her neighbor Laura (Anita Sharp-Bolster) to listen

In this still from *The Suspect* (Universal Pictures, 1944), Charles Laughton looks euphoric at the thought of taking his pajamas and slippers over to the bedroom across the hall, free after his son has moved out. His wife, played by Rosalind Ivan, is less than thrilled with this mutiny from the marriage bed.

to the "Happy Household Hour," and threatens to give his oil paintings away to the junk man, because they are smelling up the apartment. In modern dress and with a large, round picture hat of the kind Cora Witherspoon often wore in films, Ivan does resemble the American actress to some extent, though Witherspoon could never have reached the depths of disgust and derogation Ivan brings out in this performance.

Based on the French novel and play *La chienne*, *Scarlet Street* has an ingenious plot in which one man is executed for another man's murder and mainly revolves around Chris's platonic relationship with the fatally attractive Kitty March (Joan Bennett) and, by extension, with her abusive boyfriend Johnny Price (Dan Duryea). This classic film noir would have been infinitely better without the tacked-on, maudlin, moralizing ending, but nothing can hide the fact that Ivan, Robinson, Bennett, and Duryea here give some of the best performances of their careers.

Another diabolically good match for Ivan on the big screen was Sydney Greenstreet, who made Laughton look like a svelte nymph in comparison. Ivan and Greenstreet weren't married in their two films together, though Greenstreet would have liked to have been in *Three Strangers* (J. Negulesco, Warner Bros., 1946) to save himself from financial ruin. There he plays a shady lawyer and Ivan his aristocratic client. According to McClelland, "They worked superbly together, the fat man's nervous, ultimately dumbstruck embezzler a beautiful counterpoint to Ivan's fluttery, unrelenting gaiety that could not hide a pair of vixen's eyes behind her fan."[30]

On the distaff side, Ivan is best remembered for her teaming with Joan Lorring, which began so auspiciously in the film version of *The Corn Is Green* and was followed, to less stunning effect, by *Three Strangers* and *The Verdict* (D. Siegel, Warner Bros., 1946). Lorring was Oscar-nominated for her debut performance in *The Corn Is Green* (as was John Dall as Morgan Evans), though it's fair to say she never lived up to the promise of that stunning beginning. In films like *The Lost Moment* (1947), for example, famously called "The Lost Hour and a Half" by its star Susan Hayward,[31] Lorring basically plays a less interesting version of Bessie Watty. If there's one person I would have liked to have asked about Ivan, though, it's Joan Lorring. Unfortunately, she never responded to my many requests for an interview. She died in 2014.

To me, Ivan was a fundamentally urban figure in films, whether as a landlady or a titled lady. I picture her walking along a New York avenue, window-shopping in a large hat or emerging from a London townhouse into the pea soup fog in one of the timeless, foot-length dresses with a short jacket over she so often wore on film, a hat with some kind of avian decoration on her head. I associate her with the dark, dank, seedy underbelly of the big city, a sort of British Esther Howard without the visible signs of wear and tear. You'd no sooner expect to see Rosalind Ivan in a Western than Mary Boland (and no, *Ruggles of Red Gap* is *not* a western!), though surely Ivan would have been game for anything had she been given the chance.

It's hard to pinpoint exactly why Rosalind Ivan was so "watchable," but she was. She was innately dramatic, of course, sweeping in on a gale of dropped "h"s or with her long, sloping nose, which only Edith Evanson could match, pointing heavenward. But even more than her distinctive profile and characteristically piled-up, poufed-up hair, her most important feature was her eyes. Ivan's eyes could register every emotion from twinkling benevolence to nefarious hatred. Narrow and slanting, they could get considerably narrower when focusing on an object of disdain and ridicule, such as her henpecked husbands in *The Suspect* and *Scarlet Street*.

Beyond the fact that she never married, I know nothing of Rosalind Ivan's private life. I picture her as a solitary creature, without the close support of a live-in mother or sister that was so important to several other actresses in this book. She must have been a brave person to leave everything and everyone she knew in England to go to America and then to do it all over again when she went to Hollywood.

Doug McCelland writes that, despite her nickname "Ivan the Terrible," which derived from "the shrike-like nature of many of her film roles," the real Rosalind Ivan "was said to have been a charming woman, clearly cultured and a bright, amusing conversationalist with a penchant for mimicry."[32] What a wonderful thing it would have been to be invited over for tea in her room at the once fabled but fast-fading Hollywood Hotel, where she lived in 1948 (it was demolished in 1956); or at the Midston House, a "club residence" for men and woman at 22 E. 38th St. in New York City, where she resided at the end of her life.[33] It was there Ivan was found dead of natural causes by the hotel employees on Monday, April 6, 1959.[34] She had no immediate survivors and her place of burial is unknown.

Working Girl: Isabel Jewell (1907–72)

To this day, Isabel Jewell remains the most famous movie actress to come out of Shoshone, Wyoming. I have to add, though, that she is the *only* movie actress to come out of Shoshone, Wyoming. In fact, according to Wikipedia, she is the only notable person of any gender or profession to come out of Shoshone, Wyoming. This is no slur on Shoshone (also spelled Shoshoni), which had a population of only 649 inhabitants in 2010. This very small ranching community in Fremont County and roughly in the center of the state is further characterized by being very flat and very dry; in fact, "some years" it has the distinction of being "the driest town in the entire Mountain Time Zone."[1]

This is the place in which Isabel Jewell spent the first years of her life. Jewell, who would typify the rootless, aimless, and characterless urban woman on the big screen, was in her beginnings a small town girl. She didn't grow up on a ranch, though, as the press agents liked to picture it, but in a house smack dab in what passes for the center of town, on 3rd St. between California St. and Idaho St., where the public school parking lot is now.[2] According to the U.S. census, the home was valued at $4,500 in 1930, but only at $900 in 1940.[3]

Isabel's parents had moved to Shoshone from an even smaller place in Wyoming called Lost Cabin, where they had met and married in 1905. Her father, Emory Lee Jewell, was 29 and her mother, Livia A. Willoughby, was only 16. It was a double wedding with Livia's older sister Eliza and her intended Johnny Johnson and took place at the home of the local bigwig and Wyoming pioneer J.B. Oakie.[4] Jewell's parents came from two very different parts of the United States, the Midwest and the South, and were united in the West.

Lee Jewell, as he was known, was born in Pine Island, Goodhue County, Minnesota, on July 9, 1875, the son of Wallace W. Jewell and Mary Isabel Jewell.[5] Lee's father, Isabel's paternal grandfather, was born in Wisconsin in 1847 and was a prosperous druggist and leading citizen, who had moved to Pine Island, Minnesota, when he was seven, while Lee's mother, the grandmother Isabel Jewell was named for, was born in New York in 1853 and was "keeping house," as the census described it.[6] Grandma Jewell died in 1927 and Grandpa Jewell in 1931.[7] Both were buried in the Jewell family plot in Pine Island Cemetery.[8]

Lee had two younger brothers, Scott W. Jewell, born on November 24, 1878,[9] and Ray J. Jewell, born on May 12, 1881, who died before he was two.[10] After graduating from the University of Minnesota in 1903, Lee, who was a doctor, and Scott, who was a druggist like his father, settled in Lost Cabin, Wyoming, and later in Shoshone. "Doc Jewell" grew to become a highly respected member of the Shoshone community, who did pioneering research with the help of his brother on Rocky Mountain Spotted Fever.[11] Scott was accidentally shot and killed on June 2, 1909, when he was 30 and his niece Isabel was two years old.[12]

Isabel's mother Livia, who only had an elementary school education and married at 16, was a homemaker. She has been described as "an intelligent and perceptive woman" and as "the perfect mate for the 'devilish handsome,' diminutive Dr. Jewell."[13] In 1930, she was Worthy Grand Matron of the grand chapter of Wyoming of the Order of the Eastern Star, a free-masonry related fraternal organization open to both men and women.[14] That same year, the census shows that she and her husband were still living in the house on 3rd St., that their daughter grew up in.[15]

Livia Willoughby Jewell was born in Kentucky on December 31, 1888, as the middle child of seven.[16] In 1900, 11-year-old Livia was living in Lost Cabin, Wyoming, with her farm laborer father, Sidney Willoughby (41), mother Minnie E. Willoughby (39), who was also known as "Nannie," and six siblings between the ages of four and 18. The Willoughbys, married 19 years at this point, who were both born in Kentucky of parents born in Kentucky, had had a somewhat peripatetic existence, as witnessed by the birthplaces of their children. The first four, including Livia, were born in Kentucky, while the next two were born in Illinois, and the youngest was born in Indiana.[17] Isabel's Grandma Willoughby died sometime in the 1930s, but Grandpa Willoughby followed his famous granddaughter to California, where we find him living in Pasadena with his widowed daughter, Isabel's maternal aunt Eliza K. Johnson, in 1940.[18] This intrepid man, born on a farm in Madison County, Kentucky, in 1859, who had worked as a farm laborer, stock grower, and hotelkeeper, lived to be 99 and died in Los Angeles on May 18, 1958.[19]

To return to Shoshone, Wyoming, and our story. Lee and Isabel Jewell's only child was born July 19, 1907, in Shoshone and christened Isabel after her paternal grandmother.[20] Isabel attended local schools until the eighth grade.[21] As the possibilities for a higher education in Shoshone were non-existent, she was sent away to school, first to St. Mary's Hall, an Episcopal preparatory school in Fairbault in her father's native state of Minnesota and then in the fall of 1925 to Hamilton Female College in Lexington in her mother's home state of Kentucky.[22] It was in Lexington that she met and married her first husband on September 2, 1926.[23]

Jewell appears to have had no better luck with men in real life than she had on the screen. She was involved in at least four important romantic relationships before she was 35 and apparently none after that. It was not generally known during Jewell's lifetime, that she had contracted an early marriage when she was only 19. Certainly, it was never mentioned in the press during her heyday in American films. Her first husband was Lovell "Cowboy" Underwood, a senior at the University of Kentucky and a local basketball star, according to William D. Eppes, who discovered the marriage when doing research primarily for a biography of Gertrude Michael, but also by extension on the life of her close friend Isabel Jewell. Eppes even interviewed Underwood in 1972, though he found "his memories and account of Isabel's career was sketchy in detail and fact." Underwood recalled that Jewell "couldn't have been over five feet" and "had the most gorgeous eyes you ever saw."[24]

Lovell T. Underwood was born in Kentucky on December 13, 1902.[25] He was raised by his grandmother on her farm in Iron Hill and later in Charlotte Furnace, Kentucky, went to Lexington Senior High School, where he excelled in basketball, and later attended the University of Kentucky.[26] His marriage to Jewell cannot have been of long duration. In 1940, he was married to Hazel M. Underwood, had a newborn son Terry, and was working as the proprietor of a confectionary in Yakima, Washington.[27]

The greatest love of Isabel Jewell's life was fellow actor Lee Tracy. He was born William Lee Tracy, Jr., in Atlanta, Georgia, in 1898, the son of a railroad superintendent and a former school teacher, both from Pennsylvania, and grew up at 1108 E. Armour Blvd. in Kansas City, Missouri, and 311 Hayden St. in Sayre, Pennsylvania, among other places.[28] Tracy came up through vaudeville and stock companies and debuted on Broadway in George Kelly's hit comedy *The Show-Off* in 1924. Phil Dunning and George Abbott's show *Broadway* made him a star in 1926, as song-and-dance man Roy Lane, but the stage role with which he would be most closely identified was the intrepid reporter Hildy Johnson in Ben Hecht and Charles MacArthur's satire on the press *The Front Page* (1928–29).

Tracy first came to Hollywood in 1929 in the wake of his Broadway success and made his film debut with Mae Clarke in *Big Time* at Fox. He had a stint back on Broadway in the early 1930s, where he and Jewell first met and embarked on a relationship.[29] By the time Jewell came out to Hollywood in 1932, Tracy was already back and was working at Warner Bros. It is not hard to imagine that his presence there was an added inducement for her to move permanently to the West Coast.

Tracy's film career peaked early, as indeed did Jewell's, and was nearing its height when he and Jewell were reunited on the set of *Blessed Event* at Warner Bros. in the spring of 1932. *Blessed Event*, based on a play by Manuel Seff and Forrest Wilson that ran from February to May 1932 at the Longacre Theatre in New York, is credited with making Tracy a movie star and was Dick Powell's debut film. Tracy headed the cast as the ruthless gossip columnist Alvin Roberts, a role created by Roger Pryor on Broadway and which had been intended for James Cagney until he went on a one-man strike and had to be replaced. Jewell was also in the Broadway show. Film director Roy Del Ruth saw her in it and asked her to recreate her role for his film version.[30] Allen Jenkins and Milton Wallace did the same, while the other roles were filled by established actors in Hollywood and Warner Bros. contract players like Mary Brian, Ruth Donnelly, Emma Dunn, Ned Sparks, and Frank McHugh.

Thus Jewell made her film debut reprising her stage role as the small-time singer Dorothy Lane, who has to see her pregnancy "without benefit of clergy" being trumpeted in Alvin Roberts's column "Spilling the Dirt." Alvin's specialty is writing about "blessed events," hence the film's title: births expected, but mostly unexpected, unwanted, or badly timed.

Blessed Event is one of those remarkable pre–Code films simply jam-packed with talent and excitement, humor and pathos, that epitomizes so much of the Depression era and particularly its fascination with the press. Incredibly, Jewell was uncredited for her touching display of histrionics. Equally surprising, hers was not considered an auspicious debut at the time. Jewell told a reporter that, even though many people had congratulated her on her performance, she couldn't get another film role for eight months and was told she "wouldn't photograph": "Nobody thought of the role I played, or remembered that I was made up with gray paint to make me look haggard and dissipated."[31]

Tracy and Jewell were also together in *Bombshell* (V. Fleming, MGM, 1933) and *Advice to the Lovelorn* (aka *Miss Lonelyhearts*; A.L. Werker, 20th Century, 1933). Jewell made more of an impression, though, in two other films from this period: *Beauty for Sale* (R. Boleslawski, MGM, 1933) and *Counsellor at Law* (W. Wyler, Universal, 1933). In the former, her first film at MGM, her performance as Hortense, an almost robotically polite and delightfully superficial receptionist at Madame Sonia's beauty salon, is a vivid example of what she could do with a small role. One minute she bosses the poor employees around in a voice that cuts like a steel blade, the next minute she instantly shifts into a mock genteel, honeyed tone to schmooze with the customers. "Directly following the release of 'Beauty for Sale,'" George Johnstone wrote in a feature article on Jewell, MGM "was deluged with inquiries regarding the identity of the black-clad girl who greeted patrons in the beauty parlor sequence of that film. She was so snappy, so pert and so spirited that she immediately intrigued audiences the country over."[32]

Elmer Rice's gripping drama *Counsellor at Law* has been credited with being the saving of Jewell's film career. When no new film roles were forthcoming in the wake of *Blessed Event*, she took a relatively modest part in the Los Angeles stage production of *Counsellor at Law*, starring Otto Kruger, and made the most of it. It was her performance as Bessie Green, the fast-talking telephone operator in a swanky lawyer's office, that made Hollywood producers sit up and take notice all over again.[33] In a typical quip to an insufficiently ardent date, Bessie says over the phone: "Sure I missed you, like Booth missed Lincoln" (or words to that effect). In the film version, John Barrymore took over Kruger's leading role as the high-powered Jewish lawyer George Simon, who has worked himself up from the slums and is torn between materialism and idealism.

Both these performances demonstrate Jewell's striking presence on the screen, which George Johnstone once described so vividly: "The moment she breezes into a scene, the action accelerates to mile-a-minute momentum and very neatly and swiftly she folds up that bit of play with the prettiest of dispatch and tucks it into her pocket."[34] At the close of 1934, Jewell was described as being "on top of the cinema heap" and was earning $3,000 a week at MGM.[35] According to her UPI obituary, she was loaned out for nine months of her three-year contract with Metro, "making her the most in-demand contract player for borrowing of her time."[36] In terms of money, publicity, and popularity, Isabel Jewell had reached the peak of her career, though neither she nor anyone else could have known it at the time.

Tracy and Jewell lasted about four and a half years. Partly thanks to a major scandal involving Tracy, their relationship "was the talk of Hollywood and movie fans everywhere."[37] In November 1933, Tracy's fondness for drink and prankster personality got him into serious trouble on a location shoot for *Viva Villa!* in Mexico, when he urinated on a military parade passing below the balcony of his hotel room.[38] MGM immediately yanked him from the film and terminated his contract. When he returned from Mexico in disgrace on November 24, 1933, Jewell was there to meet him at the train station and "wept when she kissed him."[39]

On December 23, 1933, Louella Parsons devoted her entire column to Jewell's and Tracy's relationship. According to Parsons, Jewell "watches over the screen's bad boy like a mother hen protecting her favorite chick." Jewell adamantly denied that the "Mexican episode" had anything to do with their postponing their marriage. According to Tracy, he had asked Jewell to marry him "a hundred times," but added, "Perhaps she is right in insisting that we wait." "I want my mother to know her before we get married," he said in Parsons's report. The legendary gossip columnist, who appears to have had a soft spot of sorts for the couple, concluded, "It is Miss Jewell's ability to understand Lee Tracy's little eccentricities that has so endeared her to him. She never nags, never criticizes and she is always interested in his welfare. Undoubtedly they will marry and live happily ever after."[40]

It may have been indicative of their relationship that while Jewell called Tracy "Angel," he called her "Peanuts."[41] Spurred on by their friend George E. Stone and his fiancée Ruth

Romaine, the couple almost got married on Christmas Eve 1933, according to one report.[42] In her final column that year, Parsons was confidently expecting the "very blonde, very naive Isabel Jewell and her bad boy Lee Tracy" to marry soon, despite Jewell's avowals that that wouldn't happen "until she has had her chance at a screen career."[43]

Despite Parsons's confident predictions, Lee Tracy and Isabel Jewell never married. Rumors that the couple were no longer "that a way about each other" began to surface in the columns in the spring of 1934.[44] Tracy got his mother's agreement "Isabel is a fine girl and would make a good wife for her son" after the two met in person in the summer of 1934, but there were more signs of trouble in paradise when Parsons reported, "Isabel hasn't seen Lee once alone since mamma came to visit her boy."[45]

The first rumors of a definite break came in January 1935. Tracy was going back to the New York stage and "the two have definitely come to a parting of the ways but remain friends."[46] Only a week later, Jewell was "vociferously" denying that the couple had parted, though Louella Parsons was not convinced. "The little Jewell girl," she added, "is really headed for big things on the screen."[47] In March, Tracy was being referred to in the press as Jewell's "erstwhile boy friend."[48] In July, she was going dancing with Nelson Eddy.[49] When it came time to sum up the year in an interview with columnist Hubbard Keavy, Jewell said, "She never will love anyone as much as she loved Tracy, that 'one big romance in a life time is enough,' and that (she is very sure about this) she never will fall in love again."[50]

In 1938, Tracy married Helen Thomas Wyse, a "civilian." They remained married for 30 years, until Tracy's death from liver cancer in 1968.[51] In an interview in 1959, Jewell declared: "I am still in love with him, paunch and all. I loved him then and I shall love him always."[52]

It was towards the end of 1935, after close to four years in Hollywood and 21 feature film releases, that it began to dawn on Jewell that full-fledged stardom was going to elude her. She told Hollywood columnist Hubbard Keavy when she was 28, that she soon had to "start doing something important." She had three pictures coming out soon and if they didn't help her "get over the hurdle," she said, it was "Good-bye, Hollywood": "I'll leave here so fast, for New York and the stage, that there won't even be time for farewell parties." She feared she wouldn't make so much money on the stage, "but in the long run I'll be much better off than if I stay in Hollywood. It's awfully discouraging to be in Hollywood and getting the occasional good role and a few so-so roles."[53]

Jewell had the added pressure at this time of having become the sole support of her parents. Her father was only 60 years old, but by 1935 he was completely blind and could no longer practice.[54] Emory Lee Jewell died in his home in Shoshone, Wyoming, on October 21, 1949, with Isabel at his side.[55] He was buried in the Jewell family plot in Pine Island Cemetery, but he also has a memorial in Lake View Cemetery in Shoshone, which reads "Pioneer—Humanitarian—Friend" and "Greatness is measured in service."[56]

Even after her days as a contract player at MGM were over, Hollywood still held out the promise of stardom. The headline of a feature article in connection with the release of *Lost Horizon* in August 1936 read: "A New Hollywood Triumph (on the Wreck of a Shattered Love)." According to this account, Jewell had "for several years ... been one of the vast army of featured players": "Now, within the last few weeks, she has suddenly become a sought-after leading woman with stardom just around the corner." This tendentious and overly optimistic account credited the break-up with Tracy for giving a new upturn to Jewell's career.

Now she was no longer regarded only as "Lee Tracy's girlfriend," now "Hollywood is seeing her as a person, a gifted actress." The writer compared her with Greta Garbo and Joan Crawford no less and claimed: "She is living again the old Hollywood story of the building of fame upon the ashes of dead love." Towards the end of the piece, Jewell is described as being "too busy to be linked with any one man."[57]

This was not correct. Despite her assurance that she would never fall in love again, Jewell had embarked on a new romance in 1936 with artist turned radio executive Owen Crump. Their on-again off-again relationship lasted roughly three years. Owen E. Crump was born December 30, 1903, in Muskogee, Oklahoma, the son of an affluent attorney, and grew up at 1101 W. Broadway and on Terrace Blvd. near Turner Hill Park in Muskogee.[58] In 1930, he was living in Shreveport, Louisiana, with his first wife Jean and supporting himself as an artist.[59] Six years later, we finding him living in Los Angeles, working in radio, and dating Isabel Jewell. On July 6, 1936, the newspapers announced that the couple was engaged and the wedding was set for October. Crump was described as the son of "Judge D.E. Crump of Muskogee, Okla." and as "a radio writer, director, and producer, and a portrait painter."[60] The wedding kept getting put off. Jewell was too busy to get married. She wanted to wait till she was done with her role in *Valiant Is the Word for Carrie*.[61] Then in November the engagement was suddenly off. Jewell wanted to keep working after she got married; Crump wanted her to stay at home.[62] Jewell explained: "I did not feel I could make such a sacrifice at this time."[63] Come 1937, the wedding was on again in January.[64] Then it was off again in March.[65] During the next couple of years, the columnists had their work cut out for them keeping up with the ups and downs in this stormy relationship. Finally, by the August of 1939, it was all over and Jewell was said to be dating "a Mohammedan prince by the name of Bey Hadji Selimovitch."[66] It was about this time, Crump became a screenwriter specializing in short films. In 1942, he married sometime actress Lucile Fairbanks, the daughter of Richard Fairbanks, niece of Douglas Fairbanks, and cousin of Douglas Fairbanks, Jr. They were married until Crump's death in 1998.[67]

During her years with Owen Crump, stardom for Jewell had remained "just around the corner." She was given good, solid yet undeniably secondary roles in films like *Valiant Is the Word for Carrie* (W. Ruggles, Paramount, 1936), an over-long, over-involved melodrama that couldn't be saved even by another multi-talented peroxide blonde who ultimately missed stardom, Gladys George; *Go West, Young Man* (H. Hathaway, Emanuel Cohen Prod., 1936), in which as a starstruck waitress Jewell had to compete for audience attention not only with Mae West, but with Alice Brady and Elizabeth Patterson as well; and *Lost Horizon* (F. Capra, Columbia, 1937), surely her most overrated performance, as a tubercular prostitute who goes through a physical and spiritual regeneration in La-La-land, which is where fans of this asinine film probably also belong.

And yes, of course, she played Emmy Slattery in *Gone with the Wind* (V. Fleming, Selznick International, 1939) and ended the 1930s on a kind of high note, but her character was more spoken of than actually seen. Emmy has only one scene in the film, with her carpetbagger husband, the former Tara overseer Jonas Wilkerson (Victor Jory), and a harried yet resilient Scarlett O'Hara telling them in no uncertain terms that Emmy's "hankering" to live at Tara is never going to be satisfied. Ironically enough, Emmy Slattery's main plot function is to be the indirect cause of both Ellen and Gerald O'Hara's death. She infects Mrs. O'Hara with typhoid while surviving herself and Gerald O'Hara is killed when he rides madly after the

I'm going to resist making any off color remarks about lollipops and limit myself to saying that Isabel Jewell looks pleased with her gift from a fan in this candid taken on the set of *Go West, Young Man* (Emanuel Cohen Prod., 1936). Jewell had a nice little role in the film, but had to compete with veteran scene stealers Mae West, Elizabeth Patterson, and Alice Brady.

Wilkersons to show them who is still boss at Tara. After that, they are not seen or heard from again.

At this time, Jewell was living in an apartment in a Spanish Mission style building at 2270 N. Beachwood Dr.[68] By the end of the 1930s, she must have recognized that she would never be anything more than a supporting player. Even her career as a character actress would have to be continually fought for. The 1940s brought her no new character roles that remotely could compare with her best opportunities in the preceding decade, though she was cast in one of my all-time favorite noir crime dramas *Born to Kill* (R. Wise, RKO, 1947) and did indeed get herself killed as the instigating incident of the action.[69]

In the low budget crime drama *Marked Men* (aka *Desert Escape*; S. Newfield, Producers Releasing Corp., 1940), Jewell got above the title star billing with Warren Hull, but the real star was Wolf the German Shepherd and the true romance was between him and his owner. I think this film illustrates an interesting phenomenon, namely that with Jewell more was not necessarily more. When she had to sustain a more conventional performance as a romantic lead throughout a film, the magic wasn't there. The same was the case in other films where she had the lead as a sort of "girl next door," such as *She Had to Choose* (R. Ceder, Larry Darmour Prod./Majestic, 1934) with Buster Crabbe and *Danger! Women at Work* (S. Newfield, Jack Schwarz Prod./Producers Releasing Corp., 1943), a not very funny comedy where she starred with Patsy Kelly and Mary Brian.

Jewell's forte was the short, intense, emotion-laden scene, such as her justly famous portrayal of the little seamstress in *A Tale of Two Cities* (J. Conway, MGM, 1935). In a film jam-packed with powerful actors from Ronald Colman to Edna May Oliver to Blanche Yurka, we still remember Jewell's few scenes at the end of the film, as she is summarily condemned to death by a revolutionary tribunal and gains emotional support from Colman before she climbs the scaffold to the guillotine.

It seems that when Jewell gave herself time to think, she ended up choosing her career over marriage. Her long-term relationships with Lee Tracy and Owen Crump are cases in point. On the other hand, she was also capable of acting impulsively and getting married almost on a whim. As a result, her marriages were briefer than her non-marital romances. After evading marriage all through the '30s, Jewell's last hurrah on the marital front came just two months before Pearl Harbor, when on October 10, 1941, she flew to Atlanta, Georgia, and married Private Paul Marion of Company C, 30th Battalion, stationed at Camp Croft, South Carolina. Marion was granted a three-day leave for a honeymoon.[70] He was an actor born in the Bronx on September 12, 1915, who had been in the cast of the hit Broadway comedy *My Sister Eileen* with Shirley Booth when he was drafted on August 29, 1941.[71] Prior to his Broadway engagement, he had been living in Los Angeles and had a few roles in films, initially as "Paul Marian."[72] He reported that he had earned $600 for six weeks' work in 1939 and lodged with a Norwegian-born widow and her divorced daughter at 2234 Holly Dr.[73]

It was a sign of Jewell's fading fame, that her marriage was given minimal space in the papers. As Marion was in the army throughout their connubial bliss, he and Jewell never actually lived together for any length of time. Jewell was living in the Chateau de Fleurs apartment building at 6626 Franklin Ave. in Hollywood and would live on or near this well-known residential street in Hollywood the rest of her life.[74] She and Marion separated in May 1943 and some sources claim they divorced the following year.[75] Marion was not seen again on Broadway after the war. He moved back to Los Angeles and was living at 1833½ Grace Ave. in 1944, only a few blocks from Jewel's current apartment at 1814 Vine St.[76] He worked in the film industry as an actor, mostly in uncredited roles, until 1955 and also did some work in television.[77] His marriage to "non-professional" Elinor Marion, entered on in 1952, ended in divorce in 1984.[78]

The last 30 years of Jewell's life were an increasingly melancholy and even tragic spectacle.

Let's remember her as she was in her prime, as one of the most talented screen actors in small roles in the 1930s. In a somewhat equivocal compliment typical of the period, one observer wrote: "She certainly is not beautiful but she possesses the spark of a genuine dramatic genius, which is rarer than beauty in Hollywood."[79] In 1940, Bob Musel mused: "She is the girl tossed into a picture to make the rhinestone stars sparkle. A few minutes before the camera, an explosion of emotion."[80]

Isabel Jewell was found dead of a barbiturate overdose in her apartment at 6130 Franklin Ave. in Hollywood on Wednesday, April 5, 1972. She had died at 2:45 p.m.[81] Her mother Livia preceded her in death on August 8, 1971, in Los Angeles.[82] Unlike Lee Tracy, Jewell's three other partners all survived her by many years and lived to a vast age. Her first husband, Lovell T. Underwood, died in Bellevue, Washington, in 1997 at the age of 94.[83] Owen Crump died in West Hollywood, California, in 1998. He also lived to be 94.[84] Finally, Paul Marion died in Los Angeles on September 8, 2011, just three days short of his 96th birthday.[85]

Cougar in Evening Dress: Violet Kemble-Cooper (1886–1961)

Though never a bona fide stage star, Violet Kemble-Cooper was certainly a highly respected actress and leading lady both in her native England and in the United States in the first third of the twentieth century. She made her stage debut in a production of *Charley's Aunt* at the Comedy Theatre in London in December 1904 and her New York debut in J. Hartley Manners's *The Indiscretion of Truth* at the Harris Theatre eight years later with her father, Frank Kemble-Cooper (1857–1918), also in the cast.[1]

Between 1912 and 1934, Violet Kemble-Cooper was often seen on the Broadway stages in plays such as *Peg O' My Heart* (1912–14), Hartley Manners's smash hit for his wife Laurette Taylor; *The Professor's Love Story* (1917) with George Arliss, who she would support 18 years later in the biographical film *Cardinal Richelieu* (R.V. Lee, Twentieth Century Pictures, 1935); Arthur Wing Pinero's *The Gay Lord Quex* (1917) with John Drew; *The School for Scandal* (1923); the title role in Aristophanes' *Lysistrata* (1930–31), one of the big hits of her stage career; and many others. Her last play in New York was the short-lived drama *Mackerel Skies* in early 1934. By then Kemble-Cooper had already spent some time in Hollywood and she and her husband relocated there permanently in the mid–1930s. She was last seen on the stage, according to her *New York Times* obituary, on tour in 1934 as Elizabeth Tudor in Maxwell Anderson's *Mary of Scotland* with Helen Gahagen and Ian Keith.[2]

Her stepson Stuart Ferris refers to her as "a highly respected English Shakespearean actress,"[3] which must be a misunderstanding, as I've not identified any of the Bard's plays among Kemble-Cooper's stage productions. She played Lady Capulet in MGM's 1936 production of *Romeo and Juliet*, though, which appears to have been her final performance. She was only 50 when she retired. It would be another half a dozen years before the first symptoms of Parkinson's disease would make themselves felt.

As her surname indicates, Kemble-Cooper belonged to the British stage aristocracy and called herself "an actress by heritage."[4] Her father and her three siblings were all actors, not to mention five generations of forbears, including most notably the founder of the acting dynasty, Roger Kemble; Fanny Kemble, and Sarah Siddons (*née* Kemble). Violet trained as a portrait painter at one point, thinking she would avoid the family tradition, and in a 1921 interview said that she firmly believed she was a better portrait painter than she was an actress.[5]

Violet's younger sister Lillian Kemble-Cooper (1892–1977) also had a career on Broadway and in Hollywood and is perhaps best remembered for her small role in *Gone with the Wind*, as the nurse who is fired after she forces Rhett's daughter, Butler Bonnie, to sleep without a night light, though she is afraid of the dark. Lillian played the role of the Principessa Della Cercola in the 1928 Broadway production of *Our Betters*, the play by W. Somerset Maugham that would give her sister her first and best opportunity on the big screen when it was filmed at RKO in 1932–33.

Compared to British leading ladies like Gladys Cooper, Alison Skipworth, May Whitty, and even Constance Collier, Violet Kemble-Cooper was little used by Hollywood. I wouldn't say she was ill used, she was simply "underused." Her brief heyday, if you can even call it that, was restricted to the years 1934–36 and roughly coincided with the glory days of wonder boy producer Irving Thalberg at MGM. We can imagine that he had a hand in casting her in two of Metro's prestige projects towards the end of his all too brief life: *David Copperfield* (George Cukor, MGM, 1935) and *Romeo and Juliet* (George Cukor, MGM, 1936), though George Cukor probably had even more to do with it. Neither film gave Kemble-Cooper much play, so to speak, but she was in good company and her brief scenes may be studied by those curious to see her range and what she could do with a small part.

In *David Copperfield*, equipped with remarkably furry eyebrows, Kemble-Cooper plays Jane Murdstone, the spinster sister of David's stepfather, Mr. Murdstone (Basil Rathbone), who moves in and makes life difficult for David and his delicate mother Clara by taking over

Violet Kemble-Cooper as the Duchess in *Our Betters* (RKO Radio Pictures, 1933) regards her wayward boyfriend Pepi D'Costa (Gilbert Roland) with a characteristically mournful expression. He remarks: "I can never put my hand out without finding yours there ready to press it."

Kemble-Cooper is here seen in full Renaissance drag as Lady Capulet in *Romeo and Juliet* (Metro-Goldwyn-Mayer, 1936). For once she got to play the mother of an actor young enough to be her child in real life too, namely Norma Shearer as Juliet. In the silly Helen Hayes vehicle *Vanessa: Her Love Story*, she had played Otto Kruger's mother, and in the minor Universal horror film *The Invisible Ray*, she was Boris Karloff's. Both men were the same age as her.

the household. "Generally speaking, I don't like boys," she intones. In *Romeo and Juliet*, she was Juliet's stern mother, Lady Capulet, and for once played the mother of someone young enough to have been her daughter in real life. Norma Shearer was born in 1902.

A much better opportunity, though, indeed the best she would ever get on film, was her debut role on the big screen. *Our Betters* (RKO, 1933) is one of those delightfully naughty pre–Code comedies in which Constance Bennett gets to be cynical and sophisticated in "to die for" frocks. Closely based on a play by W. Somerset Maugham from 1917, the combined efforts of Maugham, screenwriters Jane Murfin and Henry Wagstaff Gribble, costume designer Hattie Carnegie, "technical advisor" Elsa Maxwell, and director George Cukor make for a camp extravaganza in black and white. The stellar ensemble cast includes Grant Mitchell as a catty, Anglophile queen, Phoebe Foster as a soulful princess, Tyrell Davis as the gayest dance instructor ever seen on the silver screen, and Anita Louise and Charles Starrett as the attractive ingénues.

As Lady Pearl Grayston, an American heiress, who discovers on her wedding day that her aristocratic yet not so noble husband has married her for her money and really loves another, Bennett had to see herself upstaged by one of her supporting players. Violet Kemble-Cooper dominates the film from the moment she sweeps into Lady Grayston's chic London drawing room in a dark, dramatic coat with a huge stand-up fur collar and matching muff with her dishy toy boy Pepi (Gilbert Roland) in tow. In her portrayal of a spoilt American duchess divorcée ("Minnie" to her friends), Kemble-Cooper uses a petulant little girl voice; her characteristically dark, mournful eyes are frequently on the verge of tears and her mouth is firmly set in a dissatisfied moue. "Where is Pepi?" is her litany, as her younger lover is often unaccounted for and is in fact conducting an affair with Lady Grayston. Mordaunt Hall, reviewing the film in the *New York Times,* wrote, "A good deal of fun is furnished by the way in which he is tied to the Duchess's apron strings."[6] Another reviewer wrote that the duchess's "barbed tongue and troubles with her private gigolo ... provide most of the laughs."[7]

It is always sad to contemplate a film career where the crest of the wave occurs immediately, and the remaining roles make hardly a ripple on the surface. It happened to Blanche Yurka after her standout debut as Madame DeFarge in *A Tale of Two Cities*; Sara Allgood after her Oscar-nominated performance as Mrs. Morgan in *How Green Was My Valley*; Alma Kruger after her screen debut as Amelia Tilford in the first film version of Lillian Hellman's hit play *The Children's Hour, These Three*; and Henrietta Crosman in the wake of showy roles in her early films *The Royal Family of Broadway* and *Pilgrimage,* to mention but a few examples. As an actor in the unhappy situation where the roles are getting fewer and smaller, you can either stick around and take what is offered or go elsewhere.

Violet Kemble-Cooper chose a middle route. She stayed in Los Angeles till the end of her life in 1961, but her film career was over by 1936, after only four years and eight films. She stayed, I suspect, largely because of the opportunities offered to her writer husband, Walter Ferris, though his film career was ultimately not much longer or more prolific than hers. Between 1934 and 1940, he wrote screenplays for about a dozen films, including *Maid of Salem* (1937), *Heidi* (1937), *A Yank at Oxford* (1938), *The Little Princess* (1939), and *Tom Brown's School Days* (1940). He worked on three films for Shirley Temple and, according to his son, he thought "she was one of the finest actresses of all time."[8] After 1940, things dried up. Ferris only obtained two further screen credits during the 25 years that remained to him.

Despite writing the screenplays of some well known films, Ferris's chief claim to fame is probably writing the English adaptation of an Italian play by Alberto Casella, *La Morte in vacanza,* which was produced by Lee Shubert at the Ethel Barrymore Theatre and opened December 26, 1929. *Death Takes a Holiday* is a fantasy drama about a personification of Death taking a three-day holiday on Earth to allow him to understand human beings better and why they cling to life. Death appears to the guests of Duke Lambert at Villa Happiness in Italy as the Prince Sirski and ultimately falls in love with one of them, Grazia. After a slow start, *Death Takes a Holiday* ended up being one of the hits of the 1929–30 season with Gladys Cooper's future husband Philip Merivale as Death/Prince Sirski and Rose Hobart as Grazia. The show ran for 180 performances and was also briefly revived with the same leading players in 1931 and was Ferris's last show on Broadway. Mitchell Leisen directed a film version of *Death Takes a Holiday* at Paramount in 1934 with Fredric March and Evelyn Venable in the starring roles. The screenplay was by Maxwell Anderson and Gladys Lehman. Many years later, *Death Takes a Holiday* was the inspiration for the 1998 film *Meet Joe Black* starring Brad Pitt.

Walter Lewis Ferris is described in his World War I draft registration at the age of 36 as being of medium height and slender build with blue eyes and dark hair.[9] Photographs of him in his later years show a dapper gentleman of the old school with plentiful white hair, horn-rimmed glasses, a navy blazer and grey flannels, cigarette holder in hand.[10] Ferris had had a varied life and career before he and Violet Kemble-Cooper tied the knot in the early 1930s. He was born the son of a successful businessman and minister, Hiram Jones Ferris, and his wife, Harriet Sanborn Ferris, in Green Bay, Wisconsin, in 1882 and grew up there and in Columbus, Wisconsin, with four brothers and sisters.[11] He was given a first-rate education at Beloit College in Beloit, Wisconsin, and then went to the Yale Divinity School (class of 1909), as his mother had her heart set on one of her sons becoming a minister.[12] After graduating, Ferris took up his first and, as it turned out, only ministry in Whitneyville, Connecticut, a northern suburb of New Haven.[13] Finding that he had lost his vocation, he then embarked on an alternative career as an educator. According to his son's memoir, he won the debt-ridden Roxbury Tutoring School in a game of bridge in 1916, relocating it to Cheshire, Connecticut, and making it a first-rate preparatory school.[14]

While at Yale, Ferris had met his future wife, Alice Cheney, who was three years his senior. Alice, an accomplished pianist and graduate of the Yale School of Music, was born the daughter of a wealthy New Haven physician in 1879.[15] Between 1910 and 1918, the couple had three sons and a daughter. As Stuart Ferris records, the Ferris's marriage was a rocky one, "primarily because of dad's wandering eye and Mom's intense jealousy."[16] The Ferrises divorced in the late teens. In 1920 or 1921, Walter was involved in a serious car accident "resulting in all his facial bones being broken."[17] Alice Ferris stepped up and nursed her ex-husband back to health. They were reconciled and remarried. Alice and the children moved back into their home in Cheshire on the grounds of the school. "The ensuing years until 1929 were good ones," Stuart Ferris records, "although there were rumblings underneath."[18] Walter was spending more and more time on his writing and in New York. On January 16, 1928, Eva La Gallienne produced and starred in his first play on Broadway, *The First Stone*, at the Civic Repertory Theatre.

How Violet Kemble-Cooper and Walter Ferris met has not been recorded, but it was likely in New York City, where by the late 1920s they were both a part of the theatrical scene. I wonder if Basil Rathbone may have played a role, as he and Violet did a very successful play together, *The Command to Love*, with Mary Nash and Henry Stephenson at the Longacre Theatre in 1927–28. In early 1929, Rathbone went on to star in Ferris's second play on Broadway at the same theatre. *Judas*, which "took the side of Judas and showed that he had not betrayed Jesus,"[19] only lasted 12 performances, but that was long enough for Violet Kemble-Cooper to have come back stage and met the author.

At any rate, the spring of 1929 was when Walter and Alice Ferris separated for the second and final time. He left the family home in Cheshire for good and curtailed his active involvement in the Roxbury School.[20] I have found his and Violet's names linked in the press in connection with a "program" they gave in Oak Park, Illinois, in October 1930.[21] They were not spring chickens any longer. Violet was 44 (though only admitted to 37) and living in an $10,000 apartment she owned at 25 East End Ave., a free-standing, elegant, palazzo style brick building at 80th St., directly overlooking the East River.[22] Walter was 48 and staying at the Yale Club.[23] By 1933, they were married and in 1940 we find them living with a Hawaiian servant in a $16,000 owned home at 304 Cliffwood Ave. in Los Angeles. Ferris reported to the census taker that he had earned in excess of $5,000 in 1939. Kemble-Cooper had earned nothing.[24] In comparison, we find Alice Ferris living with her youngest sons Stuart and Geoffrey in a modest, rented, $75 a month, two-and-one-half-story wooden house at 302 Willow St. in the East Rock section of New Haven. She reports no income in the preceding year.[25]

Stuart Ferris does not suggest "Vi," as she was called in the family, was the cause of the break-up of his parents' marriage and he maintained an amicable relationship with his stepmother until her death, though she apparently never met his wife and children. When Stuart came to visit them in California in later years, she would say: "I always look forward to you coming because it's the only time I hear 'his nibs' [Walter Ferris] laugh these days."[26] By that time, their glamorous life in a luxurious Brentwood mansion was far behind them. Violet's increasingly debilitating disease meant that neither she nor her husband, who devoted himself to nursing her, could work. One by one they lost all their assets, including their house, and had to move into a small apartment at 360 S. Burnside Ave., the site of the current Park La Brea Apartments.[27]

Violet Kemble-Cooper died at the Westmoreland Sanitarium on August 17, 1961, at the age of 74, three months after suffering a stroke that left her bedridden.[28] She was buried in the Sanctuary of Trust in the Abbey of Psalms Mausoleum of Hollywood Forever Cemetery.[29] Walter Ferris had suffered a stroke himself not long before Violet's death, but lingered on for another four years, dependent on the financial support of his son Stuart and the Motion Picture Welfare and Relief Fund. He died September 2, 1965, at the home of his and Violet's longtime caregiver Maisie and was laid to rest in a niche around the corner from his wife.[30]

Walter Ferris, who had left his wife and four underage children to fend for themselves through the Great Depression and beyond, remained steadfastly by his second wife's side through 30 years of marriage and long illness.[31] In 1930, not long before they married, Violet Kemble-Cooper had outlined her requirements for an ideal husband in an article: "My ideal husband would never look upon me as a companion. He would never forget that I am a woman and something of a mystery. He would be, above all, a magnificent creature, mentally and physically, who went through life playing a high hand in the grand manner. Even if his falsity were glaring I should be proud to belong to a man who stood head and shoulders above the more timorous tribe. And I should demand from him the most exquisite courtliness, courtesy in small things as well as in large, and a tinge of that woman worship that made the Middle Ages beautiful."[32] It looks as if she got her wish.[33]

Her Wicked Wicked Ways: Doris Lloyd (1891–1968)

I'll be the first to admit it took some time before Doris Lloyd registered on my radar. But then her parts were all too often just that: under the radar. Springer and Hamilton observe that she was "one of those actresses you take for granted."[1] Yet Lloyd was one of the busiest British character actresses in Hollywood in the 1930s and well into the 1940s. In her own modest, low-key way, she did very well for herself and had a longer and more prolific career than many with showier roles. In terms of the longevity of her film career and the sheer number of the roles she played (about 175 that we know of), she was arguably the most successful British character actress in Hollywood.

Admittedly, because of the "minuteness" of most of her roles, Doris Lloyd is an acquired taste. She is one for the real connoisseurs of Hollywood supporting players. "Everyone" knows fellow Brits like Gladys Cooper and Elsa Lanchester and even Dame May Whitty, but Lloyd, well Lloyd requires a little more patience and time to emerge in our consciousness as the very fine and versatile actress that she was. I honestly don't think there was anything she couldn't do. Her roles tended to go in two diametrically opposite directions, though: either she was very "ladida" and aristocratic, "keep a stiff upper lip" and that kind of thing; or she was very much a woman of the people, typically a Cockney working girl, be it a maid, landlady, or in the pre–Code era, lady of the night—"reprehensible ladies of scant morals, in every walk of life," as one newspaper wrote.[2]

Here are just a few Doris Lloyd sightings to remind you. In the striking first sound version of *Oliver Twist* (W.J. Cowen, Monogram, 1933), she was a poignant, if somewhat mature Nancy Sikes and her murder at the hands of her alcoholic husband was memorably gruesome. Her brother-in-law, George K. Arthur, played Toby Crackit, one of Fagin's gang. In *Dangerous Corner* (P. Rosen, RKO, 1934), she portrayed what used to be called a "lady author," Maude Mockridge, in a film based on one of J.B. Priestley's stage experiments with time and chronology. In *Becky Sharp* (R. Mamoulian, Pioneer, 1935), she climbed to the top of the social scale as the Duchess of Richmond and that in glorious, three-strip Technicolor. Lloyd was in both versions of *Kind Lady* (G.B. Seitz, MGM, 1935; J. Sturges, MGM, 1951), based on Edward Chodorow's hit play. In the 1935 version, the "kind lady" was Aline MacMahon and Lloyd played her relative, Lucy Weston, while 16 years later, Ethel Barrymore played the lead as Mary Herries and Lloyd was her devoted maid, Rose, and got herself strangled by Keenan Wynn.

Usually, the larger the part, the "smaller" the film and vice versa. Thus Lloyd had quite substantial roles in 1930s B movies like *A Shot in the Dark* (C. Lamont, Chesterfield, 1935),

Motive for Revenge (B.P. Lynwood, Larry Darmour Prod./Majestic, 1935), *Brilliant Marriage* (P. Rosen, Invincible, 1936), and *Murder Is News* (L. Barsha, Kenneth J. Bishop Prod./Central, 1937). *Vigil in the Night* (G. Stevens, RKO, 1940) was the exception to the rule: it was a quality production *and* gave her one of her best roles of the 1940s, as the spoilt wife of a philandering, newly rich Manchester industrialist and trustee of the hospital where Carole Lombard works as a nurse. Lloyd has Lombard fired after she finds her and "hubby" in what she takes to be a compromising position. Later, she has a change of heart when Lombard is instrumental in saving her only child's life during an epidemic.

In *The Letter* (W. Wyler, Warner Bros., 1940), Lloyd was back in the lower ranks as the sympathetic prison matron Mrs. Cooper, who takes care of Bette Davis and guards her at the trial. In *Journey for Margaret* (W.S. Van Dyke, MGM, 1942), she was rejected as a foster mother by Margaret O'Brien. In *The Lodger* (J. Brahm, Twentieth Century–Fox, 1944), she played an entertainer in a pub, who lends Anita Sharp-Bolster her concertina and is murdered in her humble lodgings by Jack the Ripper that same night.

Doris Lloyd strikes a pensive pose in this studio portrait from the 1930s. Lloyd parlayed her not too striking good looks into a successful film career lasting 47 years. However modest many of her roles in Hollywood, there weren't many British character actresses who could compete with their number and variety.

Another rare opportunity for Lloyd came in the comedy *Molly and Me* (L. Seiler, Twentieth Century–Fox, 1945). Gracie Fields stars as an out of work actress who is forced to "perform" as a housekeeper for wealthy ex-politician Monty Woolley to make ends meet. Lloyd plays Woolley's ex-wife, whose love affair with a sportsman 15 years earlier was front-page news and ended his political career. When she returns suddenly and unexpectedly to her old home from Johannesburg, it is up to Fields to shield her employer and "handle" the situation. Lloyd says she needs £1,000 and intends to get it one way or the other. As Mrs. Graham, she looks old and tired with dark rings under her eyes and has a rough edge to her. One easily imagines she once married above her station, though she doesn't overdo it. This is just the type of venal vulgarity under a thin veneer of gentility Lloyd was so expert at delineating. She quickly drops the grand dame routine when she encounters Reginald Gardiner playing a French gigolo in the elaborate and ingenious ruse Fields engineers at the end

Doris Lloyd acted in both film versions of Edward Chodorov's hit play *Kind Lady*. In the 1935 version starring Aline MacMahon, she played "kind lady" Mary Herries's relative, Lucy Weston. In MGM's 1951 remake with Ethel Barrymore (left) in the title role, Lloyd played Miss Herries's faithful maid Rose, whose loyalty to her mistress costs her her life.

of the film to get rid of her once and for all. Lloyd returns posthaste to South Africa in a terrific ending to a solid film, though one that does not make Gracie Fields's star appeal any easier to fathom.

Wonderful as she is when playing the "heavy," my favorite Doris Lloyd role must be the Cockney prostitute Kitty in the original film version of *Waterloo Bridge* (James Whale, Universal) from 1931. Compared to the glossy, cleaned up, MGM version from 1940, starring Vivien Leigh and Robert Taylor, for all its merits, the original is rawer, rougher, and more real. Lloyd has a scene alone with Douglass Montgomery as the naïve, young American soldier Roy Cronin, who has recently met her friend and neighbor Myra Deauville (Mae Clarke), that in the space of a few minutes demonstrates what a fine and subtle actress Lloyd was. By this time, former chorus girl Myra has become a disillusioned, hard-bitten prostitute, but Roy doesn't see it. Recognizing that he represents a rare chance for her down-on-her-luck friend, Kitty (dropping her "h"s left and right) paints a poignant picture of Myra as a tender, innocent young thing, alone in the world, vulnerable, sensitive, just waiting for a man to protect her from the wicked, wicked world. This scene is an amusing interlude in an otherwise somber film. One news article called Lloyd's Kitty "a remembered performance."[3]

The most important misconception about Lloyd that I need to correct is that she was born in 1896. This was the year of her younger sister's birth, which she "adopted" at some point; probably when she went to America, but possibly earlier.[4] It is well documented that she was born Hessy Doris Lloyd on July 3, 1891, and was christened (like her older brothers) in St. Stephen's Church in Liverpool on August 2, 1891.[5] She was the daughter of Edward Franklin Lloyd, who was born in Holywell, Flintshire, Wales, in 1855, and Hessy Jane McCappin, who was born in 1860.[6] The acting gene, she had from her grandfather, who "was a notable amateur actor in Liverpool, playing star parts with the Garrick Club of that city."[7] By the time Doris came along, the Lloyd family had strong ties to the Toxteth Park section of Liverpool. The parents married there in 1886 and all four of their children were born there: Edward Vernon Franklin Lloyd in 1887, William Norman Lloyd in 1889, Hessy Doris Lloyd in 1891, and Milba Kathleen Lloyd in 1896.[8]

The Lloyds were a close-knit family. Doris, who remained unmarried, would live with one or more members of her birth family for most of her life and on both sides of the Atlantic. In 1911, they were living in Walton, West Derby, Lancashire.[9] Three years later, at the age of 23, Lloyd made her stage debut as a member of the Liverpool Repertory Company.[10] She would spend six years with them and made her London debut in May 1915 with the company in *Nobody Loves Me* and *A Bit of Love* at the Kingsway Theatre.[11] By the early 1920s, she was working steadily on the London stage in plays like *The Yellow Jacket, The Philanderer*, and *South Wind.*[12] Lloyd made her silent film debut as Marian West in *The Shadow Between* (G. Dewhurst, Seal) in June 1920, but only made one other silent film in Britain before moving to the United States.[13]

It would appear that Doris's father died in 1915,[14] at least he was dead by the time Doris and her mother left England in 1923, as Hessy Lloyd is described as a widow in the 1930 and 1940 U.S. census. Doris's younger sister Milba, who was her closest friend and relative throughout her life, married Arthur George Brest in 1922. Brest was born in Brentford in Greater London in 1899 and would be known to the world as the comic actor George K. Arthur.[15] Shortly after his marriage, Arthur spearheaded the family's move to the United States.[16] His wife Milba followed him in February 1923.[17] Even before her move to the United States, she was front-page news in American newspapers as "The Youngest Sculptress in England." In a news photo, she was shown with a model of the sculpture she had made for her sister's hit play *The Edge o' Beyond* at the Garrick Theatre.[18] In Hollywood, Milba Lloyd Arthur worked in Paramount's art department and is described making statues for *The Marriage Maker* in 1923 and wax models for *Bluebeard's Eighth Wife* in 1924.[19] She also made the Egyptian statues for Cecil B. DeMille's epic *The Ten Commandments* and in a news article entitled "Husbands and Wives of Celebrities Shine in Their Own Spheres" in 1926, she was said to be "certain to become an important figure in the artistic world."[20]

When Doris and her mother Hessy arrived in New York City aboard the *Pittsburg* on September 25, 1923, at the age of 32 and 62,[21] their plan was to visit Milba and Arthur in California. They ended up staying the rest of their lives. Lloyd got her first film role in *The Lady* (F. Borzage, Norma Talmadge Film Corp., 1925) starring her friend Norma Talmadge and racked up a total of 15 silent film credits before making her sound film debut in *The Drake Case* (E. Laemmle, Universal) in 1929. She was perfectly positioned to benefit from the myriad new opportunities for character players with the coming of sound.

In 1930, we find the extended Lloyd-Arthur family living in a $6,000 owned home at 1006 Carol Drive in Beverly Hills. The household consisted of Doris Lloyd, her mother Hessy, her sister Milba and brother-in-law Arthur, their daughter Milba Jeanne, who had been born on February 18, 1925, a 25-year-old nurse, and a lodger.[22] A feature article on Lloyd from about this time entitled "Shady Lady at Home" has a delightful photograph of three generations of Lloyd women: Hessy Lloyd, her daughters Doris and Milba, and granddaughter Milba Jeanne. They are described as living in "chummy reserve" in "a retreat of charm and calm, where people who find pleasure in music and cultured talk like to gather." The atmosphere "fairly breathes tea and crumpets and brisk walks and busy people and coziness." Lloyd herself is described as "this red-haired English girl of the clear skin and level blue eyes" and as "not a person to be satisfied with just getting by": "No hesitation ever marks her conversation, no vague generalities. On subjects with which she is familiar she converses easily and readily. On others she maintains that complimentary silence of the listener who is anxious to learn." "Mother Lloyd" is "a white-haired lovely background" and manages the house. Milba Lloyd Arthur has a studio out back where she molds busts and figures of celebrities.[23]

Ten years and a staggering 80 films later, we find the now all-female Lloyd household living at 3942 Fredonia Drive in a modest but charming, white stucco, Spanish style bungalow with a red tiled roof built in 1928, which they rented for $60 a month. Eily Malyon lived just down the street. Lloyd was still pretending to be five years younger than her real age, while her mother came clean and was 69. Mother Hessy and daughters Doris and Milba all had four years of high school, while 15-year-old granddaughter Milba Jeanne was enrolled in her first year of the same. By this time Milba and her husband had divorced. Doris Lloyd reported to have earned in excess of $5,000 in 1939 for 26 weeks' work. Neither her mother, sister, or niece had a salaried income, but all three had income from other sources.[24] Doris's only niece, Milba Jeanne Brest, married Charles Robert Gray in Santa Monica on April 1, 1950.[25] Doris's mother, Hessy McCappin Lloyd, died on May 23, 1953, at the age of 92.[26] Her sister Milba never remarried and survived her by 16 years, dying on May 27, 1984.[27]

Despite the intensity of her screen career, Lloyd continued to act on stage during the 1930s and 40s, including playing Gertrude to Maurice Evans's "G.I. Hamlet" on tour in 1945.[28] She didn't get to Broadway till 1947, though, just as her film career was beginning to slow down. Lloyd's only New York show was J.B. Priestley's *An Inspector Calls,* where she replaced Frieda Inescort, who withdrew from the role of Sybil Birling only ten days before the October 21, 1947, opening at the Booth Theatre. The drama was staged by Cedric Hardwicke, who handpicked Lloyd to save the show, and Thomas Mitchell starred as Inspector Goole.[29]

Lloyd also acted in television between 1950 and 1965 with guest spots on shows like *Cavalcade of America* (1953), *Jane Wyman Presents the Fireside Theatre* (1955), *Lux Video Theatre* (1955–56), *The 20th-Century Fox Hour* (1955–56), and *Suspicion* (1958). She made no less than five appearances on *Alfred Hitchcock Presents* (1958–62) and four on *The Alfred Hitchcock Hour* (1963–65). After supporting Julie Andrews in *Mary Poppins* (R. Stevenson, Walt Disney, 1964) and *The Sound of Music* (R. Wise, Robert Wise Prod./Argyle, 1965), Lloyd was last seen in *Rosie!* (D.L. Rich, Ross Hunter Prod./Universal, 1967), as titular heroine Rosalind Russell's faithful companion Sedalia, who comes to lend support at the sanity hearing engineered by Rosie's avaricious children. She had been acting in films for 47 years. Not as long as Lillian Gish by any means, but she gave Zasu Pitts and Ethel Griffies a run for their money.

Doris Lloyd died of a "strained heart" on May 21, 1968, in Santa Barbara, California, where she had recently moved from Hollywood to live with her sister.[30] After a funeral in Santa Barbara on Saturday, May 25th, she was buried with her mother in Forest Lawn Memorial Park, Glendale. Her grave marker reads: "Beloved Daughter and Sister."[31]

The Old Doll: Helen Lowell (1865–1937)

Helen Lowell deserves to be better known. She came to Hollywood in 1934 after a long and eminently successful stage career as one of Broadway's leading comediennes. She played substantial, credited roles in more than two dozen films. At the end of her life, she adapted remarkably well to the requirements of a medium that didn't even exist until she was in middle age. And she was the most important portrayer of older women at Warner Bros. in the mid–1930s.

So how do we explain her relative obscurity compared with contemporary character comediennes like May Robson, Marie Dressler, Alison Skipworth, and Jessie Ralph? Well, apart from the fact that her film career only lasted three and a half years, Lowell never acted in a truly important or widely seen film, which could help fix her in the public's consciousness and memory. This is illustrated by the fact that her most popular and highly ranked film today in the Internet Movie Database is *Page Miss Glory* (M. LeRoy, Warner Bros, 1935), starring Marion Davies, and there her part was relatively modest. Helen Lowell, then, is a lost jewel just waiting to be rediscovered. In the subtlety of her comic technique, she certainly could compare with Ralph and Robson and at times even attains the eminence of Skipworth and Louise Closser Hale.

There were several prominent character actresses in Hollywood in the 1930s who were Canadian born and bred, such as Dressler, Lucile Watson, and Maude Eburne. Helen Lowell was only half Canadian and was born and raised in New York City. Her father, William L. Robb, came from East Oxford in Ontario and was born in about 1834 and her mother, Mary K. Robb, was born in New York in about 1842.[1] Their only child, Helen Lowell Robb, was born on June 2, 1865, and was known professionally as Helen Lowell.[2]

In the 1870, we find the Robb family living in the 20th Ward of New York City, where 36-year-old William is working as a post office clerk, his 28-year-old wife Mary is keeping house, and their daughter is five years old. The value of the family's personal estate is $2,000.[3] William Robb died in April 1874, at the age of 40, and was buried in the vast Greenwood Cemetery in Brooklyn.[4]

Ten years after her father's death, Helen Lowell made her stage debut at the Academy of Music in New York in the title role of the comic opera *Iolanthe*.[5] Mary K. Robb joined her husband in Greenwood Cemetery in September 1886 at the age of 44 and thus Helen Lowell was alone in the world at the age of 21.[6] During the next decade, she was best known for creating the role of the mother, Mrs. Errol ("Dearest"), in the stage version of *Little Lord Fauntleroy*;

and in March 1895, we find she "attracted attention in New York" in *Charlotte Corday* at the Herald Square Theater.[7] She was 30 and well on her way to becoming the character actress and spinster she would remain for the rest of her life.

From then on and for nearly four decades, Helen Lowell was a fixture of the New York stage, appearing in about 30 Broadway shows. Many of these have, of course, long been forgotten and few have been revived. Among the more familiar titles, though, Lowell created the role of Susan Throssell in the original stage production of James M. Barrie's *Quality Street* with Maude Adams starring as her sister Phoebe Throssell. Phoebe and Susan were played by Katharine Hepburn and Fay Bainter in the film version from 1937.

Lowell would be more closely associated in the public's mind with another and more classic spinster role, namely the lovelorn maiden lady in the major hit comedy *Mrs. Wiggs of the Cabbage Patch* by Anne Crawford Flexner, based on two stories by Alice Hegan Rice. Mrs. Wiggs (first played by Madge Carr Cook) is a poverty-stricken wife and mother with too many children and an absentee husband, and Miss Hazy is her pathetic neighbor in the "cabbage patch." Lowell first played Miss Hazy in Louisville, Kentucky, where the comedy itself was set, in October 1903; the show opened at the Savoy Theatre in New York on September 3, 1904; and Lowell would end up playing Miss Hazy for seven years all over the United States and in Hawaii, Australia, and New Zealand.[8]

When *Mrs. Wiggs of the Cabbage Patch* was performed for the first time in Boston in March 1908, the critic for the *Boston Daily Globe* wrote that it was "the most successful dramatized novel since Trilby." The same writer called Lowell's Miss Hazy "a representation of the pessimist of the Cabbage Patch that is one of the most comical creations the local stage has seen in years."[9] Though Lowell was in Hollywood when Paramount made its film version of *Mrs. Wiggs* in 1934, she was under contract to a rival studio and may have been considered too old for the part. The role of Miss Hazy went to Zasu Pitts and Lowell sent her a copy of the original script, some stills from the stage production, and even some of the original costumes.[10]

Helen Lowell at 51 looks preternaturally youthful (with a little help from the photographer, no doubt) in this portrait from the "play with music," *Broadway and Buttermilk*, which opened at Maxine Elliott's Theatre in New York on August 15, 1916. In a town "lousy with old dames," according to Columbia boss Harry Cohn, Lowell nevertheless was able to carve out a niche for herself in the film industry in the 1930s.

In the wake of her *Mrs. Wiggs* success and similar roles, Lowell was described in the press as having "devoted herself to the delineation of spinster types."[11] This was certainly true, but Lowell was also identified with one of the classic mother-in-law roles in American dramatic literature, namely Mrs. Fisher in George Kelly's hit comedy *The Show-Off*. The "show-off" in this case was Aubrey Piper, created by Louis John Bartels, and Lowell originated the role of his skeptical and nay-saying mother-in-law, who ultimately is proven wrong in her doubts about him. The show ran for a stunning 571 performances at the Playhouse Theatre in New York in 1924–25. Lowell was actually tested by MGM to play Mrs. Fisher in their projected film version with Lee Tracy, who had had a supporting role in the stage version, as Aubrey Piper, but Tracy got himself into a diplomatic debacle by misbehaving on a film shoot in Mexico and the project was temporarily called off.[12] Ultimately, Clara Blandick and Marjorie Main played Mrs. Fisher in the film versions from 1934 and 1946, starring Spencer Tracy and Red Skelton respectively as Aubrey Piper.

Lowell also made a hit in another George Kelly comedy, in a role specially written for her by the author, as the "fluttery promptress"[13] Nelly Fell in the all-time spoof of amateur theatricals *The Torch-Bearers*. She shared the limelight at the 48th Street Theatre in 1922 with two other expert comediennes, Alison Skipworth and Mary Boland. Lowell lost out on the role in Fox's 1935 filmatization *Doubting Thomas*, which went to Helen Flint. Boland was replaced by Billie Burke, but Skipworth was fortunately allowed to give a stunning reprise of her role as the autocratic amateur director and valkyrie of culture, Mrs. J. Duro Pampinelli.

Lowell's last Broadway show was the new comedy *Come Easy* at the Belasco Theatre in August and September 1933. On January 3, 1934, the *New York Herald Tribune* reported that she had signed with Warner Bros. and would depart for Hollywood in a few weeks.[14] The *New York Times* wrote the same day that she her first assignment would probably be in *Fur Coats* (aka *Side Streets*) with Aline MacMahon.[15] Warner Bros. announced that Lowell would have "One of the important roles" in *The Old Doll's House*, based a story by Damon Runyon.[16] Her "character lead," wrote the *Los Angeles Times*, "will be of strength equal to that which May Robson enacted in 'Lady for a Day.'"[17] In 1934, Robson became the oldest person ever to be nominated for an Academy Award for her portrayal of Apple Annie, based there too on a Damon Runyon story.

On her arrival in Hollywood, Lowell went immediately into production on *Side Streets*, which started shooting on January 10, 1934, at Warner Bros. Burbank studios under the direction of Alfred E. Green.[18] *Side Streets* is one of those films that is usually referred to as "small," but it is perfectly cast, perfectly acted, and perfectly produced, indeed it is perfectly charming in its own way. Vastly talented Aline MacMahon stars as Bertha, who calls herself "Madame Valery," an industrious, Brooklyn-born furrier with her own business, who makes the mistake of marrying a younger man with a roving eye.

As a disgruntled and at times downright disgusted witness to her boss's accelerating domestic debacle, we have her forewoman and only employee, the drab spinster Tillie (Lowell). Tillie is working on something in almost every scene, as she keeps a watchful eye on her employer and friend, even if this isn't always appreciated. Bertha repeatedly tells her to butt out when Tillie tries to make her see her marriage is on the rocks. "Helen Lowell lends humor," one critic wrote, "in the role of a worldly-wise spinster with an acid tongue and a quick temper."[19] Tillie also has a plot function apart from being a witness to and commentator on events, but explaining that would involve too many spoilers. When it's all over, she concludes: "Maybe I'm lucky I never had a husband." Tillie is a touching monument to older, self-supporting, unmarried working women.[20]

In the 1930s, Warner Bros. had a unique stock company of "characters" in every sense of the word and for a couple of years from 1934 till 1935, Helen Lowell was their resident "old lady." The breadth and variety of the talent the studio could draw upon is vividly illustrated by *The Merry Frinks*, which was the second of Lowell's films to be produced, ending in March 16, 1934, but the first to be released.[21] *The Merry Frinks* premiered on May 26, 1934, was based on an original screenplay by Gene Markey and Kathryn Scola, and was directed, like *Side Streets*, by Alfred E. Green. One reviewer summarized the action: "The picture concerns itself with the everyday life of a thoroughly individualistic family of seven who are crowded into a small Bronx flat and who are forever in each other's way at odd purposes."[22]

In what is surely her most sublime comic creation on screen, Lowell plays Amelia "Grandma" Frink, nagging mother to ne'er-do-well, alcoholic pressman Joe Frink (Hugh Herbert), mother-in-law from hell to hard-tried, long-suffering Hattie Frink (Aline MacMahon), and generally a constantly complaining and petulant old woman at daggers drawn with her family in general and with her brother-in-law Newt Frink (Guy Kibbee) in particular. Grandma likes a tipple in the morning before breakfast and keeps a bottle hidden in her room under the cushion of her rocker. She loves to listen to old tunes on the radio and fights with everyone to get hold of the newspaper, where she particularly enjoys the romantic serial stories. She is a self-imagined chronic invalid, who says she would prefer to go to the poor house, to which her daughter-in-law responds laconically: "That may be arranged." There is a hysterically funny scene involving her getting her arm stuck in the jaws of a stuffed alligator, where she knows her son has hidden a bottle, while her brother-in-law Newt unconcernedly regales her with the "oriental dishes" he is going to make to celebrate his birthday. One simply has to agree with the critic who wrote: "Helen Lowell is unusually clever in her portrayal of the role of the aged grandmother who has an unappeasable ear for gossip and an insatiable thirst for Scotch, and who criticizes everything and everybody."[23]

As I've already suggested, Lowell was preeminently a comedienne both on stage and screen. In a "straight" part, she could be as dull and even nauseating as the next character actress. Her third film to be produced and released, *Midnight Alibi* (A. Crosland, First National, 1934), that was supposed to represent her big opportunity, unfortunately left her unprotected in the front line of its barrage of cloying clichés. Advertised in the trailer as Damon Runyon's follow-up to *Lady for a Day* and *Little Miss Marker*, it was based on his story "The Old Doll's House" about a rich, reclusive old lady, Abigail Ardsley, in a big, lonely mansion, whose youthful lover was killed by her autocratic, disapproving father 45 years before the film opens. While the main storyline involving a gang leader, Lance MacGowan (Richard Barthelmess), returning to reclaim his territory, falling in love with the sister of a rival mobster, and befriending the elderly Miss Arsdale almost by accident, the subplot involving Lowell offered a classic "Rose for Emily" situation with the grim father accidentally shooting and killing what he perceives as his daughter's inappropriate suitor and a touch of *Great Expectations* with Miss Arsdale as a kind of New York Miss Havisham living in the past.

In her role of fairy godmother to her gum-chewing, slangy "no gentleman caller" Lance, poor Lowell had to get through several maudlin monologues, including uttering pronouncements like "Oh, my boy, love is the most beautiful thing in the world. When that is gone, there is nothing worth to live for. I found that out." The only humor in the film is provided by the ludicrous juxtaposition of Miss Abby's old world airs and graces and Lance's modern lingo and hapless attempts to try to be polite to the "old doll." The film makes it patently clear why Richard Barthelmess's star was on the wane.

Lowell went on to do 23 more films in rapid succession during the remaining three years of her life, at Warner Bros. and various other studios. While *Big Hearted Herbert* (W. Keighley, Warner Bros, 1934) showed her at her best yet again playing an inept maid very much in the comic maid tradition stretching from Hattie McDaniel in *Alice Adams* to Thelma Ritter in

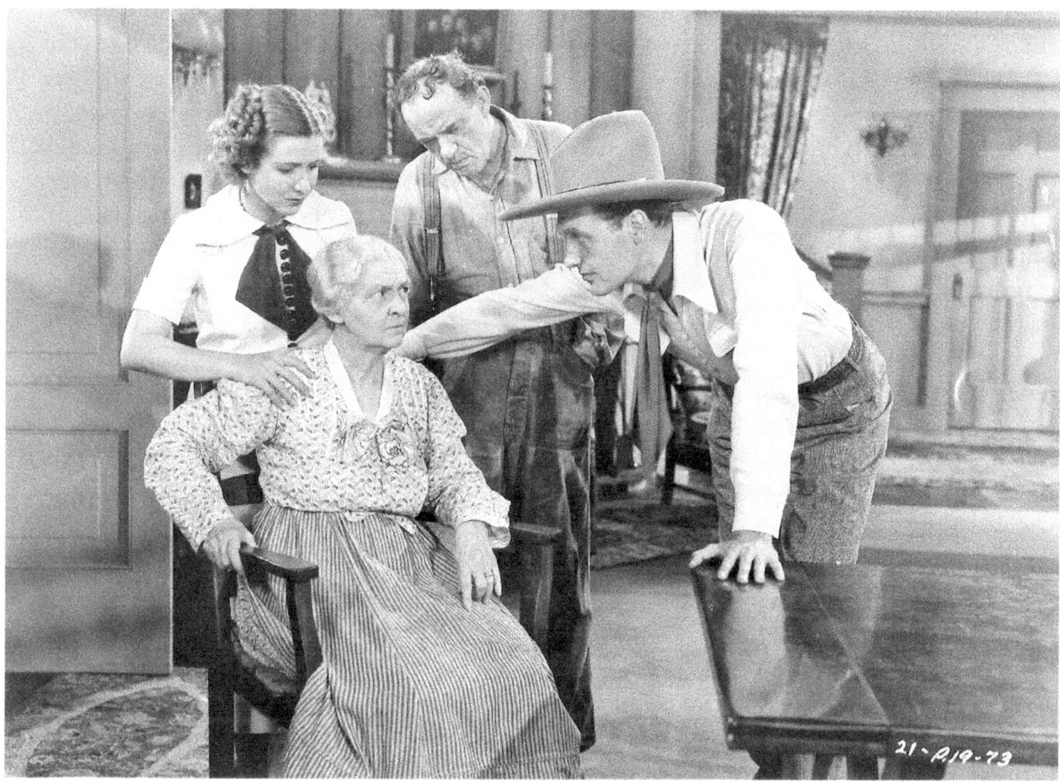

With Ralph Bellamy (right) in the title role, you can be sure there was nothing particularly "wild" about the hero of *Wild Brian Kent* (Sol Lesser Prod., 1936). Helen Lowell was cast as the rustic pioneer grandma of Bellamy's romantic interest, the ill-fated Mae Clark (left), and is here seen sizing him up, as hired hand Lew Kelly looks on. In this B movie western, perennial "also ran" Bellamy actually gets the girl.

A Letter to Three Wives, films like *Living on Velvet* (F. Borzage, Warner Bros., 1935) and *Wild Brian Kent* (B. Bretherton, Sol Lesser Prod., 1936) were more in the dull dramatic mode of *Midnight Alibi*, and films like *Madame Du Barry* (W. Dieterle, Warner Bros., 1934) and *Valiant Is the Word for Carrie* (W. Ruggles, Paramount, 1936) simply gave her little to do.

It was Lowell's "luck," if you can call it that, to be "called" to the big theater in the sky at a time when the quality and quantity of her film work was in decline. She was cheated out a retirement, of course, but then so many of the old troopers of her kind and generation wouldn't have known what to do with themselves in retirement. For Lowell, then, there were no declining years in the Motion Picture Country Home and Hospital (which didn't even exist in her day) or in increasing poverty and decrepitude. There was simply a swift and brutal "The End," which came in the Hollywood hotel where she was living and where she was found dead from an unstated illness on June 29, 1937.[24]

Her last two titles were released after her death and were the only films in which she did not receive screen credit. Her final role in *High, Wide, and Handsome* (R. Mamoulian, Paramount, 1937) was that of the "rather unsympathetic" village gossip Mrs. Lippincott. "Ironic," one columnist noted, "in view of the fact that Miss Lowell, who thus makes her final exit, was known as a gracious and considerate lady."[25] On her arrival in Hollywood, one of the first things she had done was start the "Helen Lowell Meal Club" to help feed destitute actors.[26]

Meaner Than Margaret: Eily Malyon (1879–1961)

It is sad when your *Variety* obituary is the size of a postage stamp and your entire 50-year acting career is summed up in two sentences. Such was the case with Eily Malyon. And those two sentences even contained two factual errors. Malyon did not go to Hollywood in 1936 and she had not "appeared on the Broadway stage for years."[1]

I must admit, though, that I didn't know much about Eily Malyon myself when I started work on this profile. I knew she was British, of course, and her dates. I knew that after years of hard work in modest roles, she finally got her big chance in that supernatural corker *On Borrowed Time*. I knew that her mother, Agnes Thomas, had also been an actress. That was about it.

Fortunately, I was able to find out quite a lot more. Our story begins with Eily's father Harry Craston. Harry was born in Manchester and was christened in the cathedral there on December 20, 1856.[2] In 1871, we find him age 14 living with his father, Thomas Craston (48), mother Emma Craston (47), four siblings between the ages of six and 24 and no less than seven servants in East Preston, Worthing, Sussex. The family was from Lancashire and both the parents and all but of two of the children were born in Manchester.[3] Ten years later, Harry Craston, who is now 25 and a master in boot manufacture, is living with his 26-year-old wife, Agnes S. Craston, and a 19-year-old servant, Harriet Hubbard, in Myrtle Cottage, Islington, London. The couple have a one-year-old daughter, Lily S. L. Craston, born in Islington, who is our present subject and whose full birth name was Eily Sophie Lee Craston.[4] Either Eily was also known as "Lily" or there is a misprint in the census.

By the time Agnes Craston gave birth to her daughter on October 30, 1879,[5] she had been on the stage for a year or so under the name "Agnes Thomas." She appears to have made her London stage debut in the risqué melodrama *Mazeppa* at the Royal Park Theatre in October 1878.[6] She would be an actress for 40 years, mainly in England, but also in Australia and, briefly, in New York. Even if her daughter was not literally born on the stage, she came pretty close, as Agnes Thomas continued to act during her pregnancy and even garnered high praise as "the boy Ned" in *The Black Flag; or, Escaped from Portland* when she was six and a half months pregnant![7] In her younger days, Thomas was known for her "boy's parts, not burlesque boys, but character boys," as she herself explained.[8]

After her daughter's birth, Thomas left the stage until 1882. When the census enumerator called in 1881, then, she was at home in Islington with her baby. During 1882, 1883, and early 1884, she worked steadily and had leading roles at the Drury Lane Theatre and the Opera

Comique in London and elsewhere. After April 1884, she disappears from the London stage, only to reappear again in New York a year later. What was she doing in the interim? Well, it turns out Thomas was "co-habiting" with a married man we only know as "Mr. Vose" at 24 Gilbert St., Grosvenor Sq., London from July till November 1884, before going to New York with him and continuing to live with him there. In New York, Mr. Vose "intended to start a dramatic company" and Agnes Thomas "was to be the 'leading lady.'"[9] We wouldn't know even this much, if it weren't for the fact that *Mrs.* Vose resented this untimely intrusion into her own wedded bliss, which had begun after only seven months of marriage and with a child on the way, and sued Mr. Vose for divorce on the grounds of adultery and desertion.[10]

Apparently, nothing came of Mr. Vose's plans to enter theatrical management. We have a few notices of Agnes Thomas's activities in New York, including a special matinee of George Fawcett Rowe's new play *Beauty* at Wallack's Theatre on April 16, 1885, which marked her American stage debut, and her performance in the play *Twins* at the Standard Theatre four days later.[11] By the time the case of *Vose v. Vose* came up before Mr. Justice Butt in late October 1887, Thomas was even further afield, in Australia, a journey no doubt at least partly motivated by the desire to remove herself even further from the divorce proceedings in London. By this time, Thomas had also shed Mr. Vose and was married to someone else. We don't know if she ever divorced Harry Craston, but he died in Camberwell, London, in 1885 at the age of 29.[12]

On November 24, 1886, the *South Australian Advertiser* printed a long interview with the current leading lady at the city's Theatre Royal, which she had granted the paper at the Prince Alfred Hotel. This interview gives us a unique glimpse of Agnes Thomas aged 31 (though she claimed to be 27), who describes herself as a "common-place every-day sort of leading lady." She tells of her experiences in New York and San Francisco and how she was finally enticed by the manager Dion Boucicault, Jr., into abandoning her "American prospects" and going with his company to Australia. "My experience generally has been in London," she relates, "in what is known as the melodramatic school. My first engagements were in the East-End theatres, on what is known as the Surrey side of the water—a very good school for beginners." She talks at length of her experience acting with Lily Langtry and of her admiration for Mrs. Kendal and of how "nature evidently intended me for the broken hearted, draggle-tailed heroine." She mentions that she has done so much writing for the press, "I almost look upon myself as a journalist, for my husband and my four brothers are all literary men." She also mentions a sister, but not her daughter.[13]

By the time Eily Craston was six, then, her father was dead and her mother was on the other side of the world. As soon as Eily was old enough, we know she was sent to boarding school in an Ursuline Convent in Belgium and also in France.[14] Agnes Thomas was back in England and performing on the London stage by 1890.[15] If we fast forward to January 30, 1899, we find Thomas in support of a new 19-year-old star at the Princess's Theatre in a revival of a drama from 1897 called *The White Heather*. This star was her own daughter in her London stage debut. As the heroine Marion Hume, the reviewer for the *London Standard* found Eily Malyon "earnest and refined in speech and action, though somewhat lacking in facial expression." The later so impassive Malyon face was already beginning to freeze up! The same reviewer felt "Miss Agnes Thomas's make-up as Lady Janet was too young, and she had no need to raise her voice to the extent she did."[16] In a long, detailed review, *The St. James's Gazette* pronounced Malyon's debut "a very distinct success." "Miss Agnes Thomas," they added, "although playing a little too obviously to the gallery, made a decided hit."[17]

Our subject clearly performed from the first under the name Eily Malyon. Malyon, it turns out, was the surname of her stepfather. Edward J. Malyon was a former actor, playwright, and stage manager, who was probably the husband Agnes Thomas mentions in the 1886 interview. At any rate, he died suddenly on May 23, 1902, in Birmingham, where he was at work superintending rehearsals of a new play at the Grand Theatre.[18] The following year, his now 47-year-old widow embarked on the arguably most important and successful part of her long career, when she played Betsy Trotwood in a new dramatization of *David Copperfield* called *Em'ly* at the Adelphi Theatre and completed her transformation into a character actress.[19] Up until her retirement in 1918, Thomas was very busy indeed as a character woman on the London stage and even returned to Broadway in 1912–13 in a transfer of one of her biggest stage successes in later years, K.G. Sowerby's drama *Rutherford & Son*, which ran for 63 performances at the Little Theatre in New York.[20]

Thomas was a favorite of George Bernard Shaw and created supporting roles in several of his plays, including most famously the old maid Miss Ramsden in *Man and Superman* at the Court Theatre in 1905.[21] She was highly praised for her portrayal of Gina Ekdal in Ibsen's *The Wild Duck* at the Cort that same year.[22] Thomas ended her long stage career with the biggest hit she'd ever had: the "emotional" play *Romance* by Edward Sheldon, where she supported Doris Keane first at the Duke of York's and later at the Lyric Theatre. She only appeared for seven minutes as an aunt in the second act and called it her "rest cure." The newspapers noted in March 1918 that she had never missed a single of the 1,000 performances.[23] When it was finally over, she went into a well deserved retirement. Agnes Thomas was still alive in 1939 at the age of 84, when Malyon mentioned in an interview that she hoped to get over to England to see her.[24] With the war coming on and a busy schedule, it seems unlikely that mother and daughter ever saw each other again.

To return to the narrative of Eily Malyon's career: It appears that the promise of her debut in 1899 was not quite fulfilled. She fluctuated for about a dozen years between leading and supporting roles in London and the provinces. By 1911, she appears to have felt that greener pastures were needed. She was living in the London parish of St. George Hanover Square (Belgravia) at the time.[25] Between what was probably her last London show, the Incorporated Stage Society's production of the new one-act play *The Little Stone House* ("a cameo of village life in Russia"[26]) at the Aldwych in January 1911 and her American film debut in 1931, Eily Malyon simply disappears.

So where was she? Australia? Well, actually, yes. In about 1911, Malyon followed in her mother's footsteps and decided to try her luck "Down Under." I leave it to others to explore that period in detail. I only know that she was part of the American-born actor-manager J.C. Williamson's stock company in the teens with the likes of Judith Anderson and Tempe Pigott.[27] Clearly, she formed important bonds in Australia, as she left her estate to friends or family there, though she hadn't lived there in over 30 years.[28]

In an interview in 1939, Malyon explains how she came to settle in America. It was in 1926, when she was returning to England from Australia, that she "decided to see the United States en route." "[T]houghts of the New York stage were uppermost in her mind," but she got waylaid in San Francisco and via stage work there one thing led to another.[29] She made her film debut in a tiny, uncredited role as a stern nurse in *Born to Love* (P.L. Stein, RKO Pathé, 1931), who tells fellow nurse Constance Bennett, "Visiting hour is up." Five years later, when she was doing three matinees and seven evening performances of the comedy *Call It a Day* at El Capitan Theatre in Los Angeles while filming *A Woman Rebels* with Katharine Hepburn at RKO, she was described as "probably the busiest woman in Hollywood."[30]

In fact, 1935 and 1936 were the peak years of Malyon's film career with respectively 14 and ten film releases. Among her more visible performances during her 1930s heyday were her roles in *Great Expectations* (S. Walker, Universal, 1934), as Miss Havisham's "poor relation" Sarah Pocket, who covets her money and acts as a kind of housekeeper; *The Little Minister* (R. Wallace, Radio Pictures, 1934), as the laird of the manor's spinster sister Evalina, who plays cards with him, embroiders, and generally disapproves of his planning to marry his ward, Babbie (Katharine Hepburn); *A Tale of Two Cities* (J. Conway, MGM, 1935), as the pious wife of grave-robber Jerry Cruncher (Billy Bevan), who prays for her husband's delivery from evil to his vociferous objection, as he claims she is "plopping" to take the bread out of his and their son Jerry Jr.'s mouth; and *Anthony Adverse* (M. LeRoy, Warner Bros., 1936), as the Mother Superior at the convent where the hero (Fredric March) is left as a baby, who later wants him adopted by Edmund Gwenn when he begins to charm the girls at the convent school.

It was a film from 1939 that would be the high point of Eily Malyon's film career. *On*

This still from *On Borrowed Time* (Metro-Goldwyn-Mayer, 1939) shows (from left) Beulah Bondi as Granny, Eily Malyon as Demetria Riffle, Lionel Barrymore as Julian "Gramps" Northrup, and Bobs Watson as Pud. This film elevated Malyon to the top of the list of female "meanies" in Hollywood.

Borrowed Time was to Malyon what *The Grapes of Wrath* was to Jane Darwell and *The Wizard of Oz* to Margaret Hamilton. Frank S. Nugent summed up the plot in his *New York Times* review, describing *On Borrowed Time* as "the story of a stubborn and hot-tempered old man who didn't want to die until his stout-legged grandson had grown safely out of the mercenary clutches of his Aunt Dimmy [Demetria]. So when the shadowy Mr. Brink came for him, as he had come before for Granny and the boy's parents, Gramp chased him up a tree and tried to keep him there."[31]

The cast of the Broadway play on which the film was based had been entirely replaced when filming began at Metro on April 3, 1939, with Harold S. Bucquet directing. Lionel Barrymore now headed the ensemble cast as Julian "Gramps" Northrup, Bobs Watson played his grandson Pud, and Sir Cedric Hardwicke Mr. Brink. Beulah Bondi played Granny, who tries to keep her husband and grandson in line. When Pud's father and mother are killed in a car accident, the grandparents suddenly become responsible for raising the boy. Malyon was cast as the straight-laced, avaricious maiden aunt Demetria Riffle, who wants control of the boy and the money he has inherited. She is a "pismire" according to Gramps; a pismire being the meanest ant there is. His biggest fear is that Demetria is "going to make a sissy out of Pud."

Unfortunately, *On Borrowed Time* was just a momentary flare up in Malyon's film career. She soon returned to more modest and even at times uncredited roles in films like *Shadow of a Doubt* (A. Hitchcock, Skirball Prod./Universal, 1943), *Jane Eyre* (R. Stevenson, Twentieth Century–Fox, 1943), *Going My Way* (L. McCarey, Paramount, 1944), *The Seventh Cross* (F. Zinnemann, MGM, 1944), and *She-Wolf of London* (J. Yarbrough, Universal, 1946). *On Borrowed Time* led to some rare press interest in Malyon, though, which allows us to know a little more about her life and experiences.

Throughout this book, we'll encounter several laughable headlines. The title that topped an interview with Malyon in 1939 is one of my favorites: "When They Hate Her, Eily's Really Happy." Journalist Rose Pelswick explains that, unlike stars who measure their success in fan mail full of praise, villains "know that they got over when their fan mail berates them for being such blackguards." Malyon, according to Pelswick, "is rapidly gaining the reputation of being the meanest woman on the screen." Malyon herself considered Aunt Demetria "her most hateful part": "But the avalanche [of letters] really started when she began mistreating Shirley Temple." This was in *The Little Princess* (W. Lang, Twentieth Century–Fox, 1939), where she played a cook. "Apparently," she told the reporter, "threatening Shirley was all that was needed to brand me as an untouchable." She'd even received "semi-threatening" letters. Malyon chose to take the criticism as a tribute. While her personal mail "fell off somewhat" after *The Hound of the Baskervilles*, in which she "didn't rank as an out and out heavy," she hoped "*On Borrowed Time*'s scheming Aunt Demetria will cause her to be disliked intensely once again."[32] Malyon's hopes were more than fulfilled. One reviewer wrote, "Eily Malyon etches with unerring strokes what must surely be the most unsympathetic role of the year."[33] In 1940, she was dubbed "Hollywood's No. 1 'meanie'" by the *Syracuse Herald*.[34] It was quite an achievement beating Margaret Hamilton, who came in second place, after she had just delivered her iconic portrayal as the Wicked Witch of the West.

In another interview from 1939, Malyon was described as "a pleasant person who enjoys collecting Duncan Phyfe antiques and enjoys looking down on cinemaland from her home in the Hollywood Hills." On her increasing stereotyping in "mean" roles, Malyon reflected that she didn't like being typecast, adding: "I'll welcome variety. But I like to eat regularly,

Eily Malyon's modest role in *Above Suspicion* (Metro-Goldwyn-Mayer, 1943) as a hotel proprietor was par for the course. She is seen here behind the counter with the film's stars Fred MacMurray and Joan Crawford.

too."[35] As it turns out, Malyon's screen image as a "heavy" was money in the bank. Her unpopularity was lucrative, as is evidenced by the 1940 U.S. census, where she reported that she'd earned in excess of $5,000 in 1939 for 17 weeks' work. Admittedly, 1939 was one of Malyon's better years with the release of seven films, including *The Little Princess, The Hound of the Baskervilles, On Borrowed Time,* and *We Are Not Alone,* but a yearly income of more than five "G"s was princely indeed at the time. Malyon had no dependents, unlike her neighbor, fellow British character actress Doris Lloyd, who also earned in excess of $5,000 in 1939, but was at least partly supporting her live-in mother, sister, and niece. In the census, Malyon is listed as being 60 (her correct age), divorced (probably in Australia), and having a high school education. She lived in a $4,500 owned home at 3928 Fredonia Dr. and Lloyd lived on the same side of the street at no. 3942 in a home she rented for $60 a month.[36]

My guess is that Eily Malyon was the type to save her pennies. And she owned her own home. So after *The Challenge* (J. Yarbrough, Bernard Small Prod.) in 1948, she simply retired. She would enjoy her retirement for more than a dozen years, dying of cancer on September 26, 1961.[37]

Bessie's Daughter: Una Merkel (1903–86)

It was front page news across America on March 5, 1945: "Una Merkel Is Saved, Mother Dies from Gas"! "Una Merkel Near Death After Mother Suicides"! "Mother of Screen Star Found Dead; Actress Una Merkel Burla Revived by an Inhalator"![1] The mother who had been so proud of her daughter's success was herself in the headlines for the first and last time.

At five that morning, a night bell captain had used his passkey to enter the 16th floor apartment occupied by Una Merkel and her mother Bessie Phares Merkel in the exclusive Essex House at 160 Central Park South in New York City. A night watchman had reported smelling gas coming from the apartment. The bell captain found Mrs. Merkel in the kitchen, lying on the floor in front of a gas range with all the jets turned on. She was wearing a blue and white housecoat and bleeding from her wrists. Razor blades were found on the edge of the stove. Though Bessie Merkel was pronounced dead when police from the W. 54th St. station arrived, a police emergency squad assisted by private physicians worked on her for more than an hour in a futile attempt to revive her.

Before taking her own life, Mrs. Merkel had closed the two doors between the kitchen and her daughter Una's bedroom and placed towels under them in an attempt to prevent the gas from seeping out. Una Merkel was nevertheless overcome by gas. She was partially revived by the police emergency squad using an inhalator and taken to Roosevelt Hospital, where her condition was "said to be good."[2] In a different newspaper report, Merkel was in a coma that Monday forenoon, "gaining consciousness only intermittently and never long enough to make a statement."[3] She was given a 50–50 chance of survival. An almost empty bottle of tablets found on her night table had been turned over to the city toxicologist for analysis.

Bessie Merkel had left an almost illegible suicide note in pencil, which was found either on the living room or kitchen table. "I'm ill and can't take it anymore. Forgive me," she wrote.[4] She asked that her husband Arno Merkel at the Reform Hotel in Mexico City; her brother-in-law Carl Merkel and Una's father-in-law G.F. Burla in Los Angeles; and Arno Merkel's sister's husband, William Thayer in Hartford, Connecticut, be notified.[5] She also made reference to the disposition of some money and jewelry. The newspapers reported that Mrs. Merkel was 70. She was in fact only 60 years of age. Mother and daughter had been living in the Essex House apartment since May 1944.

Bessie Merkel was a large, florid woman, with thick, wavy hair she liked to keep blonde, and sharp, light-colored eyes in a pleasant but not beautiful face. She was born Bessie Phares in Cincinnati, Ohio, on September 24, 1884.[6] By the time she was 14, the Phares family had

This happy family photograph taken around 1934, when Ronald Burla and Una Merkel had been married three years and her parents, Bess and Arno Merkel, 32, takes on a particular poignancy when one knows the end of the story. Bess Merkel killed herself in 1945, Ronald and Una divorced in 1947, and Una went on to make a home for her father until his death in 1969.

moved across the Ohio River to Covington, Kentucky, where Bessie's Ohio-born father, James C. Phares (b. 1845), worked as a bookkeeper in an attorney's office. Her mother, Mary Elizabeth Alexander Phares (b. 1853), was from Louisiana and kept house for her husband and three children. Bessie had two older sisters: Josephine A. Phares (b. 1879) and Hazel K. Phares (b. 1881).[7] The tiny wooden house the Phares family was living in in 1900 is still standing at 27 13th St. in the Eastside section of Covington and looks like two shoe-boxes placed one on top of the other.[8]

Bessie's oldest sister Josephine married a bookkeeper called John A. Hanks (1867–1908) in Covington in 1905.[9] As it happened, her little sister had beat her to the altar. On January 1, 1903, Bessie Phares married Arno Merkel in Covington, Kentucky.[10] Albert Arno Merkel was born in Cincinnati, Ohio, like his wife, on May 8th in either 1881 or 1882. In the many ship manifestos from his travels later in life, he seems unable to make up his mind which year it was.[11] His parents were Hans August Adalbert "Albert" Merkel (b. 1845), who worked as a pharmacist, and Amelia Kanther [Kanzer] Merkel (b. 1849). He was born in Missouri, she was born in Ohio, and they were both second-generation German immigrants.[12] It turns out that in 1880, the Merkel and Phares families were living within a few blocks of each other in downtown Cincinnati.[13] Maybe Arno and Bessie had known each other since childhood.

Bessie and Arno's only child, a daughter named Una, was born in Covington on December 10, 1903.[14] I imagine little Una was cute as a button as a child and she continued to be "cute as a bug's ear" even as an adult, as one newspaper noted when she was 40.[15] Bessie had a new focus for her life and no doubt developed into a classic stage mom. In a revealing remark, her daughter once said: "Actually my mother has more thrills out of my career than I do."[16]

Bessie would need her relationship with her daughter, as during the coming years she would lose her parents, both her sisters, and her brother-in-law. Her father and Una's grandfather, James Phares, died in 1909.[17] He was soon followed by Bessie's oldest sister and Una's aunt, Josephine Hanks, who died in Newport, Kentucky, in 1910, two years after her husband John. She was only 30.[18] Bessie's mother Mary died in New York City on October 13, 1920.[19] Una would have been closest to her Grandma Phares among her four grandparents, as she lived with the Merkels at 400 W. 150th St. in New York at the end of her life.[20] After Bessie's mother's death, Bessie's unmarried sister Hazel came to live with them in their apartment in the Belvedere, a large building in Upper Manhattan's Sugar Hill on the corner of 150th St. and Edgecombe Ave. Hazel worked as a bill clerk and died in New York on February 20, 1926, at the age of 44.[21]

On Hazel's death, then, Bessie Merkel found herself at 41 the only surviving member of her birth family. Her strong ties to her kin are symbolized by the fact that on her own death nearly 20 years later, she was laid to rest with her parents and sisters in Highland Cemetery, Fort Mitchell, Kentucky.[22]

Arno Merkel was a travelling salesman who fell in love with long distance. Unlike Tom Wingfield's father in *The Glass Menagerie*, though, Una's father would sooner or later always come home. When he registered for the draft on September 12, 1918, Arno was boarding with a family called Rudiger at 144 W. 129th St. in Harlem, New York, while his wife and 14-year-old daughter were living at 125 E. 4th St. in Covington.[23] On January 13, 1920, we find 16-year-old Una living with her parents and maternal grandmother in Sugar Hill in Upper Manhattan.[24] Ten years later, she is still living with her parents, now in an apartment at 450 W. 147th St., on the corner of Convent Ave., which was not far from their old apartment.[25]

Merkel had made her New York stage debut under the name "Alta Mearkl" as a cigarette girl in the four-act play *Montmartre* at the Belmont Theatre on February 13, 1922, and throughout the 1920s was kept busy as a popular comedienne on Broadway and on tour, her biggest hit show being *Coquette* starring Helen Hayes in 1927–38.[26] When Merkel made her move to Hollywood in 1930, her parents went right along with her. They lived first in a modest house at 3216 Ellington Dr., before moving to an apartment in Hollywood at 6919 Franklin Ave.[27]

On January 2, 1932, a fourth member was added to the family when Merkel married 25-year-old Ronald L. Burla in Tijuana, Mexico.[28] She had caught the bridal bouquet at her friend and co-star Helen Hayes's wedding to Charles MacArthur in 1928,[29] but it took some time before she was able to tie the knot herself. Ronald Burla was the elder of the two sons of the former bank president Given F. Burla (1868–1936) and Elizabeth Cedergren Burla (1885–1958).[30] Ronald was born in Billings, Montana, on February 2, 1907, and raised in Hardin, Montana, where his father "organized the First National Bank" in Hardin and was elected state senator from Big Horn County.[31] In 1918, Mr. Burla sold his stock in the bank, resigned as president, and moved with his family to Los Angeles, where we find them in 1920 living at 730 S. Carondelet St., a Spanish Mission style apartment court in the MacArthur Park section of the city.[32] Ronald had four years of college and was variously described in contemporary newspapers reports as an "aviation designer," "aeronautical engineer," "aviation engineer," "executive in the North American Aviation company," and "airplane factory executive."[33] In the 1930 census, his occupation is given as "Apprentice Rubber co." and in 1940 he is "assistant to vice president airplane manufacturer."[34] It was symptomatic that it was Ronald and his father-in-law Arno who went on a trip to Europe in the first year of the Burlas' marriage.[35] Una was too busy working and Bessie apparently had no interest in foreign travel.

The 1930s saw the release of nearly all Merkel's major films: *Abraham Lincoln* (D.W. Griffith, D.W. Griffith Prod., 1930), *Red-Headed Woman* (J. Conway, MGM, 1932), *42nd Street* (L. Bacon, Warner Bros., 1933), *Beauty for Sale* (R. Boleslawski, MGM, 1933), *Bombshell* (V. Fleming, MGM, 1933), *Evelyn Prentice* (W.K. Howard, MGM, 1934), and *Destry Rides Again* (G. Marshall, Universal, 1939), just to name a few. Taking this body of work into account, Merkel was arguably the most important female comic second in Hollywood during the '30s. More than Eve Arden, Patsy Kelly, Aline MacMahon, Ruth Donnelly, Helen Broderick, Nydia Westman and scores of other cute, quirky, and zany blondes, Merkel epitomized realism butting its head against the bulwark of romance, rapier wit piercing the heart of sentimentality, the healthy injection of saline that prevented the Hollywood solution from becoming too saccharine.

I imagine that Merkel's years as a contract player at MGM in the mid–1930s, living with her husband and parents in a spacious Spanish Revival bungalow at 2572 Outpost Dr. in the Hollywood Hills, were among the happiest of her life.[36] Columnist Hollis Wood described her at this time: "At home Una is a pleasant little housewife who lives in a bungalow with her mother and husband, Ronald Burla, entertains informally, plays a cracking good game of bridge, and isn't very interested in stardom."[37] Dan Thomas added the observation, "Una's real life conversation runs more toward the serious than the humorous."[38] Kyle Crichton was all too typical of the male columnist's dismissive appraisal of female supporting players' appearance, when he wrote blithely of Merkel: "She is a blond dame, but she is no beauty."[39]

I also want to share Paul Harrison's 1939 description of the joint Burla-Merkel household, written just before or soon after the extended family moved house from Outpost Dr. to 603 N. Rexford Dr. in Beverly Hills. This half-timbered, Tudor style home represented the high point of Merkel's career, in real estate terms at least. Yet she did not own this 4,300 square foot home from 1924, which still stands, but rented it for $200 a month. It was staffed with a live-in cook and butler.[40] Harrison wrote: "The Merkel-Burla household is somewhat madly reminiscent of the Sycamores. Papa Arno Merkel, a breezy, chubby little man, makes a hobby of traveling; just picks a spot on a map at random and goes there. Bessie, the mother, works tirelessly at her stamp collection. Burla himself collects coins. Una reads voraciously. Another member of the family is a trained nurse who came there seven years ago when somebody was sick and just stayed."[41] The Sycamores were, of course, the eccentric, artsy, multi-generational family depicted by Moss Hart and George S. Kaufman in the play *You Can't Take It with You*.

Merkel herself chimed in in a 1941 interview with May Mann: "'Mother and father and Ronnie and I all live together. I'm rather proud of it,' Una commented. 'We are absolutely devoted to each other. Mother takes care of the home—and sees that all of us are comfortable. Dad has his job—Ronnie has his—and I have mine. We are just about the happiest family I ever heard about.'"[42] When we consider that only four years later her mother took her own

Una Merkel played a part in both the 1937 and 1952 film versions of *The Merry Widow*. Here she is seen in the 1952 version from Metro-Goldwyn-Mayer with Fernando Lamas, who starred with Lana Turner. The original sound version starred Maurice Chevalier and Jeanette MacDonald.

life, Merkel must have been putting on a brave front or things must have deteriorated fast during the war years.

Merkel's life, both personal and professional, collapsed in the wake of her mother's 1945 suicide. She had a nervous breakdown and was off the screen for two years.[43] When she finally returned in *It's a Joke, Son!* (B. Stoloff, Bryan Foy Prod., 1947), it marked her transition from playing younger women to the mother and secretary/companion roles that would dominate the latter part of her film career. Her marriage to Ronald Burla ended in divorce in 1947.[44] Merkel made her own suicide attempt on March 4, 1952, nearly seven years to the day after her mother killed herself.[45] On recovering, she claimed she had taken too many sleeping pills by mistake.[46] She lived quietly with her father until his death in 1969.[47]

Despite her emotional ups and downs, Merkel continued to work in films, on the stage, and in television until she was 64. When she was 52, she won a "Best Featured Actress in a Play" Tony Award for her performance as Edna Earle Ponder in a play based on the short novel *The Ponder Heart* by Eudora Welty. When she was 58, she was Oscar-nominated for one of the finest performances of her long and varied career, as Mrs. Winemiller, the off-kilter minister's wife in the flawed but still fascinating film *Summer and Smoke* (P. Glenville, Hal Wallis, 1961), based on a play by Tennessee Williams. In addition to the pathetically attenuated love story between Mrs. Winemiller's frustrated spinster daughter Alma (Geraldine Page) and a local Lothario, the film centers on the troubled relationship between the mentally ill mother and her dutiful yet rebellious daughter. As we have seen, that was the story of Una Merkel's own life.

That life ended in her Los Angeles apartment on Thursday, January 2, 1986, with "no survivors."[48] Una Merkel was laid to rest in the Phares plot in Highland Cemetery with Bessie and Arno and all the rest of her mother's family, who had been lying beneath their simple stone markers for so many years.[49]

Maids and Masseuses: Greta Meyer (1883–1965)

In his magisterial reference work *Who's Who in Hollywood, 1900–1976,* David Ragan lists Greta Meyer at the back among the "'Lost' Players."[1] These are all manner of film actors, Ragan explains, where "the best efforts on the part of the author have failed to pinpoint their present whereabouts."[2] The author adds that he would like to hear from readers or from the players themselves, as to their present location and circumstances. Meyer was unlikely to have responded to his call in 1977, as she had been dead for a dozen years. In fact, her death is just about the only major event in her life that is securely documented. It took place on October 8, 1965, in Gardena, California.[3]

It is a little surprising that Ragan missed the fact that Meyer had hit the headlines for the first and only time just two years before her death, when local newspapers across America carried a human interest story about an elderly Hollywood actress who had been evicted from her rented home, which was being torn down and replaced by a new building. The story was accompanied by a photograph of a forlorn, elderly woman holding a broom and looking rather theatrical in "an old purple dress, possibly a costume."[4] For any old movie buff and fan of 1930s films, the elderly woman in the photograph was still recognizable at age 80 as Greta Meyer.

Meyer was never very widely known even in her own day, but she was ubiquitous in the Hollywood films of the 1930s and probably the most successful, German-born character actress in Hollywood between the World Wars. By the time she found herself and all her belongings on the pavement outside her home at 505 N. Westmount Dr. in West Hollywood,[5] Meyer had not had a film role in nearly 20 years. Her final bow on the big screen was in *An American Romance* (K. Vidor, MGM, 1944). Her film career only lasted 15 years or so and her heyday was the first half of the 1930s, when she was kept very busy indeed in a variety of mostly modest roles as maids, masseuses, and foreign-inflected mothers.

So the mystery isn't where or what she was doing from about 1929 and up until her death. No the mystery is exactly where she came from and what she had been doing prior to her film career. I can only share what little historical information I have been able to unearth and hope that this may inspire others to pursue the no doubt fascinating highways and byways of Greta Meyer's life and career for themselves.

To go back to the beginning then: an item in the "Hollywood Chatter" column in 1933 noted that Meyer "belongs to the most famous theatrical family in Germany, comparable to the Barrymores in America."[6] Modern internet sources all give Meyer's date of birth as August

7, 1883, and this event was to have taken place in Dessau, Germany.[7] It is interesting, though, that her official death record gives her year of birth as 1888.[8] Normally, I would tend to trust the earliest dating of an actress's birth for reasons that will become patently obvious in the rest of the book. The blatant mendacity of many, indeed most, actresses with regard to their year of birth is a well known fact and not unheard of even among actresses who were destined for supporting roles from the beginning and never traded in youthful good looks. As the birth data in the Social Security Index is probably based on information provided by Meyer herself when she registered for Social Security, it certainly isn't infallible. On the other hand, as there is no way of knowing what the basis for the Internet Movie Database's information is, that needs to be taken with a grain of salt as well when not supported by historical sources. It is possible, though, that the source is the 1963 news articles in connection with Meyer's eviction, where her age is given as 80, supposedly based on information she herself provided.

Matters aren't made easier by the fact that being called Greta Meyer in Germany is like being called Mary Smith in the United States. I've located, for example, a Greta Meyer who arrived at Ellis Island on April 29, 1909, aboard the *President Lincoln* from Hamburg, but whether this is *our* Greta Meyer, even though the age fits, is anybody's guess.[9] We know she was in the United States and, more specifically, in New York by 1911. In an article in the *New York Times* entitled "Matters of Interest to Playgoers," published on Christmas Eve 1911, there is a photograph of a youthful but easily recognizable Greta Meyer with a massive Gibson Girl type hairdo, who is identified by name in the caption followed by the word "Weber's," but not otherwise mentioned in the article.[10] Weber's Music Hall was a popular musical variety house on Broadway between 29th and 30th St., that was converted into a movie theater in 1913 and torn down in 1917.[11] Clearly, Meyer was performing in vaudeville at this stage of her career and well-known enough to get her picture in the "paper of record."

She is also on record as having performed in a "Parisian Vaudeville" in three acts called *Auction Pinochle* at Adolf Phillipp's Fifty-Seventh Street Theatre. It opened on November 23, 1912, and had a highly "continental" cast list, full of names like Berla, Brookmann, Hartzheim, Keller, Krueger, Schumann, and Steingler. This brand new theater near Third Ave. named for the owner and dedicated to "light German and Viennese operettas" was later renamed the Bandbox.[12] In October 1915, we know Meyer acted in *Der Weibsteufel* (*The Devil-Woman*), a German play by Karl Schoenbert presented by Rudolf Christian's Irving Place Theatre stock company after being "a pronounced success both in Berlin and Vienna." There were only three characters in the play, enacted by Meyer, Arnold Korff, and Christian Rub, who years later would do 11 films with her in Hollywood.[13]

Then in 1920, at the age of 37, Meyer's career takes an unexpected turn. According to Zalmen Zylbercweig's *Leksikon fun Yidishn Teater, 1931–1969* (*Encyclopedia of Yiddish Theater*), Meyer became "a popular force in the Yiddish theatre" in the 1920s. Who would have guessed? According to Zylbercweig, Meyer was not herself Jewish, being born into a Christian family in Dessau, Anhalt, Germany, in 1886, but learned Yiddish in Germany "during the disintegration of the German theatre" from actor M.B. Samuilov. Her father had been an actor too, he writes, and she went to school in Berlin and Vienna. Meyer made her debut with Schwartz's Yiddish Art Theatre at the Garden Theatre in New York on June 4, 1920, as "Debeka Vest" (Rebecca West) in Ibsen's *Rosmersholm*. Zylbercweig goes on to name a number of the roles she played in Yiddish theaters across America. Meyer became a member of the Yiddish Actors Union in 1921 and later opened a German cabaret and a restaurant.[14]

Meyer's career in the Yiddish theater ended when she was cast as the leading lady's maid in Lili Hatvany's hit play *Tonight or Never*, starring Helen Gahagan and Melvyn Douglas, which opened on November 18, 1930, at the Belasco Theatre and ran for 232 performances (until June 1931). This was legendary producer and director Belasco's last show, as he died on May 14, 1931, which was also the year the stars Gahagan and Douglas married. The queeny character actor Ferdinand Gottschalk was also in the show, as the singer's devoted yet critical manager, "The Faithful Dog."

For both Gottschalk and Meyer, *Tonight or Never* became their ticket to Hollywood, as they were asked to reprise their roles in the film version. This film was not strictly speaking Meyer's American film debut, though, as she had acted in the first foreign-language "talkie" to be made in the United States in 1929.[15] The film, entitled *Die Königsloge* (*The Royal Box*; B. Foy, Warner Bros., 1929), was shot at Vitagraph Studios, whose buildings, including the signature smokestack with the Vitagraph logo, are still standing at 15th St. and Locust Ave. in the Flatbush section of Brooklyn and now house the Shulamith School for Girls.

Tonight or Never completed production at Samuel Goldwyn Studios in mid–October 1931, which allows us to pinpoint the time Meyer would have made her move, permanent as it turned out, from New York to Hollywood. In the film version, Helen Gahagan Douglas was replaced by Gloria Swanson, who looks about as visually appealing as a dwarf in drag as the opera singer Nella Vago. Melvyn Douglas got to reprise his stage role as "The Unknown Gentleman" (Jim Fletcher in the film) and thus made his film debut. While Robert Greig and Warburton Gamble were also invited to reprise their stage roles as Nella's imposing butler and her stick-in-the-mud fiancé, there were several other interesting changes of cast. That marvelous old wreck Alison Skipworth took over Katherine Stewart's role as the dubious Marchesa and, as usual, acted everyone else off the screen. She even managed to have a shorter neck than Swanson, which takes some doing. Boris Karloff, in the very year of his breakthrough in *Frankenstein* at Universal, played a ghoulish waiter, who acts as a liaison of sorts between Swanson and Douglas, helping to engineer their first meeting. He replaced Edmund Loewe and was billed eighth and last after Meyer.

Tonight or Never suggests with typical pre–Code candor that Swanson can't reach her full potential as a singer until she becomes intimate with Douglas. This is what has to happen "tonight or never." This was also the premise of the original play, which is summarized more subtly by Burns Mantle as dealing with how the prima donna "will never sing until she has experienced love and suffering."[16] Douglas says in the film that someone needs to "rouse her and shake her." He turns out to be the man for the job.

Given the name Emma in the film, Meyer's role in all this was to be Swanson's eyes and ears and to keep her informed of the purported gigolo Douglas's movements. Emma lives vicariously, as so many maids have done, particularly in Central European romantic comedies and operettas. She has her big scene with Gottschalk, when she discovers Swanson's emerald necklace is missing and is forced to reveal that her mistress was "out all night," didn't come home until six in the morning, slept all day, and was singing in the bathtub. Meyer is togged out in Hollywood's idea of Hungarian dress, which means she looks a bit like a buxom, blonde, Spanish widow with a large comb in her hair, her ample forms swathed in black silk, and a surprising amount of make-up above her characteristically dimpled chin.

Both Meyer and Gottschalk went directly from *Tonight or Never* into *Grand Hotel*, which began rolling at MGM in mid–December 1931 under the direction of Edmund Goulding. It was a heady start to a film career for both of them. *Grand Hotel* is to my mind a film so atmospheric, so powerful, and so engaging, that you simply want to register at the desk and stay in that hotel forever watching the world go by. Every single role is perfectly cast with the best Metro-Goldwyn-Mayer had to offer, which is to say the best any studio at the time had to offer.

Meyer's modest role is just one example of the film's perfection in every detail. For once she is not simply a maid, but actually one of the hotel housekeepers. We first encounter her berating one of her staff for not cleaning Garbo's room sooner. At the same time, the burglar baron played by John Barrymore is hiding in Garbo's closet to avoid being caught red-handed stealing her jewels. To add to the excitement, Garbo's maid (Rafaela Ottiano) and manager (Gottschalk) arrive looking for her, as she has left the theater in the middle of a performance. This is when Garbo herself shows up still in her ballet costume and utters the immortal line "I vant to be alone." As you may recall, she isn't left alone at all, but has a long and romantic tête-à-tête with Barrymore in her room instead. Later, as Garbo is leaving the hotel in the morning to take the train to her next engagement in Vienna, Meyer agrees to keep the Baron's death a secret when Ottiano pleads with her. Meyer says she can control the maids, but not

Greta Meyer (right), as film audiences were accustomed to seeing her, in one of her better maid roles in *Biography of a Bachelor Girl* (Metro-Goldwyn-Mayer, 1935) with (from left) Edward Arnold, Ann Harding, and Robert Montgomery. Meyer became the personification of ordinary, female "Germanness" in the Hollywood films of the 1930s.

the people working downstairs. Thus, when Garbo asks Meyer if the Baron has left, she lies and says he left half an hour ago. Ironically, Meyer may well be the only genuine German in this film set in Berlin.

However limited, Emma and the Grand Hotel housekeeper were more individualized than the average run of maids and masseuses that Meyer portrayed in the 1930s and which often amounted to non-speaking parts or "under fives." While her looks were neutral enough not to register as foreign on the screen without the help of the hair and make-up department, her thick German accent obviously limited her to Northern European and Scandinavian roles. Luckily for her, German and Scandinavian maids and cooks and other types of servants, though not as common as the Irish or the African American domestics, were certainly common enough both in American society at the time and in American films to allow her to carve out a niche for herself as a servant on the big screen. By the time she played a cook in *Laddie* (G. Stevens, RKO, 1935), she was referred to in a review as "old-time extraordinary for such roles."[17]

Meyer also had a sideline in immigrant mothers, as exemplified by her Mrs. Haberschmidt in *Pilgrimage* (J. Ford, Fox, 1933), a non–English-speaking, German "Gold Star" mother,

Greta Meyer was billed fourth in *When Love Is Young* (Universal, 1937), which is the highest she ever got on the credits list. She played Virginia Bruce's German immigrant mother and Christian Rub (left), also German-born and Meyer's former stage co-star, was Bruce's equally concerned father.

who has lost her son fighting for the Allies in Europe; and her Hannah Werner in *When Love Is Young* (H. Mohr, Universal, 1937), heroine Virginia Bruce's mother in a film where Christian Rub, Meyer's *Der Weibesteufel* co-star, played her husband. As Hal Erickson of the *All Movie Guide* observes: "Whenever Greta Meyer was given a character name, it was usually along the mittel–European or Scandinavian lines of Mrs. Svenson, Mrs. Oxenreich, Mrs. Schroldt, Mrs. Vogelhuger or Mrs. Rovitch."[18]

The story of Meyer's eviction fortunately had a happy ending: friends rented her a new apartment, where she had room for all her costumes and memorabilia.[19] In the 1963 interview, Meyer threatened to return to Germany, where she still had a brother living, though she had been an American citizen since 1923. "There's nothing so terrible as being alone," she said. She had humor enough, though, to recognize the irony of the situation. "I've finally got some publicity,"[20] she observed. When Meyer died two years later, the newspapers were not interested.

The Quest for Dennie: Dennie Moore (1902–78)

Sometimes all you need is one small, innocuous piece of information to make all the other pieces fall into place. Such was the case in my research on Dennie Moore, the toothy-grinned, chipmunk-cheeked, nasally inflected, quintessential New York actress, frequently described as "daffy," who infamously tried to seduce Katharine Hepburn in *Sylvia Scarlett* and spilled the beans to Norma Shearer about her husband's affair with Joan Crawford in *The Women*. Try as I might, I just couldn't get any purchase on who she really was and where she came from. Then I read the last line in a review of Moore's 1932 Broadway show *The Great Magoo*: "Paul Kelly and Clare Carlton are excellent in the leading roles, but it is red-headed Dennie Moore, sister of ice-skating Joe Moore, who runs away with most of the performance honors."[1] Eureka! A 1935 *Oakland Tribune* news item gave further details: "Dennie Moore, clever young Scotch-Irish stage comedienne signed for an important role in RKO Radio's 'Sylvia Scarlett,' comes from a family of champions. Her father was the walking champion of Scotland for several years, and her brother, Joe Moore, is now the champion ice skater of the world."[2] Finally, I had something to work with.

Joe Moore was a common enough name, but I soon discovered that the speed skater in question, whose full name was Joseph John Moore, was born in New York City on January 12, 1901.[3] If I could identify him in the census, I figured I would also be able to find his sister and the rest of the Moore family. Lo and behold, there was a four-year-old Joseph Moore in the 1905 New York State census living at 351 W. 47th St. in Manhattan with his father Philip Moore (40, b. Scotland, porter dry goods), mother Mary Moore (40, b. Ireland, janitress), two step-sisters, Anna Mahoney and Mary B. Mahoney (14 and 16, b. Ireland, both packers of patterns), and, finally, a little sister, Florence, two years of age, born in the United States.[4] The ages of both Joe and Florence were appropriate. The Scotch-Irish background was dead on. Was this the girl who would grow up to play the loose-mouthed manicurist Olga in *The Women*? Was this the actress who played in no less than 25 shows on Broadway between 1927 and 1957? Was Florence Moore really Dennie Moore?

I was also able to locate Florence, Joe, and their family in the U.S. census for 1910, as they moved just one block up from W. 47th St. to 316 W. 48th St., as father Philip got a job as a watchman in a wholesale house, as mother Mary gave up her job as a janitress, as stepsister Anna moved out and 16-year-old stepbrother Thomas moved in and helped support the family as an office boy in a gas company. But what about Florence? In 1910, she was only seven and naturally didn't yet have a job.[5] But in 1920, seven years before Dennie Moore's debut on Broadway: Bingo! Florence Moore is still living at home with mom, pop, brother Joe, and stepbrother Thomas. More to the point: Our precocious, 16-year-old Florence is listed as "actrice stage." The family is now living at 48 W. 66th St.[6]

So why didn't Florence Moore use her birth name on stage? As it happens, there was an older, established actress on Broadway at this time, born in Philadelphia in about 1886, who was called Florence Moore.[7] To avoid confusion and because of Equity rules prohibiting "the issuance of a professional name that is identical (or similar sounding) to that of an already current member of the union," our Florence Moore had to come up with another name, a stage name.[8] I was guessing she came up with "Dennie Moore." But how to be sure when she continued to show up as Florence Moore in the census? In 1930, Florence Moore gave her age as 28, was employed as an "actress stage" and lived alone in a $125 a month rented apartment at 100 W. 55th St.[9] Miss Moore had clearly moved up in the world both literally and metaphorically. If she was indeed Dennie Moore, she had made her Broadway debut in the comedy *A Lady in Love* in 1927 and in April 1930 had just finished the run of her sixth consecutive Broadway show, *Phantoms*, at Wallack's Theatre, which would be converted into a movie theater that year.[10]

The deciding factor in determining that Florence Moore was Dennie Moore was finding a passenger list from a transatlantic crossing aboard the SS *Washington* from Southampton to New York in July 1934, where one of the passengers was called "Florence Rita (Deny) Moore" and was born in New York on December 31, 1903.[11] She was the right age and even though "Dennie" was spelled differently, it was too close to be a coincidence. Unfortunately, though, the ship's manifest did not give Miss Moore's profession. So what could Florence Moore have been doing in England? Most recently Dennie Moore had appeared in a show called *The Pursuit of Happiness* at the Avon Theatre in New York. On March 27, 1934, the *New York Times* wrote that after the end of its Broadway run in late May, the show with its American cast would probably open in—you guessed it—London in June.[12] We know Moore went, because a 1935 news item in the *Oakland Tribune* reported, "Dennie Moore and Edmund Gwenn [her *Sylvia Scarlett* co-star] met first in London with the 'Pursuit of Happiness' troupe."[13] When Florence Moore boarded the Washington in Southampton on July 19, 1934, then, she was going back home after her London engagement in *The Pursuit of Happiness* and she was without a doubt our Dennie Moore.

To sum up my findings: Florence Rita Moore, known as Dennie Moore, was born in New York City on December 30, 1902, to Scotch-Irish, immigrant, working-class parents and grew up in the neighborhood known as Hell's Kitchen in midtown Manhattan with her older brother Joe, the champion Olympic speed skater, and (intermittently) two step-sisters and a stepbrother. I believe she was born in 1902 rather than the year 1903, which she provided herself, because I tend to find that age information provided by parents rather than the actresses themselves tends to be more accurate. Florence Moore's "age at last birthday" when the New York State census was taken on June 1, 1905, was recorded as two years old and she was said to be seven when the U.S. census was taken on April 23, 1910. Had she been born in 1903, she would only have been one and six respectively. A birth date of December 30, 1902, is also corroborated by the Social Security Death Index.[14] My guess is that Moore, beyond making herself a year younger than she really was, pretended to be born on New Year's Eve, as that was more glamorous and interesting than December 30th.

I have also found that Florence "Dennie" Moore was an actress from an early age and only had six years of schooling.[15] She is consistently identified as single in all the primary documents I have located with the exception of the 1934 ship's manifest, where she is listed as "M" for married, but that could be an error.[16] She once made it into Walter Winchell's column, where he wrote that she "had a sprained heart since she discovered her new wooer is a groom."[17] During the years covered by my sources (1905–1940), Florence Moore was resident in New York City. Moore's heyday on the stage was the years of the Great Depression, when she appeared in show after show on Broadway with stage legends of the day like Richard Bennett, Patricia Collinge, and Eugenie Leontovich; rising young stars like Jean Arthur, Joan Bennett, Ann Harding, Bob Hope, Miriam Hopkins, Sylvia Sidney, Franchot Tone, and Spencer Tracy; and talented supporting players like Edward Arnold, William Frawley, Sydney Greenstreet, Percy Kilbride, Frank McHugh, Mayo Methot, Natalie Moorhead, Claude Rains, Joseph Schildkraut, Raymond Walburn, and Cora Witherspoon. Many of them would soon be on their way to Hollywood. It was maybe inevitable, then, that Moore herself would give the movies a try. Her time spent in the movie capital in the mid-to-late '30s and early '40s, when she acted in 20 of her total of 22 feature films, must have been limited. I have not found any addresses for her in Los Angeles telephone directories or other primary sources.

This photograph of Scotch-Irish Broadway comedienne Dennie Moore with her screen hubby in *Angel* (Paramount Pictures, 1937), Ernest Cossart, shows all her characteristic features except her red hair. Nearly all her film characters could be described as "daffy" and nearly all were a delight. Her distinctive New York twang contributed substantially to the comic effect of many of her portrayals.

In April 1940, "Florence D. Moore" was living at the Park Lane Hotel on the northeast corner of Park Ave. and 48th St. in New York. She gave her age as 36 and her profession as "entertainer theatrical." She had only worked six weeks in 1939 and earned $1,800, but had an additional source of income beyond her salary.[18] Moore had been working mostly in Hollywood since she left the cast of *Three Men on a Horse* in Chicago to do *Sylvia Scarlett* (G. Cukor) at RKO in August 1935 and had not been in a show on Broadway since 1937.[19] 1939 was her peak year with seven films released, including *The Women* (G. Cukor, MGM) and *Eternally Yours* (T. Garnett, Walter Wanger Prod.). In 1940, though, she would only have two films released: *Saturday's Children* (V. Sherman, Warner Bros.) and *Women in War* (J.H. Auer, Republic). Her brief heyday in Hollywood would soon be over with the release of *Dive Bomber* (M. Curtiz, Warner Bros.) in 1941. She did only two films in later years: *Anna Lucasta* (I. Rapper, Security Pictures, 1949) and *The Model and the Marriage Broker* (G. Cukor, Twentieth Century–Fox, 1951). Moore retired in 1956 after creating the role of Mrs. Van Daan in the successful dramatization of *The Diary of Anne Frank,* directed by Garson Kanin at the Cort Theatre with Susan Strasberg in the title role.

In *Who's Who in Hollywood,* David Ragan wrote in 1977 that Moore "is retired, lives alone at an excellent hotel on Park Avenue, and is in her late 60s (b. 1907). This does not stop her, however, from citing roller skating as one of her pet recreations."[20] Florence Rita "Dennie" Moore died in New York City in February 1978 at the age of 75.[21] By the time of her death, Moore was so forgotten that there was no obituary in the *New York Times,* where Brooks Atkinson once had called her "an uncommonly comic actress."[22]

The Oregon Belle: Ona Munson (1903–55)

I'm going to begin and end with the two things you probably already know about Ona Munson, beyond the fact that she played Belle Watling in *Gone with the Wind*. Hopefully there will be one or two things you don't know about her in between. I have a feeling that, despite *Gone with the Wind* and *The Shanghai Gesture* and *Ghosts* with Nazimova on Broadway, Munson's life was probably more exciting than her work. It may not always have been an easy or a happy life, but even the tone and tenor of her famous suicide note shows an unusual and original frame of mind. Munson was a searching soul. When she finally gave up searching, it was over.

I'm sure you know Ona Munson's real name was Owena Wolcott. It seems to me that if you're going to go to the trouble of making up a new name for yourself, you could probably do better than "Ona Munson." Ona is clearly a contraction of Owena, but where the "Munson" came from, I can't tell you. It may be a garbled version of a fairly common Norwegian surname, which is *Monsen*. Monsen is a traditional patronymic and means "son of Mons," Mons being a first name for boys in Sweden and Norway. As far as I've been able to ascertain, Munson did not have Scandinavian blood in her veins and came by her blonde tresses by way of the peroxide bottle, rather than through an hereditary predisposition.

Having gone to the trouble of finding a new stage name for herself, it was pretty ironic that Munson would spend most of her film career being mixed up with an actress called Osa Massen. Massen, for example, hijacks Munson's entire entry in Alex Barris's book on *Hollywood's Other Women*. He writes: "Osa Massen, as Mother Gin Sling … in *The Shanghai Gesture* (1942), hardly a distinguished film, but worth remembering for the bizarre characters, of whom she was one."[1] Osa Massen was Scandinavian, Danish to be exact, and her real name was Aase Madsen. She was 11 years younger than Munson, but the two women even looked somewhat alike. Massen was active in American films and television between 1939 and 1962 and didn't die till 2006, more than half a century after Munson. I imagine the confusion between them is less of a problem today, though. While a few of us still remember Munson, nobody really remembers Massen.

Owena Wolcott was named for her father Owen Parrett Wolcott. He was born in Nebraska in March 1870, the son of Edgar Wolcott and Christina Carrion Wolcott (also known as Anna or Annie). Owen's father, Munson's paternal grandfather, was born in Michigan in 1844 with a father from Vermont and a mother from Michigan; and Owen's mother, Munson's paternal grandmother, was born in Canada of French Canadian parents and immigrated to the United States in 1865. Owen's parents were married in Calhoun County, Michigan, on February 28, 1867, when both were 22.[2]

On June 27, 1870, only a few months after Owen was born, we find him living with his parents and two-year-older sister Ella on Grand Island in Hall County, Nebraska. His father is a brakeman on the railroad and is worth $2,000 in real estate and $1,000 in his personal estate.[3] Ten years later, the family was living at 306 S. 2nd St. in Marshalltown, Iowa, where Edgar Wolcott was working as an engineer on the Central Iowa Railway (CIRR).[4] Five years later, they were still in Marshalltown and living at 207 S. Center St.[5]

Owen's parents divorced in the second half of the 1880s, which would have been unusual at the time. His father married Josie Andrews in Marshalltown in 1889 and died there in 1897. He and his second wife are buried under an imposing headstone in the town's Riverside Cemetery.[6] Owen's mother married a Mr. Dalson, who died before 1910. Ona's paternal grandmother lived with them in Portland, Oregon, throughout Ona's childhood and teenage years. She died in the 1920s.

By the time Owen Wolcott was 22, that is in 1892, we find him in Los Angeles, where he is living at 416 Bernard St. in what is now known as "Old Chinatown."[7] The following year, Owen met and married a woman who was five years older than him and was either a widow or divorced.[8] Her maiden name was Sally E. Gore and she had been born in Baltimore, Maryland, on November 25, 1865.[9] Sally Gore Wolcott was Ona Munson's mother. In 1896, the Wolcotts lived at 167 N. Spring St. in downtown Los Angeles.[10] By 1900, Owen Wolcott was working as a merchant and the couple lived at 312 21st St.[11] At this point, the census shows, Sally Wolcott had given birth to three children that had all died. One or more of these may have been from her first marriage.

Sally gave birth to her fourth and final child on June 16, 1903. This was Owena Wolcott, known to the world as Ona Munson. Munson would later have a fairly "imprecise" attitude to her own age, but there is no doubt she was born in 1903. The 1910 U.S. census, for example, taken on April 15th, shows she was six at the time.[12] A passenger list for a trip between Le Havre and New York aboard the Normandie that Munson made with her mother in 1936, also gives her birth date as June 16, 1903. The list says she was born in Albany, Oregon, and not Portland, as many sources indicate, and which she gave as her birth place on other occasions.[13] Albany is in Linn County, Oregon, and 70 miles south of Portland.

By 1910, the Wolcotts, including Owen's now 63-year-old, widowed mother, were living at 129½ 12th St. in Portland, Oregon. Owen was working as a real estate salesman.[14] Ten years later, when Owena was 16, the family circle was unchanged and they were still living on 12th St. in Portland, but now at no. 258. Owen Wolcott was still a real estate broker and Sally Wolcott was working as a milliner.[15] Grandma Anna was still with them. Munson would recall how her doting grandmother would read aloud from their deluxe leather-bound copy of *Collier's Biography of Leading American Actresses*.[16] As to Owena's further education, we know she was sent to "Miss Catlin's school" in Portland, "majored in English literature," and was "so clever at dancing she took special instruction in that art."[17]

Owen and Sally's marriage ended in divorce sometime in the 1920s. In 1930, we find Owen Wolcott still living in Portland, but now with his second wife, Jesse Failing Wolcott, his 26-year-old stepson, and his 84-year-old mother-in-law.[18] Owen Parrett Wolcott died in 1937, during one of the slow periods in his daughter's career.[19]

By the time her parents divorced, Owena Wolcott had left home. She made her stage debut in 1922 on the Keith-Orpheum Vaudeville Circuit in *The Manly Revue.*[20] In the second half of the 1920s, she worked steadily in musical comedy on tour and on Broadway. She made her New York debut replacing Louise Groody in the lead of *No, No, Nanette* at the Globe Theatre on May 24, 1926.[21] By the early 1930s, she was also playing dramatic roles, for example in Rachel Crothers's comedy *As Husbands Go* in San Francisco in August 1931 and Sidney Howard's drama *The Silver Cord* in Hollywood in October 1931.[22]

Munson made her film debut in 1928 in an uncredited role in the silent comedy *The Head of the Family* (J.C. Boyle, Gotham Prod.), which was produced on the East coast while she was starring as Mary Brennan in the hit musical comedy *Manhattan Mary* at the Apollo

Ona Munson spent many of the years "between marriages" living with her divorced mother Sally Gore Wolcott (aka Sally Munson), seen here with her in a photograph from 1941. Sally was 37 when Ona was born and had already buried three children. She lived to bury Ona as well, dying at the age of 90, ten months after her daughter's 1955 suicide.

Theatre.[23] Munson had two periods in her career when she concentrated on screen work: 1930–31, which resulted in three films for Warner Bros., including *Five Star Final* (M. LeRoy, 1931); and her "major" phase, indeed the height of her acting career, the period 1938–42, with releases like *Gone with the Wind, Lady from Louisiana,* and *The Shanghai Gesture.* She also did scattered films after that until 1947.

Between these periods in the movies, Munson made a return to Broadway in two very different stage productions: the Mark Reed farce *Petticoat Fever* (1935) at the Ritz Theatre and a revival of Ibsen's *Ghosts* (1935–36) at the Empire Theatre. In *Ghosts,* the legendary Russian actress Alla Nazimova took the lead as Mrs. Alving and also directed, while Munson was cast as the family maid Regine, who is involved in a flirtation with Mrs. Alving's son, Oswald (Harry Ellerbe).[24] At 32, Munson was a pretty mature Regine, but she received "excellent notices."[25]

Between her two marriages, Munson shared her home with her mother Sally, who had not remarried after her divorce. In 1936, they travelled to Europe together and were living in a large apartment building at 111 E. 56th St. in New York between Park Ave. and Lexington.[26] In 1940, mother and daughter were living in a $150 a month apartment in the Villa Carlotta. Munson reported to the census enumerator that she had earned more than $5,000 for 26 weeks' work as an actress in radio and motion pictures in 1939, which may well have been the peak year of her career. Munson claimed to be 29 when she was really 36, while her mother, who was now calling herself "Sally Munson," claimed to be 69, when she was 74.[27] Their many film folk neighbors in the building that year included character actress Nana Bryant, producer Lester Cowan and his wife Ann, composer Aaron Copland, character actress Nydia Westman and her sister Lolita, and actress Fay Wray Saunders and her daughter Susan. Munson was still living at Villa Carlotta in 1942, but two years later we find her living in a small but pleasant house on a corner lot at 2340 Canyon Dr. She kept this house for several years, even after she married for the second and last time.[28]

Munson had a varied love life. On July 16, 1926, a month after her 23rd birthday, she married fellow Broadway musical comedy star Eddie Buzzell.[29] Edward N. Buzzell was the son of Russian Jewish immigrants with their own real estate business and was born in Brooklyn, New York, on November 13, 1895. He was only 5'1" tall and was described as being of medium build and having brown eyes and black hair in his World War I draft registration.[30] Like Munson, Buzzell got his start in vaudeville and went to Hollywood in 1929 to reprise one of his starring roles on Broadway. Munson went with him. He started directing films in 1931, the year he and Munson divorced, and is best known for the Marx Brothers films *At the Circus* (1939) and *Go West* (1940).[31] Buzzell never hit the big time, but was active as a director until 1961 and died in 1985, 30 years after his ex-wife. Munson's own comment on this brief, early marriage some years later was "My first and only husband was an actor and a nice guy, but never again."[32]

After her divorce, Hollywood historian Gavin Lambert records that Munson had an affair with German émigré director Ernst Lubitsch, who was also between marriages. Lubitsch was "fond but unfaithful" and the relationship ended when he married former agent Vivian Gaye.[33] Lambert also tells us in his biography of Nazimova, that 32-year-old Munson had a brief affair with the 56-year-old Russian star during rehearsals for *Ghosts* on Broadway in late 1935. Lambert heard from Harry Ellerbe, who played Oswald, "by the time *Ghosts* opened at the Empire, her affair with Nazimova was over. He didn't know the reason, but it seems

I love this portrait of Ona Munson in her signature role as Mother Gin Sling in *The Shanghai Gesture* (Arnold Pressburger Films, 1941). Munson had a chameleon quality on the screen, which meant that she was often unrecognizable from role to role, even without being heavily disguised by costumes, wigs, and make-up.

the glue that bound Ona to her lovers, although powerful, usually came unstuck before very long." They parted amicably.[34]

In 1940, Munson had an affair with the writer Mercedes de Acosta, who was ten years her senior and could count Nazimova, Isadora Duncan, Garbo, and Eva Le Gallienne among her lovers by the time she and Munson embarked on their relationship. According to Axel Madsen, they had originally met seven years before, when Munson was living with Lubitsch and Acosta was involved with Garbo.[35] Acosta was living at the beach in 1940 and according to her autobiography, Munson "loved to come down to the sea" and "often came to spend the night when she was shooting at Republic Studios."[36] The 1940 U.S. census shows that Acosta was living in a rented house at 740 Amalfi Dr. in Pacific Palisades, while her voter registration shows that she also lived at 785 Napoli Dr. that year, which is a more modest, hilltop house, just north of Acosta's Amalfi Dr. home.[37] Munson wrote to Acosta in 1940, "I long to hold you in my arms and pour my love into you." Six years later, she recalled having shared "the deepest spiritual moment at that life brings to human beings" with Acosta.[38]

There was nothing, of course, about Acosta and Munson in the press. Her engagement to "former Federal Housing Administrator" Stewart McDonald, on the other hand, became public knowledge in September 1941, when she collapsed on the set of *The Shanghai Gesture* and requested that he be notified.[39] Her engagement ring was described as "a handsome sapphire-and-platinum ring, the stone being a large, square cut one, mined more than 100 years ago in Persia, and of the most desirable 'corn-flower' color." Munson stated in an interview, "When I marry Mr. McDonald, I shall leave the stage forever."[40] Later that month, Munson said she was not marrying McDonald after all, though he was "a fine man."[41] They were still seeing each other in 1942, but never married.[42]

Munson did not marry again until she was 46. On Friday, January 20, 1950, she was wed for the second and final time at the Beverly Hills home of Igor Stravinsky.[43] Her husband was the "neoromantic" painter and set designer for opera and ballet Eugene Berman. Berman had been born in St. Petersburg on November 4, 1899, and immigrated to the United States in 1935, after spending the years since the Russian Revolution with his family in Paris.[44] He was naturalized in 1944 and was then living at Villa Carlotta in Los Angeles.[45] The groom was 50 and this was his first marriage.

It was Berman who found Munson dead of an overdose of sleeping pills at one in the afternoon on Friday, February 11, 1955. In a handwritten note on her own embossed stationery, Munson wrote, "This is the only way I know how to be free again." She asked that her body be cremated and closed the unaddressed letter with the now famous words: "Please don't follow me." Medical examiner Louis Winkelman determined death as having occurred between four and six in the morning. Berman had left the apartment at ten a.m. to take care of some business. He returned to pick up his wife in the afternoon, as they had made a date to go shopping together. He found her in her nightgown, as he told the police, "exactly as though she were asleep, with her beautiful hair streaming over the side of the bed." According to Berman, his wife had been ill for the past four years and "had been taking medicine constantly and often had been unable to sleep" after a serious operation. They had only lived in their apartment in the enormous and luxurious Belnord building at 225 W. 86th St. in New York for a month.[46]

Funeral services for Munson were held on Monday, February 14th at the Frank E. Campbell funeral home at Madison Ave. and 81st St.[47] She was laid to rest in Ferncliffe Cemetery and Mausoleum in Hartsdale, Westchester County, New York, where her husband joined her 18 years later.[48] He died of internal hemorrhages at his home in Rome on December 12, 1972.[49] Sally E. Gore Wolcott, aka Sally Munson, was fated to survive all her four children. She died in Los Angeles on December 21, 1955, not long after her 90th birthday and ten months after her daughter's death.[50]

In *Actresses of a Certain Character*, I profiled Hattie McDaniel, Butterfly McQueen, Laura Hope Crews, and Jane Darwell. With the inclusion of Munson, Barbara O'Neil, and Isabel Jewell in this volume, I have now written about all the major character actresses in *Gone with the Wind* (V. Fleming, Selznick Int. Pictures/MGM, 1939). I think Munson really came into her own as Belle Watling. She was everything the role required and left an indelible impression. *Five Star Final* excepted, though, the rest of Munson's "oeuvre" leaves me cold. Naturally, I haven't seen everything and there may be undiscovered gems still to be found, but I feel that beyond *GWTW* Munson was given few opportunities to shine and never really found her place in the film industry. Even the films I have seen, don't stick in the mind. I can't remember a thing about *Lady from Louisiana* (B. Vorhaus, Republic, 1941), for example, one of Munson's few starring vehicles, apart from the fact that it was a period costume drama and must have been a blatant attempt to cash in on her identification with Belle Watling and *GWTW*. Munson frequently complained in the wake of her success as Belle, that she was only getting roles as "'good bad' girls" in period costume dramas.[51]

Even *The Shanghai Gesture* (J. von Sternberg, Arnold Pressburger Films, 1941) doesn't really hold up to closer scrutiny, however much the Von Sternberg fans hold it in high regard. Gavin Lambert suggests Munson was miscast as Mother Gin Sling.[52] Honestly, with that get-up most of her performance is being given by the wardrobe, hair, and make-up departments anyway. I don't think it made much difference whose face and body they went to work on. It was a bit like Agnes Moorehead in *The Lost Moment* (1947). With all the rubber she has on her face playing a 105-year-old woman, her part of the performance might as well be radio.

Munson was not recognizable in *The Shanghai Gesture*. That was one of the film's gimmicks. Yet she was a chameleon on the big screen in other roles as well, which is not often the case with women who are as beautiful as she was. One of the things that fascinates me about her is how different she looks in her various films. I'm sure, for example, that had I not bought the DVD of *Five Star Final* with the express purpose of seeing her in it, I could easily have sat through the entire film without the slightest idea who I was watching. As the news-hungry, bottle-blonde reporter Kitty Carmody, hired by editor Edward G. Robinson to cover a sensational story, she is totally unrecognizable as the same Ona Munson who eight years later played Belle Watling.

Journalists and fans that met her in real life also commented on how differently she looked from what they expected. "Curiously," Louis Raymond wrote in the early 1940s, "Ona Munson looks less like a hussy, less like a scarlet woman than anyone you can imagine this side of Hawthorne or Hemingway."[53] Another journalist commented at about the same time: "Ona Munson in person is perplexingly unrecognizable."[54] She was also described as "a make-up man's delight—that is, an actress who can make any disguise come alive."[55]

It was often the case with character actresses that they disappeared into their character, but Munson was no typical character actress. Like so many other tough blonde broads in the 1930s—Grace George, Isabel Jewell, Veda Ann Borg, Glenda Farrell, Claire Trevor—Munson was an "also ran" in the star sweepstakes, who ended up playing "other" women of various kinds more or less by default. Maybe she never really wanted to be a movie star in the first place. I imagine she mainly wanted to be taken seriously as an actress. When asked in an interview in 1942 whether she was sorry she had ended up as a character actress, she responded: "Parts like these really give you a chance to act and that is what I'm interested in."[56]

When she died, Ona Munson had not been seen on the big screen in nearly eight years. Her last film was *The Red House* (D. Daves, Sol Lesser Prod.) in 1947. Rarely in Hollywood has so fine a cast been so ill used. By the early 1950s, Munson had gotten herself into a professional rut, being cast in the least interesting of the female supporting roles, if she was working at all. She made her TV debut in 1952 as Mrs. Frazier in *Craig's Wife*. In her last show on Broadway that same year, a revival of Katharine Dayton and George S. Kaufman's satire of gender and other politics in the nation's capitol, *First Lady*, she was cast as Sophy Prescott. You're good if you can tell me what those minor characters contributed to their respective plays without looking it up. Munson only did three episodes of television before she died. *First Lady* at the City Center was a flop and closed after five performances.

Sunset Boulevard: Mary Nash (1884–1976)

Behind the ornate, wrought-iron gates of a sprawling, Spanish-style mansion on Sunset Blvd., a lonely old woman of 92 died in her sleep on Friday, December 3, 1976. The neighbors said she had been a star once, on Broadway. She had also been in the movies. They seemed to recall that she had been in that 1930s film with all the nasty women in it and some Shirley Temple pictures—and wasn't she the mother in *Philadelphia Story* with Katharine Hepburn and Cary Grant? Someone could remember her fighting with Edward Arnold over a fur coat, which ended up getting thrown out the window; and tarted up like an old drag queen in one of those ridiculous Maria Montez pictures from the '40s. Those who had lived in her Brentwood neighborhood the longest could recall that she once lived with her elderly mother and a sister who looked a lot like her and who was also an actress. That was all a very long time ago. Surely, it must have been 25 or 30 years since they passed away and left her all alone behind the high walls and swaying palm trees of her estate.

Mary Nash was born Mary Ryan in Troy, New York, on August 15, 1884.[1] Her mother was Ellen Frances McNamara Ryan, born in the state of New York in 1863 of parents born in Ireland.[2] Mary's biological father James H. Ryan was a lawyer,[3] but he "died when she was very young"[4] and the father figure she grew up with was her mother's second husband, Philip F. Nash. Nash was born in Pennsylvania in 1859 and was also of Irish extraction. He was once upon a time a drama critic for the *Philadelphia Evening Star* and had worked for B.F. Keith and F.F. Proctor as a theater manager. Nash married the widowed Ellen Ryan about 1900 and the census enumerator caught up with the newlyweds living in a rented home at 276 Hamilton St. in Albany, New York, on June 11, 1900. Besides Philip and Ellen Nash and a maid, the household consisted of Mary H. Ryan, born in August 1884, and Florence A. Ryan, born in October 1886.[5] More specifically, Mary's younger sister Florence was born in Troy, New York, on October 2, 1886.[6]

In a business full of actresses with a less than veracious attitude to their age, Mary Nash was surely one of the most creative. She came to her success relatively late and naturally wanted to extend her "sell by" date as long as possible. In the 1920 U.S. census, she claimed to be 22, when she was actually 36.[7] I think the limit of plausibility, though, was reached in the 1930 census, when 45-year-old Mary and 43-year-old Florence both claimed to be 30. Their mother was also in on the game, claiming to be 50 when she was actually 66![8] Long live the power of mind over matter.

It was not long after the U.S. census was taken in 1900 that the Nash family moved to

New York City. Mary had received her elementary school education at the Convent of St. Anne in Montreal and attended what was to become the American Academy of Dramatic Arts in New York in 1900.[9] Philip Nash started working for the newly organized United Booking Office, which booked vaudeville acts. During the last dozen years of his life, he was the company's executive manager.[10] Nash was thus uniquely positioned to help further his stepdaughters' theatrical ambitions and the results were not long in coming.

By the time of the 1910 census, both the Ryan girls had taken their stepfather's surname and made their New York debuts as Mary Nash and Florence Nash. Again, we find the family in the U.S. census, this time living in a rented apartment at 1700 Broadway (between 53rd and 54th St.), a building that has since been replaced by an enormous, modern-day skyscraper. Both young women have listed as their profession "actress theater," their stepfather "manager theater," and their mother "none." They have a 26-year-old, live-in maid. Funnily enough, all their ages are rendered correctly here expect Philip Nash's, who claimed to be 52 when he was actually 61.[11] Four years later, the Nash family was living further up on Broadway at no. 2020, a building which is still extant on the corner of 69th St. It was here on the afternoon of October 4, 1914, two days after Florence's 28th birthday, that Philip Nash died suddenly of acute indigestion.[12]

Not every New York actress could be Ethel Barrymore or Katharine Cornell. In the first three decades of the 20th century, there was a firmament full of smaller stars on Broadway with their own specialties and their own followings. Mary Nash was one of those stars. She was known as an "emotional actress" and as such was mostly seen in melodramas and in "emotional, tense and wearing roles."[13]

Unlike her sister, Florence Nash was primarily a comedienne and made her Broadway debut at the Lyceum Theatre in 1907 in a comedy called *The Boys of Company "B."* Her biggest hits on Broadway were *Within the Law* (1912–13), where she supported Jane Cowl; and *Merton of the Movies* (1922) with Glenn Hunter as Merton Gill at the Cort Theatre. She was called "America's greatest comedienne" at that time and "was distinguished by the unusual beauty and expressiveness of her hands."[14] Florence acted with her sister in Rachel Crothers's *A Lady's Virtue* at the Bijou Theatre in 1925–26, which was a success; and in a revival of *The Two Orphans* at the Cosmopolitan Theatre in 1926, which was not. Her last show on Broadway was in 1930.

In 1916, Florence Nash had the good fortune to inherit a substantial part of her rich maternal uncle John Mack's estate, which was valued at close to one million dollars.[15] This may explain why she worked relatively little as an actress compared to her older sister and for all intents and purposes retired in 1930. She only acted in three films: one silent film in 1914 and two sound features in the 1930s. You can get a good impression of her comedic talents, though, in *The Women* (G. Cukor, MGM, 1939), where she plays the witty writer and confirmed bachelorette Nancy Blake and acts as a kind of chorus and commentator on the state of moral decay and decadence she sees all around her. Ironically, it was a better part than her sister got in any of her two dozen films.

Two decisive moments in Mary Nash's early career were being cast in support of John and Ethel Barrymore in James M. Barrie's *Alice Sit-by-the-Fire*, Nash's Broadway debut in 1905, and being hand-picked by the dandified, eccentric, and immensely successful playwright Clyde Fitch to be in his final play, *The City*.[16] By the time it opened at the Lyric Theatre on December 21, 1909, Fitch had been dead several months. Big Broadway producers like Charles

Frohman and David Belasco also had faith in Mary Nash, as did William A. Brady, who cast her in the play that made her a star in 1916, when she was 32: *The Man Who Came Back.* It ran for 457 performances at Brady's own Playhouse Theatre at 137 W. 48th St., followed by a two-year tour all over the United States.[17] After doing *I.O.U.* and *The Big Chance* on Broadway, Nash took *The Man Who Came Back* to London in April of 1920, "where she scored one of the biggest successes attained there by an American actress."[18]

Between the productions of *I.O.U.* and *The Big Chance* an event occurred of greater rarity in Nash's life than a "mere" stage success: she married for the first and only time. On October 5, 1918, she had opened in a stage version of the sensational silent film *The Cheat* (1915) entitled *I.O.U.* The play was not well received and closed after ten performances at the Belmont Theatre, but it did lead to a collaboration of another kind with her male co-star, the dashing French actor José Ruben. Ruben had made his Broadway debut as Batouche in the original production of the hit play *The Garden of Allah* at the Century Theatre in 1911. Since then, he had been associated with the Washington Square Players and played Oswald in their production of Ibsen's *Ghosts* (1916–17), supported Mrs. Fiske in *Madame Sand* (1917–18), and played Romeo to Laurette Taylor's Juliet in *Laurette Taylor in Scenes from Shakespeare* (1918), that is before *I.O.U.*

Nash and Ruben were married on Saturday, October 19, 1918, at the Church of the Blessed Sacrament at 152 W. 71st St., just around the corner from the Nash home on Broadway and 69th.[19] Born in Paris of French parents, Ruben had been in the United States for eight years and appears to have arrived in New York aboard *La Provence* from Le Havre on November 10, 1910. If this José Rubens [sic], last resident in Paris, France, is indeed our José Ruben, which there is reason to believe, then there is either an error in the passenger list or he was born in 1884, the same year as his wife, and not 1886 or 1888 or 1890, as he claimed at various times.[20]

José Ruben was a strikingly handsome in the Rudolf Valentino mode with soulful eyes, sensuous lips and his dark hair slicked back and parted at the side.[21] He wasn't very tall, though, only 5'6", according to his World War II draft registration, which also records that he weighed 170 pounds, had hazel eyes and a "light" complexion.[22] I don't suppose the ethnically Irish and no doubt racially conscious Nash would have married him otherwise. No doubt as a result of his marriage, Ruben became a naturalized American citizen on March 18, 1919.[23]

Nash and Ruben received better notices for their next collaboration, the melodrama *Thy Name Is Woman,* that Ruben staged himself at the Playhouse. The story of a love triangle between a tanner, who is mostly a smuggler (Ruben); his beautiful, young wife (Nash); and a young, handsome soldier (Curtis Cooksey) in the Spanish Pyrannees, this production saw Nash doing "some of the finest acting of her interesting career" and proving once again "she is an emotional actress of great ability." Ruben, the same critic observed, "climbs to new heights in this difficult role."[24]

In late 1921, Nash and Ruben were included in a survey of actor couples to disprove the assertion "stage marriages are always unhappy and doomed to end in divorce."[25] Their marriage did end in divorce, though, probably not long after their last play together, *The Two Orphans* (1926), in which Florence Nash also acted. When Ruben returned to New York from France on August 20, 1926, he is listed as divorced in the passenger list of the SS *Aquitania.*[26] Even when the census was taken in 1920, after they had only been married a year and a half, they were not living together. Mary Nash is listed as living with her mother and sister, a cook and a maid.[27]

Maybe the Nash-Ruben liaison was just a marriage of convenience. Maybe they thought it would help their careers, if they teamed up. Maybe they had dreams of becoming a new Lunt and Fontanne with an Irish-Latin twist. Maybe Ruben just wanted to become an American citizen. Who knows? As an actor, director, and writer on Broadway, José Ruben certainly lasted longer than his ex-wife. His last show was the Howard Lindsay and Russel Crouse comedy *The Great Sebastian* with Lunt and Fontanne in 1956. He remarried late in life and died on April 26, 1969.[28]

Nash's own particular star continued to shine brightly on Broadway throughout the 1920s, with starring roles and commercial successes in the new plays *Thy Name Is Woman* (1920–21), *The Lady* (1923–24), *A Lady's Virtue* (1925–26), and *The Command to Love* (1927–28) and a revival of the farce *Captain Applejack* (1921–22). The early 1930s, though, were not propitious for Nash on Broadway, which may have been instrumental in convincing her to try her luck in Hollywood instead. One disaster was *Isadora*, a biographical play about Isadora Duncan's love life, which had to be renamed *Diana* after members of the Duncan family objected. After that debacle, Nash was known as "the theatre woman who pretended to be Isadora Duncan."[29] Her next play, *A Woman Denied* (1931), was described as "calamitous."[30] Nash's efforts as Barbara, who is "living in sin" in Paris with an artist, garnered her some of the worst reviews of her career. One critic wrote: "Miss Mary Nash is deplorable. She makes faces, she poses, she acts upstage, she acts downstage, she acts as no actress has any cause to carry on. In all my critical career I am yet to see a female titleholder indulge in such curious behavior."[31]

In all fairness, though, I must also quote an accolade Nash once received from the legendary Alexander Woollcott in his lengthy review of her starring vehicle *The Lady* at the Empire Theatre in 1923: "You have seen her in her various impersonations, now gentle, now frenzied, and nearly always sincere. But it seems from her performance in 'The Lady' that she is also good at song and dancing. She counterfeits sad old ladies as expertly as she does gay young ones. She looks as well in the cerise tights of a music-hall artiste as she does in the drab livery of an aged flower woman."[32] He continues in a similarly laudatory vein.

Nash's last show on Broadway was *The Devil Passes*, written and staged by Benn W. Levy at the Selwyn Theatre in 1932, with a stellar cast, including Eric Blore, Ernest Cossart, Cecilia Loftus, Basil Rathbone (who had starred with Nash in *The Command to Love*), Ernest Thesiger, and Diana Wynyard. The comedy was a success, but for the first time in many years Nash was relegated to a supporting role with the 26-year-old Wynyard starring in her Broadway debut. With nothing else happening on Broadway (Florence's final show had been back in 1930), the entire Nash household pulled up stakes and moved to Los Angeles in early 1934. Mary Nash went straight into production on her first sound film, *Uncertain Lady* (K. Freund, 1934) at Universal in February.[33] The three women bought a beautiful Spanish Revival mansion at 12831 Sunset Blvd. in Brentwood, just west of Bristol Circle. Built in 1930, it is still standing and covers 8,300 square feet with seven bedrooms and eight bathrooms.[34] It was valued at $50,000 in 1940 and sold for $2,3 million in 1995.

To the extent that Nash is remembered today, my readers probably associate her mainly with the two pictures where she was mean to Shirley Temple, *Heidi* (A. Dwan, Twentieth Century–Fox, 1937) and *The Little Princess* (W. Lang, Twentieth Century–Fox, 1939), and the role of Katharine Hepburn's long-suffering, patrician mother in *Philadelphia Story* (G. Cukor, MGM, 1940). My particular Mary Nash favorites are two other, entirely different films. *The Rains Came* (C. Brown, Twentieth Century–Fox, 1939) deserves to be better known, as it has a stellar cast, great special effects (for the time), beautiful filming (including gorgeous opening credits), Tyrone Power looking stunning as "pale copper Apollo," and Myrna Loy in one of her rare, later "bad girl" roles. The film stars Power as Major Rama Safti, a medical doctor and heir to the throne of the mythical Indian state of Ranchipur, Loy as the bored, cosseted, and sensual Lady Edwina Esketh, and throws in George Brent for good measure, but the only name above the title is that of producer Darryl F. Zanuck.

Nash is billed eighth as Power's furiously devoted nurse and assistant, Miss McDaid, who is jealous of Loy and hates her for having the potential to distract Power from his larger purposes in life. Nash's character is Scotch and spinsterish and she carries off both with aplomb. She is described by Brent as "a great and good woman." Miss McDaid doesn't have many lines, but is often seen in the background and makes the most of every opportunity. She narrowly escapes the flooding with the help of Power, is present at the Maharajah's deathbed and not long after puts Loy to work scrubbing floors and doing menial labor, because she has no training as a nurse. Nash's moment of truth comes when she realizes that Loy is dying of the plague that has struck after the torrential rains, ensuing flooding, and a major earthquake. Loy, who is volunteering at the Ranchipur State Hospital as a nurse's aide, has written a list with the number of sick patients in one column and the dying in the other. Nash resolutely crosses out 25 and writes 26. Then realizing her own vengeance and lack of humanity, she breaks down. Not a word is spoken and this is the last time we see her.

Left: **Mary Nash as the cruel headmistress Amanda Minchin in *The Little Princess* (Twentieth Century–Fox Film Corp., 1939), one of the two films for which she is best known, because she was mean to Shirley Temple. The other was *Heidi* (1937).** ***Right:*** **Mary Nash looks very glamorous in this photograph from her early film *Uncertain Lady* (Universal Pictures, 1934), in which she played a sophisticated friend of the heroine. Genevieve Tobin and Edward Everett Horton starred.**

Paul Roen calls *Cobra Woman* (R. Siodmak, Universal, 1944) "the quintessential Maria Montez vehicle" in his classic study *High Camp*.[35] Here Nash plays the queen of the Island of Cobra, but appears to have considerably less power than her granddaughter, the evil High Priestess Naja, played in a double role by the irrepressible Montez. The old queen has Naja's twin sister Tollea (Montez again) bought back to Cobra by force and we first see her explaining how they are related, why Tollea was taken away from the island as a child, and what needs to be done now to save the inhabitants from Naja's bothersome human sacrifices. "Fear has made our people religious fanatics," she says to her granddaughter.

The queen continues to have an explanatory role in the film. In Nash's final scene, she goes to sleep after her birthday in her suitably queenly canopy bed, sighing: "Each birthday finds life's candle burning a little lower." She adds, "My heart is deep in shadow, cold shadow." Soon after, she is stabbed to death by Naja's left-hand man and fiancé Martok (Edgar Barrier), but does not expire until she has given him a piece of her mind. What makes this role so memorable and laughable is not least of all the costume department's efforts to make Nash look suitably queenly and exotic. How to describe her get-up? Well, I guess you have to see it to believe it. There's a lot of gauzy veils involved, but the effect is not quite that of Salomé.

Nash's mother, Ellen Frances McNamara Ryan Nash, died in Los Angeles on December 6, 1946, four days after her 83rd birthday.[36] *Swell Guy* (F. Tuttle, Universal), a drama starring Sunny Tufts and Ann Blyth, premiered the day before her death. It would turn out to be Mary Nash's last film. Not long after their mother's death, Florence was diagnosed with heart disease. She died of a heart attack in Los Angeles on April 2, 1950, at the age of 63.[37] The death of the two individuals that meant the most to her within such a short space of time must have been emotionally devastating to Nash. No doubt she was amply provided for both with her own fortune and what she inherited from her mother and sister, so she simply retired at the age of 62. It would be a long retirement. When Mary Nash died on December 3, 1976, with "no immediate survivors,"[38] she had been out of the public eye for 30 years.

Tragic Second: Barbara O'Neil (1910–80)

We've all heard of comic second leads in films, those wisecracking best friends of the heroine or secretaries of the hero played by the likes of Una Merkel, Eve Arden, and Patsy Kelly. Had there been a parallel "tragic second lead" category, I would put forward Barbara O'Neil as an eminent example. Just as there were certain second-rank male stars, like Ralph Bellamy or Richard Carlson, who never got the girl, there were also female "also rans" who never got the guy. Or if they had him, they were bound to lose him. Again, such a player was Barbara O'Neil. So she didn't get the guy and she ended badly and the story really wasn't about her; or as Alex Barris summed it up in 1975: "Coldly attractive, Miss O'Neil made a full-time living losing men to bigger stars in the 1930s and 1940s."[1]

O'Neil is best known, of course, as Scarlett O'Hara's angelic mother in *Gone with the Wind* (V. Fleming, Selznick International, 1939). In truth, this signature role is not very large and limited to the first part of the film, though Ellen O'Hara's spirit remains throughout the epic. We first encounter her returning from assisting at the birth of Emmy Slattery's and Yankee overseer Wilkerson's illegitimate child, who has "thankfully," according to Mrs. O'Hara, promptly died. Her daughters and Mammy resent the time and energy she spends on "poor no account white trash." Mrs. O'Hara insists that Wilkerson be fired and does it herself, while her husband and daughters attend the big party at Ten Oaks without her. Because she is not in this long party sequence, her role is smaller than it might have been. Mammy's part, for example, is much larger, as arguably are those of Aunt Pittypat and even Prissy. We never see Ellen O'Hara alive again after she suggests to Scarlett that she go and spend some time with Aunt Pittypat in Atlanta in the wake of her broken heart over Ashley's betrothal to Melanie and her own short-lived marriage to Melanie's brother Charles Hamilton.

To put it bluntly, O'Neil didn't always photograph well. She was a handsome woman, but she had the kind of "mature" beauty that often made her look older than her years on the big screen. This can explain why she could be credibly cast as the mother of Vivien Leigh, an actress who was only a year younger than her, after Lillian Gish, who was born in 1893, had declined to play the role.[2] When the lighting people and the cinematographer were focusing on the female star, as was often the case, O'Neil suffered as a result. *The Toy Wife* (R. Thorpe, MGM, 1938) is an illuminating example. Luise Rainer never looked better, while O'Neil looks tired and unwell.

On the other hand, Bette Davis said several times that in *All This, and Heaven Too* (A. Litvak, Warner Bros., 1940) O'Neil looked *too* attractive for credibility in her role as the insanely jealous duchess.[3] Why would the duke choose the frumpy governess over her? Well, stranger things have happened and Davis was primarily revealing her own insecurities here. Even though Hollywood did give O'Neil the glamour treatment as the Duchesse de Pralin, I can't see that it detracts from the character's basic and deep unattractiveness. The duchess remains one of O'Neil's finest screen performances.

I would also single out her later performances in *Whirlpool* and *Angel Face* as being among her most interesting. A decade after *GWTW*, in *Whirlpool* (O. Preminger, Twentieth Century–Fox, 1949) she plays an "aging siren," who has gotten herself involved with the hypnotist and quack doctor played by José Ferrer, resulting in his extortion of $60,000 of her daughter's inheritance. When she threatens to reveal all, he strangles her in her home and frames heroine Gene Tierney for the murder. A point is made of O'Neil being old enough to be Tierney's mother (she was ten years older in real life) and having faded charms. She looks quite striking, though her skin is bad, with a distinctive white, "Bride of Frankenstein" stripe in her otherwise jet black hair.

In addition to women on the edge, O'Neil also had the inside track on playing WASP ice princesses, albeit of a certain age. Her debut role as Helen Morrison in *Stella Dallas* (K. Vidor, Samuel Goldwyn, 1937) was such a one. Her function was clearly to establish through the implied contrast, that Barbara Stanwyck's title character is simply impossible, but also a lot more heart-warming and sympathetic than Miss Morrison. In *Angel Face* (O. Preminger, RKO, 1952), O'Neil plays rich stepmother of "Angel Face" Jean Simmons, who Simmons wants her lover Robert Mitchum to believe is evil and controlling. O'Neil plays her with aplomb, clearly suggesting she is a strong, dominant woman, but also sensible and not unsympathetic. At 42, she looks older and is every bit as matronly, sophisticated, and elegant as the part requires.

O'Neil was to the patrician manner born and had a social background unlike any actress I've written about. Even though this volume includes daughters of the upper middle class and even from "Blue Book" families, like Margaret Hamilton of the Cleveland Hamiltons and Sara Haden of the Galveston Hadens, O'Neil came from a family of even greater social eminence and wealth, based in a major American city. As the daughter of lumber baron David Nicholson O'Neil (1874–1947) and the granddaughter of banker Joseph O'Neil (1817–93), Miss O'Neil had never needed to work a day in her life. The city in which her family made their fortune and rose to social prominence was St. Louis, Missouri, where she was born the youngest of four children on July 17, 1910.[4] Young Barbara was raised in increasingly more substantial homes, until the family moved away for good in 1920, first to Berkeley, California, and later to an estate in Cos Cob near Greenwich, Connecticut.[5]

Barbara O'Neil's mother, once described as "a famous suffragette in St. Louis,"[6] was born Barbara Blackman (1880–1963), the daughter of Missouri-born leather merchant and later secretary of the McClean Medical Co., George Blackman (1854–1931), and Ohio-born portrait painter Carrie Horton Blackman (1856–1935).[7] David O'Neil and Barbara Blackman married in 1903 and their first child, David Blackman O'Neil, known as "Little David," was born the following year.[8] Barbara would never know her eldest brother, as he died in 1908. He lies buried with his father and namesake in the enormous, Gothic-inspired O'Neil family grave in St. Louis's Calvary Cemetery.[9]

Barbara's paternal grandfather died before she was born, but her paternal grandmother Catherine Horan O'Neil (1839–1925) lived throughout Barbara's childhood and early teens

Barbara O'Neil is visited on the set of her debut film, *Stella Dallas* (Samuel Goldwyn Co., 1937), by her father, the wealthy businessman and poet David O'Neil. The O'Neils were a St. Louis family, but Barbara's branch relocated to Greenwich, Connecticut, when she was still young. When playing poised, privileged women of the upper-classes, like Helen Morrison in *Stella Dallas*, O'Neil was to the manner born.

in the stately house she had built for her family in 1897 at 4470 Westminster Place.[10] This mansion still stands just a stone's throw from the apartment building on McPherson Ave. where Agnes Moorehead lived with her Presbyterian minister father, mother, and younger sister from 1912 till 1919. The O'Neil residence also lies only a block away from the building at the corner of Westminister Pl. and Walton Ave. in which Barbara O'Neil's contemporary Tennessee Williams lived from the age of ten and that he famously used as a setting for *The Glass Menagerie*.

The O'Neils were not all business. Far from it. They were passionately devoted to the arts. According to one source, Barbara was "granddaughter of the O'Neils who founded the Artists Guild" in St. Louis.[11] Apart from Barbara's thespian talents, there was her father, who was a fine though not prolific poet with one poetry collection to his name, *The Cabinet of Jade* (1918). Indeed, David O'Neil "retired from business at an early age to travel and write poetry."[12] Barbara's eldest surviving brother, George Blackman O'Neil (1906–88), was a teacher in private schools. Her other brother, Horton O'Neil (1907–97), was a stage designer and architect who between 1938 and 1940 actually built a 500-seat marble amphitheater in

Barbara O'Neil as the troubled Duchesse de Praslin and Fritz Lieber as her spiritual guide Abbé Gallard in *All This, and Heaven Too* (Warner Bros., 1940), which starred Bette Davis and Charles Boyer. Davis repeatedly voiced the opinion that O'Neil had been too attractive to make it seem likely that her husband, played by Boyer, would stray, but surely O'Neil's outstanding performance as the maniacal and paranoid duchess made the reasons for the duke's disaffection abundantly clear.

the woods behind the family home in Connecticut.[13] He married a dancer, Madelyn Hyde Phillips (1912–2011), in 1940, the same year Barbara embarked on her ill-conceived and short-lived marriage to wonder boy producer Josh Logan (1908–88).[14] Horton and Madelyn O'Neil's son, yet another David O'Neil, is an award-winning architect. Barbara's cousin George Rowley O'Neil (1896–1940) was a playwright and screenwriter in Hollywood in the 1930s, known for the play *American Dream*, produced by the Theatre Guild on Broadway in 1933; and for films like *Only Yesterday*, the 1935 version of *Magnificent Obsession*, and *Intermezzo*. Barbara had a small part in his play *Mother Lode* at the Cort Theatre in December 1934, but it didn't run.

O'Neil came to films via the fabled University Players—where she worked with soon-to-be stars Margaret Sullavan, Henry Fonda, and James Stewart and met her future husband Joshua Logan—and a smattering of small roles on Broadway between 1932 and 1936.[15] According to Springer and Hamilton, Sidney Kingsley's drama *Ten Millions Ghosts* with Orson Welles "brought her to the attention of Hollywood."[16] O'Neil's career on the big screen began with *Stella Dallas* (King Vidor, Samuel Goldwyn), which started filming in early April 1937. Though her American film career lasted till *A Nun's Story* (F. Zinnemann, Warner Bros.) in 1959, O'Neil only acted in 16 films during her 22 years back and forth between Hollywood and Connecticut. She returned several times to Broadway in the 1940s and '50s, had successes in plays like Lillian Hellman's *The Searching Wind* (1944–45), *Deep Are the Roots* (1945–46), and *Affairs of State* (1950–52), and retired from the stage in 1960.[17] In later life, she divided her time between her home in Carmel and the family estate Lia Fáil in Cos Cob. It was at Lia Fáil on September 3, 1980, that O'Neil died suddenly from a heart attack as she was preparing to go to the beach.[18] She was buried with her mother and other members of the Blackman family in Pacific Grove's scenic El Carmelo Cemetery. Today there is no marker on her wind-blown grave overlooking the Pacific Ocean.[19]

"The woman you love to hate": Rafaela Ottiano (1888–1942)

On April 30, 1899, two Italian girls arrived in New York aboard the *Kaiser Wilhelm II* from Genoa. They had travelled in steerage with a family friend, 38-year-old musician Pasquale Sammartino, on the long journey from the home they had left forever, the village of Viggiano in the province of Potenza in southern Italy.[1] Rafaela was 11 and could read and write; Francesca was nine and could not. Their lives in their new country would follow very different paths. Rafaela would grow up to act on the silver screen with some of the biggest stars of the 20th century: Greta Garbo, Mae West, Jean Harlow, Norma Shearer, Shirley Temple. Francesca, also known as Frances, would marry a factory worker, stay at home and raise a family, and never leave the East Boston neighborhood where both sisters spent their first 15 years in the United States.

In unraveling the facts of Rafaela Ottiano's early life, the first mystery I had to solve was that there was reliable but contradictory evidence indicating that she was born in Boston in 1886 and in Italy in 1888. On August 1, 1886, musician Antonio Ottiano and his wife Maddalena had a daughter named Rafaela at 27 Eastern Ave., which is now Congress St. and lies in the Financial District of downtown Boston.[2] Other equally reliable sources, though, such as the 1900 U.S. census, indicated that their daughter Rafaela (who was also known as Loti in 1900 and Ellen in 1910) had been born in Italy in 1888.[3] How was it possible that the same person could be born in two different places in two different years? Well, obviously it wasn't the same person. The Rafaela Ottiano who would grow up to become the most successful Italian American character actress in Hollywood was in fact born in Italy in November 1888. It turns out she was named for an older sister, born in Boston in 1886, who had died in infancy and who had been named for her paternal grandmother, Rafaela Bellizia Ottiano.[4]

Her first child's death may have influenced Maddalena Ottiano's decision to return to Italy and have her next child there. In addition to "our" Rafaela, her younger sister Maria Francesca was also born in the old country. That was in September 1889.[5] Then, it appears, the girls' parents returned to the United States, leaving their young daughters in the care of their family in Viggiano. The entire Ottiano family was not reunited in the United States until the girls' arrival there in April 1899. By that time, the family also consisted of three sons: Pasquale (Patsie), born at 4 Baker's Alley in the North End of Boston on October 23, 1892[6]; James, born in Boston, probably at 210 North St., on March 3, 1896[7]; and Augustino (August), born at 196 Maverick St. in Boston's East End on August 30, 1898.[8]

Like Blanche Yurka, Rafaela Ottiano came from a Continental European, first-generation immigrant family where there was never a lot of money, but where culture and the arts were valued. Her father, Antonio Ottiano, born in Italy on February 25, 1859,[9] worked all his life as a professional musician and her brothers Pasquale and James also became musicians. Rafaela's mother, Maddalena Polcari Ottiano, born in Italy in February 1869,[10] was a homemaker. Maddalena immigrated in 1880 and Antonio came to the United States four years later.[11] The couple married in 1885, when Maddalena was only 16.[12]

Like the Yurkas, the Ottianos were ultimately able to buy their own home, which became the center of family life and where the unmarried children remained until their parents' death. The Ottiano home was at 196 Maverick St. in Boston's East End. A three-story, bow-fronted row house, it stands out from the other, wooden houses on the street by virtue of its brown brick façade. It must have given them a sense of pride, accomplishment, and security two own such a substantial building. The family is duly recorded living in Maverick St. both in the 1900 and the 1910 U.S. census . In 1900, Antonio is listed as a naturalized alien (that happened in 1896),[13] while his wife and children are not. He is supporting the family as a musician. In 1910, he is working as a musician in a band. Rafaela, who is now 21, is working as a saleslady in dry goods. Her sister Frances is a milliner in dry goods, and Patsie is a musician in a hotel.[14]

The marriage of youngest daughter Frances in 1913 was the last happy time for the united Ottiano family at 196 Maverick St., just as was the case for the Yurka family in New York when Blanche's brother Charles married in 1915. Frances was 22 and married Carmen De Stefano, a 23-year-old shoe cutter, who lived just a few doors down at 186 Maverick St.[15] Though James and August would marry later, Frances was the only one of the five siblings to marry while their parents were alive. Rafaela and Pasquale never married.

On October 15, 1914, Maddalena Ottiano died at home at the age of 46, two days after suffering a cerebral hemorrhage.[16] She was buried in what would become the family grave in a relatively new Italian Catholic burial ground called St. Michael Cemetery, which had opened in 1907 and lay next to the much larger Forest Hills Cemetery in South Boston.[17] Her husband Antonio joined her there only a year later, when he died age 56 from a hemorrhage in Massachusetts General Hospital after being hospitalized for one month and eight days for an abscess on his lung.[18]

Sometime between 1917 and 1920, the family home on Maverick St. was sold. Frances and Carmen took their part of the profits and bought a house at 382 Lovell St. in East Boston, valued at $6,000 in 1930, where they would live for more many years and raised two children, Vincent (b. 1913) and Madeline (b. 1915). The three unmarried Ottiano brothers moved in with them, as did their uncle and aunt, Nelson and Jennie Mottola.[19]

Rafaela, as the oldest child and an unmarried daughter, had remained dutifully at home helping to support the family and take care of the house until she was 26 years old. The death of both her parents, wrenching as it no doubt was, meant that she could finally strike out alone and realize her dream of becoming an actress. She took her little nest egg and headed for New York City. We find her there in 1920, when she was living at 49 W. 37th St. in the home of an architect and his wife with five other "roomers," including an actress and a couple of artists. To support herself, she worked as a saleslady in a department store. She claimed to have immigrated in 1910, for whatever reason, and was not yet a naturalized alien. She also claimed to be 25, when she was in fact 31.[20] The reason for that is evident.

Ottiano got her first big break in 1924, when she was cast as Mrs. Lovett in the original

New York production of the two-act melodrama *Sweeney Todd* by George Dibdin-Pitt. It was her first Broadway show and ran for 67 performances at the Frazee Theatre at 254 W. 42nd St., which closed as long ago as 1930, but wasn't torn down until 1997. It is fascinating to think that Ottiano was the "foremother" of all the later Mrs. Lovetts on Broadway: Angela Lansbury, Dorothy Loudon, Beth Fowler, Patti LuPone, and Judy Kaye.

Ottiano had a face well suited to portraying the less benevolent aspects of human nature. A review of the 1933 film *Bondage* (A. Santell, Fox) noted, for example, "You will enjoy hating Rafaela Ottiano, who is a thoroughly detestable paragon of virtue as the superintendent of the charity home."[21] UP columnist Alexander Kahn wrote in a 1940 article, "If you hate Rafaela Ottiano, one of the screen's better villainesses, you are not alone in your attitude, for Miss Ottiano hates herself." According to Kahn, she didn't watch the daily rushes and sometimes waited up to six months to see one of her own films. As a "dyed-in-the-wool full-time menace," Kahn adds, "she can put more menace in a simple act like winding a clock, than most other actors could while strangling a child." Quite a comparison! Ottiano herself was philosophical about her typecasting: "I feel that if I am destined to be a menace I might as well do a workmanlike job of it."[22] Charles G. Sampas called her "the woman you love to hate."[23] More recently, Springer and Hamilton have called her "an indelible part of the thirties, although usually in roles that required only atmosphere. Even so you were always aware of her—black eyes snapping, head cocked—somewhere in the background."[24]

When Ottiano was 39, she was handpicked by Mae West to play her female adversary in her hit show *Diamond Lil*. The play opened at the Royale Theatre on April 9, 1928, and ran for 176 performances, before going on the road.[25] West probably did more for Ottiano's career than anyone else, as she did for Libby Taylor, who is also profiled in this book. Ottiano was the only supporting player from the Broadway cast of *Diamond Lil* who was asked to reprise her role when it came time to film the play as *She Done Him Wrong* at Paramount on November 25, 1932.[26]

It wasn't *Diamond Lil* that gave Ottiano her first sound film role, though, but another more prestigious and even more popular Broadway show.[27] W.A. Drake's English adaptation of Vicki Baum's German play *Menschen in Hotel* opened as *Grand Hotel* at the National Theatre on November 13, 1930, and became an unexpectedly tremendous hit. Ottiano was cast as Suzanne, the devoted French maid of a troubled prima ballerina. The play ran for over a year and closed in December 1931 after 459 performances.[28] As soon as the show closed on Broadway, production on the film version started at MGM under the direction of Edmund Goulding and lasted until February 18, 1932.[29] This would have been the point when Ottiano pulled up stakes and left New York for good. She was 43 and would spend the final decade of her life in Los Angeles, where she lived in an apartment at 439 N. Van Ness Ave. in Oakwood.[30]

For me the two quintessential Ottiano performances on film are in *Grand Hotel* and *She Done Him Wrong*. Though she acted in a total of 41 sound features, you can more or less keep the rest. This may sound arrogant and dismissive, but putting things this way is meant rather to indicate how much I love her in my two favorite Ottiano films. I freely admit I haven't seen her in *The Devil-Doll* (T. Browning, MGM, 1936), where as Malita she responds gleefully to the discovery that her husband has invented a "miniaturization" process by saying: "We'll make the whole small!"[31] She was singled out in the reviews as one of the actors who provided "unforgettable characterizations to the finished product": "Rafaela Ottiano, with her mad eyes, will linger long in your memory."[32] But then there's a limit to how excited I can get about

Practically the entire credited cast of *The Last Gentleman* (Twentieth Century Pictures, 1934) is seen in this still, the "gentleman" of the title being George Arliss (front row center) and the rest being (from back row left) Rafaela Ottiano, Donald Meek, Janet Beecher, Edna May Oliver, Ralph Morgan, Charlotte Henry, and Frank Albertson.

a film starring that old curmudgeon Lionel Barrymore (even in drag) and annoyingly fresh-faced Maureen O'Sullivan. And who ever heard of an *MGM* horror film? That's about as anomalous in the 1930s as a drawing room comedy from Republic or a western from Paramount.

In *Grand Hotel,* though, there can be no discussion: Ottiano is simply grand. She must have been equally so when she played the role on stage. Out of the entire 21-member Broadway cast, she was the only actor asked to reprise her role in the film version. And it wasn't that there was no competition for this relatively modest role among the already established actors in Hollywood. It was reported "when 'Grand Hotel' was filmed, Miss [Hedda] Hopper, along with Marie Dressler and a host of other important film players, offered their services for supporting roles. Both Miss Dressler and Miss Hopper went so far as to volunteer to play the role of Garbo's maid."[33]

It must have been a strange experience to be doing the same play she'd done so many times at the Royale Theater, only now she was performing with entirely different actors. The temperamental and troubled prima ballerina Grusinskaya was being played by Garbo, not Eugenie Leontovich. Grusinskaya's manager Witte had changed names to Pimenov and was being played by the fey Ferdinand Gottschalk. Albert Van Dekker was no longer the Baron. John Barrymore was. Even the "inspectress," the housekeeper responsible for the maids on Grusinskaya's floor of the hotel, was different. German immigrant Greta Meyer had taken over that role from Florence Pendleton.

As for Ottiano's role as Grusinskaya's maid, the only thing that had changed was her name. Suzanne was now Suzette. Dressed in somber black with a white lace bib collar, she has an emaciated, almost Oriental face, which is entirely devoid of make-up and scrubbed so clean her cheeks shine. This is a typical mirror role, where she responds to all the many changes in her mistress's mood. Suzette's one goal in life is to get her employer to the theater and onto the stage, so that she will fulfill her contract and share her talent with the world.

As a film, *She Done Him Wrong* is, of course, ham to Grand Hotel's filet mignon, but it is delicious ham. This is Mae West at her very best and like other stars secure in their own wattage, she fully understands the value of having equally luminous supporting players. As Russian Rita, Ottiano and her decorative "assistant" Serge (Gilbert Roland) are in league with the shady saloon-keeper and local "boss," Gus Jordan (Noah Beery). Rita tries to sow

After her breakthrough role in *She Done Him Wrong* with Mae West, Rafaela Ottiano was seldom allowed to look as glamorous as she did as mercenary Madame Makanoff in *Victory* (Paramount Pictures, 1940), starring Fredric March and Betty Field. The role was unusual in several ways in that she played the manager of an all-female orchestra in Java.

the seeds of dissension between him and his live-in lover, songstress and star Lady Lou (Mae West), from the first. "Rita never talks," she says, "but are you sure about Lou."

As Rita, Ottiano speaks with a vaguely Continental European accent or maybe what was supposed to pass for a Russian accent in Hollywood at the time. Rita hadn't been Russian at all in the stage play, but Brazilian. In order not to alienate the South American movie audience, her nationality had to be changed, as was that of Serge, who was originally called Juàrez.[34] The response of the Russian audience in 1934 was naturally not a concern. Rita is beautifully dressed in both her scenes courtesy of Edith Head working on her own as a costume designer for the first time.[35] When we first see Rita, she wears an amazing hat with a bird in flight on the brim. In her second scene, she is in a décolleté, "Gay Nineties" style dress with spaghetti straps and is surprisingly buxom and attractive. This is how I want to remember Rafaela Ottiano: as a cosmopolitan, sophisticated, and charismatic actress and woman, who unfortunately was given too few chances to show how "talented" she really was.

Ottiano was one of only six actresses who tested for the coveted role of Pilar in *For Whom the Bell Tolls*. It finally went to Greek actress Katina Paxinou, who won an Academy Award for her performance.[36] The film was in production at Paramount when Ottiano died of intestinal cancer on Saturday, August 15, 1942.[37] The *New York Times* noted in Ottiano's obituary that she died "at the East Boston home of her late parents."[38] This was not strictly speaking true, as no member of the Ottiano family had lived in the Maverick St. house in 25 years. I think we can assume, though, that Ottiano died at her sister's house at 382 Lubec St., where Frances De Stefano and her husband Carmen lived alone now that their children had left home.[39]

The Lubec St. house, which the De Stefanos owned and which was a simple dwelling valued at only $2,000 in 1940, is gone now, but it was in the same East Boston neighborhood where Rafaela and Frances grew up. Their brother Pasquale was dead, but James was still living in Boston and still unmarried at 46. Youngest brother Augustine had married, though, and was working as a telephone installer earning $2,800 a year. In 1940, he and his wife Angeline (both 41) and their children Jacqueline (16) and John (13) were living in a pleasant, $6,500 home they owned at 27 Pierrepont Rd. in Winchester, Massachusetts, on the northern outskirts of Boston.[40] Rafaela's siblings had all stayed close to home, then, and lived very different lives from their glamorous and talented older sister. Yet Rafaela, too, came home in the end. When she was gone at 53, they laid her to rest with her parents and brother in St. Michael Cemetery.[41]

The Eternal Landlady: Tempe Pigott (1869–1962)

Tempe Pigott is probably the most obscure character actress I have ever profiled. Tempe Pigott is probably the one I know least about. Yet not many actors born in the 1860s (or later for that matter) can boast of a film career spanning 30 years. Not many can say they worked with Erich von Stroheim, Joseph von Sternberg, *and* Douglas Sirk. And though I haven't found much, I can at least claim to have uncovered two important new facts about Tempe Pigott, namely that she wasn't born in London and she wasn't born in 1884.

So who cares about Tempe Pigott today? No one cares much, I suppose, except me. You'll find nary a mention of her in any film book, even those devoted to supporting players. David Ragan is an exception, but his *Who's Who in Hollywood 1900–1976* is distinguished both by the numeric extensiveness of its coverage and the necessary brevity of most of its entries. In the case of Pigott, Ragan manages to sum up her entire film career in one sentence: "In Cooper's *Seven Days' Leave* ('30), she was a delight as the gin-guzzling old Cockney charwoman; played Cockneys in many in the '30s: *Cavalcade, One More River, Limehouse Blues, Becky Sharp, The Devil Is a Woman,* etc."[1] Hal Erickson of the *All Movie Guide* also has a word for her, noting that she "was generally cast as gabby cockneys. In the talkie era, she could usually be found playing drunken harridans or slovenly slum landladies."[2]

Tempe Pigott is here to represent the legions of elderly women who eked out some kind of a living in the autumn and winter of their lives as extras, "under fives," and minor character actresses in Hollywood. I love them all, the Nora Cecils and May Beattys and Mary Gordons and Dorothy Vaughans and the hundreds whose names I don't even know. I celebrate every last life-lined, weary-eyed, steely-haired, saggy-breasted, bent-backed one of them and Tempe Pigott will be their representative. Tempe, who was usually far from temperate, on the screen at least, and whose name makes her sound like a character in one of Dickens's novels. It just had to be the name she was born with. No actress would willingly *choose* to be called Tempe Pigott.

In films there has to be someone to open the door and say that so and so is calling or make a drunken spectacle of themselves in a pub or gossip about the neighbors or shout imprecations in crowd scenes or press the heroine for the rent. Such an actress was Tempe Pigott. In *Vanessa: Her Love Story* (W.K. Howard, MGM, 1935), a silly drama dominated by Helen Hayes's surprisingly large nose and May Robson being got up like an octogenarian Princess Leia, Pigott plays a market woman selling cakes at a fair, who makes a catty remark to the heroine. In the *A Tale of Two Cities* (J. Conway, MGM, 1935), she has her moment in the elaborate crowd scene by the guillotine at the end of the film, as an elderly working-class woman with long grey hair busily knitting as she watches the executions. Her one line is: "I've dropped a stitch. Cursed aristocrats."

Pigott plays a gossip who stirs up trouble in *Man of the Forest* (H. Hathaway, Paramount, 1933), a minor western crime drama, in which devoted live-in housekeeper Blanche Friderici ends up shooting her employer Noah Beery dead when he scorns her for Verna Hillie. One of my favorite drunk scenes is the result of the combined efforts of veteran actresses Zeffie Tilbury, Ethel Griffies, and Pigott in a sordid tavern at the opening of *Werewolf of London* (S. Walker, Universal, 1935). Tilbury and Griffies are rival landladies gorging on tripe and hitting each other over the head, while Pigott demands "two drinks for two ladies" at the bar. Both these ladies are apparently her. She comments sagely, as Wolfman Henry Hull asks the barman about rooms to let, that he apparently "has troubles."

In *A Study in Scarlet* (E.L. Marin, K.B.S. Prod., 1933), her Mrs. Hudson was no more than a door opener and announcer of new arrivals to see Sherlock Holmes (Reginald Owen). More than anything, Pigott was the quintessential Hollywood landlady, who was usually there to keep tabs on the protagonist and provide information for the audience and the other characters. In *Born to Love* (P.L. Stein, RKO Pathé, 1931), she was middling sympathetic for once,

Character actresses often provided their own costumes. This get-up, then, was probably Tempe Pigott's own idea for the landlady she plays in *Born to Love* (RKO Pathé Pictures, 1931). Her beautiful tenant is Constance Bennett.

as Constance Bennett's landlady concerned about her finding a job. Her tiny part as Leslie Howard's landlady, who lets his "fatal attraction" Bette Davis into his room in the first sound version of *Of Human Bondage* (J. Cromwell, Radio Pictures, 1934), was also par for the course. In *The Rage of Paris* (H. Koster, Universal, 1938), she was given a little more play as an unusually disheveled landlady, who locks Danielle Darrieux out of her room for not paying her rent before fellow lodger Helen Broderick intervenes.

Out of Pigott's 70 known feature film appearances, 40 were uncredited. In *Bride of Frankenstein* (1935) and *One Foot in Heaven* (1941), her scenes were deleted.[3] Pigott made her film debut in *The Great Impersonation* (G. Melford, Famous-Players Lasky) in 1921. She acted in a dozen more silent films during the next seven years, the most important and memorable being Erich von Stroheim's opus magnum *Greed* (Metro-Goldwyn, 1924), based on Frank Norris's novel *McTeague* and starring Zasu Pitts as the increasingly avaricious Trina and Gibson Gowland as her miner turned dentist husband McTeague. Pigott was billed fifth as McTeague's mother and is first shown in one of the opening scenes of the film sweltering in a hot kitchen in the rustic cabin home she shares with her son near the gold mines in 1908. Mother McTeague is fired up with ambition on her son's behalf. They part ways when he

Tempe Pigott's inebriation in this opening scene from a tavern in *Werewolf of London* (Universal Pictures, 1935) doesn't prevent her from perceiving that werewolf Henry Hull has "troubles." The bartender is James May.

goes to San Francisco to become a dentist on her instigation. The last we see of her, she is standing in the road after he is gone eating her handkerchief.[4]

All my talk of Pigott's obscurity is not to suggest that there weren't some passably good opportunities and recognizable roles among her 30 credits. *Greed* is one example. In fact, all her silent film appearances were in named, credited roles, including playing Mrs. Sedley in the 1923 version of *Vanity Fair* (H. Ballin, Hugo Ballin Prod., 1923) and the "duenna" in *The Black Pirate* (A. Parker, Elton Corp., 1926) with Douglas Fairbanks and Billie Dove. Pigott got a rare mention in the press in a news item about the latter "stupendous production," when the *Lima News* pointed out that, in addition to Dove, "Tempe Pigott is the only other feminine player in the picture."[5]

Her heyday, though, was the first half of the 1930s, peaking in 1935 with roles in ten new releases. Pigott made her sound film debut in the drama *Seven Days Leave* (R. Wallace, Paramount, 1930), starring Gary Cooper and Beryl Mercer. She plays one of Mercer's three cronies and with Nora Cecil and Daisy Belmore "supply the humor."[6] My two favorite Pigott performances, though, are from *Dr. Jekyll and Mr. Hyde* and *Cavalcade*. In the first, innovative sound version of Robert Louis Stevenson's classic *Dr. Jekyll and Mr. Hyde* (R. Mamoulian, Paramount, 1931), with a break-out performance by Fredric March in the title role and an excellent one from Miriam Hopkins as lady of easy virtue Ivy Pearson, Pigott plays Ivy's garrulous Cockney landlady Mrs. Hawkins. Mrs. Hawkins detests Mr. Hyde and does what she can to derail Ivy's affair with him. She's fears her lover with end up killing Ivy and Mrs. Hawkins finds her when he has.

In Noël Coward's *Cavalcade* (F. Lloyd, Fox Film, 1933), which is about changes in British society during and after World War I, as reflected by the upper-class Marryot family and their upwardly mobile servants, Pigott is omnipresent in the "downstairs" scenes as the maid Una O'Connor's aged mother. Mrs. Snapper is an inveterate pessimist, who always has a maudlin story on hand to undercut any hope or optimism that might manifest itself. The cook, played by Beryl Mercer in one of three films with Pigott, remarks after one of her stories: "You're a nice, cheerful body, I must say." Mrs. Snapper is often seen looking after her baby granddaughter Fanny in her carriage and one of her favorite lines is "Well, I mustn't grumble."

Pigott was also given better than usual parts in *Oliver Twist* and *The Devil Is a Woman*. She is seen in the first scene of *Oliver Twist* (W.J. Cowen, Monogram, 1933) as the midwife Mrs. Corney, who gives the newborn hero briefly to his dying mother and then steals her wedding ring while making a halfhearted attempt to revive the dead woman. This results in her being considered an unwed mother and Oliver being sent to an orphanage. Mrs. Corney shows up again destitute 36 minutes into the film, when she sells the stolen ring to Fagin. Pigott also had a named, credited role in *The Devil Is a Woman* (Joseph von Sternberg, Paramount, 1935), as Tuerta, the one-eyed owner of the theater where Concha Perez (Marlene Dietrich) performs, who sells Concha's contract to Don Pasqual (Lionel Atwill). According to Concha: "She really only has one eye and with that eye she can only see money."

The most important source for factual information about Tempe Pigott is the 1940 U.S. census. This is the only census in which I've been able to find her, though she was living in the United States from at least 1918. It provides us with a unique insight into her life at a difficult point in her career. The enumerator, who was called Harry Burnett, called at 1824 N. Cherokee Ave., in the heart of Hollywood, on April 5, 1940. This fairly modest house on the right side of the street going north between Hollywood Blvd. and Franklin Ave. was valued at $7,000 and was owned by Mary T. Tracy, a 54-year-old, unmarried woman born in Turkey with no occupation or income.[7] Living with her in the house, Miss Tracy had three lodgers. One was a 56-year-old widow from Scotland, who worked as a clerk in a housing project. Another was a 33-year-old, unmarried radio actress from California. The third was our heroine.

In the census, Tempe Pigott is described as being 56 years old and was born in England. She has had four years of high school and is an "alien," that is to say not an American citizen. She is a widow. Her profession is listed as "actress stage + film." She worked nine weeks in 1939, for which she was paid $500. She has no other sources of income than her wages. Pigott has been unemployed for 13 weeks so far that year, which is practically all of 1940 up until the time of the census[8]; this despite getting a small part in the remake of *Waterloo Bridge* (M. LeRoy, MGM), playing a Cockney in the air raid shelter scene with Vivien Leigh and Robert Taylor. We know, too, that things only got a little better for her in the remainder of 1940. *Waterloo Bridge* was released on May 17th. Her part was small, but it was a quality picture with a stellar cast from a major studio. More importantly, she got work on two more quality films that year: *Arise, My Love* (M. Leisen, 1940) at Paramount and *Shining Victory* (I. Rapper, 1941) at Warner Bros.

As I've already hinted, despite her claims in the census, Tempe Pigott was not born in England in 1884. Pigott was born in Auburn, Queensland, Australia, a tiny hamlet northeast of Brisbane, in 1869. I know this thanks to a passenger list for a trip aboard the SS *Monterey* from Sydney, Australia, to Los Angeles, California, in March 1937. There we find an actress called Tempe Pigott, who is 68 years old, was born in "Auburn, Q'land," and is an Australian citizen. We know this information is reliable, because it is based on Pigott's Australian passport issued in Sydney on February 20, 1937, as recorded in the ship's manifest.[9] With such a rare name and the right profession, too, this has got to be our girl.

How to explain this discrepancy? Well, actresses lying about their age is the oldest story in the world. As this book amply shows, character actresses were no different. I think I can guess what happened. In 1918, the year Pigott was in her only recorded show on Broadway,[10] or possibly earlier, she moved to the United States, either directly from her native Australia or after an interim stay in England. With no public record of her birth in her new homeland, the temptation to make herself just a little younger in order to prolong her possibility for gainful employment must have been irresistible. Pigott didn't do things by halves. She decided to make herself not two, not five, not ten, but *15* years younger and arrived on the American shores with a birth year of 1884 rather than 1869. She stuck to her story till the bitter end, it seems, which explains that she is recorded with a birth date of February 2, 1884, in the California Death Index.[11]

After a few years of fairly steady employment in the first half of the 1930s, Pigott decided to make a return trip to her native Australia. She was 78 and probably felt this was her last chance. Whether there was the promise of work or it was simply a sentimental journey, she did not stay in the land of her birth. On March 5, 1937, she boarded the SS *Monterey* to return to Los Angeles, where she would remain for the rest of her life. Film work became scarcer upon her return. During the last dozen years of her film career, she only acted in 19 films. All but two were uncredited roles.

In her final film and back at her old studio Universal, *Thunder on the Hill* (D. Sirk, 1951). Pigott is briefly seen as a nameless villager seeking refuge at a convent during a flood. When a fellow refugee, Mr. Smithson (Patrick O'Moore), expresses concern about his pregnant wife to heroine and nun, Sister Mary Bonaventure (Claudette Colbert), and the hope that she will be present when his wife gives birth, Pigott is standing next to him and says one unintelligible line, which has something to do with Mrs. Smithson (Queenie Leonard), her baby, and the murderess who is sharing their roof. She looks very old and has her grey hair braided and tied up in a twist at the back. Pigott was 82 and never acted again.

Tempe Pigott died in Woodland Hills, Los Angeles on October 6, 1962, at the age of 93.[12] Woodland Hills is the site of the Motion Picture Country Home and Hospital, which was founded in the 1940s to care for elderly film industry workers who needed health care and a place to live in their old age. We can only hope that a hard-working and faithful film actress found a well-deserved and safe harbor at the end of her long life.

A Woman's Face: Anita Sharp-Bolster (1895–1985)

It seems to me there is always ambivalence in dealing with actresses like Anita Sharp-Bolster. On the one hand, you don't want to focus exclusively on how unusual or unattractive, in conventional terms, they looked, while at the same time realizing that their appearance probably had a substantial influence on their acting careers, severely limiting the range and types of roles they were offered, but at the same time being a primary reason why they got some types of jobs in the first place. I feel much the same doubts about derogative terms like "hatchet-face," "termagant," "battle-axe," or "shrew," that are only applied to women, while at the same time recognizing that there are some individual women, on the screen at least, for whom these terms may be appropriate. It is all too easy to uncritically and even unconsciously adopt the more openly misogynistic language practices of the period in which these actresses lived, while at the same time there is a need to recognize the stereotypes of women that existed in the popular culture of the day. Maybe terms like "termagant" or "battle-axe" even need to be reclaimed and "owned" on behalf of these now long gone actresses, as their individual and perfectly legitimate niche in the film industry and as a survival strategy or a form of rebellion among the uncontrolled and uncontrollable characters they portrayed so vividly on the screen.

So let me begin then, by shooing the elephant out of the room by saying that Anita Sharp-Bolster was blessed with an unconventional, even decidedly odd appearance and that she built a career on portraying the types of odd, quirky, "flat," and usually minor characters where that appearance could be put to maximum effect. The same could be said of Margaret Hamilton and Una O'Connor, of course, though they had a wider range than Sharp-Bolster and more high-profile careers, and also of her fellow players in the "third tier" of the character actress hierarchy, like Nora Cecil, Minerva Urecal, Almira Sessions, and Eily Malyon.

It is interesting to see the extent to which Sharp-Bolster was viewed as a good alternative if producers couldn't get Hamilton or O'Connor. In August 1951, for example, Sharp-Bolster was brought in to replace O'Connor as a "conventional shrew house-wife" in the comedy *A Case of Scotch* at the Westport Country Playhouse in Connecticut, because of trouble with Equity. After nearly a week's rehearsal, "it was discovered Miss O'Connor is listed at Equity as an 'alien' actress."[1] Sharp-Bolster had probably obtained American citizenship by marriage. In August 1952, Sharp-Bolster played the Wicked Witch of the West in a stage musical version of *The Wizard of Oz* at the State Fair Auditorium in Dallas, Texas, as the fifth show of the "State Fair Musical" season.[2] O'Connor was a fellow Irishwoman, but 15 years older than Sharp-Bolster, while Hamilton was born in Cleveland in 1902.

Even her name was a comical contradiction in terms. After all, bolsters are anything but sharp. Anita Sharp-Bolster (known as Anita Bolster until 1955) was born in County Cork, Ireland on August 28, 1895, into an "ancient Irish family," whose genealogy apparently is written up in *Burke's Peerage*.[3] Her father was "a gentleman farmer who raised some of the best horse stock in England." As a result, his daughter Anita became an excellent rider, who frequently participated in "point to point" races in her native Ireland.[4]

Sharp-Bolster joined the famous Abbey Players in Dublin "at an early age," according to one source.[5] Sources differ, though, on whether she made her stage debut with the Abbey Players in a play called *The Mineral Workers*, with the Hamilton and Dean repertory company in Scotland and Wales, or in Oscar Wilde's *An Ideal Husband*.[6] Later, she appeared in London as a "witty monologist at the leading cafés," such as the Café Anglais, Ciro's, and the Trocadero.[7] In London, she also performed in such plays as *Cautious Campbell, This Monkey Business, Time, Gentleman Please, Night Must Fall, The Dog Beneath the Skin,* and *Out of the Picture*.[8] She toured England with the Compton Company of Players.[9]

What is more unexpected is that Sharp-Bolster was a "remarkable nurse," as the result of having worked as one both during the Irish Rebellion and World War I. She also volunteered as a nurse on the Loyalist side during the Spanish Civil War and "was under shell fire for months."[10]

We know she was not a stranger to film work by the time she came to the United States. She made her film debut in England at the tail end of the silent screen era, symptomatically playing a cleaner in a drama starring Madeleine Carroll called *What Money Can Buy* (E. Greenwood, Gaumont British Picture Corp., 1928). Two more silents and six sound features followed in England, before she immigrated to the United States in 1938.[11] She spent the first 42 years of her long life in her native Ireland and in England and the last 47 in America.

Sharp-Bolster's first stop in her adopted country was New York City. She did four shows on Broadway: two hits and two misses. Her debut show, *Where There's a Will*, which opened at the John Golden Theatre on January 17, 1939, was one of the misses. Producer Edward Stirling had written the English adaptation based on a French comedy by Sacha Guitry, *Le Nouveau Testament*, about adultery, illegitimacy, and other marital complications and containing a quite extraordinary series of coincidences.[12] Stirling also directed the show and played the lead as Dr. Jean Marcelin. Jessie Royce Landis played his equally wayward wife and Sharp-Bolster a certain Mademoiselle Morot, who seems unlikely to have been involved in all the sexual intrigue. At any rate, the play only lasted seven performances.[13]

A little over a year later, Sharp-Bolster had another stab at Broadway and this time with greater success. *Lady in Waiting* by Margery Sharp was based on her novel *The Nutmeg Tree* about Julia Packett, an English chorus girl during World War I, who when her officer husband goes off to war gives up her child to his family to be raised as a lady and who years later gets a call from that same daughter to help her "when her marriage plans are interfered with."[14] The lead was played by Gladys George and Sharp-Bolster played the role of the Packett maid and family factotum, Griffin. This was George's first show in New York since her huge success in *Personal Appearance* in 1934–35, which was later made into the film *Go West, Young Man* with Mae West in the lead. George had been in Hollywood herself during the intervening years, where she just missed stardom and became instead the "doyenne" of hard-bitten, bottle blondes, who usually didn't get the guy.

Lady in Waiting opened at the Martin Beck Theatre on March 27, 1940, and ran for 87 performances.[15] Brooks Atkinson liked the play, though he thought it had little to offer beyond "the blonde phenomenon" Gladys George's "breezy vitality" that "keeps everything lively." Bolster was mentioned among several members of the supporting cast, who "run through other stock parts as briskly as possible."[16] There is a terrific drawing of George and Sharp-Bolster by Al Hirschfeld from this show, which captures perfectly the, dare I say, sharp visual impact of Bolster's imposing profile, erect bearing, and lean body. MGM made an exasperating film version of *Lady in Waiting* as *Julia Misbehaves* in 1948 with Greer Garson in the lead. Sharp-Bolster's part was cut from the film, which was considerably changed from the original play to create a "love interest" both for Garson and her screen daughter Elizabeth Taylor.

During the run of *Lady in Waiting* in New York, Bolster was also working in radio. She was mentioned in the column "On the Air Waves" in April 1940, as being "among the new voices seeking a place in American radio." According to the report, she had been "augmenting her stage appearances with an occasional dramatic microphoning as a cockney miss" and traced her radio experience to the BBC.[17]

We next pick of the trail of Sharp-Bolster on the West coast. In August 1941, we find her playing Miss Preen in *The Man Who Came to Dinner* at the Pasadena Playhouse. Miss Preen, you will recall, is the disgruntled nurse played so memorably by Mary Wickes in the 1942 film version, who has to try to dole out "tender loving care" to a most reluctant patient, radio personality and arbiter of taste Sheridan Whiteside (Monty Woolley in the film). According to the review in the *San Marino Tribune*, "A whole paragraph could be devoted to praising the work of Anita Bolster as poor, insulted Miss Preen of the nursing profession." Sheridan Whiteside in this production was played by Gilmor Brown.[18]

It may indeed have been this popular revival at the Playhouse that got Hollywood producers to sit up and take notice of the new arrival and ultimately cast her in her first American film. Production on *Saboteur*, starring Priscilla Lane and Robert Cummings and directed by Alfred Hitchcock, who may well have known Sharp-Bolster from London, started at Universal Studios on December 17, 1941.[19] In one of the most startling and unusual debut roles imaginable, Sharp-Bolster was cast as a bearded lady in a traveling circus. "Unable to find a real-life bearded lady," wrote the *Oakland Tribune*, Hitchcock hired Sharp-Bolster and had "make-up expert Jack Pierce create a beard for her."[20]

We meet her hirsute character Esmeralda when Cummings and Lane try to stow away on the circus tour bus, as it winds its way slowly through the desert en route to its next destination. Esmeralda casts the deciding vote when the troupe has to determine whether or not to hand the fugitive Cummings over to the police. She decides in his favor, because she looks at Lane standing by him: "It's the good people that stick when anybody's in trouble and there aren't many good people in the world." This is ironic considering Lane has been trying to turn Cummings over to the police since she unwillingly became the chauffeur on his getaway. As far as visibility is concerned, it was a good start for Bolster and she even got screen credit. Most of the 53 feature film roles to follow would be less unique, less visible, and about half uncredited.

Saboteur, which premiered in Washington, D.C., on April 22, 1942, was one of six of Sharp-Bolster's films released in 1942. Other familiar titles from this year were *This Above All* (A. Litvak, Twentieth Century–Fox), *The Pride of the Yankees* (S. Wood, Samuel Goldwyn Co.), and *Journey for Margaret* (W.S. Van Dyke, MGM), though she only had tiny, uncredited roles in all three. Nineteen forty-two and the next three years were in fact Sharp-Bolster's most active in films, with five or six releases a year throughout the war. Among her better opportunities during the 1940s, I would mention *Going My Way*, *My Name Is Julia Ross*, *The Lost Weekend*, and *The Woman in White*.

Going My Way (L. McCarey, Paramount, 1944) probably requires little introduction, but it starred Bing Crosby as a relatively young Catholic priest, who has to sort out the parish of a far from young Catholic priest played by Barry Fitzgerald. In this Catholic cornucopia, where fellow worker in the field of "frozen faces" Eily Malyon played a stern yet ultimately sympathetic housekeeper to the two priests, Sharp-Bolster had what was for her a quite substantial role as a nasty neighborhood gossip and battle-axe (yes, indeed), Hattie Quimp, whom Crosby first encounters in the opening scene and later saves from being thrown out of her apartment.

At the behest of director Alfred Hitchcock, Universal's genius make-up artist and legendary monster-maker Jack P. Pierce devised this beard for Anita Sharp-Bolster's unconventional American film debut role as the bearded lady in a circus in *Saboteur* (Frank Lloyd Prod./Universal Pictures, 1942). Sharp-Bolster had come a long way from her roots as the daughter of a gentleman-farmer in County Cork, Ireland.

My Name Is Julia Ross (J.H. Lewis, Columbia, 1945) is a minor thriller with a major cast. It offered Sharp-Bolster a good part for as the ramrod-backed factotum Sparkes, who helps May Whitty and her psychopathic son George Macready with their nefarious plan to cover up his murder of his wife. Sharp-Bolster first appears as a worker at the bogus Allison Employment Agency, where she helps lure unsuspecting job seeker Nina Foch into the trap and later shows up at Whitty's home in Henrique Sq. and at Sea House, Beverton, Cornwall (shades of "Manderley" there), where Foch is kept captive.

Film fans seem to remember Sharp-Bolster in *The Lost Weekend* (Paramount, 1945) to a surprising degree given her relatively modest role in Billy Wilder's famous film about alcoholism. She has a brief scene at beginning of this drink-sodden drama, where she shows up to clean Ray Milland's apartment and get her wages, revealing that Milland's brother leaves the money for her in the lid of the sugar bowl. This then allows Milland to go on a major bender with her money.

Finally, it is sheer delight to see Sharp-Bolster share the screen with Agnes Moorehead in *The Woman in White* (P. Godfrey, Warner Bros., 1948). Sharp-Bolster plays Mrs. Todd, the forbidding housekeeper at Limmeridge House hired after the dastardly Count Fosco takes over control with Sir Percival Glyde, while Moorehead plays the Count's repressed wife, who knows how to time and carry out a pointed revenge. I wonder if Moorehead thought of Sharp-Bolster: "There but for the grace of God...." We know she and her secretary and friend Georgia Johnstone would reward each other with the promise of "tea with Anita Bolster, and perhaps an autographed photo."[21]

In about 1944, Sharp-Bolster and the British director Peter Godfrey (1899–1970) organized the Hollywood Gate Theatre, which was described as "the most advanced and radical theatre in Hollywood today" in a 1947 news article written about the time Sharp-Bolster was "elected Dean of the Drama Department of the newly created Hollywood Academy of Arts."[22] In addition to *The Woman in White*, Godfrey directed Sharp-Bolster in *The Two Mrs. Carrolls* (Warner Bros., 1947).

Between her film engagements, Sharp-Bolster returned to Broadway in 1945 and 1948. After four fairly intensive years of film-making, she was cast in late 1945 in a revival of *Pygmalion* starring Gertrude Lawrence as Eliza Doolittle and Raymond Massey as Henry Higgins. Sharp-Bolster played Professor Higgins's housekeeper Mrs. Pearce at the premiere on December 26, 1945, but did not stay till then end of the play's run at the Ethel Barrymore Theatre in June 1946. She was replaced by Dorrit Kelton.[23] In 1948, she played the housekeeper Lily in a new play by Michael Sayers called *Kathleen* at the Mansfield Theatre, but only for seven performances.[24] When so many of the theaters on Broadway have been demolished, it is a rare thing that all four theaters that Sharp-Bolster performed in are still standing and in operation as theaters. The Mansfield is now the Brooks Atkinson and the Martin Beck has been renamed the Al Hirschfeld Theatre.

Sharp-Bolster also acted in summer stock in places like the Westport, Connecticut, and Bar Harbor, Maine. She had a family connection with the latter popular seaside resort near Acadia National Park on Mount Desert Island through her husband, whom I only know as "Dr. J. Schwartz." The earliest mention I have found of Sharp-Bolster being married to this mystery man is in a piece in the *Bar Harbor Times* in 1947 and there are also several news items about the couple's movements and activities in the same newspaper in 1948. No sooner had *Kathleen* closed peremptorily on Broadway in February 1948, for example, when Mr. and Mrs. Schwartz decided to spend several months in Bahamas. Dr. Schwartz had "a small antique shop" in Bar Harbor in the summers.[25]

Among her later films, I particularly enjoy Sharp-Bolster in *The Perfect Woman* and *The Rising of the Moon*. The British film *The Perfect Woman* (B. Knowles, Two Cities Films, 1949) would have been a rare opportunity for what that fellow portrayer of working women, Connie Gilchrist, called a "dress up." It was also rare for Sharp-Bolster to be billed fifth in the credits. She portrays Lady Diana, a talkative and inquisitive friend of the hero Nigel Patrick's aunt, who lives in Paris and gives him an allowance. The aunt, I mean. Lady Diana's role is to add to Patrick's complications in connection with the robotic "perfect woman" (Patricia Roc) he is testing out for eccentric inventor Miles Malleson.

The Rising of the Moon (Four Province Films, 1957), an anthology film with three stories courtesy of veteran director John Ford, started shooting in Ireland in April 1956 and thus offered Sharp-Bolster the opportunity to return to her native land, probably for the first time in many years.[26] In the second segment, "A Minute's Wait," Sharp-Bolster plays Englishwoman Lydia Frobisher, who is travelling first class on an Irish local train with her husband, Colonel Charles Frobisher (Michael Trubshawe). The Frobishers are subject to rough treatment, as they are evicted from their first-class compartment to benefit a champion goat and put in third class and then joined there by a bunch of lobsters intended for the Bishop's Golden jubilee celebration. They are the only ones who don't make their escape during the frequent delays of the train (hence the segment title), until they final succeed in being shown to a small table outside in a quiet spot where Mrs. Frobisher orders China tea. The last we see of them is standing forlornly on the platform, as the train leaves them behind. Mrs. Frobisher carries an increasingly bedraggled bouquet of flowers, which is apparently intended for a wedding they are to attend, though the porter, Paddy Morrisey, treats her like a blushing bride and pretends it is her own bridal bouquet.

During the last 20 years of her career, Sharp-Bolster worked mostly in television on shows like *Little Women* (1950–51), where she had the recurring role of the March family maid Hannah Mullet; *Robert Montgomery Presents* (1952–53), *Armchair Theatre* (1959), *The Saint* (1962), and on the soap opera *Dark Shadows* (1968). She got to play Countess Fosco, Agnes Moorehead's showy role in *The Woman in White*, on an episode of the ABC series *Hour of Mystery* in 1957.

Thirty-one years after she played Miss Preen at the Pasadena Playhouse, Sharp-Bolster returned to *The Man Who Came to Dinner* (1972) in a televised version on NBC, which "hewed to the original plot."[27] This time she played the host Mr. Stanley's eccentric, live-in sister Harriet. Orson Welles played Sheridan Whiteside, Lee Remick his assistant Maggie Cutler, and Joan Collins the "sexpot actress" Lorraine Sheldon. TV columnist Bob MacKenzie was not impressed with the new version. Orson Welles's "famous nose for theater should have detected the scent of mothballs," he wrote in his review. According to MacKenzie "none of the actors around Welles had the slightest idea how to play a lightweight farce": "All those naturalistic modern actors trying to be stylish and trivial went at it like a troupe of teamsters attempting the minuet." The only players who came in for praise were "Anita Sharp Bolster as the sweetly vague old-maid sister of the host and Miss Collins who can be artificial with the best."[28]

Sharp-Bolster's final feature film was as late as 1977. She had a small, uncredited role as an "old crone" in Terry Gilliam's fantasy adventure film *Jabberwocky* (Python Films/Umbrella Films) when she was 81. Anita Sharp-Bolster died in Miami, Florida, on June 1, 1985, at close to 90 years of age.[29]

I'm No Lady's Maid: Libby Taylor (1900-?)

I was determined to include at least one African American character actress in this volume. Having previously written about Louise Beavers, Hattie McDaniel, and Butterfly McQueen in *Actresses of a Certain Character* and Juanita Moore and Ethel Waters in *Mothers, Mammies and Old Maids*, there was no obvious choice for a follow-up. I could choose among less familiar figures such as Madame Sul-Te-Wan, Hattie Noel, Gertrude Howard, Libby Taylor, Theresa Harris, Marietta Canty, and Maidie Norman. I made things a little easy for myself for once. For this volume, I chose the actress from the list that I was most familiar with.

One of the special joys of doing research on the life and career of an obscure actress, such as Libby Taylor, Tempe Pigott, or Anita Sharp-Bolster, is that every new piece of reliable information feels important. There are special challenges, though, presented by the case where almost nothing is known of the individual's off-screen life. It is particularly important when writing about such persons, that one base oneself only on reliable historical evidence. When I started working on Taylor, for example, there was no birth or death information available for her in the Internet Movie Database (IMDb). I see now that she appears with a birth date of April 20, 1902, in Chicago, Illinois, and that she is thought to have died in Falls Church, Virginia, on January 1, 1990.[1] I assume that someone has checked the Social Security Death Index (SSDI), where an individual named Elizabeth A. Taylor appears, who was born and died on these dates. But how do we know for certain that this is Libby Taylor? Elizabeth Taylor is a common name, after all, and why should a woman who had spent her life in Chicago, New York, and Los Angeles, choose to finish it in Virginia?

I've decided to conduct my own little investigation and see how far I can get based on census information and other forms of primary sources. It may well be that the Elizabeth A. Taylor in SSDI is Libby Taylor and that she lived to be 87 years old, but if we leave that to one side for a moment, what else can we find out about her?

I begin with one piece of what I consider incontrovertible historical evidence and that is Libby Taylor's entry in the 1940 U.S. census. On April 19, 1940, she and her lodger were visited by census enumerator René Charles Dahle at the home Taylor owned at 1042 Morton Ave. in Pasadena, California. Taylor gave her name as "Elizabeth Taylor," said she was 36 years old on her last birthday, that she had been born in Illinois, and had an eighth grade education. According to the record, Taylor was a widow and had also been living in Los Angeles on April 1, 1935. She had been unemployed for six weeks up until March 30, 1940. She had earned $3,000 for 15 weeks' work in 1939 and had no income from other sources than "money wages or salary." She owned her own home, which was valued at $3,000. What clinched it, though, in the identification was that Taylor gave her occupation as "character actress" in "motion picture production."[2] When I read that, I felt certain I had found Libby Taylor.

We now have some hard evidence to work from, including a possible birth year of 1903 or 1904, the fact that Taylor was originally from Illinois, and that she is most likely to appear as "Elizabeth Taylor" in the public record. If we move backwards in time, I next located an individual whom appears to be Libby Taylor in the 1930 U.S. census. At this time, "Elizabeth Taylor" was living in a 30 dollar a month, rented apartment at 100 W. 128th St. in New York, which still stands on the corner of Lenox Ave. in Harlem. Harlem is exactly where one would expect to find Libby Taylor at this time and the Elizabeth Taylor in question is black, single, and 28, was born in Illinois, and, to clinch the matter, gives her occupation as "actress stage."[3] Eureka! If she was indeed 28, though, this moves her birth year up to 1901 or 1902.

I am unable to locate Elizabeth Taylor in the 1920 census, but I do find her in 1910. In 1910, a nine-year-old African American girl called Elizabeth A. Taylor is living with her mother Mattie Taylor in a rented home at 15 W. 70th St., which is in the Englewood section of Chicago's South Side. Today the Dan Ryan Expressway (Highway 94) runs more or less straight through the block of 70th St. on which Taylor's childhood home once stood. Elizabeth was born in Illinois. Her father, who is dead at this point, was born in Georgia. Her mother Mattie, who is a 47-year-old widow and "works out" as a washerwoman, was born in Virginia in 1862 or 1863, thus possibly in time to have been born a slave. Both Mattie's parents were also born in Virginia. She has given birth to four children of which Elizabeth is the only survivor.[4] If this is Libby Taylor, and I'll admit there's no way of knowing that for certain, she keeps getting older! This Elizabeth Taylor was born in 1900 or 1901. As I mention elsewhere, in the case of actresses, the earliest possible year of birth is usually the correct one.

I've just said that I couldn't locate Elizabeth Taylor in the 1920 census. I have found *Mattie* Taylor, though, living at the rear of 6713 Eberhart Ave. in Park Manor, which is also on Chicago's South Side near Highway 90 and the Oak Woods Cemetery. Today there is only grass growing on this narrow, empty lot and a melancholy cement path leading to nothing to remind us that there once was a home here. Mattie is working as a laundress in a private family. What is more important is that she is living with her son-in-law William Bradley and her married daughter *Elizabeth* Bradley. Eureka again. Mattie is now 56. Elizabeth Taylor Bradley is 19, as we would expect, and is not working. Her husband William Bradley is a 26-year-old truck driver born in Virginia of parents born in the same state. All three are described as "mulatto."[5]

I have located William Bradley's World War I draft registration dated June 5, 1917, which tells us something more about him. He was born in Rustburg, Virginia, on August 1, 1894. At the time of this record, he was married and living at 1221 Miller Dr. in Lynchburg, Virginia. He was working as a driver for the Standard Ice Co. in Lynchburg and was described as being tall, stout and having black hair and eyes.[6] This means that Elizabeth Taylor was married by the time she was 17 and may have temporarily relocated to Virginia, her mother's home state.

On July 4, 1918, that is about a year after the draft record I've just cited, William and Elizabeth Bradley had a son in Chicago, Illinois, who was named William Ollie (Oliver) Bradley. From his birth certificate, we know further that his mother's full name was "Elizabeth Anna Taylor" (hence the "A." we found in the 1910 census), she was 18 years old and born in Chicago; and his father was William Allen Bradley, 25 and born in Gladys, Virginia, which is a tiny hamlet about 20 miles directly south of Lynchburg with Rustburg lying about midway between the two.[7]

Sadly, William and Elizabeth's little son only lived three months. He died in Chicago on October 9, 1918, and was buried two days later in Lincoln Cemetery. But what happened to the marriage? We've already seen that Elizabeth Taylor gave her marital status as single in the 1930 census. The answer will be found in the same census, where I have located William Bradley living with his new wife Geraldine, two daughters aged ten and 11 and born in Indiana, who must be Geraldine's from a previous relationship, and his six-year-old son Walter.[8] Thus we can assume that the Bradley-Taylor marriage was over by 1924.

In the 1930 U.S. census, I have also located Elizabeth's now 68-year-old mother, Mattie Taylor, who is living in a $75-a-month apartment at 6215 Elizabeth St. in Chicago, a property since razed to make way for Woods Academy. Mattie is no longer working, but she has the charge of two grandchildren: Martha N. Bradley, ten years old and born in Illinois; and Junior McMare, who is nearly three, also born in Illinois, with a father born in Mississippi.[9] Elizabeth Taylor, then, had a daughter with William Bradley in about 1920, before they divorced. She was married a second time to a man called McMare, had a son in 1927, before leaving both her children with her mother to seek her fortune in New York. We note, too, that neither of the children was living with her in 1940. Martha would have been 20 and old enough to take care of herself, but what of 13-year-old Junior? I have not found any further record of either of these children.

Mattie Taylor's story ended on June 9, 1934, when she died in Chicago at the age of 72. She was buried two weeks later in the now abandoned Oak Forest Cemetery.[10] Sadly, she did not live to see the release of her daughter's big film *Belle of the Nineties* in September 1934, where Taylor had the role of her career as Mae West's maid Jasmine.

There is a sense in which everything we know about Libby Taylor, apart from what I have just told you, is a direct result of her personal and working relationship with Mae West. To the extent that Taylor appears at all in the newspapers of her own day and in modern-day film scholarship, it is as West's maid both on and off the screen during a relatively brief period from early 1933 till about mid–1935. Taylor and West met in New York when West came east for personal appearances in connection with *She Done Him Wrong* in early 1933, though they may originally have met in the 1920s. According to modern sources, Taylor was not working as an actress at the time, but as a barbecue cook in Harlem's Black and Gold restaurant. West hired her to play her maid in the stage show after showings of *She Done Him Wrong* and at some point she started doubling as West's maid at home as well.[11]

During the years of their association, Mae West's star shone so brightly it cast a reflected light on her friend and employee as well. Taylor became, in biographer Jill Watts's words, "a very visible presence" in West's life.[12] Taylor made frequent appearances in the newspaper columns at this time, though always as "Mae West's maid." Columnists and reporters were clearly fascinated by the interphase between West's screen life and real life; the fact that Taylor was her maid both on and off the screen.

We find an early mention of Taylor in Captain Roscoe Fawcett's syndicated "Screen Oddities" column. On August 30, 1933, he announced, "Fans will see Mae West's own personal Negro maid when they view 'I'm No Angel'": "The maid, Libby Taylor, was an outstanding actress in her native Harlem and has appeared in a number of Broadway plays. Unable to find an acting job, Libby became a maid and Mae West hired her on a recent trip to New

York. Now Libby is a movie actress and has won an attractive role in which she will have the opportunity to do some good work."[13] That was the entire item.

My first reaction to the information in Fawcett's column that Taylor had "appeared in a number of Broadway plays" was that this was probably studio hype. I had checked already and found no hits for "Libby Taylor" in the Internet Broadway Database (IBDb) or in the printed volumes of the "Best Plays" series, edited by Burns Mantle. Based on my census research, though, I now tried "Elizabeth Taylor" and found, besides the white star of the same name, another Elizabeth Taylor, who had 13 credits in IBDb between 1924 and 1932. Could this be Libby Taylor? How many of these roles could conceivably have been played by an African American woman in her mid–20s to early 30s?

Well, surprisingly many, if not all of them. Nineteen twenty-four seems fairly early for her to be in New York, though, and the first role credited to IBDb's "Elizabeth Taylor" was as a "peasant girl" in a play set in Hungary. Surely, this could not be our party. Roles like "Mamie O'Brien" in *Puppets* (1925) and "Madge Cox" in *The Masque of Venice* (1926) seemed similarly unpromising. Maids, which we would expect Taylor to play, mostly came with just a first name, if any. Things began to look more plausible with the show *The New Moon* (1928–29), which you may recall from the 1940 film version starring Jeanette MacDonald and Nelson Eddy was a musical set around New Orleans. Here Elizabeth Taylor was a member of the ensemble. Between September 1929 and May 1930, we find her cast as "Harlem Lady" in the hit murder mystery *Subway Express* at the Liberty Theatre, which took place entirely in the car of a New York subway. Surely this could be our Libby Taylor; similarly with roles like "Cinia" in *The Up and Up* (1930), which was set in a Harlem speakeasy; "Cornelia" in *Schoolgirl* (1930); and "Lula" in *The Social Register*, which sounds like a stereotypically African American maid's name. The last recorded credit for Elizabeth Taylor was as "Gertrude" in *Here Today*, a new comedy by George Oppenheimer set in the Bahamas, which opened at the Ethel Barrymore Theatre on September 6, 1932. None of these roles were mentioned in the "Best Plays" plot summaries, which also indicates their subordinate character. At the end of the day, I am certain that some, if not all, these credits belong to Libby Taylor, particularly the nine shows starting with *The New Moon* in 1928 and up until *Here Today*, which ran for 32 performances and closed in October 1932. Thus, Taylor might well have been looking for work when she encountered West in early 1933.

Taylor made her film debut later that year as one of four maids working for West in her second film *I'm No Angel* (W. Ruggles, Paramount, 1933). The film was in production between July and September 1933,[14] so this is when Taylor would have made her move from New York to Los Angeles. In *I'm No Angel*, she played the hairdressing maid Libby, while the other attendants were portrayed by Gertrude Howard, Hattie McDaniel, and an actress who has never been identified. The film was released in October 1933. In November 1933, fans could read "Mae West keeps her maid, Libby Taylor, for two reasons. Libby helps her to dress and undress, both at the studio and at home, and in addition she knows how to make Mae laugh at just the right times."[15] On the screen, though, it was West who made Taylor laugh and not the other way around.

Production on *Belle of the Nineties*, which was originally known as *It Ain't No Sin*, began at Paramount on March 13, 1934, with Leo McCarey directing.[16] In April 1934, readers were informed that Taylor was "adding Scram's look-after to her on-and-off-the-screen duties as Mae's maid."[17] Scram was a duck West had been given by Carl Brisson. Under the heading

"Hollywood Has Star Servants, Too," Associated Press staff writer Hubbard Keavy assured his readers that same month, "The stars' secretaries, companions, stand-ins and dressers are as colorful as many of the characters their employers play on the screen." One of the examples cited was Libby Taylor, "a successful actress on Broadway," who "gave up her career to become maid and companion to the buxom blonde" Mae West.[18] Columnist Walter Clausen painted an idyllic scene of Taylor bringing in the steak and potatoes and "getting ready to cut the pie" for Mae West and her family in West's "cheery Hollywood apartment" in September 1934.[19] We may assume Taylor lived with West in her famous apartment no. 611 at the "Ravenswood" at this time, a grandiose white apartment building which still stands at 570 N. Rossmore Ave.[20]

Apart from her time with Mae West at the Ravenswood in 1934–35, I have not been able to find out much about Taylor's private life in Hollywood. Film historian Thomas Cripps includes her among the "grandes dames of the ghetto": "a social élite who gave without stint to help the race while at the same time supporting their style of life by playing traditional roles as domestic servants."[21] These distinguished ladies were among the most prominent African American actresses in Hollywood. In addition to Taylor, there was Hattie McDaniel, Theresa Harris, Louise Beavers, Lillian Yarbo, and Marietta Canty.[22] The *Galveston Guide*, an African American paper, described Taylor in 1937 as a Catholic and a "very regular attendant" at church.[23]

Belle of the Nineties was released on September 21, 1934. In Violet LeVoit's telling summary, the film is "a Victorian period piece where jewelry-loving vaudeville chanteuse Ruby Carter (West) enjoys the company of saloon owners (John Miljan), prize fighters (Roger Pryor) and millionaires (Johnny Mack), all while wearing stunning hourglass gowns and purring tunes like 'My Old Flame.'"[24] In the film, Taylor was cast as Ruby Carter's maid Jasmine, who is allowed a bit of her own storyline, including attending a Negro prayer meeting. Jasmine even has her own love interest in the figure of Sam McDaniel, playing a nameless gambler who fetches her and Miss Carter's luggage from the boat on their arrival in New Orleans and later attends the prayer meeting with Jasmine. Jasmine is a confidante to Ruby and is supposed to learn from her mistakes. They discuss Ruby's various men friends and what she has learned from her experiences. In this connection, Jasmine is a receptive audience for Ruby's one liners and acts as a straight woman and "feed" for West's comedy. In portraying Jasmine, Taylor speaks in the customary ungrammatical, pidgin English often used by black maids in films at this time. She is quite buxom at this point and wears elaborate maid uniforms.

In one important scene with her maid and confidante, Ruby ponders her situation after she discovers villain club owner Ace Lamont (John Miljan) has stolen her diamonds with the help of her boyfriend, boxer Tiger Kid (Roger Pryor). Ruby finds she should never have taken them from a man she doesn't love, the high-toned, young millionaire Brooks Claybourne (Johnny Mack Brown). Ruby then allows Jasmine to go to the prayer meeting, and even gives her money to put in the collection. This segues into an unexpectedly artistic montage sequence with images of West and the African Americans at the meeting, often superimposed over each other.

It was news in itself that West chose to include the revival sequence in the film. Under the heading "Negro Songs in Mae West Film," one article informed the readers that it was a radio revival program heard on the set between scenes that "resulted in Mae West's injecting

It did neither actress's reputation any harm that Libby Taylor was Mae West's maid both on screen and off and garnered them a lot of press interest. It did cause some friction in their relationship, though, and Taylor finally decided to focus on performing as a maid on film rather than being one in real life. This still is from her breakthrough role in *Belle of the Nineties* (Paramount Pictures, 1934).

a negro song revival in the sequences of the picture." Director McCarey "rallied ninety-two singers," 50 men, 25 women, and 17 children. Taylor and character actor George Reed, who played the preacher, would have most of the dialogue, while readers were assured "the blond star does not appear in the revival scenes, but one of her hit songs, 'Troubled Waters,' has as its background the voices of the singers."[25] The following entry from one of the myriad film columns of the day, "Hollywood Chatter," is versed in the condescending race lingo of the day: "Mae West getting a big bang out of her dusky maid, Libby Taylor, taking over the 'starring' spot in the negro revival sequences Mae is injecting into 'It Ain't No Sin'—and Libby going big while nearly 100 ebony extras hail her as their movie queen."[26]

I am not going to try to determine once and for all how we should feel about Taylor's character in *Belle of the Nineties*.[27] Whether we approve of her or not and the film in which she appears, Jasmine was simply the most important character in the most important film Libby Taylor would ever act in. In terms of screen time, character development, and plot significance, there is no doubt that West did more for Taylor in this one film than any star, director, or producer was willing to do ever again in the almost 20 years that remained of Taylor's career. According to Jill Watts, West "created a much larger role for Libby Taylor."[28] For an actress, visibility is the ultimate good after all.

In December 1934, the *New York Herald Tribune* reported that Taylor had been signed for a part in *Mississippi* to be directed by Edward Sutherland.[29] According to the *Salt Lake Tribune*, "Mae West's maid, who proved her worth as an actress in the two West productions in which she appeared, has 'gone on her own.'"[30] Taylor stayed with her and West's home studio, though, Paramount. *Mississippi* was a comedy musical starring Bing Crosby, W.C. Fields, and Joan Bennett and was released in March 1935. Predictably, Taylor played a maid, specifically Bennett's maid Lavinia, though she actually has a plot function in writing to Crosby at a crucial moment in his and Bennett's romance to tell him she is about to marry someone else.

Several columnists noted that West had not included a part for Taylor in her latest film *Goin' to Town*.[31] It was explained "a French maid will be in the new picture as she fits the background better."[32] Taylor was to have responded ("somewhat dolefully"), that it was "a good idea to give some other girl a chance."[33] Pauline Paquette played the French maid. The papers noted that Taylor had been cast in "an important character role" in *Shanghai* (J. Flood, Walter Wanger Prod./Paramount, 1935), starring Loretta Young and Charles Boyer, but in truth there was nothing very exciting about her thoroughly generic role as Alison Skipworth's maid Corona, who cheers Young on in her battle against her autocratic aunt.

It was inevitable that Taylor's double role would eventually cause friction with her employer. The more success she had as a maid in films, the less easy and satisfying it would have been to be a maid also during her off-screen hours. According to West's biographer, "Taylor had begun to manifest an unforgivable devotion to her own pursuits."[34] The break finally came in 1935, which incidentally would prove the peak year of Taylor's film career with 12 feature film releases. West commented in an interview with the *New York Times* on June 9, 1935, "When she began wanting me to wake her up in the morning I told her she'd better stop being a maid and give all her time to the public."[35]

Columnist Willa Okker assured her readers in November 1935 "Libby intends to continue her film career, between spells of 'maiding' for Miss West."[36] Taylor's name dropped from the news columns after that. She would keep on working fairly steadily in films until the mid–1940s, but she was no longer "news." I have found one intriguing exception to this rule, though, in the *New York Times* for June 30, 1939, where it was reported "Libby Taylor will be seen as Belle Watling's maid in 'Gone with the Wind.'"[37] I'm pretty sure, though, that Taylor does not appear in *Gone with the Wind* as Belle Watling's maid or in any other capacity.

In general, there was nothing to separate Taylor's many maid roles in the following, non–Mae West films from the anonymous average of this type of role. Even the more visible, credited maid roles she was cast in had nothing approaching the individualization and extent of interaction with the star/mistress of *Belle of the Nineties*. I've already mentioned *Mississippi* and *Shanghai*. Her "Libby" in *Ruggles of Red Gap* (L. McCarey, Paramount, 1935) was reduced to a non-speaking part. In *Dangerous* (A.E. Green, Warner Bros., 1935), she only had one line when she brings Bette Davis her suitcase and is told to get lost. In *Libeled Lady* (J. Conway, MGM, 1936), she only had one scene as Jean Harlow's maid and her role in *Three Smart Girls* (H. Koster, Universal, 1936), as Alice Brady's maid, was no more substantial. These four screen appearances were uncredited, as indeed were 42 out of her nearly 60 feature film roles.

If anything distinguished or set Taylor's African American maids apart from the "general," it was her state of dishevelment; the extent, for example, that she was shown to be "nappy" and having no very close acquaintance with the hair straightener. This was long before "black is beautiful" and it is thus quite interesting to see the extent to which Taylor was allowed to stray from the white beauty ideal. I assume this was done to add to her comic effect. One example of an extraordinary degree of unkemptness is her tiny role as May Robson's maid Bertha in *Reckless* (V. Fleming, MGM, 1935), who unsuccessfully tries to stop William Powell from invading her elderly employer's bedroom and waking her up.

Taylor had been attractive in her youth, but she aged quickly and became really quite homely in the course of the 1930s. This was no disqualification, of course, for a character actress.

By the time she was in her 30s, Taylor's hair had already begun to turn grey, as we can see in *The Toy Wife* (R. Thorpe, MGM) from 1938. This period drama set in and around New Orleans, provided Taylor with one of her better roles during her post–Mae West years. As Suzanne, one of a wealthy planter H.B. Warner's many house slaves and personal maid to his sensible daughter Louise, played by Barbara O'Neil, Taylor is most prominent in the early part of the film set at the Brigard family plantation, when Louise and her flighty sister Gilberte, nicknamed "Frou Frou" (Luise Rainer), have returned home after spending several years in Europe. In one good scene, as Louise Brigard takes dictation from wounded gentleman-lawyer George Sartoris (Melvyn Douglas), Suzanne sits between them and objects to Mr. Sartoris talking of "our children" (in connection with his belief in a great future for America after their deaths), when there hasn't been any proposal yet. This is part of the build-up to the surprising revelation that George is actually in love with Frou Frou, rather than Louise. Louise says jokingly at one point that Suzanne is getting in the way of her love life. For what may well have been the first and last time, Taylor was singled out for praise as doing "some fine work in the picture."[38]

Taylor's last credited role was in another period drama set in the South. *Another Part of the Forest* (M. Gordon, Universal, 1948) was based on a play by Lillian Hellman that she wrote as a "prequel" to her more famous *The Little Foxes*. Here Taylor plays Coralee, the Hubbard family's trusty maid, who is a particular friend and confidante to her troubled mistress Lavinia Hubbard (Florence Eldridge). We first see her going to get "Miss Vinny" away from the Confederate memorial on Confederate Day in 1880, where Lavinia's cruel husband, Marcus Hubbard (Fredric March), does not want her to be. It Miss Vinny's birthday, so Coralee comes out with a cake with candles. It turns out that only the servants have remembered her birthday. Later, Coralee sits with Lavinia as she reads the story of Sodom and Gomorrah, waiting for her husband to return. Next morning, Coralee informs Hubbard that Lavinia is feeling poorly. She is only seen in the background after that. At the age of 48, Taylor looks older than her years. Watching her here, it doesn't seem to me that this is a woman with more than 40 years left to live. But I could be wrong.

Libby Taylor was last seen on the big screen in *Bright Road* (G. Mayer, MGM, 1953), starring Dorothy Dandridge, Philip Hepburn, and Harry Belafonte, which had an almost entirely black cast. She never worked in television.

Granny's Got Her Gun: Zeffie Tilbury (1863–1950)

There is a scene from one of Zeffie Tilbury's films that I find illustrative of the situation for older actresses in the 1930s. In *Made on Broadway* (H. Beaumont, 1933), a crime comedy-drama from MGM and Tilbury's third sound film to be released, she plays one of three elderly actresses hired by publicity maverick Robert Montgomery to play Sally Eilers's aunts from Schenectady during her trial for murder and to cry at appropriate moments. Tilbury opines, "It's worth more than $25 to cry and really put your heart in it," to which Montgomery responds: "Now listen, I can get all the aunts in town for $10 a day and furnish their own costumes." What was true in the acting profession in general was all the more true in Hollywood. You may recall Columbia studio boss Harry Cohn's charming remark from this same period, when Frank Capra was disappointed he couldn't get MGM star Marie Dressler for his latest film *Lady for a Day*: "The world's lousy with old dames. Go dig one up!"[1]

Zeffie Tilbury's humble status in the Hollywood is in a sense symbolized by the low status of the two characters she is best remembered for playing: dirt poor Grandma Joad in *The Grapes of Wrath* (J. Ford, Twentieth Century–Fox, 1940) and the equally destitute and decrepit Granny Lester in *Tobacco Road* (J. Ford, Twentieth-Century-Fox, 1941). While one might choose to see this as a prestigious finale to a fairly ordinary film career; despite the high profile of these two films, it really was "business as usual" for perpetual screen granny Tilbury. To see the distance between Tilbury and the top-tier character women, we need only ask if May Robson would have taken either of these roles? Of course, she wouldn't.

So I suspect that when Springer and Hamilton wrote that Tilbury was "unforgettable" in *The Grapes of Wrath*,[2] it was more a case of them having forgotten what she had played in anything else. *The Grapes of Wrath*, of course, is Jane Darwell's big film, her reward after all those years of doing small parts at Twentieth Century–Fox. The only important thing Grandma (Tilbury) has to do is to die in the desert before the Joads get to California, creating a moment of suspense about whether her death will be discovered and the family prevented from entering the promised land.

David Ragan's recollection of Tilbury's films must have been pretty hazy, too, when he writes that she was "unforgettable as 'Gramma' in *The Grapes of Wrath*, who didn't make it to California, and as the Grandma in *Tobacco Road*."[3] In *Tobacco Road*, it is perfectly possible to blink and miss the one second, the one brief shot, where, covered head to foot in an enormous black, knitted shawl, Tilbury is for a moment identifiable, if you are really concentrating on the film. Granny Lester in *Tobacco Road* is no more than a walk-on and hardly even that.

Her character's existence is never acknowledged, she has no lines, and she is only briefly seen in the background of the early scene when the Lesters all gang up on Lov (Ward Bond) to steal his sack of turnips. Even the dog gets more screen time than she does!

This is not to suggest that Tilbury deserved to languish in the background and that her mostly modest screen roles were the result of her limited abilities. Far from it. There were actually a handful of films where she was allowed to showcase her acting talents more in depth. Tilbury even starred in a film once. *Federal Bullets* (K. Brown, Monogram, 1937) has proven hard to come by these days, but the *All Movie Guide* describes it as "a leisurely paced Monogram crime melodrama with not a few

Top: This portrait is proof that Zeffie Tilbury was in John Ford's _Tobacco Road_ (Twentieth Century–Fox Film Corp, 1941), though you have to watch the film with rapt attention to be able to spot her as Grandma Lester. Like other daughters of stage beauties in this book—Sara Haden and Eily Malyon—Tilbury's face had more character than pulchritude even in youth. _Bottom:_ Zeffie Tilbury (second from right) as a shady society dame in _Federal Bullets_ (Monogram Pictures, 1937), her sole starring vehicle. To her right stand Milburn Stone and Helen MacKellar and to her left Selmer Jackson.

clever plot twists." Tilbury plays a "Ma Barker clone" who heads a crime ring using a charitable organization as a front.[4]

Tilbury also had substantial roles in *Rhythm in the Clouds* (J.H. Auer, Republic, 1937) and *The Sheriff of Tombstone* (J. Kane, Republic, 1941), possibly because her niece Olive Cooper was the screen writer on both of them. In the former hour-long, low budget comedy from Republic, she is billed fifth as Maggie Conway, the Duchess de Lovely, a cosmetician seeking a new angle on advertising her skin creams from her ad agency. The Duchess, who wasn't "to the manor born," is the kind of feisty, down-to-earth, no nonsense kind of gal Tilbury played so well and who in a more prestigious picture at a larger studio would have been played by May Robson or Jessie Ralph.

In *Sheriff of Tombstone*, the sheriff is Roy Rogers. Tilbury plays Granny Carson, the matriarch of a renegade clan sitting on a rich silver mine in Tombstone, Arizona, whom the sheriff has to deal with because she and her family haven't paid their taxes. She also happens to be the grandmother of his love interest, milliner Mary Carson (Elyse Knox). When Grandma hears that the sheriff is approaching, she says: "Mary, bring me bonnet and me gun." Mary points out, "Your bonnet's crooked," to which Granny responds: "Me shooting's straight." This role shows Tilbury as the B movie queen of crotchety yet lovable little old ladies. This was her penultimate film and her last credited role. She retired at the end of 1941, the year of its release.

Thus, with Tilbury, as with so many others: the larger the part, the "smaller" the film. In most cases, if she is billed in the top ten, we're probably dealing with a B movie or a film from a less prestigious studio or both. One notable exception, is the Marlene Dietrich—Gary Cooper picture *Desire* (F. Borzage, Paramount, 1936). Not as well known today as their earlier collaboration *Morocco* (1930), *Desire* has been widely praised by the Dietrich and Cooper experts and Dietrich herself described it as "the only film I need not be ashamed of" among her post–Von Sternberg films.[5] Dietrich biographer Steven Bach calls *Desire* "her most entertaining American picture yet" and Cooper biographer Jeffrey Meyers calls it "his best comedy."[6] Dietrich was cast as sophisticated jewel thief Madeleine de Beaupre and Cooper was the guileless, expatriate American businessman Tom Bradley, who mistakenly makes off with a vastly valuable pearl necklace Madeleine has stolen in his luggage. From there, the storyline naturally develops into a romance, where Madeleine must decide whether or not to come clean to Tom about her criminal activities and risk losing his love and respect forever.

This sophisticated, cosmopolitan comedy gave Tilbury a rare chance in a first-rate film to do what she did really well and that was to play against type, specifically against the generic, innocuous, conventional little old lady or granny type she was perpetually being cast as. Tilbury plays Aunt Olga, a member of Madeleine's gang, who comes to check up on her when fellow gang member Carlos Margoli (John Halliday) fails to get Madeleine to go to Madrid and sell the stolen necklace. Upon arrival, Olga says she is old enough to be Madeleine's grandmother and that she would offer her grandmother a brandy. "Brandy is the only thing I'm straight about." Olga tries to advise Madeleine and to convince her of the futility of her relationship with Tom. She tells a touching tale of a doctor, a fine man, whom she met long ago when she fell ill in Vienna, but whom she gave up when she realized her past would give them no future. "I still dream of him now and then," she sighs. In the following tense dinner scene, Tom tells Olga she was wrong not to have told the doctor about herself, paving the way for a happy ending. Not one to be surprised or taken aback by anything, Olga observes nonchalantly to Carlos: "I really hope you don't shoot him unless it's absolutely necessary." Tilbury, who cleaned up nicely when given the chance, looks very elegant dressed head to toe in modish black with a plumed hat and a coat with a large fur collar.

This contrast between appearances and reality, this interesting study of older, even old women in control of their lives and even actively manipulating and commanding their surroundings was, of course, the particular specialty of that gorgeous wreck and Tilbury's fellow Briton, Alison Skipworth. Skipworth was a very different and more expansive type physically than Tilbury, though, and came to these types of "con woman" roles from the stereotype of the dowager rather than the grandmother. They actually acted in one film together before Skipworth's retirement in 1937. I would have liked to have seen Tilbury's reaction when she understood that in *The Gorgeous Hussy* (C. Brown, MGM, 1936), an historical romance about President Andrew Jackson starring Joan Crawford and Robert Taylor, she was going to play Skipworth's mother! They were both born in 1863.

Skipworth, like May Robson, also serves to illustrate the distance between the top and the more modest lower-middle range of the character actress hierarchy inhabited by Tilbury. It is worthy asking, then, when most of the talented older actresses in Hollywood never reached the heights of Skipworth and Robson, of Lucile Watson and May Whitty, of Gladys Cooper and Jessie Ralph, if there was any systematic reason why this was so? Did one need to have been a stage star prior to starting in films to be taken seriously in Hollywood? Did one have to "know someone" or have the financial security on arrival to sit quietly and wait for just the right opportunity? How important were agents for character actresses as compared to stars? How much did age and possible infirmity matter in relation to whether or not a studio was willing to give you a chance? Obviously, this is not the place to discuss these questions in depth, but I would like to mention one factor that could be decisive for the development of a character actress's career in Hollywood: how you got started.

Tilbury had acted in a few silents in the late 1910s and into the 1920s, most notably playing Prudence to Nazimova's Camille (R.C. Smallwood, Nazimova Prod.) in 1921. She returned to Hollywood just as sound was being introduced, though her film career didn't really gain momentum until 1933. Tilbury's earliest sound films were for MGM and RKO. While her sound film debut was in a credited role, many of the following roles were uncredited, which would have set a pattern. Once an actor begins to accept uncredited roles, then that, in addition to her weekly salary, establishes her at a certain level in the hierarchy and in turn determines the size and type of roles she will be considered for in the future.

To make matters worse, Tilbury also took parts in short films and started working for "Poverty Row" studios like Monogram. For her, it meant betters parts. Her role in *Mystery Liner* (W. Nigh, Paul Malvern Prod., 1934), for example, which was produced by an independent production company and released by Monogram, was better than any MGM or RKO had offered her. Tilbury plays Granny Plimpton, a passenger on a luxury liner, who has been sent on an involuntary trip for her health, which her prissy grandson Edgar (Jerry Stewart) assures her will do her "a world of good." After that, Tilbury went to Universal and did the horror films *Mystery of Edwin Drood* (S. Walker, 1935) and *Werewolf of London* (S. Walker, 1935), which probably didn't raise her status either, though they contain delicious performances as "The Opium Woman," undoubtedly her most off beat role; and the old lush of a lovelorn landlady, Mrs. Moncaster, who rents Werewolf Henry Hull a room and lives to regret it.

Beyond the fact that Tilbury didn't arrive in Hollywood on the wave of some big Broadway success and may have gotten the wrong kind of start, it would seem that she did also have age and infirmity against her. It has been claimed that she was "almost totally blind" by the time her film career really got started, though she was able to hide this fact from the public.[7] What is certain is that Tilbury was 70 years old in 1933; an age when many retire, if they can, and certainly not the time to start a new career in a new medium. If she did have impaired eyesight, it would naturally have been easier for her to take on smaller roles, where there were fewer lines, fewer close-ups, fewer marks to hit, where she might be sedentary part of the time, and where nothing was riding on her performance. Stage work would have been impossible.

This being said, I certainly don't want to paint a picture of Zeffie Tilbury as some doddering invalid. The most striking characteristic she manifested on screen was, in fact, completely the opposite of weak, sickly, or decrepit. *Feistiness* is the quality I most associate with her. Tilbury was a tiny little thing, but she was able to project a strength and will power to match any character actress of her age and generation and many who were younger too.

So what had made Zeffie Tilbury such a strong and resilient woman? What had she been doing with herself for the first 70 years of her life? One of the distinctive things about her is that she spent most of her long life surrounded by actors, not just at work, but also at home. Her mother was burlesque queen Lydia Thompson (1838–1908), an international star from the 1860s onwards and Zeffie Tilbury would always be "Lydia Thompson's daughter."[8] Her mother's younger half-sister, Clara T. Bracy (1848–1941), was a pioneering actress in the early days of silent films and Clara's son, Sidney Bracey (1877–1942), was also an actor on stage and a bit player in more than 300 films between 1909 and his death in 1942. Both Tilbury's husbands, Arthur Lewis (c. 1846–1930) and L.E. "Bud" Woodthorpe (c. 1864–1915), were actors, as was her second husband's older sister, Georgia Woodthorpe (Cooper) (1859–1927). Georgia Woodthorpe was in turn the mother of actress Georgie Cooper (Stevens) (1882–1968) and screenwriter Olive Cooper (1892–1987), and grandmother of director George Stevens (1904–75).[9]

Tilbury herself was born Zeffie Agnes Lydia Tilbury in London on November 20, 1863, and christened in the Holy Trinity Church in Bishop's Road, Paddington two weeks later.[10] Her mother, 25-year-old Lydia Thompson, had been born Eliza Hodges Thompson in London in 1838 and had made her stage debut at an early age, about 11 years before her daughter and only child Zeffie was born.[11] On January 3, 1863, Lydia had married the riding master and fashionable "man about town," John Christian Tilbury, at the Old Church, St. Pancras. Tilbury died in a steeple-chasing accident when he was rolled on by his horse, only a little over a year later.[12] His daughter was not yet five months old.

By the time she became a young widow, Lydia Thompson had already returned to the stage and would in the course of the 1860s become the "Queen of Burlesque" in England, but also in the United States, where she spent nearly six years between 1868 and 1874 mesmerizing American audiences with her company of "British Blondes." By the time Zeffie Tilbury made her stage debut in *Nine Points of the Law* at the Theatre Royal in Brighton in 1881, her mother was semi-retired, but Lydia Thompson's official retirement didn't come until 1899.[13] Zeffie nursed her through a serious illness that same year, but when her mother died in London in 1908, Tilbury was living and working in the United States and could not attend the funeral at Kensal Green Cemetery.[14]

Tilbury was married twice. Her first husband was an English actor called Arthur Frederick Lewis, who was born around 1846 and thus was considerably older than her.[15] They were married in West Derby, Lancashire in 1887.[16] By 1905, the couple had divorced and Lewis went on to a productive career as a character actor on Broadway, which lasted until his death in New York on June 13, 1930.[17]

Tilbury's second husband was American. Louis Edward Woodthorpe, who would be known as "Bud," was born in 1864 and grew up with his parents and five siblings in San Francisco. The Woodthorpes were a cosmopolitan family. Father John Woodthorpe, who worked as the secretary of the product exchange in San Francisco and later as a shipping clerk, was born in France; his wife Harriet was born in Wales; their eldest child was born in Tahiti, while the remaining five, including Louis Edward, were born in California.[18] He worked as a telegraph boy before he became an actor.[19]

By the time he and Zeffie Tilbury married in 1905,[20] Bud Woodthorpe was in his early 40s, as was she. In 1910, the census shows that he was working as a private secretary to the stage star Nat Goodwin and the Woodthorpes were both living with Goodwin and his much younger wife Edna at their beachside home at 114 Hart Ave. in Santa Monica.[21] No profession is listed for Tilbury at this time. In the early years of the century, Woodthorpe had supported Goodwin in *The Altar of Friendship* and *When We Were Twenty-One* on Broadway, while in 1903 Tilbury had joined the company as Goodwin's leading lady on tour with the same plays.[22] This was probably how Bud and Zeffie met. They were only vouchsafed ten years together. Woodthorpe died suddenly on April 8, 1915, in Saginaw, Michigan, and was buried the next day in Detroit.[23]

Both during and after her marriage to Woodthorpe, Tilbury had a few, scattered roles on Broadway. She supported Viola Allen in *Twelfth Night* and *The Winter's Tale* in 1904–5. Both Tilbury and Woodthorpe supported Patricia Collinge and Douglas Fairbanks in *The New Henrietta* at the Knickerbocker Theatre in 1913–14. Tilbury's biggest commercial success on Broadway was in a play by Tolstoy called *Redemption* with Helen Westley and Thomas Mitchell at the Plymouth Theatre in 1917–18.[24]

She made her silent film debut in 1917 in *Blind Man's Luck* (G.B. Seitz, Astra Film) and made almost a dozen silent films up until her last, which was *The Single Standard* (J.S. Robertson, MGM, 1929) with Greta Garbo. Her maternal aunt Clara T. Bracy was a pioneering actress in silent films, acting in nearly 75 short films for D.W. Griffith in the years between 1908 and 1913. By 1920, Bracy and her son Sidney Bracy (often spelled Bracey) were both living in Los Angeles and working in films there, which may have been partly the reason for Tilbury relocating to the West coast.[25]

Tilbury's last show on Broadway was in December 1925.[26] We know she did *The Goat Song* for the Theatre Guild in San Francisco in January 1928 and that she played Mrs. Alving in *Ghosts* at the Golden Bough Theatre in Carmel in March 1928.[27] During the years of her sound film career between 1930 and 1941, Tilbury acted in nearly 60 features and half a dozen short films. In her best known short, *Second Childhood* (G. Meins, Hal Roach, 1936), she plays a rich, cantankerous old woman, who gets a new outlook on life when Spanky and the rest of the "Our Gang" regulars fly a toy airplane through her window and break a vase.

In 1930–32, she was living at 5724 Sunset Blvd. in West Hollywood, a house long since razed, which stood on the block of Sunset between Van Ness and Wilton that now runs over the Hollywood Freeway.[28] By 1933, her address was 6229 Banner Ave.[29] By some miracle, this small, modest bungalow is still standing on a quiet side street in the heart of Hollywood near Hollywood Forever Cemetery. By 1936, her home was at 7038½ Hollywood Blvd. and she was still living there in 1942.[30] In 1940, though, when the census was taken, Tilbury was staying at the historic Roosevelt Hotel at 7000 Hollywood Blvd., just a few houses down from no. 7038. Also living there at the time was fellow character actress Elizabeth Patterson. The two had been together in *Tobacco Road,* of course, where Patterson played the long-suffering Ada Lester, and in three other films. Patterson, who was considerably higher up on the character actress ladder in Hollywood, told the census enumerator in 1940 that she had earned in excess of $5,000 for 30 weeks' work in the preceding year. Tilbury, on the other hand, claimed to have earned nothing in 1939.[31] This seems odd when we know she had six films released in 1939 and five films in 1940, including *The Grapes of Wrath.*

Zeffie Tilbury Woodthorpe died on July 22, 1950, in Los Angeles "after long illness."[32] She was buried in the Memorial Hall of the Chapel of The Pines Crematory, which is adjacent to Rosedale Cemetery in central Los Angeles.[33]

Big Enough: Norma Varden (1898–1989)

There are several stories of mothers and daughters in this book, but none quite like that of Norma Varden and her mother Julia Maria Shackleton. The one constant for the first 71 years of Varden's life was her mother's presence. Indeed the two women lived together for most of those years. When, after several false starts, Varden decided to move permanently to the United States in 1939, her mother came with her. Norma was 41 when they made their big move and her mother was 63. They couldn't have known then that they would spend 30 years together in their new California home.

In the spring of 2007, when I was doing research for a book on the films of Agnes Moorehead in the UCLA Film and Television Archive, I lived at the Le Montrose Suite Hotel at 900 Hammond St. in West Hollywood. Little did I know that only two blocks south and just around the corner where Hammond St. meets Dicks St., there is a small, cozy Craftsman style bungalow where Norma Varden and her mother used to live. 8957 Dicks St. is a 920 square foot, two bedroom home built in 1923 on a 3,200 square foot lot. Varden was living there on January 28, 1949, the day she became a naturalized U.S. citizen. The house was last on the market in 2000, when it was sold for $605,000.[1]

As a biographer, I like to know how and where my subjects lived. I picture Norma Varden coming home to Dicks St. after a day of work at the studio to find her mother pottering about the kitchen, putting the kettle on and setting out the porcelain tea service I'm sure they brought with them from England. I picture the two women going shopping on Sunset Blvd. (just four blocks north) or Santa Monica Blvd. (just four blocks south), having lunch at the Hollywood Brown Derby, or going out to see one of "Norma's films" at a local cinema. They were probably social and had friends over for tea or spent quiet evenings at home while Julia helped Norma memorize her lines, though there were never that many to memorize.

Who were their neighbors? Among people in the business, it was mostly cinematographers, the odd producer, and some journalists. Fellow character actresses were thin on the ground in the aptly named "Norma Triangle." They tended to favor the many handsome apartment buildings along Franklin Ave. in Hollywood, Hollywood Heights (where Norma lived herself in 1942[2]), Studio City (where fellow Britons Doris Lloyd and Eily Malyon lived) or, if they could afford it, the "Flats" of Beverly Hills. The supreme British character actress Alison Skipworth used to live over on Larrabee St., just below Sunset, but she left Hollywood in 1938 and went back to New York.[3] One possible thespian neighbor, though, was Harold

Minjir (1895–1976), a queer character and a character actor in a small way. Harold lived just a block and a half west in a quaint cottage on the corner of Dicks and N. Doheny Dr. with his mother Clara.[4] Maybe Harold and Norma knew each other. Norma was a bit of a faghag and would be close friends with Sal Mineo in later life.[5]

I seem to have jumped right in and need to go back to the beginning of the story. Varden's beginnings are not obscure exactly; indeed, I've discovered more about them than has hitherto been known, but there are still several unanswered questions that I have to leave to a future researcher. The only source of information on Varden's early life when I started my work was an article in *Film Fan Monthly* by Jim Bigwood, which is based on interviews with Varden, but mainly deals with her career. Bigwood does mention, though, supposedly on Varden's say-so, that she was the "daughter of a retired sea captain and his young wife."[6]

It is well documented that Norma Varden was born Norma Varden Shackleton in Wandsworth in south west London on January 20, 1898.[7] As I've already revealed, her mother was called Julia Maria Shackleton and she was born Julia Maria Shackleton in the south London borough of Lambeth on March 31, 1876.[8] Here appears the first anomaly. If Varden's mother was born Shackleton, how is it that her daughter was also born with the surname of Shackleton? Did Julia Shackleton marry a relative or by sheer coincidence a man who was also called Shackleton? Or did she keep her maiden name and bequeath it to her daughter? Or, better yet, was she an unwed mother?

Well, I hate to disappoint, but it appears Varden's origins weren't quite as romantic or unconventional as all that. I have been able to uncover one piece of documentary evidence relating to her father. In the England and Wales census for 1901, the Shackleton family of three are found to be living in Streatham, which is in the same London borough of Wandsworth where little Norma was born. According to the census, the family consists of the head of the household "Z. Shackleton," age 44, born in America; wife Julia Shackleton, 35, born in Brixton; and last but not least, daughter Norman [sic], 3, born in Clapham.[9] From this, then, we can gather that Varden's father was born in the United States about 1857, was almost 20 years older than his wife, and was 41 when his daughter Norma was born. As far as Z. Shackleton is concerned, the rest is silence. In the ship manifest for Julia Shackleton's journey to the United States in 1939 and in the U.S. census for 1940, she appears as "single."[10]

After training at the Guildhall School of Music, Varden had started her acting career in Shakespearean repertory, appeared on the London stage in serious dramatic roles from 1920 and as a feed for comedians like Tom Walls and Ralph Lynn, known collectively as the "Aldwych farceurs," beginning in 1930. Her straight woman roles led directly to her British sound film debut in *A Night Like This* (T. Walls, Herbert Wilcox/British & Dominions Film) in 1932 and a full-time film career in England for the remainder of the '30s.[11]

Varden had made no less than four trips to the United States prior to her final move to Hollywood in 1939. Her first visit was to New York City in the spring of 1928, where she stayed with her aunt Miriam Oppenheim and Miriam's German-born husband Maurice F. Oppenheim, an importer, in their apartment at 536 W. 112th St., which is now the site of a Columbia University book store.[12] She finally came to America to stay in the summer of 1939. Varden took the ship Aseania to Montreal and then entered the United States through the port of Detroit on July 1, 1939, en route to Los Angeles.[13] Her mother left England from Manchester aboard the SS *Pacific President* on September 8, 1939, and arrived in the port of Los Angeles on October 11, 1939, the day production on Varden's first Hollywood film, *The Earl of Chicago*, began at MGM.[14] When the census was taken in May 1940, we find the two women living at 1238½ Harper Ave. in West Hollywood.[15]

Varden's two most important contacts on first arriving in Hollywood were directors William Beaudine and Victor Saville. William "One-Shot" Beaudine (1892–1970) was a prolific American director whom Varden had worked with on four films in England in the mid–1930s. She became a personal friend of Beaudine and his family and it was he who encouraged her to visit California.[16] Ironically, Beaudine didn't direct her in Hollywood until 1958 in a film called *In the Money* (Allied Artists). Victor Saville (1895–1979) was born in Birmingham and directed Varden in five films from *The Iron Duke* (Gainsborough) and *Evergreen* (Gaumont British) in England in 1934 up until *The Silver Chalice* (Victor Saville Prod./Warner Bros.) 20 years later and also helmed her American debut film *The Earl of Chicago* (MGM, 1940) and *The Green Years* (MGM, 1946).

Like fellow Britons Eily Malyon and Doris Lloyd and Australian Tempe Pigott in this volume, Varden bypassed the New York stage entirely on her way to Hollywood and was nevertheless able to make a career for herself. We have to recognize, though, that her lack of Broadway credentials limited the opportunities she was given. There was a level she could never rise above, a kind of "glass ceiling" relating to previous stage experience rather than

Norma Varden's powerful profile is evident in this still of her as the Duchess of Richmond in *The Iron Duke* (Gainsborough Pictures, 1934) with Lesley Wareing as Lady Frances Webster. The film starred George Arliss as the Duke of Wellington.

gender. Varden herself recognized that. Her observations in 1975 about the differences between the film industry in England and the United States are worth quoting at length:

> People are so loyal over there [in England]. Here, you'll go up a step and it's so hard to get up the next step. Over there, you build and if they love you, you go up and on. Here it's much more factory, much more commercial than over there. I always say that here they look down the salary list and say, "Oh yes, she's only earning so much, she couldn't play this part, she's not big enough." They go by the money-money-money all the time. I never realized that here you really have to brag about yourself. I thought your work would be sufficient to let them know what you were. I kept busy, but not with the lovely parts that I had in England. I played some wonderful parts over there, and here—well—some of them were interesting.[17]

As Varden's own remarks suggest, it's not easy to point to standout roles that everyone remembers. Her presence in the American films of the 1940s, '50s and '60s is more a question of cumulative effect. She acted in roughly 100 feature films between 1932 and 1968, starting in England in the 1930s, but spending most of her career in the American film industry. About a third of her screen roles were uncredited. Nevertheless, Varden was given a few opportunities to shine, however briefly, and she made the most of them. In *Forever Amber* (O. Preminger, Twentieth Century–Fox, 1947), for example, in many ways a deplorable film, Varden is suitably villainous in extreme décolleté as a dress-shop owner who swindles Linda Darnell out of £200 and, if that wasn't enough, gets her thrown in Newgate Prison.

Like Gladys Cooper, Isobel Elsom, and Mary Forbes, Norma Varden personified the patrician British dowager in American films. Unlike them, though, Varden could display genuine warmth on the screen. She had a nose that was created for looking down people at and her hooded, hazel eyes could paralyze you with their glare, but they could also register warmth and geniality. Even when she was being most censorious, you might just be able to discern a faint twinkle in her eye and feel as if, given half a chance, she might like to get up to some mischief herself. So while Varden could be aristocratic, dignified, and haughty, she could just as easily be game, genial, and "one of the boys." She was what another age called a "comfortable" woman.

In unsympathetic roles as haughty dowagers, Varden was no better than the average, as exemplified by her American debut film *The Earl of Chicago*. As a British aristocrat whose young son is pushed to the side when the vulgar American gangster played by Robert Montgomery inherits the title, she was no more than adequate. It was as granddames with an earthy, amorous quality and a spirit of fun that Varden came into her own. If we compare two of her British films where she played straight woman to comedian Will Hay, we can see the difference. Varden is an absolute delight as Lady Dorking, the chairman of the board of a school determined to hire Hay as principal against the board's opposition, in *Boys Will Be Boys* (Gainsborough, 1935) and only passable as Hay's stern, dismissive sister-in-law in *Where There's a Will* (Gainsborough, 1936). Both films were directed by her friend and future mentor in Hollywood, William Beaudine.

Films such as *Boys Will Be Boys* established the light-hearted, empathetic, warm, and flirtatious screen persona that would also be evident in Varden's American films, not least of all in *Strangers on a Train* and *Witness for the Prosecution*. Her role in *Strangers on a Train* (A. Hitchcock, Warner Bros., 1951) was limited, but she makes the most of her scene as Mrs. Cunningham, a giggly, diamond-bedecked society woman, who encounters Robert Walker at a party and gets more and more drawn into a conversation about the best way to murder someone, before she ends up with Walker's hands around her throat.

According to one news item, Norma Varden "set back her scheduled picture-making expedition to Europe" to join Bob Hope in *Fancy Pants* (Paramount Pictures, 1950). Here she is seen with Hope (center) and Hugh French. She also lent the star comedian staunch support in *Road to Zanzibar* and *Where There's Life* in the 1940s.

My favorite Varden character, though, is the lonely widow and murder victim she portrays in the Billy Wilder classic *Witness for the Prosecution* (Edward Small Prod., 1957). Emily Jane French is 56 and lives alone in a home full of Nigerian tribal art collected when she and her late husband Hubert lived in Africa. She keeps a bottle of sherry ready for her attentive and, as it turns out, murderous friend Leonard Vole (Tyrone Power) and leaves him £80,000 in her will. Though Varden never married, I imagine there is a lot of her own personality in this warm, charming portrayal of the vulnerability and pathos of a lonely, middle-aged woman. Comedian Eddie Bracken, who did *Hold That Blonde!* (G. Marshall, Paramount, 1945) and *Bring On the Girls* (S. Lanfield, Paramount, 1945) with Varden, described her as "all out, a very giving person": "When an actor works with people like Norma, you have nothing to worry about because they do more for you than you can possibly imagine anybody else doing. When you talk about people like Norma, you talk about the Rock of Gilbraltar."[18]

The only certain sadness and pain that we know of in Varden's long life (and I'm not talking about her losing the part of the Mother Superior in *The Sound of Music* to Peggy Wood) came on September 14, 1969, when her beloved mother died at the age of 93 not long after they moved to Santa Barbara.[19] Julia Maria Shackleton had stood by her daughter's side for more than 70 years. For the next 20 years, Varden had to go it alone. After her mother's death, she never worked again, though David Ragan noted in 1977 that her picture kept appearing in every new edition of the *Academy Players Directory*, indicating that she was still available.[20] In the 1970s, Varden devoted herself to fighting for better medical benefits for actors.[21] She stayed on in Santa Barbara and died there of heart failure in Cottage Hospital's coronary care unit on January 19, 1989, the day before her 91st birthday.[22] She was laid to rest beside her mother in Santa Barbara Cemetery.[23]

Divinely Dotty: Nydia Westman (1902–70)

In his syndicated column for September 12, 1970, Jack O'Brien mentioned "the bunch in Sardi's Bar hoisting a farewell toast to their old fine friend Nydia Westman, an always busy busy actress who died without an obit in the N.Y. papers."[1] If indeed it was true that the New York papers did not take note of Westman's death, it was a glaring oversight and deeply disrespectful towards an actress who had appeared on Broadway for 37 years, who had scores of film and television credits, and whose career in the American entertainment industry had spanned five decades.

Truth to tell, Nydia Westman has always had trouble being taken seriously. Capsule descriptions of her often make her sound like an airhead or a dessert or a light and fluffy mixture of both. According to John Springer and Jack Hamilton, she was "a dumpy little woman with a pudding of a face" and "specialized in maids and old maids, often frightened." They correctly point out that she "had few chances to shine on her own," before adding, "*Three Live Ghosts, Craig's Wife, A Feather in Her Hat, The Cat and the Canary* did give her moments."[2] David Ragan writes, "She played giggly, giddy little women and smalltown gossips."[3] David Quinlan claims she "had spinsters-on-the-shelf down to a T, and could make them comic, pathetic, twittering or fey."[4] Hal Erickson provides this description: "A short, pudgy lady with an air of perpetual consternation, she was ideally cast as maids, busybodies and spinsters."[5] Finally, columnist Vic Wilmot was being chivalrous, then, when he described Westman in print in 1965 as an "ultra-grand character actress."[6]

The best word to describe Westman's characteristic screen persona, I suppose, is "dotty." In a wide variety of young maid, old maid, and homemade roles, she brought dottiness to another level. While in the case of Una Merkel, whom she superficially resembled (columnist Jimmie Fiddler once called them "peas-in-a-pod"[7]), the humor was always verbal—in the tart retort; with Westman, it was something much more physical, a kind of zaniness and quirkiness that radiated out of her face and body and required no words at all to register as funny.

Yet Westman was a serious dramatic actress with a string of Broadway credits in everything from John Golden produced comedies in the 1920s to Aristophanes' *Lysistrata* (1930–31), the original production of Thornton Wilder's *The Merchant of Yonkers* (1938–39), the megahit *Life with Father* (1944–47), and *The Madwoman of Chaillot* (1948–50). She even created the role of Nell in Beckett's *Endgame* off-Broadway in 1958. She was able to sustain a lifetime in the entertainment industry through a versatility that anyone who only knows her from her films would hardly imagine she had.

Nydia Eileen Westman was born in New York on February 19, 1902, the second of the four children of Theodore Westman and Lily Wren Westman.[8] Theodore was born of Swedish immigrant parents in Chicago, Illinois, in 1870 and Lily in Brooklyn, New York, about a year later with a father from England and mother from New York. On her mother's side, Nydia was descended from four generations of actors and Sir Christopher Wren to boot.[9] Nydia was born into the entertainment business, as Theodore was an actor and composer and Lily an actor and writer and they performed together in vaudeville. They had met when both were playing in the melodrama *The Evil Eye*. "Because of the opposition in those days to married people in the same cast," their daughter told a reporter years later, Theodore and Lily "received their 'notice' as a wedding present" after they had been married in Pittsburgh on Theodore's 30th birthday January 15, 1900.[10]

In addition to doing their vaudeville act together on the Keith-Orpheum circuit and elsewhere,[11] the couple had five children before 1910, four of whom survived: Lolita Ann (b. c. 1901 in California), Nydia Eileen (named for a character in *Quo Vadis*[12]), Theodore Jr. (b. c. 1904 in New York), and Neville (b. c. 1908 in Rhode Island). In 1910, the family was living at 154 Rogers Ave. in Brooklyn.[13] Their apartment building and the entire block of this quiet street in Crown Heights near the Eastern Parkway and the Brooklyn Museum is little changed since Westman's day.

Nydia was educated at the Children's Professional School in New York, which her mother had helped found, and when on tour with her parents via correspondence courses.[14] *Who's Who* says she made her first stage appearance age 13 with her parents, two sisters, and brother as part of the family act "The Westman Family" at the Bronx Opera House in 1915, but she claimed herself to have been five.[15] I do not know when Westman's parents died, but that fact that her 12-year-old younger sister Neville was living with railroad clerk William Johnson, his wife Emma, and son Fred in Mount Pleasantville, New York, in 1920 would seem to indicate that Theodore and Lily Westman were probably dead by that point.[16] Eighteen-year-old Nydia's whereabouts at this time are also unknown, but her younger brother Theodore Westman, Jr., had started on the brief but successful acting career that ended with his tragic death in 1927 at the age of 24.[17] He made his Broadway debut in the comedy *Thank You* in October 1921 and is best known for his role in the silent film *The Flapper* (1920), where he starred with Olive Thomas, though he was only 17 at the time.[18] In an Associated Press interview from 1934, her parents are described in the past tense, while it is reported that Lolita Ann Westman is a "playwright and scenarist" and Neville Westman is "an actress in the East."[19]

Nydia Westman's Broadway debut took place on September 1, 1924, as Mildred Cushing in the new three-act comedy *Pigs* produced by John Golden at the Little Theatre (now the Helen Hayes).[20] Is it surprising she found it hard to be taken seriously? If you make your debut in a play called *Pigs*, you're asking for it, even if the show was a great success, ran for 312 performances followed by a year-long tour, and Westman's "magnetic personality" was considered "one of the chief delights."[21] At any rate, between her porcine debut and her last show in 1961, a resounding flop starring Tallulah Bankhead called *Midgie Purvis*, Westman racked up 18 credits on Broadway. She belonged as much to New York as to Hollywood.

In 1930, she married writer and later producer Robert Sparks.[22] Born Salathiel W. Sparks in Peebles, Adams County, Ohio, on February 4, 1898, Sparks was the son of John H. Sparks, a liveryman from Ohio who later turned to farming, and his wife Elsie A. Sparks, also from Ohio.[23] Robert and Nydia's daughter Robina Jane Sparks was born in New York on September

19, 1931, and in the following year the little family packed their bags and moved to California.[24]

Westman had had a "Movietone" test with favorable results in 1928.[25] She didn't get to Hollywood, though, until the sound era was well underway, as part of the tidal wave of actors and other creative people from the New York stage that washed over the film capital in the early 1930s. Her older sister Lolita, who had married Sam A. Burton, a stage actor from California in 1925, was already living in Los Angeles and trying to make her way as a playwright.[26]

Westman made her film debut in 1932 as Gwen in the drama *Strange Justice* (V. Schertzinger, J.G. Bachmann Prod./King Motion Pictures), starring Marian Marsh and Reginald Denny. Her most active period in films was the 1930s, when she acted in 31 features, including *Little Women* (G. Cukor, RKO, 1933), *Three Live Ghosts* (H.B. Humberstone, MGM, 1936), *The Gorgeous Hussy* (C. Brown, MGM, 1936), and *The Cat and the Canary* (E. Nugent, Paramount, 1939) and nearly always with screen credit.

One of my favorites Westman roles is in the 1936 drama *Craig's Wife* (D. Arzner, Columbia). It was based on a hit play about the dangers of being overly house-proud by the then widely popular American playwright George Kelly and starred John Boles as the doormat Walter Craig and Rosalind Russell as his borderline psychopathic wife Harriet. Westman played the maid Mazie, in fact her name is the first word of the film, as it is shouted in warning by the housekeeper Mrs. Harold (Jane Darwell). Mazie is about to move the Grecian-style urn from its exact position at the center of Mrs. Craig's drawing room mantelpiece. "Mazie, never forget. This room is the holy of holies," Mrs. Harold admonishes her. The urn is a central symbol in the film, which Mr. Craig ultimately smashes in his increasing frustration with his cold, rigid, and unloving wife. Fairly early in the film, Mazie is summarily fired when Mrs. Craig returns from a visit to her ailing sister in Albany and discovers Mazie's boyfriend Tom helping her peel potatoes in the kitchen.

I also love Westman in *Manhattan Tower* (F.R. Strayer, Remington Pictures, 1932), only her second release, a "day in the life" type film about the people working in the Empire State Building starring Mary Brian, Irene Rich, and James Hall. Westman plays lawyer Hale Hamilton's clumsy secretary, Miss Wood, who is given to engaging her boss in conversations about her health that he's not much interested in. She's quite the hypochondriac, with an entire pharmacy in her office desk drawer. A typical exchange between Miss Wood and her boss Mr. Witman consists of her saying, "Oh, I think I'll take a pill" and he responding, "I wish you would." All Miss Wood's savings are in the Tower Security Bank, so she is quite disturbed by the fact that the bank president is having hectic meetings in her boss's office. She single-handedly sets off a run on the bank based on something she overhears from such a meeting. As the bank president, Mr. Witman, and two major depositors they have convinced to stay with the bank convivially leave the inner office, Westman happily returns to her outer office with her withdrawn savings, she thinks, safe in her purse. It turns out she dropped the purse in the lobby and someone who looks a lot like George E. Stone (though he is not in the credits) stole the money while pretending to help her. She faints dead away. The entire action is limited to one working day in the building. *Manhattan Tower* is a delightful Depression-era timepiece.

Even with her starring days on Broadway behind her, Westman was prominent enough in Hollywood to rate the occasional feature article. My favorite Westman headline has to be "She Doesn't Need Beauty to Succeed." Who can imagine the same title with a male pronoun?

Nydia Westman was 34 years old when this portrait was taken of her in her role as the maid Mazie in the filmatization of George Kelly's drama *Craig's Wife* (Columbia Pictures Corporation, 1936), starring Rosalind Russell and John Boles. Her uniform is elaborate even for the period.

The author of this casually and all too commonly chauvinistic piece from the period is Whitney Williams. His starting point is "You don't have to be beautiful to succeed in Hollywood." After discussing Zasu Pitts briefly, dragging poor Una Merkel into the fray ("Not that Una isn't an attractive creature, but in no sense of the word could she be described as beautiful") and tarring Helen Hayes, Aline MacMahon, Pauline Lord, and Louise Fazenda with the same brush, "little Miss Nydia Westman" is the main recipient of the writer's backhanded compliments. And there's more. Westman is described as "a mousy little soul, an inch or so over five feet tall" and "rather full of face and not particularly pretty—although by no means unpresentable." In all fairness, Williams also describes her as "one of the cleverest comediennes in talking pictures today." Westman, when allowed to speak for herself, says that she is "still looking for the 'perfect' role" and doesn't want to be typed. She wants variety. She has chosen to freelance rather than sign a long-term contract with a studio, so she can choose what parts she wants to play.[27]

Edna Silverton wrote a piece in a somewhat similar vein in 1936 and entitled it "They Don't Want to Be Stars." Her feature article was subtitled "These Minor Players Are Happy Knowing They Will Never See Their Names in Lights" and dealt with Westman, George Barbier, Ralph Morgan, Marjorie Gateson, Alison Skipworth, Moroni Olsen, Eric Blore, and Andy Devine, "the forgotten men and women of the screen." Westman is quoted describing herself as a Cinderella "with no chance at all of being changed into a Princess in the next to last reel." Though she has no complaints, she wouldn't say no to "the opportunity to wear a pretty dress rather than a gunny sack in a picture sometime." She continues: "I get a little tired of being a Cockney, too, … mostly because my mouth is getting crooked from talking out of one side of it all the time." "I was a star once on Broadway," she concludes, "and it's a lot more fun to be an 'also ran.'"[28]

While Westman's film career was a success in the 1930s, her marriage was not. The trouble was so serious that daughter Robina was sent to live with her paternal great-aunt Olive M. Williamson before she was five years of age. Her parents divorced in 1937.[29] In 1940, we find Robyna [sic] J. Sparks, aged 8, living with the widowed, 69-year-old Mrs. Williamson and her grandson, 13-year-old Merwin Dean Fields, in Seaman Village, Ohio.[30] Her mother was sharing an apartment with her sister Lolita, now also divorced, in the legendary Villa Carlotta apartment building at 5959 Franklin Ave. in Hollywood. Also living in the building at this time were producer Lester Cowan and his screenwriter wife Ann, actress Margot Stevenson, composer Aaron Copland, actress Marjorie Gateson, actress Nana Bryant, actress Fay Wray Saunders and her daughter Susan, and actress Ona Munson and her mother Sally. Nydia had earned in excess of $5,000 for 14 weeks' work in 1939, while Lolita had no income that year as a writer of fiction.[31] By this time, ex-husband Robert Sparks had established himself as the producer of the popular "Blondie" films at Columbia and on January 1, 1941, he married their star, Penny Singleton.[32] They remained married until his death from a heart attack in Hollywood in 1963.

Good parts in movies became scarcer for Westman in the 1940s. After *The Velvet Touch* (J. Gage, Independent Artists/RKO, 1948), she took a 14-year break from films, returning to her first love the theater and embarking on an active career in TV dramas and comedy series. She had made her TV debut in 1947, as Mary Kay Stearns's mother on the first sitcom on American television *Mary Kay and Johnny*.[33] Among the many television shows that benefited from her talents during the next 23 years, we find *Robert Montgomery Presents, The Philco Television Playhouse, Kraft Television Theatre, Studio One, The Ford Television Theatre, The United States Steel Hour, The Alfred Hitchcock Hour, Perry Mason, Bonanza, The Donna Reed Show, Lancer, Dragnet 1967,* and *Bewitched*. As the rectory housekeeper Mrs. Featherstone, she was part of the regular cast of the TV version of *Going My Way* (1962–63), which starred Gene Kelly and Leo. G. Carroll and also included Dick York.[34] Mrs. Featherstone was the role played by Eily Malyon in the famous feature film original starring Bing Crosby and Barry Fitzgerald, where she was called Mrs. Carmody.

During her later stage career, Westman was seen in New York shows like *Strange Bedfellows* (1948); the original production of *The Madwoman of Chaillot* (1948–50), starring Martita Hunt; *Mr. Pickwick* (1952) Terence Rattigan's *The Sleeping Prince* (1956); Beckett's *Endgame* (1958) with P.J. Kelly; and Benn Levy's last play *Rape of the Belt* (1960). During the summer of 1950, she did *Harvey* and Mark Reed's *Yes, My Darling Daughter* with her daughter Jane Sparks and the Kennebunkport Players in Kennebunkport, Maine.[35] She called the experience "her greatest thrill."[36] Jane Sparks married an actor, Al Ruscio (b. 1924), in 1954 and the couple had four children.

Nydia Westman, who was living in Hollywood, lost her battle with cancer at St. Joseph Hospital in Burbank, California, on May 23, 1970, at the age of 68. She was buried in Oakwood Memorial Park, Chatsworth, California, after a funeral at J.T. Oswald Chapel in North Hollywood.[37] Westman was survived by her daughter, who would go on to a career as an actress in film and television in 1977 as Kate Williamson; son-in-law Al Ruscio; and her grandchildren. Williamson and Ruscio died within a month of each other in late 2013.

Ma Jarrett: Margaret Wycherly (1879–1956)

Margaret Wycherly was one of the major actresses on the American stage in the first half of the 20th century, yet she is remembered today, if at all, only as James Cagney's mother and partner in crime in the classic, late gangster film *White Heat* (R. Walsh, Warner Bros., 1949). While Wycherly's film career, which tallied 21 feature films, was only a parenthesis in the long sentence of her acting career on the stage, it has at least given us lasting access to this uniquely talented actress. Sadly, though, most of Wycherly's films do not really show us what she was capable of. I would suggest that she had a range and versatility unrivalled by any actress of her time. Her more than 40 shows on Broadway extended from popular melodramas and murder mysteries (*The Thirteenth Chair*, *Jane Clegg*) to the latest experimental plays by Maeterlinck, Glaspell, Pirandello, and Elmer Rice (*The Blue Bird*, *The Verge*, *Six Characters in Search of an Author*, *The Adding Machine*), from commercial successes (*Another Language*, *Tobacco Road*) to shorter Broadway runs in modern classics (*Rosmersholm*, *Getting Married*, *Hedda Gabler*, *The Glass Menagerie*).

Margaret Wycherly, then, was the quintessential Broadway actress. I want to organize this profile as a guided tour of some of the places important to her life and career that still remain in New York City half a century after her death. But first we must know a little about her background.

Like so many of the millions of talented people who have been drawn to the Big Apple, Wycherly was not born and raised there. She was born Margaret L. De Wolfe in St. Martin's in the Fields in London on October 26, 1879, the daughter of Dr. J.L. De Wolfe and his wife, Caroline M. De Wolfe.[1] In 1881, we find two-year-old Margaret and her 32-year-old mother, who was born in Southsea, Hampshire, in July 1850, and a servant living at Bacomb Terrace in Wendover, England.[2] According to John Parker's *Who's Who in the Theatre*, Wycherly was educated privately and at Boston Latin School.[3] There is conflicting evidence about when she and her mother immigrated to the U.S., but it happened while Margaret was still a child. She claimed her herself in the 1910 U.S. census that she first came to America in 1890, but her mother's claim in the 1900 census that it was in 1892 seems more likely, as we know her mother was still in England in 1891.[4]

Wycherly's father, who was a surgeon,[5] remains a shadowy figure and appears not to have accompanied his wife and daughter to their new home across the Atlantic. Caroline De Wolfe appears as "married" both in the 1900 and 1920 U.S. census, so the couple would appear to have lived separate lives without being divorced. Wycherly's mother worked as a trained nurse. I have discovered that in 1900 she was a live-in nurse for the former New York senator, U.S. Attorney General, and Secretary of State Williams Maxwell Evarts at his home at 231 2nd Ave. in New York City. In the census, it appears that 49-year-old De Wolfe has been in the United States since 1892, has been married 23 years, and is the mother of two children of which one is living.[6] This means that Margaret's parents were married around 1877, two years or so before her birth, and that she had an older or younger sibling that died in infancy. De Wolfe lost her patient and, one assumes, her job when Evarts died on February 28, 1901. In 1920, she was no longer working as a nurse and was living in a hotel at 15–19 E. 11th St. in New York.[7] She died on February 25, 1923, as her daughter was just finishing her run in Pirandello's *Six Character in Search of an Author* at the Princess Theatre in New York.[8]

We begin our tour of Margaret Wycherly's New York with the earliest precise address I have for her: 1270 Madison Ave. on the Upper East Side of Manhattan. Wycherly and her small family were captured in the amber of the 1910 U.S. census on April 23, 1910. She gave her correct age as 30, was born in England of parents born in England, had one child, and was a stage actress. Her husband, Bayard Veiller, was then 41, born in New York, and was working for a newspaper. They were actually living in the rented apartment of Wycherly's mother-in-law, Elizabeth DePuy Veiller, who was 62, born in Pennsylvania, a widow, and the mother of three children.[9] Margaret's and Bayard's nearly seven-year-old son Anthony Veiller was, for reasons unknown, not living with them at this time.

The building at 1270 Madison Ave., on the corner of 91st St., stands out by clearly being the oldest apartment building on the block, indeed probably for several blocks.[10] It is painted beige and brown today and is from the second half of the 19th century in the modified Renaissance palazzo style with a heavy pediment, a distinctive curved wall at the corner where the two streets meet, and the regulation fire escapes. Wycherly would never live on the Upper East Side in later life. Her husband's family, though, despite many rises and falls in their fortunes, was "fashionable." In her father-in-law Phillip Veiller's day, they had last lived at 1037 Fifth Ave., just north of the Metropolitan Museum of Art, where he had died in 1906.[11]

By 1910, Wycherly had been on the stage for a dozen years and she and her husband had been married for eight years.[12] A friend who knew them in their early days in New York, wrote on Wycherly's death half a century later: "She and Bayard had no money, but they had intelligence and dreams."[13] In addition to being one of the first to produce the Irish plays of William Butler Yeats in America (that was in 1905), Wycherly had starred in her husband's first play on Broadway, *The Primrose Path*, which was a "succès d'éstime" for her, but a commercial failure at the Majestic Theatre in 1907; and played the titular heroine in a revival of Shaw's *Candida* at the Berkeley Lyceum Theatre in 1907–08, which didn't do much better.[14]

Old Mrs. Veiller lived to see her son's breakthrough play on Broadway in 1912, *Within the Law* starring Jane Cowl, but not the follow-up hit melodrama he wrote for his wife four years later, *The Thirteenth Chair*. Here, as the *New York Times* pointed out, the "whodunit" methods of detective fiction were for the first time systematically applied to stage melodrama.[15] Wycherly played the fraudulent medium Rosalie La Grange, who must help the police in solving two mysterious murders to save her own daughter from a murder charge. Mrs. Veiller died in May 1916 and *The Thirteenth Chair* opened at the 48th Street Theatre on November 20, 1916, ran for 328 performances there and at the Fulton Theatre, before a lengthy tour, which lasted till 1918 and took Wycherly as far afield as Australia and New Zealand.[16] In addition to the eponymous heroine of *Jane Clegg* and Ada Lester in *Tobacco*

Road, Rosalie La Grange was the stage role Wycherly was most identified with and the only major role she reprised on film. *The Thirteenth Chair* gave Wycherly her sound film debut when it was filmed by MGM under the direction of Tod Browning in 1929. She would only make one film in the 1930s, *Midnight* (aka *Call It Murder*; C. Erskine, All Star Prod./Universal, 1934), and the bulk of her not very large body of films was produced in the 1940s.

Our next stop on the tour is in Midtown, more precisely an apartment building at 146 E. 49 St. When Wycherly returned from her tour of Australia and New Zealand in late 1918, she listed this as her address.[17] This fairly innocuous, nine-story building in beige brick with stone trim and the traditional blue awning over the entrance would have been quite new then. It was conveniently located in relation to the theaters, of course, though we cannot be certain she was still living there when she returned to Broadway in 1920 in the successful domestic drama *Jane Clegg* by the Irish dramatist St. John Ervine. It was produced by the Theatre Guild at the Garrick Theatre, which stood near 6th Ave. at 67 W. 35th St. until 1932, where the Hilton Garden Inn New York stands now. No lesser a critic than Alexander Woollcott wrote in his *New York Times* review, "It is seldom that our stage … produces a play as perfectly as 'Jane Clegg' has been produced by the Theatre Guild." He wrote of Wycherly's performance as "a strong and resolute woman who works out to her own satisfaction her theory that there is no sense in living with a man who isn't loyal": "Miss Wycherly's portrait of Jane Clegg is forcefully, reticently, spontaneously presented, with the most delicate of shadings and a deft suggestion throughout of all that is going on in the mind of the determined but inarticulate woman. As she moves through the play you can see her thinking it out, thinking it out."[18]

In November and December 1921, Wycherly starred in an experimental play by Susan Glaspell called *The Verge*. It was produced by the Provincetown Players at their own Provincetown Playhouse and that is the next stop on our tour, as the original building, beautifully restored by New York University, still stands at 133 MacDougal St., half a block down from the southwest corner of Washington Square. Woollcott was clearly baffled by the play and did not care for it (e.g., "'The Verge' is a play which can be intelligently reviewed only by a neurologist or by some woman who has journeyed near to the verge of which Miss Glaspell writes"), but he thought it was "momentarily and disproportionately glorified by the vital and radiant playing of Margaret Wycherly in its central role."[19] The play only lasted 38 performances.[20]

It was the following year, in 1922, that Margaret Wycherly and Bayard Veiller were divorced after more than 20 years of marriage.[21] Veiller soon married the writer Marguerite Vale (aka "Martin Vale"; 1883–1969) and died in New York in 1943. Wycherly never remarried. With her son Tony almost grown and no husband, she was now free to dedicate herself entirely to her art. As one newspaper had written of her in 1917: "if there is one actress on the American stage today who has striven for the uplift of the drama more than any other person, that actress is Margaret Wycherly." She was also free to live wherever she wanted in New York. For the rest of her life, she would live in or near the arty and bohemian Greenwich Village. She also preferred to live in her own house, rather than an apartment, which in New York meant a row house.

To locate what may have been Wycherly's first home after her divorce, we simply continue south on MacDougal St. till it ends and then turn right past Father Fagan Park and 6th Ave. 24 Charlton St. is one of three gorgeous, three-story, Georgian townhouses with sash windows and green shutters, that by some miracle have been preserved on the south side of the street. We know Wycherly was living there in 1926 and in 1927,[22] which were the years she began what would become an annual ritual only interrupted by the war years: a lengthy trip to Europe in the summer or early fall.

The years immediately following her divorce were rich ones for Wycherly, with appearances in the original productions of what would become two modern classics: Luigi Pirandello's *Six Characters in Search of an Author*, where she created the role of the mother at the long gone Princess Theatre on the south side of 39th St. between 6th Ave. and Broadway; and Elmer Rice's *The Adding Machine*, where she played Daisy Diana Dorothea Devore at the Garrick and later the Comedy theatres. They too have been demolished. In fact, the list of New York theatres that Wycherly performed in that have been razed is much longer than the list of those that survive. We are going to look at some of the survivors later on.

Wycherly starred as Rebecca West in Ibsen's *Rosmersholm* in 1925, before she hit a dry run of five consecutive flops on Broadway. The curse was finally broken by *The Jade God* in 1928. By then she had moved to 46 Commerce St., which will be our next stop.[23] From her Charlton St. address, we simply walk up Varick St. till it merges into 7th Ave., take a left at Bedford St. and then a left again at Commerce St., which takes a turn before it emerges again on Barrow St. Here in this quiet cul-de-sac, practically next door to the historic Cherry Lane Theatre formed in 1924, Wycherly lived for a while in yet another red brick row house, before finding what would be her New York home for the next quarter of a century just a few blocks further uptown.

Reemerging on 7th Ave., we walk northwards till we get to Perry St. The home with which Wycherly would be most closely identified lies at 10 Perry St., on the south side of the short block between 7th Ave. and Greenwich Ave. This is a large, elegant, nineteenth-century row house built of warm, pink bricks with a full basement, beautiful wrought iron railings, and a typical stoop leading up to the handsome, dark-stained, double front door. We know that Wycherly lived here from 1930 till about 1955, when she moved to her final New York home at 108 W. 15th St.[24] For 25 years, then, during her last 17 years on Broadway and throughout the years of her film work in Hollywood in the 1940s, this remained her home base. It was here she lived when she gave some of her greatest performances on the New York stage in plays like *Another Language*, *Tobacco Road*, and *The Glass Menagerie*. It was here she was living when the 1940 U.S. census was taken on April 13, 1940, paying $40 a month in rent, and claiming to be 51, when she was really 61. She also said she had only earned $1,000 in 1939.[25] It was here she was living when in 1942 she was nominated for an Academy Award as Best Actress in a Supporting Role for *Sergeant York* (H. Hawks, Warner Bros., 1941), which was only her fifth film, if we include her only silent *The Fight* (G.W. Lederer, George W. Lederer Stage Filmotions, 1915), based on one of her husband's early plays. She lost to Mary Astor in *The Great Lie*.

I have only found one address for Wycherly in Los Angeles. In 1939, she was living at 1152 Gordon St., which is a two-story, faintly Spanish style apartment building in Hollywood near Santa Monica Blvd. and Hollywood Forever Cemetery. In the 1940s, her twice Oscar-nominated screenwriter and producer son, Anthony De Wolfe Veiller, was living in great style at 807 N. Foothill Rd. in Beverly Hills and later more modestly at 9931 Durant Dr. in Beverly Hills, so my guess is that Wycherly stayed with him or at a hotel when she was filming.[26] He had married fellow screenwriter Laura Hornickel Kerr (1902–91) on New Year's Eve 1933 and the couple had a daughter, Caroline Margaret, in Los Angeles on March 17, 1936.[27] In addition to the money, then, acting in Hollywood films would have had the added inducement of allowing Wycherly to spend time with her son and granddaughter. Anthony Veiller and Laura Kerr were divorced in 1945.[28] Veiller married Grace Dorothy Hornburg (1911–81) on June 10, 1948, and they had a son, Philip Bayard Veiller, on November 22, 1948.[29] You do the math. As her time in Hollywood was nearing its end in 1948, Wycherly's verdict on the movie industry was as follows: "Pictures don't call for acting. There's no need to sustain a part or a scene in pictures. It's just technical ... that's not acting."[30]

It is time to have a look at some of the Broadway theaters that were such an integral part of Wycherly's life and career. As I've already indicated, the majority of the theaters Wycherly performed in have been demolished, but a few survive. If we leave Perry St. and Greenwich Village, then, and move uptown, we need to zoom in on the block of 45th St. between 7th and 8th Ave. This one block is jam-packed with theaters and here we will find no less than three where Wycherly celebrated some of her greatest stage triumphs. Standing on the sidewalk by the Marriott Hotel and looking west, you can actually see the neon signs of all three of them at the same time: the Booth, the Jacobs, and the Golden.

The Booth Theatre at 222 W. 45th St. was also the Booth on April 25, 1932, when Wycherly opened there in one of the biggest commercial successes of her career: Rose Franken's domestic drama *Another Language*. Wycherly created the role of Mother Hallam, which I personally will always think of as belonging to Louise Closser Hale, but that is only because she got to do the excellent film version at MGM in 1933. I can imagine that Wycherly was equally if differently perfect as the hypochondriac, manipulative matriarch of a lower middle-class family on the Upper West Side, who in classic "silver cord" fashion wants to keep her sons tied to her apron strings even after they marry and have families of their own. For this reason and because of a basic clash of personalities, she is at daggers drawn with her "artistic" daughter-in-law Stella (Dorothy Stickney) in a fight to the death (to pile on another martial metaphor) for control over her son and Stella's husband Jerry (John Beal). Wycherly was physically different from Hale and didn't look as innately comical, but I can imagine that she would have seemed more sinister and threatening with her intense, coal black eyes, spare, hawkish expression, and determined chin. Margaret Hamilton made both her Broadway debut and her film debut as the laconic but sympathetic daughter-in-law Helen Hallam in *Another Language*.

The 1930s would be dominated for Wycherly by an even greater commercial success than *Another Language*. *Tobacco Road* is still one of the longest running straight plays on Broadway and Margaret Wycherly created the central role of Ada Lester in this marathon production, which opened at the Theatre Masque on December 4, 1933. The Theatre Masque at 242 W. 45th St. was renamed for the producer John Golden in 1937. Wycherly's obituary in the *New York Herald Tribune* said she stayed with the show for three years.[31] We can be certain she had left her role to Leora Thatcher by the fall of 1937, because on October 1, 1937, she opened in a "musical extravaganza" called *A Hero Is Born* at the Adelphi Theatre, produced by the Federal Theatre Project of The WPA. Again, her leading role in *Tobacco Road* went to another actress in the film version, which is why Ada Lester for me is Elizabeth Patterson, again quite a different actress physically and a considerably more benign figure than Wycherly. The Twentieth Century–Fox film version of *Tobacco Road* from 1941 is not memorable, despite a fine cast, but then fashions have changed and this type of rustic, Rabelaisean humor will probably never again finds it audience. *Tobacco Road* was last revived on Broadway in 1950, but closed after only seven performances.[32]

A play that has held its own and remained a landmark of American drama is Tennessee Williams's *The Glass Menagerie*. It is well known that this first hit play from Williams's hand provided drink-sodden Laurette Taylor with a sorely needed comeback role and a capstone to her stage career, but what fewer people know is that Wycherly replaced her as Amanda Wingfield on June 3, 1946.[33] This was at the Playhouse on 48th St., which was razed in 1969 to expand Rockefeller Center, but the play transferred July 1st to the Royale Theatre, which still exists as the Bernard B. Jacobs Theatre at 242 W. 45th St. and is our last stop on this theater-filled block. The critic Walter Prichard Eaton wrote in an appreciation shortly after Wycherly's death, "She may have been one of the very few actresses who could follow Laurette Taylor in the role,"[34] but the author of the play was not impressed. Tennessee Williams wrote to his friend Audrey Wood in June 1946, after seeing Wycherly in the part: "I thought she was doing a reasonably good job but it seemed just a substitution. She does not have Taylor's humor. That was the big deficiency.... I don't think she is really right for the part."[35]

Margaret Wycherly (far left) looks considerably more elegant and civilized in her role as Grandma Read in *Something in the Wind* (Universal International Pictures, 1947) than she would two years later in her signature role as Ma Jarrett in *White Heat*. With her in this breakfast scene are (from left) Donald O'Connor, Beth Taylor, and Charles Winninger.

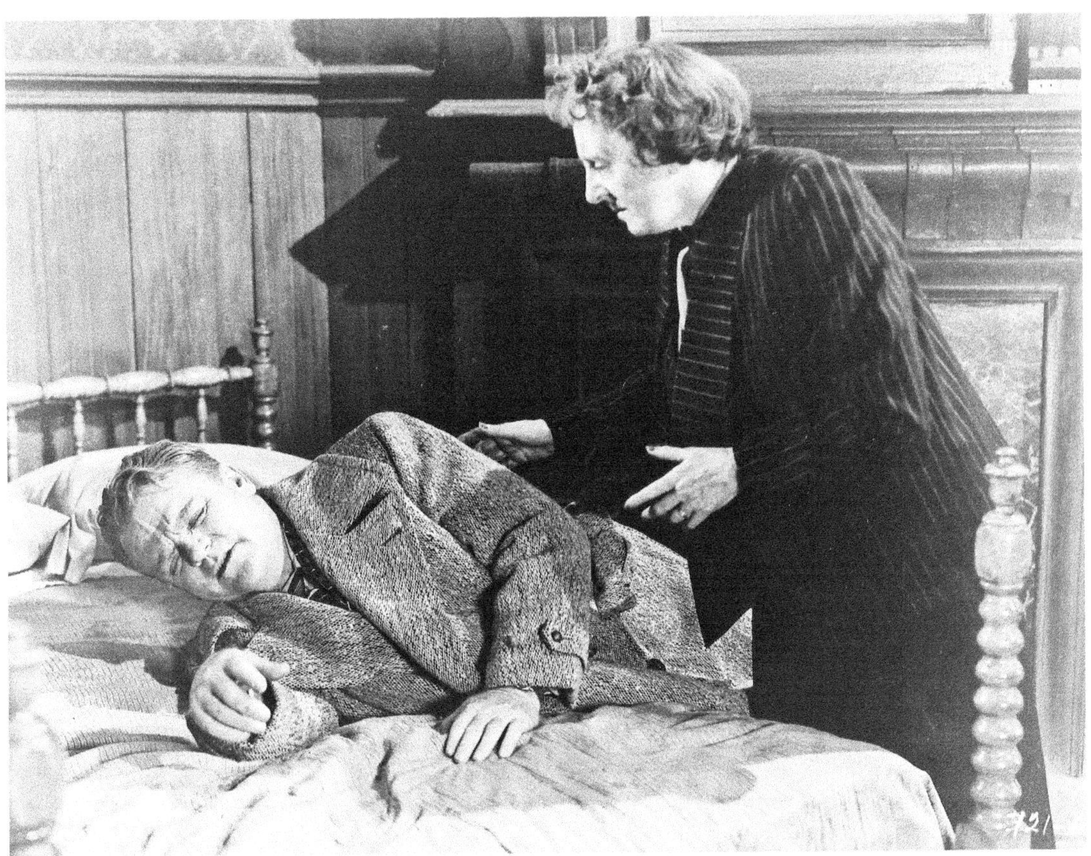

Ma Jarrett (Margaret Wycherly) gets ready to give some tender loving care to her boy, the brutal gangster Cody Jarrett, in this classic scene from *White Heat* (Warner Bros, 1949), proving once again that a boy's best friend is his mother. Cagney and director Raoul Walsh wanted to see how far they could go and even have Cody sitting in his mother's lap at one point.

We need to pay one more visit, though, to another existing Broadway theater, before we're done. If we walk two blocks up to 256 W. 47 St., we'll be standing before the lovely, mock Palladian Brooks Atkinson Theatre, which used to be the Mansfield. Wycherly's final Broadway show was staged here, a new, two-act Biblical drama called *Dear Judas,* written, produced, and directed by Mike Myerberg. Unfortunately, it was a failure and only lasted 17 performances in October 1947.[36] Wycherly never returned to Broadway in the nine years that remained to her. She still had *White Heat* and a couple more feature films left to do in Hollywood, though, and worked in television between 1949 and 1955.

If you walk five blocks northwards on 8th Ave. from the Brooks Atkinson Theatre and turn left on 52nd St., you'll come to a large, nondescript, six-story, red brick building covering a large part of the south side of the 400 block. This was once upon a time a hospital, St. Clare's Hospital to be exact. It was here Margaret Wycherly died of a stroke on June 6, 1956.[37] She was 76 years old. Hers had been an unusually full, creative, and rewarding life. How fitting that she passed out of it only blocks from the Broadway theaters that had been her real home.

Wycherly was buried with her mother in the graveyard of St. Mary's Church in Bepton,

West Sussex, where her son Anthony Veiller was laid to rest nine years later and her daughter-in-law, Grace Rowley Veiller, in 1981. The inscription on their grave reads: "They were born in this land and have returned to it."[38] This reminds me of something Hedda Hopper wrote in her column in 1949: "If Margaret Wycherly were English, she'd be Dame Margaret."[39] So much had Americans taken Wycherly to heart, they had forgotten where she was born.

Bohemian Rhapsody: Blanche Yurka (1887–1974)

The Jurkas of St. Paul, Minnesota, and later New York City were like other immigrant families in the United States in the late 19th and early 20th century. The parents worked hard for little financial reward, skimped and saved their pennies, and pinned their hopes on their children having a better life and larger opportunities then they had had themselves. The Jurkas were fundamentally different, though, from practically every Continental European immigrant family at least, in that they nurtured one of the most important presences in the 20th-century American theatre in their midst.

At a time when the stars of the American stage were overwhelmingly of Anglo-Saxon Protestant and Irish Catholic descent, Blanche Yurka was different in being a second-generation immigrant of Czech origin. Both her parents were born in what was then Bohemia and were early immigrants from that region to the United States. According to information in the U.S. census, Yurka's mother, born Karolina Nowak in November 1848 (also known as Caroline, Carrie, and Charlotte), was the first of the two to arrive in the mid–1850s.[1] Caroline's father was Joseph Nowak (b. c. 1817), who prospered as a hardware merchant in Chicago; her mother was Frances Nowak (b. c. 1821–22). The couple had 13 children according to their granddaughter's autobiography.[2]

With hyperbole typical of the period, Anton (also called Antonin or Anthony) Jurka was described in a 1910 news item, as "one of the first Bohemian pioneers in this country and a leading Bohemian journalist."[3] Yurka's father immigrated from Bohemia to the United States in 1866, when he was in his mid–20s.[4] This was the year Caroline Nowak, urged by her parents, married one of her father's colleagues in the hardware business, Civil War veteran, and a fellow Czech, Alois Uher.[5] Caroline was only 18, Alois was 23. This marriage of convenience turned out to be a recipe for disaster and would cast a long shadow over Caroline and her family's lives. The Uhers had three children, of which only one, their daughter "Mila" (Mildred), lived to maturity. Mila was born in December 1873.[6] The following year, Caroline discovered that Alois was having an affair with her best friend. She took her daughter and moved back in with her parents.[7] In 1880, we find the extended Nowak family—Joseph (65) and Frances (58), their children Charlotte Uher (29), Joseph (28), Robert (22), Rosa (22), and Louisa (20), and granddaughter Mildred Uher (6) living on Halstead St. in Chicago.[8] The Uhers subsequently divorced and Alois Uher died in Chicago in 1883.[9]

Meanwhile, Anton Jurka had loved Caroline from a distance and worked to better himself. He had moved to St. Paul, Minnesota, and found work as a teacher.[10] Now he had his chance. The couple were married in St. Paul on April 10, 1882.[11] "Carrie" was now 34, her second husband in his early 40s. During their 18 years in St. Paul, they lived at 16 Douglas St. and raised four children in a modest wooden house that miraculously has survived and appears little changed from when the Jurkas lived there more than a hundred years ago.[12] Rosa (Rose) Jurka was born on March 12, 1883,[13] Charles A. Jurka on July 30, 1884,[14] Blanche Jurka on June 19, 1887,[15] and Anton (Anthony) Jurka on July 30, 1891.[16] According to Blanche, her father was jealous and irrationally resented Mildred as the living embodiment of her mother's first disastrous marriage. Throughout the 1890s, she lived with her maternal grandmother in Chicago and did not rejoin the family until they pulled up stakes and moved to New York City in 1900.[17] Anton had lost his job as a teacher; there were no promising prospects for him in St. Paul and he had secured a position as the executive secretary of the Czech Benevolent Society in New York.[18]

The move to New York at the turn of the last century was, of course, a fateful one for the entire family, but particularly for the youngest daughter, Blanche, who was "gifted" and who would now have greater opportunities for artistic development. The family moved into the basement and ground floor of a typical New York brownstone on the Upper East Side, not the fashionable Upper East Side, mind you, but down by the river at 522 E. 82nd St.[19] Yurka first attended the 68th Street Grammar School for a year and graduated in 1903 from Wadleigh High School, which still stands at 215 W. 114th St.[20]

Yurka originally intended to be an opera singer and studied for two years at the Metropolitan Opera School. She made her stage debut in 1903 as the Grail-bearer in a Metropolitan production of *Parsifal*, before having her scholarship discontinued because the development of her voice was not deemed satisfactory.[21] She got a second chance when she was accepted at the Institute of Musical Art, the predecessor to Juillard, but again her voice was deemed insufficiently developed and she was not allowed to continue beyond the second year.[22]

Yurka was 20 years old when she had to give up on becoming an opera singer. This brings our story to 1907, which was about the time her father had to stop working due to encroaching blindness. To make matters worse, her mother, who had never learned English properly and had not adjusted well to the move to New York, suffered a nervous break-down, which meant that Yurka had to take over many of her household duties.[23] The chances of an artistic career of any kind seemed dim, when by more or less laying siege to legendary producer David Belasco, Yurka finally obtained a position as an understudy for Sara Haden's mother, the stage star and celebrated beauty Charlotte Walker, in a production of *The Warrens of Virginia* at the Belasco Theatre.[24] One thing led to another and Yurka made her Broadway debut at the same theatre on August 24, 1909, as Helen Hoyt in Leo Dietrichson's comedy *Is Matrimony a Failure?* starring Jane Cowl.[25] She was now 22.

The story of Yurka's stellar stage career has been told in several other places, not least of all in her readable autobiography, and need not be repeated in great detail here.[26] From her debut until her final stage role more than 60 years later, Blanche Yurka was one of the most vibrant and dynamic presences in the 20th-century American theatre. Idealistic, strong-minded, uncompromising, and with a seriousness bordering on humorlessness, which is often considered to be stereotypically Czech, Yurka made a stunning career for herself and one unparalleled at the time by any other daughter of Eastern European immigrants. There was Alla Nazimova, of course, but she was born in Russia and came to the United States as an adult.

A history of the American theatre could be written based on Yurka's career alone, albeit an impressionistic and one-sided one. Yurka worked with a large number and variety of major actors of the first half of the 20th century and not only as an actor. She was a director as well, and a teacher and a writer, with passionate ideas about what the theatre should be and do, as best expressed in her 1959 book *Dear Audience: A Guide to the Enjoyment of Theatre*. She got her start as a protégée of David Belasco and Jane Cowl. In turn, Yurka gave Bette Davis an important break when she hired her to play Hedvig and directed her on a tour of *The Wild Duck* in 1929. Davis described her as "a giant bird of prey": "Her long neck pressed forward and her glowing eyes devoured everything around her."[27] Unfortunately, the two never acted together on film.

The roster of the more familiar actors Yurka worked with on Broadway includes (in chronological order) E.H. Sothern, John Barrymore, Tyrone Power, Sr., Alfred Lunt and Lynn Fontanne, Mrs. Patrick Campbell, Alma Kruger, Charles Waldron, Leo G. Carroll, Charles Coburn, Otis Skinner, Esther Dale, Mildred Natwick, Barbara O'Neil, James Stewart, Basil Rathbone, Wendell Corey, Kirk Douglas, Farley Granger, Janice Rule, Jerry Stiller, Sada Thompson, Ruth Ford, Arlene Francis, June Havoc, Jeffrey Lynn, and Walter Pidgeon.

Ruth Gordon tells a funny story about Yurka and Mrs. Patrick Campbell. There was no love lost between these two strong women. They had worked together in 1932 in a short-lived production of Sophocles' *Electra* at the Selwyn Theatre with Yurka in the title role and Mrs. Patrick Campbell as Clytemnestra. Gordon writes in her autobiography that Mrs. Pat had the habit of making up new words. At the close of 1932, she went to see Katharine Cornell in *Lucrece*, which ran for 30 performances at the Belasco Theatre with Brian Aherne, Brenda Forbes, and Charles Waldron. When Gordon heard about this, she asked her if it was an all-English cast. Stella Campbell replied: "No. Blanche Yurka was yurking around."[28]

In 1909, just as Blanche Yurka was embarking on her stage career, she and her family were able to purchase their own home at 242 E. 72nd St.[29] This narrow, four-story New York brownstone, two windows wide, with its characteristic stoop, iron railings, and Renaissance palazzo pediment would be Yurka's home for 20 years and witnessed both the happiest and the saddest days of her professional and personal life.[30] Four of the people Yurka loved most in the world died in the 72nd St. house: her autocratic but loving father "Tatinek" in August 1917[31]; her mother "Maminka" in the spring of 1926[32]; her beloved half-sister Mildred, who was 14 years her senior and like a second mother to her, working all her life as a dressmaker to help support the family, in December 1926[33]; and finally, her younger brother Anthony, who was a dentist and threw himself out of his fourth-story bedroom window in 1928. His sister never knew why.[34] The home was also the site of joyous occasions, as when Yurka's older brother Charles married Edith Schevcik, also of Bohemian descent, in 1915.[35]

After Yurka married fellow actor Ian Keith (1898–1960) in Chicago in 1922 with Patricia Collinge and her husband as witnesses, the newlyweds moved into their own home, but the small, three-room apartment was only three blocks from the Jurka family home.[36] Yurka's marriage to the much younger and ridiculously handsome Keith soon failed, indirectly over his professional jealousy of his wife's success and his mother's interference and directly because of his rather public affair with his co-star in *As You Like It*, Marjorie Rambeau (1889–1970) in the spring of 1923. Yurka (like her mother before her) moved back to her parental home.[37] The couple didn't divorce till 1928.[38] Yurka never had another long-term relationship, though she hints at affairs and flirtations in her memoirs.[39]

With Charles living in a lovely home in Mount Pleasant, Westchester and all the other members of the family dead, Blanche and her school teacher sister Rose decided to sell the brownstone in 1929.[40] Characteristically, they moved just a block further east on the same street to a six-room, rented apartment at 325 E. 72nd St., which cost $175 a month in 1930 and which would be their home for the rest of their lives.[41] In Blanche's case, this apartment was her home for 45 years, minus the time she spent in Hollywood.

Blanche Yurka originally went west, as we well know, for "the plum of the season,"[42] the role of Madame De Farge in *A Tale of Two Cities* (J. Conway, 1935), which was produced at MGM in June, July, and August 1935. When MGM failed to pick up her option, she chose to return to New York and the stage.[43] Yurka didn't get back to Hollywood until 1939, when production started on the modest gangster flick *Queen of the Mob* (aka *The Woman from Hell*; J.P. Hogan, Paramount, 1940), where she played the title character Ma Brewster, "a kind of female Little Caesar."[44] Yurka stayed in Hollywood through the war years and lived first in a $60 a month rented home at 1517½ N. Hayworth Ave. in West Hollywood with two female lodgers: Pennsylvania-born fellow actress Frances Carson (1895–1973), who had moved to

Blanche Yurka (right) in her stellar role as Madame De Farge in *A Tale of Two Cities* (Metro-Goldwyn-Mayer, 1935), behind the counter of their wine shop with her husband, Ernest De Farge (Mitchell Lewis), and (from left) Fay Chaldecott, Edna May Oliver, and Elizabeth Allan. When asked by another visitor to the store what kinds of things she knits, Madame De Farge responds: "Everything. Mostly shrouds."

Los Angeles from London and was hoping to get work in films; and a 23-year-old wigmaker and cosmetician, Maria Masha, who was Czech. Yurka reported to the census enumerator on April 26, 1940, that she had earned $1,400 for 12 weeks' work in the previous year.[45]

In 1942, her peak year with the release of four films, Yurka moved to 1436 N. Harper Ave., which was also in West Hollywood and only four blocks from her old home. The rented house was a renovation project she discovered on her walks in the neighborhood and describes in loving detail in her autobiography. She called it "Casa Elastica" for its expansive capacity for containing guests.[46] By 1945, the "major phase," if you can call it that, of Yurka's film career was over and she moved back to New York, though she would act sporadically in films up until *Thunder in the Sun* (R. Rouse, Carrollton/Seven Arts) in 1959.[47] She also worked to some extent in television during these years; starting in 1949 in a 30-minute drama with John Beal and Henry Hull entitled "The Birthday Party" as part of the *Chevrolet Tele-Theatre* and for the next dozen years.

So what did Hollywood make of Blanche Yurka? Practically nothing. I honestly don't think they knew what to do with her. There are many examples of stage star appeal not transferring to the big screen—Lunt and Fontanne, for example, Katharine Cornell, even Tallulah Bankhead—but that was not the problem here. Yurka had only briefly been a conventional ingénue and star and was almost from the beginning a character player on Broadway, however much a leading lady. No, the problem for Yurka in Hollywood was that there weren't really substantial roles for anyone with her particular talents and background. There simply weren't stories being told that might showcase her unique combination of foreignness and familiarity. Brooks Atkinson gave her the highest accolade, when in the afterword to her autobiography he called her "a total actress."[48]

Yurka was particularly expert at playing ordinary women in extraordinary circumstances, like many of Ibsen's heroines and Ancient Greek ones as well. She needed parts she could really dig her teeth into and bring to life with her formidable analytical abilities and finely honed technique. And what did she get? Mostly crazy old crones, assorted hysterics, and cardboard cut-out villainesses. I'm thinking of her silly roles in run-of-the-mill film fare like *Lady for a Night* (L. Jason, Republic, 1942), *A Night to Remember* (R. Wallace, Columbia, 1942), and *One Body Too Many* (F. McDonald, Pine-Thomas, 1944).

In the first of these, Yurka plays Joan Blondell's dastardly, snobbish sister-in-law, who will stop at nothing to get rid of her and to hide her murder of her sister's fiancé on his wedding night. One might well ask why in this period picture set in the Deep South, Yurka is togged out like Lady Dracula with a hairstyle probably never seen in Memphis or any other Southern city. In *A Night to Remember*, starring Loretta Young and Brian Aherne, she gets to portray a hysterical housekeeper at a lodging house, who mistakes a turtle for a monster. In *One Body Too Many*, a low budget crime comedy starring Jack Haley, that body may very well be Yurka's, as in the role of a dead millionaire's housekeeper she is given practically nothing to do but look dark and sinister.

There is one role, though, that even more than the examples just mentioned epitomizes the idiocy of Hollywood's casting of Yurka and why she called her time in Hollywood "The Wasted Years."[49] It's one of her later films, a western melodrama called *The Furies* (A. Mann, Hal Wallis Prod., 1950), starring Walter Huston as a "law unto himself," big time rancher and Barbara Stanwyck as his strong-willed daughter, who is conducting a "cross-cultural" affair with one of the Mexican American squatters on the ranch, played by Gilbert Roland. Yurka

Blanche Yurka looked a lot like herself in daily life for her role as a spy in *Pacific Rendezvous* (Metro-Goldwyn-Mayer, 1942) with (from left) Felix Basch, Lee Bowman, and Mona Maris.

is thrown into the mix as Roland's mother and the matriarch of the Herrera family, a vengeful old crone with unruly black hair and a large plaid shawl over her shoulders, who finally shoots and kills Huston after he is responsible for having her son hanged. It is all too easy to see this as a grotesque parody of her role in *A Tale of Two Cities.*

As I observed in the case of Violet Kemble-Cooper, it is always sad when an actor's first film role turns out to be the best of the lot. This was even more the case with Yurka, who burst onto the screen as Madame De Farge in *A Tale of Two Cities* and then fizzled out in lackluster, limited roles for the remainder of her film career. Maybe she was wrong to have returned to the stage after her "success d'éstime" in Dickens's classic. She herself called it "a costly decision,"[50] but roles like Madame De Farge don't grow on trees and such an opportunity would have been a hard act to follow. Once Yurka had been typed as a portrayer of fanatical women, it limited producers' perceptions of her. She wrote the most poignant epitaph over her film career herself, when she said: "Hollywood missed out on Blanche Yurka."[51]

By the 1960s, with her sister and flat-mate Rose dead, Yurka found herself the sole surviving member of her family.[52] Shockingly, her brother Charles had also died a suicide; that was all the way back in 1930. He had recently turned from dentistry to real estate and suffered serious financial reverses in the wake of the stock market crash, losing his sister Blanche's savings as well as his own.[53] He left his widow Edith (1887–1976), who never remarried, and three children: Edith M. Jurka (1915–2012), Carol F. Jurka (Coggeshall) (b. c. 1918), and Charles E. Jurka (1924–2006).[54]

Blanche Yurka acted for the last time in an off-Broadway production of Jean Giraudoux's *The Madwoman of Chaillot*, which was also done in London in 1970, and lived to be nearly 87 years old. She died of arteriosclerosis at Mount Sinai Hospital in New York City on June 6, 1974, and was buried June 8 in the Actors' Fund section of Kensico Cemetery, after a memorial service at the Universal Funeral Chapel, Lexington Ave. and 52nd St.[55] She shares her grave with fellow actress Florence Reed (1880–1967).[56]

Chapter Notes

Jessie Busley

1. This account is based on "Mr. Joy Held No Joy for Jessie Busley," *Boston Post* (March 23, 1908), p. 7. The description of Joy's appearance is from Ernest C. Joy's 1918 draft registration. See "United States World War I Draft Registration Cards, 1917–1918," index and images, *FamilySearch* (https://familysearch.org/pal:/MM9.1.1/KZVN-NBG: accessed 24 February 2015), Ernest C Joy, 1917–1918; citing Los Angeles City no 14, California, United States, NARA microfilm publication M1509 (Washington, D.C.: National Archives and Records Administration, n.d.); FHL microfilm 1,530,902.

2. "Opening Night at Theaters," *Washington Post* (March 12, 1907), p. 5.

3. "Timely Talk of Stageland," *San Antonio Light* (February 24, 1907), p. 20.

4. "Timely Talk of Stageland," p. 20.

5. "Opening Night at Theaters," *Washington Post*, p. 5; "Stage News and Gossip, Season 1907–8," *Anaconda Standard* (October 27, 1907), p. 2. See also "In the Bishop's Carriage," *San Antonio Light* (December 22, 1907), p. 22.

6. "Miss Busley Reported Wed," *New York Times* (November 22, 1907), www.nytimes.com. See also "Mr. Joy Held No Joy for Jessie Busley," *Boston Post*, p. 7 and *Washington Post* (December 1, 1907), p. 4.

7. "United States World War I Draft Registration Cards, 1917–1918," Ernest C Joy.

8. "United States Census, 1880," index and images, *FamilySearch* (https://familysearch.org/pal:/MM9.1.1/MDLQ-TGG: accessed 24 February 2015), Ernest Joy in household of Fred R Joy, St. Ansgar, Mitchell, Iowa, United States; citing enumeration district 313, sheet 558B, NARA microfilm publication T9 (Washington, D.C.: National Archives and Records Administration, n.d.), roll 0356; FHL microfilm 1,254,356; "Minnesota, State Census, 1895," index and images, *FamilySearch* (https://familysearch.org/pal:/MM9.1.1/MQ8T-WL1: accessed 24 February 2015), Ernest C Joy, Minneapolis city, Ward 02, Hennepin, Minnesota; citing p. 1, line 13, State Library and Records Service, St. Paul; FHL microfilm 565,776; "United States Census, 1900," index and images, *FamilySearch* (https://familysearch.org/pal:/MM9.1.1/M9SD-LKF: accessed 24 February 2015), Earnest Joy in household of Fred R Joy, Election District 7 Minneapolis city Ward 2, Hennepin, Minnesota, United States; citing sheet 12B, family 272, NARA microfilm publication T623 (Washington, D.C.: National Archives and Records Administration, n.d.); FHL microfilm 1,240,766.

9. "Plays That Hold," *New York Times* (September 20, 1903), p. 21; *Trenton Times* (September 26, 1903), p. 6.

10. "Jealous Husband Shoots," *Syracuse Herald* (December 19, 1907), p. 1.

11. I base this account on "Actress's Husband Is Badly Beaten," *New York Times* (August 1, 1908), www.nytimes.com and "Jessie Busley's Escorts Unkind to 'Hubby' Joy," *Boston Sunday Post* (August 2, 1908), p. 7.

12. "Indiana, Marriages, 1811–1959," index and images, *FamilySearch* (https://familysearch.org/pal:/MM9.1.1/27VR-BJY: accessed 24 February 2015), Ernest C Joy and Mabel Brown Southard, 03 Sep 1919; citing, Wayne, Indiana, county clerk offices, Indiana; FHL microfilm 1,839,238; "United States Census, 1920," index and images, *FamilySearch* (https://familysearch.org/pal:/MM9.1.1/MHQX-PMP: accessed 24 February 2015), Earnest C Joy, Los Angeles Assembly District 63, Los Angeles, California, United States; citing sheet 1A, family 7, NARA microfilm publication T625 (Washington, D.C.: National Archives and Records Administration, n.d.); FHL microfilm 1,820,106.

13. www.imdb.com.

14. www.findagrave.com.

15. John Parker, *Who's Who in the Theatre: A Biographical Record of the Contemporary Stage* (7th ed.; London: Pitman, 1933), p. 325.

16. "United States Census, 1900," index and images, *FamilySearch* (https://familysearch.org/pal:/MM9.1.1/MSQZ-TH9: accessed 24 February 2015), Jessie Busley in household of Louise Anderson, Precinct 12 Chicago city Ward 24, Cook, Illinois, United States; citing sheet 10A, family 129, NARA microfilm publication T623 (Washington, D.C.: National Archives and Records Administration, n.d.); FHL microfilm 1,240,274.

17. "New York, State Census, 1875," index and images, *FamilySearch* (https://familysearch.org/pal:/MM9.1.1/VT8N-GC9: accessed 23 February 2015), Jessie Busley in household of James R Busley, Albany, Albany, New York, United States; citing p. 19, line 25, State Library, Albany; FHL microfilm 521,936.

18. "New York, State Census, 1875," Jessie Busley.

19. "United States Census, 1900," index and images, *FamilySearch* (https://familysearch.org/pal:/MM9.1.1/MS2Z-LMS: accessed 23 February 2015), James Busley, Borough of the Bronx, Election District 29 New York City Ward 35, New York County, New York, United States;

citing sheet 37A, family 804, NARA microfilm publication T623 (Washington, D.C.: National Archives and Records Administration, n.d.); FHL microfilm 1,241,126.

20. "Massachusetts, Marriages, 1841–1915," index and images, *FamilySearch* (https://familysearch.org/pal:/MM9.1.1/N498-6N1: accessed 23 February 2015), John Mcfedries and Jessie D. Busley, 12 Sep 1892; citing v426 p198 n3558, Boston, Massachusetts, State Archives, Boston; FHL microfilm 1,651,235; "New York, State Census, 1905," index and images, *FamilySearch* (https://familysearch.org/pal:/MM9.1.1/SPFG-61J: accessed 23 February 2015), John Fedris in household of Ellen Craig, Manhattan, A.D. 25, E.D. 09, New York, New York; citing p., line, county offices, New York.; FHL microfilm.

21. "Miss Busley Reported Wed," *New York Times* (November 22, 1907), www.nytimes.com; *Washington Post* (December 1, 1907), p. 4.

22. "New York, State Census, 1905," John Fedris.

23. Parker, *Who's Who in the Theatre*, p. 325.

24. Parker, p. 325. See also "Theatrical Gossip," *New York Times* (November 4, 1889), www.nytimes.com.

25. "Two New Plays in Boston," *New York Times* (September 4, 1892), www.nytimes.com.

26. "'Charley's Aunt' a Success," *New York Times* (October 3, 1893), www.nytimes.com; "Jessie Busley, Actress Since 1888, Dies at 80," *New York Herald Tribune*, undated (*T-Clippings, Billy Rose Theatre Division, New York Public Library for the Performing Arts; henceforward abbreviated NYPL).

27. "The 'New Boy's' Girl," *Fort Wayne News* (October 30, 1894), n.pag.; "'The New Boy' Not Rare Fun," *New York Times* (September 18, 1894), www.nytimes.com.

28. "In Charley's Aunt Here 48 Years Ago, Jessie Busley Returns to See the Play," unnamed, undated clipping [1941] (NYPL).

29. "'Pollyanna' Stories Charming on Stage," *New York Times* (September 19, 1916), www.nytimes.com; Parker, *Who's Who in the Theatre*, p. 325; www.ibdb.com.

30. Parker, *Who's Who in the Theatre*, p. 325; www.ibdb.com.

31. www.ibdb.com.

32. "Jessie Busley Offers a Word About Youth," unnamed, undated clipping [1935] (NYPL).

33. J. Brooks Atkinson, *Daisy Mayme* review, *New York Times* (October 26, 1926) (NYPL).

34. Atkinson, *Daisy Mayme* review.

35. "About Maude St. Trevor: What Jessie Busley Says of Her Calling and Her Aims," *New York Times* (March 4, 1900), p. 16.

36. Sidney Howard, "Alien Corn," *The Best Plays of 1932–33*, ed. Burns Mantle (New York: Dodd, Mead, 1933), p. 206.

37. Katharine Dayton and George S. Kaufman, *First Lady* (New York: Random House, 1935), p. 32, 33.

38. Richard Harland Smith, "King of the Underworld (1939)," www.tcm.com.

39. "'It All Came True' Comes to Colonial," *Portsmouth Herald* (May 7, 1940), p. 6.

40. B.R. Crisler, *It All Came True* review, *New York Times* (April 6, 1940), www.nytimes.com.

41. "In Charley's Aunt Here 48 Years Ago."

42. Crisler, *It All Came True* review.

43. "In Charley's Aunt Here 48 Years Ago."

44. "United States Census, 1940," index and images, *FamilySearch* (https://familysearch.org/pal:/MM9.1.1/KQSL-RXF: accessed 24 February 2015), Jessie Busley, Assembly District 15, Manhattan, New York City, New York, New York, United States; citing enumeration district (ED) 31–1384, sheet 4A, family 133, NARA digital publication T627 (Washington, D.C.: National Archives and Records Administration, 2012), roll 2657. She had lived at this address since 1927.

45. "Kay Francis Opens Monday at Playhouse," *Berkshire Evening Eagle* (July 9, 1949), p. 11; "Jessie Busley, Actress Since 1888," *New York Herald Tribune*.

46. "Jessie Busley, Long on Broadway Stage," *New York Times* (April 21, 1950) (NYPL).

47. "Jessie Busley, Actress Since 1888," *New York Herald Tribune*.

48. "About Maude St. Trevor," *New York Times*, p. 16.

Georgia Caine

1. Preston Sturges, *Preston Sturges by Preston Sturges* (New York: Simon and Schuster, 1990), pp. 197–98.

2. Diane Jacobs, *Christmas in July: The Life and Art of Preston Sturges* (Berkeley, CA: University of California Press, 1992), p. 334 and 471n26. The source of this information is a letter actor Torben Meyer wrote to Sturges on November 15, 1948.

3. See, for example, "New York, New York Passenger and Crew Lists, 1909, 1925–1957," index and images, *FamilySearch* (https://familysearch.org/pal:/MM9.1.1/KX9S-S65: accessed 19 March 2015), Georgia C Hudson, 1925; citing Immigration, New York, New York, United States, NARA microfilm publication T715 (Washington, D.C.: National Archives and Records Administration, n.d.); FHL microfilm 1,755,425; "United States Social Security Death Index," index, *FamilySearch* (https://familysearch.org/pal:/MM9.1.1/VMMD-N25: accessed 19 March 2015), Georgia Hudson, Apr 1964; citing U.S. Social Security Administration, *Death Master File*, database (Alexandria, Virginia: National Technical Information Service, ongoing).

4. "Georgia Caine Relates the Story of Her Childish Debut," *New York American* (November 14, 1920) (*T-Clippings, Billy Rose Theatre Division, New York Public Library for the Performing Arts; henceforward abbreviated NYPL).

5. "Theatrical Topics," *Oak Park Reporter* (July 2, 1897), n.pag.

6. "United States Census, 1880," index and images, *FamilySearch* (https://familysearch.org/pal:/MM9.1.1/M6PC-RW9: accessed 19 March 2015), George Caine in household of John H Darragh, San Francisco, San Francisco, California, United States; citing enumeration district, sheet, NARA microfilm publication T9 (Washington, D.C.: National Archives and Records Administration, n.d.), roll; "United States Census, 1910," index and images, *FamilySearch* (https://familysearch.org/pal:/MM9.1.1/M5HG-5X6: accessed 19 March 2015), George Cane [sic], Queens Ward 2, Queens, New York, United States; citing enumeration district (ED) 1190, sheet 2B, family 27, NARA microfilm publication T624 (Washington, D.C.: National Archives and Records Administration, n.d.); FHL microfilm 1,375,079; "United States Census, 1920," index and images, *FamilySearch*

(https://familysearch.org/pal:/MM9.1.1/MVMS-WC9: accessed 19 March 2015), George R Caine, Queens Assembly District 3, Queens, New York, United States; citing sheet 1B, family 13, NARA microfilm publication T625 (Washington, D.C.: National Archives and Records Administration, n.d.); FHL microfilm 1,821,232.

7. "United States Census, 1870," index and images, *FamilySearch* (https://familysearch.org/pal:/MM9.1.1/M6W4-9WZ: accessed 19 March 2015), Jame [sic] Darragh in household of John Darragh, Illinois, United States; citing p. 190, family 35, NARA microfilm publication M593 (Washington, D.C.: National Archives and Records Administration, n.d.); FHL microfilm 545,735; FHL microfilm; "United States Census, 1880," Jane Caine in household of John H Darragh; "California Death Index, 1940–1997," index, *FamilySearch* (https://familysearch.org/pal:/MM9.1.1/VP7M-TR9: accessed 19 March 2015), Jane Caine, 01 Feb 1949; Department of Public Health Services, Sacramento.

8. "United States Census, 1880," Georgiana Caine in household of John H Darragh.

9. "Georgia Caine," *Fort Wayne Sentinel* (September 18, 1896), n.pag.

10. "New York, New York Passenger and Crew Lists, 1909, 1925–1957," index and images, *FamilySearch* (https://familysearch.org/pal:/MM9.1.1/KX9S-S6P: accessed 19 March 2015), Alphonse Bell Hudson, 1925; citing Immigration, New York, New York, United States, NARA microfilm publication T715 (Washington, D.C.: National Archives and Records Administration, n.d.); FHL microfilm 1,755,425.

11. "United States Census, 1860," index, *FamilySearch* (https://familysearch.org/pal:/MM9.1.1/MCGC-K85: accessed 19 March 2015), Alphonzo Hudson in household of James D Hudson, Greenfield Madison Township, Highland, Ohio, United States; from "1860 U.S. Federal Census—Population," Fold3.com; citing p. 155, household ID 1095, NARA microfilm publication M653, National Archives and Records Administration, Washington, D.C.; FHL microfilm 803,986; "United States Census, 1870," index and images, *FamilySearch* (https://familysearch.org/pal:/MM9.1.1/M622-DDN: accessed 19 March 2015), Alphonzo Hudson in household of James D Hudson, Ohio, United States; citing p. 80, family 614, NARA microfilm publication M593 (Washington, D.C.: National Archives and Records Administration, n.d.); FHL microfilm 552,721.

12. "United States Census, 1900," index and images, *FamilySearch* (https://familysearch.org/pal:/MM9.1.1/MSQZ-NNY: accessed 19 March 2015), A B Hudson, Precinct 12 Chicago city Ward 24, Cook, Illinois, United States; citing sheet 3A, family 35, NARA microfilm publication T623 (Washington, D.C.: National Archives and Records Administration, n.d.); FHL microfilm 1,240,274.

13. "United States Census, 1930," index and images, *FamilySearch* (https://familysearch.org/pal:/MM9.1.1/X4PG-LWR: accessed 19 March 2015), Alfonso Hudson, Queens (Districts 0001–0250), Queens, New York, United States; citing enumeration district (ED) 0180, sheet 19A, family 314, line 47, NARA microfilm publication T626 (Washington, D.C.: National Archives and Records Administration, 2002), roll 1590; FHL microfilm 2,341,325.

14. "United States Census, 1930," Alfonso Hudson.

15. http://en.wikipedia.org/wiki/Elmhurst,_Queens.

16. *Lowell Sun* (May 3, 1934), p. 16.

17. "Hammerstein's Victoria," *New York Times* (March 3, 1899), www.nytimes.com.

18. "Singer Loses Her Voice: Affliction of Georgia Caine of 'Peggy from Paris,'" *New York Times* (November 1, 1903), www.nytimes.com.

19. "'The Sho-Gun' Produced," *New York Times* (October 11, 1904), www.nytimes.com.

20. "About the Principals," *Boston Sunday Post* (May 21, 1905), p. 19.

21. "A Rollicking Show Opens New Casino," *New York Times* (November 5, 1905), www.nytimes.com.

22. "A Rollicking Show Opens New Casino."

23. "Sam Bernard's New Play: 'The Rich Mr. Hoggenheimer' a Success at Wallack's," *New York Times* (November 23, 1906), www.nytimes.com.

24. "Miss Hook Brings Mirth and Melody," *New York Times* (January 1, 1908), www.nytimes.com.

25. "Georgia Caine as 'The Merry Widow,'" *New York Times* (September 1, 1908), www.nytimes.com.

26. "Georgia Caine is Old-Time Cohan Favorite," *Boston Globe* (April 14, 1929) (NYPL).

27. "There's Sorrow Ahead for Many a Stage-Struck Girl," *Des Moines Daily News* (August 23, 1913), p. 6.

28. *Syracuse Herald* (December 21, 1913), p. 4.

29. "'Adele' Brings Joy Unalloyed," *New York Times* (August 29, 1913), www.nytimes.com.

30. "Georgia Caine is Old-Time Cohan Favorite," *Boston Globe.*

31. "'Whispering Friends' Is Presented at the Broad," *Newark News* (August 21, 1928) (NYPL).

32. "Dogs in Silk-Lined Baby Crib," *New York Star* (March 15, 1928) (NYPL). See also "Dogs Write First Tragic Role for Georgia Caine," *New York Telegraph* (December 11, 1927) (NYPL).

33. "Dogs in Silk-Lined Baby Crib."

34. "'Baby Cyclone' at the Hollis," *Boston Herald* (August 16, 1927) (NYPL).

35. "About the Principals," *Boston Sunday Post*, p. 19.

36. "Jimmie Fidler in Hollywood," *Joplin Globe* (December 18, 1948), p. 4.

37. "United States Census, 1930," Georgia Hudson.

38. "United States Census, 1940," index and images, *FamilySearch* (https://familysearch.org/pal:/MM9.1.1/K9CD-DQZ: accessed 19 March 2015), Georgia K Hudson, Councilmanic District 2, Los Angeles, Los Angeles Township, Los Angeles, California, United States; citing enumeration district (ED) 60–114, sheet 12A, family 300, NARA digital publication T627 (Washington, D.C.: National Archives and Records Administration, 2012), roll 398.

39. www.findagrave.com.

40. www.findagrave.com.

41. "California Death Index, 1940–1997," Jane Caine, 01 Feb 1949.

42. www.findagrave.com.

43. "Georgia Caine Relates," *New York American.*

44. "United States Social Security Death Index," Georgia Hudson, Apr 1964; www.findagrave.com.

Patricia Collinge

1. "Acts for Radio Audience," *Kansas City Star* (October 28, 1924), p. 15.

2. "Ireland, Civil Registration Indexes, 1845–1958," index, *FamilySearch* (https://familysearch.org/pal:/MM9.1.1/FB6K-DZH: accessed 9 March 2015), BIRTHS entry for Eileen Cecilia Collings [sic]; citing Dublin South, Oct–Dec 1892, vol. 2, p. 595, General Registry, Custom House, Dublin; FHL microfilm 101,064.

3. See, for example, Parker, *Who's Who in the Theatre*, p. 400.

4. "United States Census, 1920," index and images, *FamilySearch* (https://familysearch.org/pal:/MM9.1.1/MJYG-9BW: accessed 9 March 2015), Fredrick Collinge, Manhattan Assembly District 7, New York, New York, United States; citing sheet 9A, family 201, NARA microfilm publication T625 (Washington, D.C.: National Archives and Records Administration, n.d.); FHL microfilm 1,821,197; Daniel Blum, Daniel, *Great Stars of the American Stage: A Pictorial Record* (New York: Greenburg, 1952), profile 115; www.findagrave.com.

5. "Ireland, Civil Registration Indexes, 1845–1958," index, *FamilySearch* (https://familysearch.org/pal:/MM9.1.1/FYYM-NJ9: accessed 9 March 2015), BIRTHS entry for Emma Cecilia Mary Russell; citing Dublin South, 1869, vol. 12, p. 720, General Registry, Custom House, Dublin; FHL microfilm 101,046; "United States Census, 1920," Emmie Collinge in household of Fredrick Collinge.

6. "United States Census, 1920," Norbert J Collinge in household of Fredrick Collinge; "United States Census, 1920," Fredrick Collinge in household of Fredrick Collinge.

7. "United States Census, 1920," Patricia Collinge in household of Fredrick Collinge.

8. "New York, Passenger Arrival Lists (Ellis Island), 1892–1924," index, *FamilySearch* (https://familysearch.org/pal:/MM9.1.1/JXRZ-S2D: accessed 9 March 2015), Emmie Collinge, 19 Sep 1908; citing departure port Southampton, arrival port New York, ship name Philadelphia, NARA microfilm publication T715 and M237 (Washington, D.C.: National Archives and Records Administration, n.d.); "New York, Passenger Arrival Lists (Ellis Island), 1892–1924," Patricia Collinge, 19 Sep 1908.

9. www.ibdb.com.

10. Parker, *Who's Who in the Theatre*, p. 400.

11. "The Revelations of Patricia," *Daily Times* [1926] (*T-Clippings, Billy Rose Theatre Division, New York Public Library for the Performing Arts; henceforward abbreviated NYPL).

12. "Moulin Rouge Show Aims to Be Naughty," *New York Times* (December 8, 1908), www.nytimes.com.

13. www.ibdb.com.

14. "Walter Browne, Dramatist, Ill," *New York Times* (February 8, 1911) and "Modern Morality at Herald Square," *New York Times* (February 28, 1911), www.nytimes.com.

15. "Modern Morality at Herald Square."

16. Parker, *Who's Who in the Theatre*, p. 400.

17. "Much to Please in The New Henrietta," *New York Times* (December 23, 1923), www.nytimes.com.

18. "Douglas Fairbanks in a Gay Comedy," *New York Times* (September 17, 1914), www.nytimes.com.

19. Parker, *Who's Who in the Theatre*, p. 400; www.ibdb.com.

20. "Acts for Radio Audience," *Kansas City Star*, p. 15.

21. "Patricia Collinge Weds," *New York Times* (June 11, 1921), www.nytimes.com.

22. "United States Social Security Death Index," index, *FamilySearch* (https://familysearch.org/pal:/MM9.1.1/JR7P-5JW: accessed 10 March 2015), James Smith, Feb 1975; citing U.S. Social Security Administration, *Death Master File*, database (Alexandria, Virginia: National Technical Information Service, ongoing); www.findagrave.com.

23. "Patricia Collinge Weds," *New York Times*; "United States Census, 1920," index and images, *FamilySearch* (https://familysearch.org/pal:/MM9.1.1/MCFJ-K3X: accessed 10 March 2015), Harry A Smith, West Hartford, Hartford, Connecticut, United States; citing sheet 1A, family 3, NARA microfilm publication T625 (Washington, D.C.: National Archives and Records Administration, n.d.); FHL microfilm 1,820,180.

24. "United States Census, 1920," index and images, *FamilySearch* (https://familysearch.org/pal:/MM9.1.1/MJ8M-DVG: accessed 10 March 2015), James N Smith, Chicago Ward 21, Cook (Chicago), Illinois, United States; citing sheet 11A, family, NARA microfilm publication T625 (Washington, D.C.: National Archives and Records Administration, n.d.); FHL microfilm 1,820,331.

25. "United States Census, 1920," Patricia Collinge. There is no such address today. I'm assuming this building was razed to make way for 91 Central Park West, a Neo-Renaissance building from 1928. See http://en.wikipedia.org/wiki/Central_Park_West_Historic_District.

26. "Patricia Collinge Weds," *New York Times*.

27. "Patricia Collinge Weds."

28. Parker, *Who's Who in the Theatre*, p. 400; www.ibdb.com.

29. Irving Drutman, "Patricia Collinge Really Played with Fire in Latest Film Role," unnamed, undated clipping [1944] (NYPL).

30. Blum, *Great Stars of the American Stage*, profile 115.

31. John Corbin, "Drama: Mennonite Romance," *New York Times* (January 7, 1919), www.nytimes.com.

32. Parker, *Who's Who in the Theatre*, p. 400.

33. www.findagrave.com.

34. www.findagrave.com.

35. "Pollyanna Returns to the Stage Where's She's Lucky to Be Alive," unnamed, undated clipping (NYPL); "Patricia Collinge Is Back," unnamed, undated clipping (NYPL).

36. "United States Census, 1930," index and images, *FamilySearch* (https://familysearch.org/pal:/MM9.1.1/X42Z-JPZ: accessed 10 March 2015), Patrica Smith in household of James Smith, Jr., Manhattan (Districts 0501–0750), New York, New York, United States; citing enumeration district (ED) 0614, sheet 14A, family 31, line 14, NARA microfilm publication T626 (Washington, D.C.: National Archives and Records Administration, 2002), roll 1562; FHL microfilm 2,341,297; Parker, *Who's Who in the Theatre*, p. 400.

37. "Pollyanna Returns to the Stage."

38. Axel Storm, "Broadway Nights," *Logansport Pharos Tribune* (March 9, 1939), p. 8. The first quote is from Bosley Crowther, *The Little Foxes* review, *New York Times* (August 22, 1941), www.nytimes.com.

39. Crowther, *The Little Foxes* review.

40. Nathaniel Benchley, "Miss Collinge Back from Coast with Awe and Usual Millions," unnamed, undated clipping (NYPL).

41. Quoted in Brendan Gill, *Tallulah* (New York: Holt, Rinehart, and Winston, 1972), p. 175.

42. "United States Census, 1940," index and images, *FamilySearch* (https://familysearch.org/pal:/MM9.1.1/KQSV-YX2: accessed 10 March 2015), Patricia Smith in household of James N Smith, Assembly District 12, Manhattan, New York City, New York, New York, United States; citing enumeration district (ED) 31–1000, sheet 17A, family 490, NARA digital publication T627 (Washington, D.C.: National Archives and Records Administration, 2012), roll 2648; "United States Census, 1940," James N Smith; "United States Census, 1940," Edith Dover in household of James N Smith.

43. Louella O. Parsons, "Ann Sheridan Is Cast in King's Row," *Charleston Gazette* (March 26, 1941), p. 7.

44. Louella O. Parsons, "Barbara Stanwyck, Fonda, to Team Up Again at Columbia," *Waterloo Daily Courier* (April 16, 1941), p. 17.

45. www.tcm.com.

46. For a more detailed account of this conflict, see Bette Davis, *The Lonely Life* (London: MacDonald, 1963), pp. 206–7; Barbara Leaming, *Bette Davis* (New York: Orion Books, 1999), pp. 176–85; Ed Sikov, *Dark Victory: The Life of Bette Davis* (New York: Henry Holt, 2007), pp. 178–84.

47. Patricia Collinge, "W.U. Boy Given Spot in the Scene," unnamed, undated clipping (NYPL).

48. Eileen Creelman, "Picture Plays and Players: Patricia Collinge Talks of Working in Hitchcock's 'Shadow of a Doubt,'" unnamed, undated clipping [c1943] (NYPL).

49. Drutman, "Patricia Collinge Really Played with Fire."

50. "Elderberry Wine, With or Without Arsenic," unnamed, undated clipping [1941] (NYPL).

51. www.findagrave.com.

52. "United States Social Security Death Index," index, *FamilySearch* (https://familysearch.org/pal:/MM9.1.1/JBPD-K47: accessed 10 March 2015), Patricia Smith, Apr 1974; citing U.S. Social Security Administration, *Death Master File*, database (Alexandria, Virginia: National Technical Information Service, ongoing); www.findagrave.com.

53. Creelman, "Picture Plays and Players."

54. "United States Social Security Death Index," James Smith, Feb 1975.

55. "The Revelations of Patricia," *Daily Times*.

Ruth Donnelly

1. "United States Census, 1900," index and images, *FamilySearch* (https://familysearch.org/pal:/MM9.1.1/M9FL-DZS: accessed 3 March 2015), Ruth Donnelly in household of Harry Donnelly, Precinct 2 Trenton city Ward 2, Mercer, New Jersey, United States; citing sheet 13B, family 282, NARA microfilm publication T623 (Washington, D.C.: National Archives and Records Administration, n.d.); FHL microfilm 1,240,982; "United States Census, 1910," index and images, *FamilySearch* (https://familysearch.org/pal:/MM9.1.1/MKB9-LHH: accessed 3 March 2015), Ruth Donnelly in household of Harry A Donnelly, Trenton Ward 2, Mercer, New Jersey, United States; citing enumeration district (ED) 51, sheet 14A, family 315, NARA microfilm publication T624 (Washington, D.C.: National Archives and Records Administration, n.d.); FHL microfilm 1,374,909.

2. "United States Passport Applications, 1795–1925," index and images, *FamilySearch* (https://familysearch.org/pal:/MM9.1.1/QV5Y-TKVR: accessed 4 March 2015), Ruth Donnelly, 1922; citing Passport Application, New York, United States, source certificate #167957, Passport Applications, January 2, 1906–March 31, 1925, 1964, NARA microfilm publications M1490 and M1372 (Washington, D.C.: National Archives and Records Administration, n.d.); FHL microfilm.

3. "United States Census, 1900," Harry Donnelly; www.findagrave.com.

4. "United States Census, 1900," index and images, *FamilySearch* (https://familysearch.org/pal:/MM9.1.1/M9FL-358: accessed 3 March 2015), Richard A Donnelly, Precinct 2 Trenton city Ward 1, Mercer, New Jersey, United States; citing sheet 9B, family 186, NARA microfilm publication T623 (Washington, D.C.: National Archives and Records Administration, n.d.); FHL microfilm 1,240,982.

5. Biographical information on Ruth's paternal grandparents and uncle from their respective pages at www.findagrave.com.

6. "United States Census, 1900," Harry Donnelly; www.findagrave.com.

7. "United States Census, 1910," index and images, *FamilySearch* (https://familysearch.org/pal:/MM9.1.1/MKB9-LHQ: accessed 3 March 2015), Harry A Donnelly, Trenton Ward 2, Mercer, New Jersey, United States; citing enumeration district (ED) 51, sheet 14A, family 315, NARA microfilm publication T624 (Washington, D.C.: National Archives and Records Administration, n.d.); FHL microfilm 1,374,909.

8. www.findagrave.com.

9. "United States Census, 1870," index and images, *FamilySearch* (https://familysearch.org/pal:/MM9.1.1/MNDG-R34: accessed 4 March 2015), Elizabeth D Weart in household of John A Weart, New Jersey, United States; citing p. 39, family 298, NARA microfilm publication M593 (Washington, D.C.: National Archives and Records Administration, n.d.); FHL microfilm 552,371; "United States Census, 1900," Bessie B Donnelly in household of Harry Donnelly.

10. See the 1900 and 1910 U.S. Census cited above for information about the birth dates of Donnelly's siblings.

11. www.findagrave.com.

12. www.findagrave.com.

13. Eleanor Blau, "Ruth Donnelly, Comedienne and Character Actor in Films," *New York Times* (November 19, 1982), p. B8.

14. Blau, "Ruth Donnelly," p. B8; www.allmovie.com.

15. "Ruth Donnelly in Hilliard's Cast," *Trenton Evening Times* (August 23, 1917), p. 7.

16. "'The Scrap of Paper' Is Fairly Diverting," *New York Times* (September 18, 1917), www.nytimes.com.

17. www.ibdb.com.

18. "'Going Up' Is Enjoyable," *New York Times* (December 26, 1917), www.nytimes.com.

19. "United States Census, 1920," index and images, *FamilySearch* (https://familysearch.org/pal:/MM9.1.1/MJYG-33M: accessed 4 March 2015), Ruth Donnelly

in household of Anna F Farrell, Manhattan Assembly District 7, New York, New York, United States; citing sheet 18A, family 227, NARA microfilm publication T625 (Washington, D.C.: National Archives and Records Administration, n.d.); FHL microfilm 1,821,197.

20. "New York, New York Passenger and Crew Lists, 1909, 1925–1957," index and images, *FamilySearch* (https://familysearch.org/pal:/MM9.1.1/KXGM-DLH: accessed 4 March 2015), Ruth Donnely, 1927; citing Immigration, New York, New York, United States, NARA microfilm publication T715 (Washington, D.C.: National Archives and Records Administration, n.d.); FHL microfilm 1,755,876.

21. "United States Census, 1930," index and images, *FamilySearch* (https://familysearch.org/pal:/MM9.1.1/X42F-37H: accessed 4 March 2015), Ruth Donnelly, Manhattan (Districts 0501–0750), New York, New York, United States; citing enumeration district (ED) 0644, sheet 13B, family 229, line 78, NARA microfilm publication T626 (Washington, D.C.: National Archives and Records Administration, 2002), roll 1564; FHL microfilm 2,341,299.

22. www.imdb.com.

23. "United States Passport Applications, 1795–1925," index and images, *FamilySearch* (https://familysearch.org/pal:/MM9.1.1/QVJG-LS31: accessed 3 March 2015), Basil Baines De Guichard, 1924; citing Passport Application, Michigan, United States, source certificate #417201, Passport Applications, January 2, 1906–March 31, 1925, 2519, NARA microfilm publications M1490 and M1372 (Washington, D.C.: National Archives and Records Administration, n.d.); FHL microfilm.

24. "United States Census, 1920," database with images, *FamilySearch* (https://familysearch.org/ark:/61903/1:1:MZSY-BCQ: accessed 29 January 2016), Basil W Deguichard in household of Albert Champion, Flint Ward 2, Genesee, Michigan, United States; citing sheet 8B, NARA microfilm publication T625 (Washington, D.C.: National Archives and Records Administration, n.d.); FHL microfilm 1,820,765; "California, County Marriages, 1850–1952," database with images, *FamilySearch* (https://familysearch.org/ark:/61903/1:1:K8JW-BMR: accessed 29 January 2016), Basil Winter De Guichard and Ruth Donnelly, 27 Jun 1932; citing Los Angeles, California, United States, county courthouses, California; FHL microfilm 2,074,987.

25. "Bicycle Notes," *Boston Post* (May 30, 1902), p. 2.

26. Peter Joffre Nye, *The Fast Times of Albert Champion* (Amherst, NY: Prometheus Books, 2014), p. 258.

27. Nye, p. 258.

28. Nye, p. 288.

29. "United States Census, 1910," index and images, *FamilySearch* (https://familysearch.org/pal:/MM9.1.1/MLPT-W11: accessed 3 March 2015), Basel De Guichard in household of James T Jones, Flint Ward 2, Genesee, Michigan, United States; citing enumeration district (ED) 13, sheet 1A, family 4, NARA microfilm publication T624 (Washington, D.C.: National Archives and Records Administration, n.d.); FHL microfilm 1,374,655; "United States World War I Draft Registration Cards, 1917–1918," index and images, *FamilySearch* (https://familysearch.org/pal:/MM9.1.1/K6XW-5BS: accessed 3 March 2015), Basil Winter Deguichard, 1917–1918; citing Flint City no 1, Michigan, United States, NARA microfilm publication M1509 (Washington, D.C.: National Archives and Records Administration, n.d.); FHL microfilm 1,675,434; "United States Census, 1920," Basil W Deguichard.

30. "Michigan, Marriages, 1868–1925," index and images, *FamilySearch* (https://familysearch.org/pal:/MM9.1.1/N3BW-YGB: accessed 3 March 2015), Basile W. Deguichard and Mae Nash Miller, 06 Mar 1920; citing Flint, Genesee, Michigan, v 2 p 295 rn 9128, Department of Vital Records, Lansing; FHL microfilm 2,342,736. The quote is taken from "Nash Heiress Weds Salesman at Yuma," *Wisconsin Rapids Daily Tribune* (May 17, 1932), p. 1.

31. The 1930 census indicates that his "age at first marriage" was 26. See "United States Census, 1930," index and images, *FamilySearch* (https://familysearch.org/pal:/MM9.1.1/XQYJ-8TH: accessed 3 March 2015), Basil W De Guichard, Flint, Genesee, Michigan, United States; citing enumeration district (ED) 0039, sheet 25B, family 492, line 81, NARA microfilm publication T626 (Washington, D.C.: National Archives and Records Administration, 2002), roll; FHL microfilm 2,340,720.

32. "United States World War I Draft Registration Cards, 1917–1918," Basil Winter Deguichard; "United States Census, 1920," Basil W Deguichard.

33. Nye, *The Fast Times of Albert Champion*, p. 340.

34. Nye, p. 359.

35. "Youngest Executive in Automotive Industry," *Bode Bugle* (December 6, 1929), n.pag.

36. "United States Census, 1930," Basil W De Guichard.

37. "Nash Heiress Weds Salesman at Yuma," *Wisconsin Rapids Daily Tribune*, p. 1.

38. See "Moran Wins 25-Mile Race at Revere Track," *Boston Sunday Post* (May 22, 1904), p. 14 and "Bobby Walthour Again in Europe," *Salt Lake Tribune* (August 21, 1904), p. 4.

39. "United States World War I Draft Registration Cards, 1917–1918," Basil Winter Deguichard.

40. "United States Passport Applications, 1795–1925," Ruth Donnelly.

41. "United States Passport Applications, 1795–1925," Basil Baines De Guichard.

42. "California, County Marriages, 1850–1952," Basil Winter De Guichard and Ruth Donnelly, 27 Jun 1932.

43. *Los Angeles City Directory 1934* (Los Angeles: Los Angeles Directory, 1934), p. 470.

44. "United States Census, 1940," index and images, *FamilySearch* (https://familysearch.org/pal:/MM9.1.1/K9CP-HXZ: accessed 4 March 2015), Ruth De Guichard in household of Basil De Guichard, Councilmanic District 3, Los Angeles, Los Angeles Township, Los Angeles, California, United States; citing enumeration district (ED) 60–221A, sheet 38B, family 934, NARA digital publication T627 (Washington, D.C.: National Archives and Records Administration, 2012), roll 407.

45. movielanddirectory.com.

46. "New York, New York Passenger and Crew Lists, 1909, 1925–1957," index and images, *FamilySearch* (https://familysearch.org/pal:/MM9.1.1/24RN-W6V: accessed 4 March 2015), Ruth De Guichard, 1949; citing Immigration, New York City, New York, United States, NARA microfilm publication T715 (Washington, D.C.: National Archives and Records Administration, n.d.); FHL microfilm 2,296,458.

47. "New York, New York Passenger and Crew Lists, 1909, 1925–1957," index and images, *FamilySearch* (https://familysearch.org/pal:/MM9.1.1/2414-WSQ: accessed 4 March 2015), Ruth De Guichard, 1952; citing Immigration, New York City, New York, United States, NARA microfilm publication T715 (Washington, D.C.: National Archives and Records Administration, n.d.); FHL microfilm 2,297,649.

48. "California, Death Index, 1940–1997," index, *FamilySearch* (https://familysearch.org/pal:/MM9.1.1/VPWX-9XQ: accessed 3 March 2015), Basil W Deguichard, 29 May 1958; Department of Public Health Services, Sacramento; "Firm's Founder Dies," *Daily Oklahoman* (May 31, 1958), p. 20.

49. Louella Parsons, "Hollywood: Vidor to Direct Columbia Films," *Anderson Daily Bulletin* (June 2, 1958), p. 11. They had actually been married for 26 years.

50. Alex Barris. *Hollywood's Other Women* (South Brunswick and New York: A.S. Barnes, 1975), p. 82.

51. Jack O'Brian, "The Voice of Broadway," *Lebanon Daily News* (October 3, 1973), p. 30; www.ibdb.com.

52. Blau, "Ruth Donnelly," p. B8.

53. David Ragan, *Who's Who in Hollywood, 1900–1976* (New Rochelle, NY: Arlington House, 1977), p. 119.

54. Archer Winsten, "Donnelly the Pro," *New York Post* (April 15, 1982), p. 29.

55. Blau, "Ruth Donnelly," p. B8; www.findagrave.com.

Maude Eburne

1. "'A Pair of Sixes' Uproarious Fun," *New York Times* (March 21, 1914), www.nytimes.com.

2. "Among the Plays and the Players," *Chester Times* (April 11, 1914), p. 5.

3. "'A Pair of Sixes' Uproarious Fun," *New York Times*.

4. "Coddles Awakes at Last to Find Herself Famous," *New York Times* (March 29, 1914), www.nytimes.com.

5. "Coddles Awakes at Last to Find Herself Famous."

6. "Canada Census, 1881," index, *FamilySearch* (https://familysearch.org/pal:/MM9.1.1/MVFV-LRB: accessed 23 March 2015), Maud Riggs in household of John Riggs, Trafalgar, Halton, Ontario, Canada; citing p. 22; Library and Archives Canada film number C-13257, Library and Archives Canada, Ottawa, Ontario; FHL microfilm 1,375,893. Her full maiden name appears in her daughter's birth record. See "Ontario Births, 1869–1912," index, *FamilySearch* (https://familysearch.org/pal:/MM9.1.1/QV9H-F8KF: accessed 23 March 2015), Marion Birdsee Hall, 1907. See also "A Fall Brings Fame to New York Actress," *San Antonio Light* (April 5, 1914), n.pag.

7. "Canada Census, 1881," Maud Riggs.

8. "Canada Census, 1891," index, *FamilySearch* (https://familysearch.org/pal:/MM9.1.1/MWL9-574: accessed 23 March 2015), Maud Riggs, Trafalgar, Halton, Ontario, Canada; Public Archives, Ottawa, Ontario; Library and Archives Canada film number 30953_148143.

9. "Canada Census, 1901," index, *FamilySearch* (https://familysearch.org/pal:/MM9.1.1/KH21-M4Q: accessed 23 March 2015), Maud Riggs in household of Joseph Riggs, I, Halton, Ontario, Canada; citing p. 2, Library and Archives of Canada, Ottawa.

10. "Ontario Deaths, 1869–1937 and Overseas Deaths, 1939–1947," index, *FamilySearch* (https://familysearch.org/pal:/MM9.1.1/J6BR-X2W: accessed 23 March 2015), John Riggs, 07 Feb 1901; citing Oakville, Halton, Ontario, cn 11689, Archives of Ontario, Toronto; FHL microfilm 1,854,090; "Coddles Awakes at Last to Find Herself Famous," *New York Times*.

11. "Coddles Awakes at Last to Find Herself Famous."

12. "Coddles Awakes at Last to Find Herself Famous."

13. All quotes and other information in this paragraph from "Coddles Awakes at Last to Find Herself Famous." See also the *Boston Daily Globe* (January 10, 1915), p. 38.

14. In the 1930 U.S. census, Eburne claimed to have married at 30. See "United States Census, 1930," index and images, *FamilySearch* (https://familysearch.org/pal:/MM9.1.1/X45Y-NSJ: accessed 23 March 2015), Maud Hall in household of Gene Hall, Richmond (Districts 1–250), Richmond, New York, United States; citing enumeration district (ED) 0244, sheet 21A, family 149, line 28, NARA microfilm publication T626 (Washington, D.C.: National Archives and Records Administration, 2002), roll 1615; FHL microfilm 2,341,349; "Ontario Births, 1869–1912," Marion Birdsee Hall, 1907. In later life, Marion Hall sometimes spelled her first name "Maryon."

15. "United States Census, 1900," index and images, *FamilySearch* (https://familysearch.org/pal:/MM9.1.1/MSQZ-V3L: accessed 23 March 2015), Eugene J Hall in household of George Allen, Precinct 13 Chicago city Ward 24, Cook, Illinois, United States; citing sheet 3A, family 24, NARA microfilm publication T623 (Washington, D.C.: National Archives and Records Administration, n.d.); FHL microfilm 1,240,274.

16. "United States Census, 1900," Eugene J Hall.

17. www.ibdb.com.

18. "Wilbur Theatre," *Boston Sunday Post* (May 16, 1915), p. 28.

19. "Wilbur Theatre," *Boston Sunday Post* (February 7, 1915), p. 26.

20. "'The Girl' Is an Artificial Play," *Syracuse Herald* (December 17, 1915), p. 22.

21. "A Fall Brings Fame to New York Actress," *San Antonio Light*.

22. "'A Pair of Queens' at the Longacre," *New York Times* (August 30, 1916), www.nytimes.com; www.ibdb.com.

23. "Funny and Noisy Farce at the Cohan," *New York Times* (September 26, 1917), www.nytimes.com.

24. "Dillingham Show Romps in a Winner," *New York Times* (November 5, 1918), www.nytimes.com.

25. "'The Canary' Comes to the Colonial," *Boston Daily Globe* (December 30, 1919), n.pag.

26. "The Half Moon Arrives," *New York Times* (November 2, 1920), www.nytimes.com.

27. "'Love Dreams' Diversified," *New York Times* (October 11, 1921), www.nytimes.com.

28. Burns Mantle, *The Best Plays of 1929–30* (New York: Dodd, Mead, 1969), p. 486.

29. "United States Census, 1930," Maud Hall.

30. Chester B. Bahn, "Dorothy Jordan Signed to New Metro Contract," *Syracuse Herald* (January 13, 1932), p. 10; www.findagrave.com. His name is mistakenly given as Eugene J. *Hill* in findagrave.

31. Robin Coons, "Hollywood Notebook," *Emporia Daily Gazette* (May 2, 1932), p. 3.

32. Coons, p. 3.

33. Coons, p. 3.

34. Hubbard Keavy, "Screen Life in Hollywood," *Sandusky Register* (March 14, 1933), p. 5.

35. "Henry Aldrich's New Adventures at Paramount," *Syracuse Herald* (November 26, 1942), p. 32.

36. "California, County Marriages, 1850–1952," index and images, *FamilySearch* (https://familysearch.org/pal:/MM9.1.1/K86Q-DZ5: accessed 24 March 2015), Sam Raymond Sebby and Marion Birdseye Hall, 11 Apr 1953; citing Los Angeles, California, United States, county courthouses, California; FHL microfilm 1,343,076.

37. "California, County Marriages, 1850–1952," Sam Raymond Sebby and Marion Birdseye Hall, 11 Apr 1953; "United States Social Security Death Index," index, *FamilySearch* (https://familysearch.org/pal:/MM9.1.1/JGSJ-RTP: accessed 24 March 2015), Sam R Sebby, 02 Feb 2004; citing U.S. Social Security Administration, *Death Master File*, database (Alexandria, Virginia: National Technical Information Service, ongoing).

38. "United States Census, 1940," index and images, *FamilySearch* (https://familysearch.org/pal:/MM9.1.1/K9Z9-9Z7: accessed 23 March 2015), Sam R Sebby, Councilmanic District 7, Los Angeles, Los Angeles Township, Los Angeles, California, United States; citing enumeration district (ED) 60–503, sheet 2B, family 38, NARA digital publication T627 (Washington, D.C.: National Archives and Records Administration, 2012), roll 414.

39. They had moved there from a five-bedroom home at 2272 Moreno Dr. in Silver Lake, not far from the reservoir. See *Los Angeles City Directory 1938* (Los Angeles: Los Angeles Directory, 1938), p. 629; www.zillow.com.

40. "United States Census, 1940," index and images, *FamilySearch* (https://familysearch.org/pal:/MM9.1.1/K9CC-ZG1: accessed 23 March 2015), Marian Eburne Hall in household of Maude Eburne Hall, Councilmanic District 2, Los Angeles, Los Angeles Township, Los Angeles, California, United States; citing enumeration district (ED) 60–94, sheet 3B, family 80, NARA digital publication T627 (Washington, D.C.: National Archives and Records Administration, 2012), roll 393.

41. "United States Census, 1940," Maude Eburne Hall.

42. "California Death Index, 1940–1997," index, *FamilySearch* (https://familysearch.org/pal:/MM9.1.1/VPS3-8L2: accessed 23 March 2015), Helen Richards Sebby, 24 Jun 1992; Department of Public Health Services, Sacramento.

43. "Texas Birth Index, 1903–1997," database, *FamilySearch* (https://familysearch.org/ark:/61903/1:1:VD9X-5XM: accessed 29 January 2016), Holly Linora Sebby, 20 Sep 1944; from "Texas Birth Index, 1903–1997," database and images, *Ancestry* (http://www.ancestry.com: 2005); citing Texas Department of State Health Services; "California Birth Index, 1905–1995," index, *FamilySearch* (https://familysearch.org/pal:/MM9.1.1/V2W3-TRX: accessed 23 March 2015), Scott Lawrence Sebby, 08 Apr 1947; citing Los Angeles, California, United States, Department of Health Services, Vital Statistics Department, Sacramento.

44. "California Death Index, 1940–1997," index, *FamilySearch* (https://familysearch.org/pal:/MM9.1.1/VPWY-HPR: accessed 23 March 2015), Maryon B Sebby, 14 Feb 1960; Department of Public Health Services, Sacramento; www.findagrave.com. Her name is mistakenly given as Maryon *Hill* Sebby in findagrave.

45. "Maude Eburne," *Variety* (October 26, 1969) (*T-Clippings, Billy Rose Theatre Division, New York Public Library for the Performing Arts).

46. "California Marriage Index, 1960–1985," index, *FamilySearch* (https://familysearch.org/pal:/MM9.1.1/V62W-R5B: accessed 24 March 2015), Sam R Sebby and Frances Severns, 05 Aug 1968; from "California Marriage Index, 1960–1985," *Ancestry*; citing Ventura, California, Center of Health Statistics, California Department of Health Services, Sacramento; "California Death Index, 1940–1997," index, *FamilySearch* (https://familysearch.org/pal:/MM9.1.1/VG5Z-G6P: accessed 23 March 2015), Frances Price Sebby, 14 Dec 1997; Department of Public Health Services, Sacramento.

47. "United States Social Security Death Index," Sam R Sebby, 02 Feb 2004; www.findagrave.com.

Effie Ellsler

1. Her death record says she was born in Pennsylvania, while the earliest census in which I have identified her says she was born in Ohio. See "California Death Index, 1940–1997," database, *FamilySearch* (https://familysearch.org/ark:/61903/1:1:VP81-MWY: accessed 29 January 2016), Effie Ellsler Weston, 08 Oct 1942; Department of Public Health Services, Sacramento; "United States Census, 1880," database with images, *FamilySearch* (https://familysearch.org/ark:/61903/1:1:MZ6X-YT9: accessed 29 July 2015), Effie Ellsler in household of Thomas A Bell, New York, New York, New York, United States; citing enumeration district 338, sheet 540B, NARA microfilm publication T9 (Washington, D.C.: National Archives and Records Administration, n.d.), roll 0883; FHL microfilm 1,254,883.

2. "United States Census, 1880," Effie Ellsler.

3. "United States Census, 1900," database with images, *FamilySearch* (https://familysearch.org/ark:/61903/1:1:MSK4-MZF: accessed 29 July 2015), Effie E Weston in household of John A Ellsler, Borough of Manhattan, Election District 20 New York City Ward 23, New York County, New York, United States; citing sheet 23A, family 515, NARA microfilm publication T623 (Washington, D.C.: National Archives and Records Administration, n.d.); FHL microfilm 1,241,108.

4. "United States Census, 1910," database with images, *FamilySearch* (https://familysearch.org/ark:/61903/1:1:MKTB-K2S: accessed 29 July 2015), Effie Weston in household of Frank Weston, Nutley Ward 3, Essex, New Jersey, United States; citing enumeration district (ED) 203, sheet 10A, family 193, NARA microfilm publication T624 (Washington, D.C.: National Archives and Records Administration, n.d.); FHL microfilm 1,374,894.

5. "United States Census, 1920," database with images, *FamilySearch* (https://familysearch.org/ark:/61903/1:1:M4RH-PCN: accessed 29 July 2015), Effie Weston in household of Frank Weston, Nutley Ward 3, Essex, New Jersey, United States; citing sheet 3B, family 56, NARA microfilm publication T625 (Washington, D.C.: National Archives and Records Administration, n.d.); FHL microfilm 1,821,039.

6. "United States Census, 1930," database with im-

ages, *FamilySearch* (https://familysearch.org/ark:/61903/1:1:XCVC-1B2: accessed 29 July 2015), Effie E Weston, Los Angeles (Districts 0001–0250), Los Angeles, California, United States; citing enumeration district (ED) 0174, sheet 11B, family 136, line 66, NARA microfilm publication T626 (Washington, D.C.: National Archives and Records Administration, 2002), roll 139; FHL microfilm 2,339,874.

7. "United States Census, 1940," database with images, *FamilySearch* (https://familysearch.org/ark:/61903/1:1:K9H4-7WW: accessed 29 July 2015), Effie E Weston in household of Peter Ruenitz, Councilmanic District 2, Los Angeles, Los Angeles Township, Los Angeles, California, United States; citing enumeration district (ED) 60–112, sheet 7A, family 197, NARA digital publication T627 (Washington, D.C.: National Archives and Records Administration, 2012), roll 394. It's amusing to see how her younger siblings Annie and William, whom she lived with most of her life, are forced to follow suit in this process of rejuvenation. Ellsler made sure not to include their year of birth on their gravestones, only the year of their deaths, as indeed is the case with her own grave marker. See www.findagrave.com.

8. "Ohio, County Death Records, 1840–2001," database with images, *FamilySearch* (https://familysearch.org/ark:/61903/1:1:F6DT-76Y: accessed 29 July 2015), John A Ellsler, 21 Aug 1903; citing Death, Cleveland, Cuyahoga, Ohio, United States, source ID item 1 p 253, County courthouses, Ohio; FHL microfilm 1,977,439; "Death List of a Day: John Ellsler," *New York Times* (August 22, 1903), www.nytimes.com (source of quotation); https://en.wikipedia.org/wiki/John_A._Ellsler. Some sources give 1821 as Ellsler's year of birth.

9. "Mrs. John A. Ellsler Is 93," *New York Times* (November 22, 1916), www.nyt.com; "Mrs. John A. Ellsler Dies," *New York Times* (December 13, 1918), www.nyt.com; "Effie Ellsler Is Dead," *Kokomo Daily Tribune* (December 13, 1918), p. 9; "The First Effie Ellsler Dead," *Kansas City Star* (December 16, 1918), p. 10. Clara Morris's trials and tribulations in the Ellsler company, where the leading lady was married to the boss, are vividly described in Barbara Wallace Grossman, *A Spectacle of Suffering: Clara Morris on the American Stage* (Carbondale, IL: Southern Illinois University Press, 2009). In two productions of *Hamlet*, for example, the elder Effie Ellsler insisted on playing Ophelia, while Morris, who was 26 years younger, had to play Gertrude (p. 46).

10. "United States Census, 1880," database with images, *FamilySearch* (https://familysearch.org/ark:/61903/1:1:MZ1Y-V5Z: accessed 29 July 2015), William E Ellsler in household of John A Ellsler, Cleveland, Cuyahoga, Ohio, United States; citing enumeration district 17, sheet 12D, NARA microfilm publication T9 (Washington, D.C.: National Archives and Records Administration, n.d.), roll 1006; FHL microfilm 1,255,006; "Pennsylvania, County Marriages, 1885–1950," database with images, *FamilySearch* (https://familysearch.org/ark:/61903/1:1:VFMY-JK8: accessed 29 July 2015), William C. Ellsler and Martha B. Chamberlin, 09 Dec 1898; citing Marriage, Pennsylvania, county courthouses, Pennsylvania; FHL microfilm 878,634; "New York, State Census, 1905," database with images, *FamilySearch* (https://familysearch.org/ark:/61903/1:1:SPFJ-PBM: accessed 29 July 2015), William C Ellsler in household of Eliza Shires, Manhattan, A.D. 23, E.D. 32, New York, New York; citing p. 15, line 5, county offices, New York.; FHL microfilm 1,433,099.

11. "United States Census, 1880," Annie Ellsler in household of Thomas A Bell; "United States Census, 1900," Annie M Ellsler in household of John A Ellsler; "New York, State Census, 1905," Annie Ellsler in household of Eliza Shires.

12. "United States Census, 1880," Annie Ellsler; Steele MacKaye, "Hazel Kirke," *Representative American Plays from 1767 to the Present Day*, ed. Arthur Hobson Quinn (New York: Appleton-Century-Crofts, 1953), p. 438.

13. https://en.wikipedia.org/wiki/List_of_Broadway_shows_that_have_held_title_of_longest-running_show.

14. "United States Census, 1880," Effie Ellsler.

15. "Artificial Naturalness," *New York Times* (February 17, 1918), www.nytimes.com; Elizabeth F. Hoxie, "Effie Ellsler," *Notable American Women: A Biographical Dictionary, 1607–1950*, ed. Edward T. James (Cambridge, MA: Belknap Press of Harvard University Press, 1971), Vol. 1, p. 580.

16. Hoxie, p. 580.

17. "Illinois, Cook County Marriages, 1871–1920," database, *FamilySearch* (https://familysearch.org/ark:/61903/1:1:N7X8-588: accessed 29 July 2015), Frank Weston and Effie Elizabeth Ellsler, 25 May 1881; citing Chicago, Cook, Illinois, Cook County Courthouse, Chicago; FHL microfilm 1,030,117.

18. "United States Census, 1880," Frank Weston in household of Thomas A Bell; "Frank Weston Dead as His Wife Plays," *New York Times* (January 29, 1922), www.nytimes.com.

19. "Frank Weston Dead."

20. "Frank Weston Dead"; www.ibdb.com.

21. "Artificial Naturalness," *New York Times*; Hoxie, "Effie Ellsler," p. 580.

22. "Mr. Goodwin as Shylock," *New York Times* (May 25, 1901), www.nytimes.com.

23. "Artificial Naturalness," *New York Times* (incl. quotation); www.ibdb.com.

24. "'The Gipsy Trail' Is Pleasant Comedy," *New York Times* (December 5, 1917), www.nytimes.com.

25. "Plucky Effie Essler Goes On With Acting Though Husband Dead," *Helena Independent* (January 29, 1922), p. 1.

26. "Frank Weston Dead," *New York Times*.

27. "Plays Her Part as Husband Lies Dead," *Boston Globe* (January 29, 1922), p. 2.

28. "Plucky Effie Essler," *Helena Independent*, p. 1.

29. "Plucky 'Bat' Actress Back," *Boston Sunday Post* (September 3, 1922), n.pag.; www.ibdb.com.

30. *Los Angeles City Directory City 1926* (Los Angeles: Los Angeles Directory, 1926), p. 822, 2070.

31. *Los Angeles Directory City 1927* (Los Angeles: Los Angeles Directory, 1927), p. 2088; *Los Angeles Directory City 1928* (Los Angeles: Los Angeles Directory, 1928), p. 832, 2167.

32. "United States Census, 1930," Effie E Weston; *Los Angeles Directory City 1934* (Los Angeles: Los Angeles Directory, 1934), p. 548.

33. *Los Angeles City Directory 1938* (Los Angeles: Los Angeles Directory, 1938), p. 583, 1921.

34. www.findagrave.com.

35. "United States Census, 1940," Effie E. Weston; *Los Angeles City Directory* (Los Angeles: Los Angeles

Directory, 1942), p. 2543. The Pacific Old People's Home is today Kingsley Manor Retirement Community and markets itself as "LA's oldest full-service retirement community" founded in 1912 (http://www.kingsley manor.org).

36. "California Death Index, 1940–1997," Effie Ellsler Weston; "Veteran Actress Dies," *Albuquerque Journal* (October 10, 1942), p. 7; Hoxie, "Effie Ellsler," p. 580; www.findagrave.com.

Edith Evanson

1. "United States Census, 1900," database with images, *FamilySearch* (https://familysearch.org/ark:/61903/1:1:MMPP-GXX: accessed 23 July 2015), Eva Carlson, Precinct 4 Tacoma city Ward 5, Pierce, Washington, United States; citing sheet 1B, family 18, NARA microfilm publication T623 (Washington, D.C.: National Archives and Records Administration, n.d.); FHL microfilm 1,241,749; "Washington, Death Certificates, 1907–1960," database, *FamilySearch* (https://family search.org/ark:/61903/1:1:N35W-V9L: accessed 23 July 2015), Eva Carlson, 10 Apr 1930; citing Tacoma, Pierce, Washington, reference 421, Bureau of Vital Statistics, Olympia; FHL microfilm 2,022,724.

2. "United States Census, 1900," Eva Carlson; "United States Census, 1920," database with images, *FamilySearch* (https://familysearch.org/ark:/61903/1:1:MHNS-Y17: accessed 23 July 2015), Eva Carlson, Tacoma Ward 5, Pierce, Washington, United States; citing sheet 5A, family 110, NARA microfilm publication T625 (Washington, D.C.: National Archives and Records Administration, n.d.); FHL microfilm 1,821,937.

3. "Minnesota, State Census, 1885," database with images, *FamilySearch* (https://familysearch.org/ark:/61903/1:1:MQXD-C6Y: accessed 23 July 2015), Eva Carlson in household of John Carlson, Minneapolis, Hennepin, Minnesota; citing p. 10, volume Hennepin, State Library and Records Service, St. Paul; FHL microfilm 565,741.

4. "Minnesota State Census, 1885," John Carlson.

5. My summary of the lives of Evanson's brothers is based on data from the census and other sources too numerous to cite here.

6. "California Death Index, 1940–1997," database, *FamilySearch* (https://familysearch.org/ark:/61903/1:1:VP2Y-9W7: accessed 23 July 2015), Edith A Evanson, 29 Nov 1980; Department of Public Health Services, Sacramento.

7. www.findagrave.com.

8. "United States Census, 1900," Edith H Carlson in household of Eva Carlson.

9. www.zillow.com.

10. "United States Census, 1910," Edith Carlson in household of Eva Carlson.

11. "United States Census, 1910," database with images, *FamilySearch* (https://familysearch.org/ark:/61903/1:1:MGJZ-39P: accessed 23 July 2015), Morris O Evanson in household of Olive [sic] A Evanson, Tacoma Ward 5, Pierce, Washington, United States; citing enumeration district (ED) 267, sheet 3A, family 73, NARA microfilm publication T624 (Washington, D.C.: National Archives and Records Administration, n.d.); FHL microfilm 1,375,678.

12. "Wisconsin, Births and Christenings, 1826–1926," database, *FamilySearch* (https://familysearch.org/ark:/61903/1:1:XRLW-D4Y: accessed 23 July 2015), Morris Otto Evanson, 02 Mar 1893; citing Shell Lake, Washburn, Wisconsin, reference 1529; FHL microfilm 1,305,599.

13. "United States World War II Draft Registration Cards, 1942," database with images, *FamilySearch* (https://familysearch.org/ark:/61903/1:1:V4DH-2Z7: accessed 23 July 2015), Morris Otto Evanson, 1942; citing NAID identifier, NARA microfilm publication M1936, M1937, M1939, M1951, M1962, M1964, M1986, M2090, and M2097 (Washington, D.C.: National Archives and Records Administration, n.d.); FHL microfilm.

14. "United States Census, 1910," Olive [sic] A Evanson; www.findagrave.com.

15. www.findagrave.com.

16. www.findagrave.com.

17. "United States World War I Draft Registration Cards, 1917–1918," database with images, *FamilySearch* (https://familysearch.org/ark:/61903/1:1:29JZ-JLD: accessed 23 July 2015), Morris Otto Evanson, 1917–1918; citing Tacoma City no 3, Tacoma City no 4, Washington, United States, NARA microfilm publication M1509 (Washington, D.C.: National Archives and Records Administration, n.d.); FHL microfilm 1,992,113.

18. After having been boarded up and abandoned, this three bedroom, 1½ bathroom house from 1904 was sold in 2012 for $52,600 and is currently being renovated (www.zillow.com).

19. "United States Census, 1920," Edith Carlson in household of Eva Carlson.

20. "United States Census, 1930," database with images, *FamilySearch* (https://familysearch.org/ark:/61903/1:1:XC3B-THS: accessed 23 July 2015), Eva Carlson, Tacoma, Pierce, Washington, United States; citing enumeration district (ED) 0165, sheet 1B, family 22, line 80, NARA microfilm publication T626 (Washington, D.C.: National Archives and Records Administration, 2002), roll 2512; FHL microfilm 2,342,246.

21. "Washington, Death Certificates, 1907–1960," Eva Carlson, 10 Apr 1930.

22. John Dunning, *On the Air: The Encyclopedia of Old-Time Radio* (New York and Oxford: Oxford University Press, 1998), p. 474. See also "Gracie Finds New Worry in Vocalist," *San Antonio Light* (October 17, 1941), p. 16A.

23. Dunning, p. 474.

24. "United States Census, 1940," database with images, *FamilySearch* (https://familysearch.org/ark:/61903/1:1:K9C6-XDC: accessed 23 July 2015), Edith Evanson in household of Morris Evanson, Councilmanic District 2, Los Angeles, Los Angeles Township, Los Angeles, California, United States; citing enumeration district (ED) 60–135, sheet 8B, family 237, NARA digital publication T627 (Washington, D.C.: National Archives and Records Administration, 2012), roll 398.

25. "United States Census, 1940," Edith Evanson.

26. "United States World War II Draft Registration Cards, 1942," Morris Otto Evanson; *Los Angeles City Directory 1942* (Los Angeles: Los Angeles Directory, 1942), p. 767.

27. www.tcm.com.

28. Robert A. Harris and Michael S. Lasky, *The Films*

of *Alfred Hitchcock* (Secaucus, NJ: The Citadel Press, 1976), p. 143.

29. www.imdb.com.

30. Farley Granger with Robert Calhoun, *Include Me Out: My Life from Goldwyn to Broadway* (New York: St. Martin's Press, 2007), p. 69.

31. Arthur Laurents, *Original Story By: A Memoir of Broadway and Hollywood* (New York and London: Applause, 2000), p. 131.

32. "Stewart Has Starring Role in Alfred Hitchcock's 'Rope,'" *Annapolis Evening Capital* (November 17, 1948), p. 10.

33. All quotes and information from James Bacon, "Film Voice Coach Tells of Marilyn," *Daily Review* (November 14, 1962), p. 56.

34. "California Death Index, 1940–1997," database, *FamilySearch* (https://familysearch.org/ark:/61903/1:1:VP61-M9H: accessed 23 July 2015), Morris O Evanson, 30 Dec 1975; Department of Public Health Services, Sacramento.

35. "California Death Index, 1940–1997," Edith A Evanson, 29 Nov 1980.

36. www.findagrave.com.

Blanche Friderici

1. Hale and Mercer were profiled in my book *Mothers, Mammies and Old Maids.*

2. "Heart Attack Fatal to a Noted Actress," *Joplin News Herald* (December 25, 1933), p. 1.

3. "Blanche Friderici: Veteran Character Actress of Stage and Screen," *New York Times* (December 25, 1933), p. 23; "Mrs. Blanche F. Campbell, Film Actress, Dies at 55; Also Appeared in Stage Plays as Miss Friderici," *New York Herald Tribune* (December 24, 1933) (*T-Clippings, Billy Rose Theatre Division, New York Public Library for the Performing Arts; henceforward abbreviated NYPL).

4. "Blanche Campbell Veteran Actress Taken by Death," *New Castle News* (December 26, 1933), p. 5.

5. "Blanche Friderici," *New York Times*, p. 23.

6. "New York, Births and Christenings, 1640–1962," database, *FamilySearch* (https://familysearch.org/ark:/61903/1:1:FDT7-9KM: accessed 21 July 2015), Blanche Friderici, 12 Sep 1873; citing Brooklyn, Kings, New York, reference; FHL microfilm 1,373,921.

7. "United States Census, 1900," database with images, *FamilySearch* (https://familysearch.org/ark:/61903/1:1:MSFD-2QK: accessed 21 July 2015), Rosetta E Friderici, Borough of Brooklyn, Election District 16 New York City Ward 7, Kings, New York, United States; citing sheet 3B, family 62, NARA microfilm publication T623 (Washington, D.C.: National Archives and Records Administration, n.d.); FHL microfilm 1,241,046.

8. "New York State Census, 1892," database with images, *FamilySearch* (https://familysearch.org/ark:/61903/1:1:MQ3R-L1Q: accessed 30 January 2016), Blanche L Friderici, 1892; citing Brooklyn, Ward 18, E.D. 41, county offices, New York; FHL microfilm 1,930,238.

9. "United States Census, 1900," Blanche L Friderici in household of Rosetta E Friderici.

10. "Actress of Many Names Uses Own Again and Will Stick to It Henceforth," *New York Evening Telegram* (March 12, 1922) (NYPL).

11. Information in this paragraph from "Stock Actress in Loew's State Film," *Boston Herald*, March 18, 1928 (NYPL); "Actress of Many Names"; www.ibdb.com.

12. *Syracuse Herald* (July 20, 1932), p. 10.

13. *Carbondale Daily Free Press* (June 1, 1908), n.pag.

14. "Plays by Radcliffe Alumnae," *New York Times* (April 17, 1909), p. 9.

15. "Actress of Many Names," *New York Evening Telegram*; www.ibdb.com.

16. Rachel Crothers, *Expressing Willie/Nice People/39 East: Three Plays by Rachel Crothers* (New York: Bentano's, n.d.), p. 190; *Joel Lobenthal, Tallulah: The Life and Times of a Leading Lady* (New York: HarperCollins, 2004), pp. 28–29.

17. www.ibdb.com.

18. "Magic of Make-Up Shown by Young Brooklyn Actress," *New York American*, undated clipping [c1922] (NYPL).

19. "United States World War I Draft Registration Cards, 1917–1918," database with images, *FamilySearch* (https://familysearch.org/ark:/61903/1:1:K3T9-2HB: accessed 21 July 2015), Donald Campbell, 1917–1918; citing St. Louis City no 28, Missouri, United States, NARA microfilm publication M1509 (Washington, D.C.: National Archives and Records Administration, n.d.); FHL microfilm 1,683,862.

20. United States Census, 1900," database with images, *FamilySearch* (https://familysearch.org/ark:/61903/1:1:M3D3-1J7: accessed 21 July 2015), Donald T Campbell in household of Malcolm Campbell, Precinct 12 St. Louis city Ward 18, St. Louis, Missouri, United States; citing sheet 2A, family 33, NARA microfilm publication T623 (Washington, D.C.: National Archives and Records Administration, n.d.); FHL microfilm 1,240,896; "United States Census, 1910," database with images, *FamilySearch* (https://familysearch.org/ark:/61903/1:1:M21Q-XJS: accessed 21 July 2015), Donald L Campbell in household of Malcolm Campbell, St Louis Ward 1, St Louis (Independent City), Missouri, United States; citing enumeration district (ED) 15, sheet 1B, family 25, NARA microfilm publication T624 (Washington, D.C.: National Archives and Records Administration, n.d.); FHL microfilm 1,374,824.

21. "United States World War I Draft Registration Cards, 1917–1918," Donald Campbell.

22. "United States Census, 1930," database with images, *FamilySearch* (https://familysearch.org/ark:/61903/1:1:XCV3-542: accessed 21 July 2015), Donald T Campbell, Los Angeles (Districts 0001–0250), Los Angeles, California, United States; citing enumeration district (ED) 0074, sheet 21B, family 237, line 81, NARA microfilm publication T626 (Washington, D.C.: National Archives and Records Administration, 2002), roll 134; FHL microfilm 2,339,869.

23. "United States Census, 1930," Donald T Campbell.

24. "Celluloid Claims Her," *Portland Express*, undated clipping [cSept. 1927] (NYPL).

25. "Celluloid Claims Her"; "Blanche Friderici," p. 23; "Mrs. Blanche F. Campbell"; "Blanche Campbell Veteran Actress," p. 5.

26. "Celluloid Claims Her."

27. movielanddirectory.com.

28. *Los Angeles City Directory 1929* (Los Angeles: Los

Angeles Directory, 1929), p. 909; *Los Angeles City Directory 1932* (Los Angeles: Los Angeles Directory, 1932), p. 389; "United States Census, 1930," Blanche F Campbell in household of Donald T Campbell; www.zillow.com.

29. "Screen Gossip," *Hammond Times* (September 11, 1930), p. 8.

30. "United States Census, 1930," Donald T Campbell.

31. *Los Angeles City Directory 1932* (Los Angeles: Los Angeles Directory, 1932), p. 768; www.zillow.com.

32. Ragan, *Who's Who in Hollywood*, p. 619; John Springer and Jack Hamilton. *They Had Faces Then: Super Stars, Stars and Starlets of the 1930's* (N.p.: Castle, 1974), p. 113; www.allmovie.com.

33. Richard Barrios, *Screened Out: Playing Gay in Hollywood from Edison to Stonewall* (New York and London: Routledge, 2003), p. 62.

34. Barrios, p. 62.

35. "Heart Attack Fatal," *Joplin News Herald*, p. 1.

36. "Blanche Friderici," *New York Times*, p. 23.

Grace George

1. Her gravestone says December 27th. She herself either said it was Christmas Day or December 26th at different times. Parker, *Who's Who in the Theatre*, p. 597 gives her birth date as December 25, 1879 and Blum, *Great Stars of the American Stage*, profile no. 26 gives December 25, 1878. See www.findagrave.com; "United States Passport Applications, 1795–1925," database with images, *FamilySearch* (https://familysearch.org/ark:/61903/1:1:QV5B-K7VL: accessed 2 August 2015), Grace George Brady, 1919; citing Passport Application, New York, United States, source certificate #77847, Passport Applications, January 2, 1906–March 31, 1925, 757, NARA microfilm publications M1490 and M1372 (Washington D.C.: National Archives and Records Administration, n.d.); FHL microfilm; "United States Border Crossings from Canada to United States, 1895–1956," database, *FamilySearch* (https://familysearch.org/ark:/61903/1:1:FS8S-JJ6: accessed 2 August 2015), Grace Brady, 13 Jun 1919; from "Border Crossings: From Canada to U.S., 1895–1954," database and images, *Ancestry* (http://www.ancestry.com: 2010); citing Ship Olympic, arrival port Halifax, Nova Scotia, England, line 6, NARA microfilm publication M1464, roll 370, NARA record group 85, National Archives and Records Administration, Washington, D.C.; "New York, New York Passenger and Crew Lists, 1909, 1925–1957," database with images, *FamilySearch* (https://familysearch.org/ark:/61903/1:1:24FQ-K71: accessed 2 August 2015), Grace Brady, 1929; citing Immigration, New York, New York, United States, NARA microfilm publication T715 (Washington, D.C.: National Archives and Records Administration, n.d.); FHL microfilm 1,756,345.

2. "United States Naval Enlistment Rendezvous, 1855–1891," database with images, *FamilySearch* (https://familysearch.org/ark:/61903/1:1:XG3R-TYF: accessed 2 August 2015), George C Dougherty, Oct 1858; citing p. 261, volume 8, place of enlistment New York, NARA microfilm publication M1953 (Washington, D.C.: National Archives and Records Administration, n.d.), roll 8; FHL microfilm 2,367,947; "United States Census, 1870," database with images, *FamilySearch* (https://familysearch.org/ark:/61903/1:1:M8XG-VWQ: accessed 2 August 2015), George Dougherty in household of Mary Dougherty, New York, United States; citing p. 108, family 899, NARA microfilm publication M593 (Washington, D.C.: National Archives and Records Administration, n.d.); FHL microfilm 552,478; "United States Census, 1900," database with images, *FamilySearch* (https://familysearch.org/ark:/61903/1:1:MSNS-SCP: accessed 2 August 2015), George C Dougherty in household of Mary G Dempsey, Borough of Brooklyn, Election District 15 New York City Ward 19, Kings, New York, United States; citing sheet 8A, family 167, NARA microfilm publication T623 (Washington, D.C.: National Archives and Records Administration, n.d.); FHL microfilm 1,241,056; "United States Census, 1910," database with images, *FamilySearch* (https://familysearch.org/ark:/61903/1:1:M5QX-157: accessed 2 August 2015), George C Daugherty in household of Mary G Dempsey, Brooklyn Ward 19, Kings, New York, United States; citing enumeration district (ED) 439, sheet 5A, family 94, NARA microfilm publication T624 (Washington, D.C.: National Archives and Records Administration, n.d.); FHL microfilm 1,374,980; "New York, New York City Municipal Deaths, 1795–1949," database, *FamilySearch* (https://familysearch.org/ark:/61903/1:1:2WMM-V86: accessed 2 August 2015), George C. Dougherty, 04 Dec 1911; citing Death, Manhattan, New York, New York, United States, New York Municipal Archives, New York; FHL microfilm.

3. There is a Helen Dougherty, who died age 51 in 1893, in the New York Municipal Deaths record, who may be George's mother; or a Helen Kenny (b. 1848–49) in the 1870 U.S. Census, but neither identification is certain. See "New York, New York City Municipal Deaths, 1795–1949," database, *FamilySearch* (https://familysearch.org/ark:/61903/1:1:2WLL-WGS: accessed 2 August 2015), Helen Dougherty, 21 May 1893; citing Death, Brooklyn, Kings, New York, United States, New York Municipal Archives, New York; FHL microfilm; "United States Census, 1870," database with images, *FamilySearch* (https://familysearch.org/ark:/61903/1:1:M8N6-YM8: accessed 2 August 2015), Helen Kenny in household of Jas Kenny, New York, United States; citing p. 119, family 904, NARA microfilm publication M593 (Washington, D.C.: National Archives and Records Administration, n.d.); FHL microfilm 552,449.

4. "New York, Marriages, 1686–1980," database, *FamilySearch* (https://familysearch.org/ark:/61903/1:1:F671-FZZ: accessed 2 August 2015), Charles Dougherty and Caroline Thomey, 12 Jun 1898; citing reference; FHL microfilm 1,504,028; "United States Census, 1910," database with images, *FamilySearch* (https://familysearch.org/ark:/61903/1:1:M5QL-77P: accessed 2 August 2015), Carrie Dougherty, Brooklyn Ward 28, Kings, New York, United States; citing enumeration district (ED) 909, sheet 11B, family 261, NARA microfilm publication T624 (Washington, D.C.: National Archives and Records Administration, n.d.); FHL microfilm 1,374,995.

5. "United States Census, 1910," database with images, *FamilySearch* (https://familysearch.org/ark:/61903/1:1:M5SX-6R7: accessed 2 August 2015), Grace Dougherty in household of Williams Brady, Manhattan Ward 22, New York, New York, United States; citing enumeration district (ED) 1316, sheet 7B, family 168,

NARA microfilm publication T624 (Washington, D.C.: National Archives and Records Administration, n.d.); FHL microfilm 1,375,059.

6. Again there is contradictory evidence, but this is the birth date William Brady, Jr., gave himself. His gravestone says 1901. See "New York, New York Passenger and Crew Lists, 1909, 1925–1957," database with images, *FamilySearch* (https://familysearch.org/ark:/61903/1:1:KXLF-4PN: accessed 2 August 2015), William A Brady, 1926; citing Immigration, New York, New York, United States, NARA microfilm publication T715 (Washington, D.C.: National Archives and Records Administration, n.d.); FHL microfilm 1,755,612; "New York, New York Passenger and Crew Lists, 1909, 1925–1957," database with images, *FamilySearch* (https://familysearch.org/ark:/61903/1:1:2462–3R7: accessed 2 August 2015), William A Brady, 1928; citing Immigration, New York, New York, United States, NARA microfilm publication T715 (Washington, D.C.: National Archives and Records Administration, n.d.); FHL microfilm 1,755,956; www.findagrave.com.

7. I profiled Alice Brady in *Actresses of a Certain Character*.

8. Parker, *Who's Who in the Theatre*, p. 597; Lewis C. Strang, *Famous Actresses of the Day in America: Second Series* (Boston: L.C. Page, 1902), p. 286, 287.

9. Strang, p. 294.

10. Blum, *Great Stars of the American Stage*, profile no. 26.

11. "New York, New York Passenger and Crew Lists, 1909, 1925–1957," Grace Brady, 1929; https://en.wikipedia.org/wiki/William_A._Brady.

12. "Young Brady Dies in Blaze," *Gettysburg Times* (September 27, 1935), p. 4.

13. L.L. Stevenson, "Lights of New York," *Connellsville Daily Courier* (September 13, 1935), p. 8.

14. "California Death Index, 1940–1997," database, *FamilySearch* (https://familysearch.org/ark:/61903/1:1:VP6Z-42W: accessed 2 August 2015), Donald William Crane, 17 Jan 1942; Department of Public Health Services, Sacramento; DeWitt Bodeen, *From Hollywood* (South Brunswick and New York: A.S. Barnes, 1977), p. 193.

15. George registered to vote while she was staying with Fields in 1934. See "News and Comment of Stage and Screen," *Fitchburg Sentinel* (February 16, 1935), p. 5; movielanddirectory.com.

16. Wood Soanes, "Curtain Calls," *Oakland Tribune* (July 10, 1935), p. D7.

17. For an account of how and why George finally "capitulated to Hollywood" that emphasizes the size of the role and Cagney's recent Academy Award, see Erskine Johnson, "In Hollywood: Presenting Grace George," *Ironwood Daily Globe* (March 30, 1943), p. 10.

18. Homer Dickens, *The Films of James Cagney* (Secaucus, NJ: The Citadel Press, 1972), p. 178.

19. Strang, *Famous Actresses*, p. 287.

20. Quoted in Dickens, *The Films of James Cagney*, p. 177.

21. Quoted in Dickens, p. 178.

22. Quoted in Dickens, p. 177.

23. Bosley Crowther, *Johnny Come Lately* review, *New York Times* (September 24, 1943), www.nytimes.com.

24. Minty Clinch, *Cagney: The Story of His Film Career* (London and New York: Proteus Books, 1982), p. 81.

25. L.L. Stevenson, "Lights of New York," p. 8; "United States Census, 1940," database with images, *FamilySearch* (https://familysearch.org/ark:/61903/1:1:KQSL-B2P: accessed 2 August 2015), Grace Brady in household of William Brady, Assembly District 15, Manhattan, New York City, New York, New York, United States; citing enumeration district (ED) 31–1384, sheet 2B, family 67, NARA digital publication T627 (Washington, D.C.: National Archives and Records Administration, 2012), roll 2657.

26. "William A. Brady, Noted Theatrical Dean, Dies at 86," *Cedar Rapids Gazette* (January 8, 1950), p. 1.

27. "New York, New York Passenger and Crew Lists, 1909, 1925–1957," database with images, *FamilySearch* (https://familysearch.org/ark:/61903/1:1:24R2-7P4: accessed 2 August 2015), Barbara A B Brady, 1949; citing Immigration, New York City, New York, United States, NARA microfilm publication T715 (Washington, D.C.: National Archives and Records Administration, n.d.); FHL microfilm 2,296,469. Many thanks to Gail Powers for the information that Barbara Brady died in 1978 and is buried with her mother in Forest Park Cemetery, Fort Smith, Arkansas.

28. George quoted in Blum, *Great Stars of the American Stage*, profile no. 26.

29. "Grace George, 81, Dies; Long-Time Broadway Star," *Madison Capital Times* (May 20, 1961), p. 2; www.findagrave.com.

Connie Gilchrist

1. Quoted in Don Stanke, "Connie Gilchrist: A Lady of Many Parts," *Films in Review* no. 3 (March 1974), p. 160.

2. The standard accounts of Gilchrist's life and career are contained in James Robert Parish and Ronald L. Bowers, *The MGM Stock Company: The Golden Era* (New York: Bonanza Books, 1972), pp. 280–83 and Stanke, "Connie Gilchrist," pp. 151–64. In this profile, I have tried to supplement, and in a few cases correct, the information contained in these still readable and informative pieces, rather than rehashing all the facts and anecdotes they contain.

3. "United States Social Security Death Index," index, *FamilySearch* (https://familysearch.org/pal:/MM9.1.1/JK5Y-923: accessed 6 March 2015), Connie Gilchrist, Mar 1985; citing U.S. Social Security Administration, *Death Master File*, database (Alexandria, Virginia: National Technical Information Service, ongoing).

4. "United States Census, 1900," index and images, *FamilySearch* (https://familysearch.org/pal:/MM9.1.1/MSFV-64Z: accessed 6 March 2015), Gertrude Volmer in household of Martha Volmer, Borough of Brooklyn, Election District 13 New York City Ward 10, Kings, New York, United States; citing sheet 17B, family 365, NARA microfilm publication T623 (Washington, D.C.: National Archives and Records Administration, n.d.); FHL microfilm 1,241,049.

5. Parish and Bowers, *The MGM Stock Company*, p. 280.

6. "United States Census, 1900," index and images, *FamilySearch* (https://familysearch.org/pal:/MM9.1.1/MSFV-64C: accessed 7 March 2015), Martha Volmer, Borough of Brooklyn, Election District 13 New York

City Ward 10, Kings, New York, United States; citing sheet 17B, family 365, NARA microfilm publication T623 (Washington, D.C.: National Archives and Records Administration, n.d.); FHL microfilm 1,241,049; "United States Census, 1910," index and images, *Family Search* (https://familysearch.org/pal:/MM9.1.1/M5QW-K89: accessed 7 March 2015), Martha A Gilchrist in household of John Gilchrist, Brooklyn Ward 5, Kings, New York, United States; citing enumeration district (ED) 44, sheet 1A, family 2, NARA microfilm publication T624 (Washington, D.C.: National Archives and Records Administration, n.d.); FHL microfilm 1,374,969; "United States Census, 1920," index and images, *Family Search* (https://familysearch.org/pal:/MM9.1.1/MJPB-XFL: accessed 7 March 2015), Martha Gilchrist in household of William Nallman, Brooklyn Assembly District 3, Kings, New York, United States; citing sheet 7A, family 145, NARA microfilm publication T625 (Washington, D.C.: National Archives and Records Administration, n.d.); FHL microfilm 1,821,148.

7. "United States Census, 1900," Annie Volmer in household of Martha Volmer.

8. "United States Census, 1910," John Gilchrist.

9. "United States Census, 1920," Gruliere [sic] R Gilchrist in household of William Nallman.

10. Parish and Bowers, *The MGM Stock Company*, p. 280; Stanke, "Connie Gilchrist," p. 151; Ragan, *Who's Who in Hollywood*, p. 160.

11. "New York, New York Passenger and Crew Lists, 1909, 1925–1957," index and images, *FamilySearch* (https://familysearch.org/pal:/MM9.1.1/2465-S8B: accessed 7 March 2015), Gertrude R O'Hanlon, 1928; citing Immigration, New York, New York, United States, NARA microfilm publication T715 (Washington, D.C.: National Archives and Records Administration, n.d.); FHL microfilm 1,755,993.

12. "United States Census, 1930," index and images, *FamilySearch* (https://familysearch.org/pal:/MM9.1.1/X42Q-TJR: accessed 7 March 2015), Gertrude O'Hanlan [sic] in household of Edward O'Hanlan, Manhattan (Districts 1001–1249), New York, New York, United States; citing enumeration district (ED) 1199, sheet 9B, family 459, line 92, NARA microfilm publication T626 (Washington, D.C.: National Archives and Records Administration, 2002), roll 1559; FHL microfilm 2,341,294.

13. "United States Social Security Death Index," index, *FamilySearch* (https://familysearch.org/pal:/MM9.1.1/JR3L-63R: accessed 7 March 2015), Edwin Ohanlon, Dec 1983; citing U.S. Social Security Administration, *Death Master File*, database (Alexandria, Virginia: National Technical Information Service, ongoing).

14. "United States Census, 1910," index and images, *FamilySearch* (https://familysearch.org/pal:/MM9.1.1/MRQ4-3DT: accessed 7 March 2015), Edward [sic] O'Hanlon in household of Bridget Gallagher, Brooklyn Ward 17, Kings, New York, United States; citing enumeration district (ED) 397, sheet 3A, family 49, NARA microfilm publication T624 (Washington, D.C.: National Archives and Records Administration, n.d.); FHL microfilm 1,374,979.

15. "United States Census, 1920," index and images, *FamilySearch* (https://familysearch.org/pal:/MM9.1.1/MJ5R-9Y2: accessed 7 March 2015), Edwin A O Hanlon in household of Anna B Gallagher, Brooklyn Assembly District 11, Kings, New York, United States; citing sheet 2A, family 31, NARA microfilm publication T625 (Washington, D.C.: National Archives and Records Administration, n.d.); FHL microfilm 1,821,161.

16. "Actors, No Doubt," *Corpus Christi Caller Time* (December 28, 1947), n.pag.; "United States Census, 1940," index and images, *FamilySearch* (https://familysearch.org/pal:/MM9.1.1/KQS6-BF3: accessed 7 March 2015), Edwin O'Hanlon, Assembly District 7, Manhattan, New York City, New York, New York, United States; citing enumeration district (ED) 31–615, sheet 3A, family 42, NARA digital publication T627 (Washington, D.C.: National Archives and Records Administration, 2012), roll 2638.

17. "New York, New York Passenger and Crew Lists, 1909, 1925–1957," Gertrude R O'Hanlon, 1928; "United States Census, 1930," Gertrude O'Hanlan [sic]; *Kingston Daily Freeman* (July 28, 1933), p. 11.

18. "United States Census, 1940," Edwin O'Hanlon.

19. "New York, New York Passenger and Crew Lists, 1909, 1925–1957," index and images, *FamilySearch* (https://familysearch.org/pal:/MM9.1.1/2465-S81: accessed 7 March 2015), Dorothy O'Hanlon, 1928; citing Immigration, New York, New York, United States, NARA microfilm publication T715 (Washington, D.C.: National Archives and Records Administration, n.d.); FHL microfilm 1,755,993.

20. Stanke, "Connie Gilchrist," p. 151.

21. Stanke, p. 151.

22. http://en.wikipedia.org/wiki/Rose_McClendon.

23. Burns Mantle, *The Best Plays of 1935–36* (New York: Dodd, Mead, 1936), p. 425; Langston Hughes, "Mulatto," *Three Negro Plays* (Harmondsworth: Penguin, 1969), pp. 19–61.

24. www.ibdb.com.

25. Burns Mantle, *The Best Plays of 1936–37* (New York: Dodd, Mead, 1937), p. 328, including quote from Watts.

26. Victor Wolfson, "Excursion," *The Best Plays of 1936–37*, ed. Burns Mantle (New York: Dodd, Mead, 1937), p. 332.

27. www.ibdb.com.

28. www.ibdb.com.

29. Burns Mantle, *The Best Plays of 1937–38* (New York: Dodd, Mead, 1938), p. 394.

30. *Los Angeles City Directory 1942* (Los Angeles: Los Angeles Directory, 1942), p. 912, 1807.

31. Parish and Bowers, *The MGM Stock Company*, p. 281; Stanke, "Connie Gilchrist," p. 156.

32. Quoted in Stanke, "Connie Gilchrist," p. 155.

33. Stanke, p. 155.

34. Parish and Bowers, *The MGM Stock Company*, p. 281; Stanke, "Connie Gilchrist," p. 152.

35. "California, Birth Index, 1905–1995," index, *FamilySearch* (https://familysearch.org/pal:/MM9.1.1/V2R5-NT5: accessed 8 March 2015), Todd Joseph Sanson, 08 Dec 1948; citing Los Angeles, California, United States, Department of Health Services, Vital Statistics Department, Sacramento; "California, Divorce Index, 1966–1984," index, *FamilySearch* (https://familysearch.org/pal:/MM9.1.1/VPTW-KDP: accessed 7 March 2015), Dorothy R Ohanlon and Joseph F Sanson, Mar 1970; from "California, Divorce Index, 1966–1984," *Ancestry*; citing Los Angeles City, California, Health Statistics, California Department of Health Services, Sacramento; *Santa Fe New Mexican* (December 17, 1983), p. A6.

36. Stanke, "Connie Gilchrist," p. 158; Ragan, *Who's Who in Hollywood*, p. 160.
37. Parish and Bowers, *The MGM Stock Company*, p. 281; Stanke, "Connie Gilchrist," p. 151.
38. "United States Social Security Death Index," Edwin Ohanlon, Dec 1983.
39. "United States Social Security Death Index," Connie Gilchrist, Mar 1985.
40. www.findagrave.com.

Minna Gombell

1. Springer and Hamilton, *They Had Faces Then*, p. 121.
2. James Robert Parish, *Hollywood Character Actors* (New Rochelle, New York: Arlington House, 1978), p. 229.
3. David Quinland, *Quinlan's Character Stars* (London: Reynolds and Hearn, 2004), p. 169.
4. Both quotes from "Minna Gombel, 'Golden Girl,' Talks Shop," *Syracuse Herald* (April 14, 1918), p. 3.
5. "California Death Index, 1940–1997," database, *FamilySearch* (https://familysearch.org/ark:/61903/1:1:VP25-X3Y: accessed 16 January 2016), Minna Gombell, 14 Apr 1973; Department of Public Health Services, Sacramento. 1893 is sometimes mistakenly given as her year of birth.
6. "United States Census, 1880," database with images, *FamilySearch* (https://familysearch.org/ark:/61903/1:1:MNQX-61T: accessed 16 January 2016), William Gombel, Baltimore, Baltimore, Maryland, United States; citing enumeration district ED 215, sheet 474C, NARA microfilm publication T9 (Washington, D.C.: National Archives and Records Administration, n.d.), roll 0505; FHL microfilm 1,254,505; Henry M. Fine, "They Found Her Hidden Under a Wig," *Oakland Tribune* (February 10, 1935), n.pag.
7. "United States Germans to America Index, 1850–1897," database, *FamilySearch* (https://familysearch.org/ark:/61903/1:1:KD3G-H78: accessed 16 January 2016), Wilhelm Gombel, 15 May 1880; citing Germans to America Passenger Data file, 1850–1897, Ship Mosel, departed from Bremen & Southampton, arrived in New York, New York, New York, United States, NAID identifier 1746067, National Archives at College Park, Maryland; www.findagrave.com.
8. "United States Census, 1880," database with images, *FamilySearch* (https://familysearch.org/ark:/61903/1:1:MNQX-61T: accessed 16 January 2016), William Gombel, Baltimore, Baltimore, Maryland, United States; citing enumeration district ED 215, sheet 474C, NARA microfilm publication T9 (Washington, D.C.: National Archives and Records Administration, n.d.), roll 0505; FHL microfilm 1,254,505.
9. "United States Census, 1900," database with images, *FamilySearch* (https://familysearch.org/ark:/61903/1:1:M3KP-9VJ: accessed 16 January 2016), William Gombel, Precinct 10 Baltimore city Ward 21, Baltimore, Maryland, United States; citing sheet 7A, family 142, NARA microfilm publication T623 (Washington, D.C.: National Archives and Records Administration, n.d.); FHL microfilm 1,240,617.
10. "United States Census, 1900," Emma Gombel in household of William Gombel; www.findagrave.com.
11. "United States Census, 1870," database with images, *FamilySearch* (https://familysearch.org/ark:/61903/1:1:MN3W-T8D: accessed 16 January 2016), Bernhardt Dabreng [sic], Maryland, United States; citing p. 241, family 1877, NARA microfilm publication M593 (Washington, D.C.: National Archives and Records Administration, n.d.); FHL microfilm 552,077; "United States Census, 1880," database with images, *FamilySearch* (https://familysearch.org/ark:/61903/1:1:MNQC-1CM: accessed 16 January 2016), Bernard Debring, Baltimore, Baltimore, Maryland, United States; citing enumeration district ED 141, sheet 17B, NARA microfilm publication T9 (Washington, D.C.: National Archives and Records Administration, n.d.), roll 0503; FHL microfilm 1,254,503; "United States Census, 1900," database with images, *FamilySearch* (https://familysearch.org/ark:/61903/1:1:M3KQ-NYK: accessed 16 January 2016), Bernhardt Debring, Precinct 7 Baltimore city Ward 1, Baltimore, Maryland, United States; citing sheet 4A, family 75, NARA microfilm publication T623 (Washington, D.C.: National Archives and Records Administration, n.d.); FHL microfilm 1,240,608; www.findagrave.com.
12. "United States Census, 1880," Emma Debring in household of Bernard Debring.
13. "United States Census, 1900," Minna M Gombel in household of William Gombel; "United States Census, 1910," database with images, *FamilySearch*(https://familysearch.org/ark:/61903/1:1:M2F4-TYC: accessed 16 January 2016), Minna M Gombel in household of William Gombel, Baltimore Ward 14, Baltimore (Independent City), Maryland, United States; citing enumeration district (ED) ED 236, sheet 8A, NARA microfilm publication T624 (Washington, D.C.: National Archives and Records Administration, n.d.); FHL microfilm 1,374,570.
14. "United States Census, 1920," database with images, *FamilySearch*(https://familysearch.org/ark:/61903/1:1:M6Q9-6CZ: accessed 16 January 2016), Emma Gombel, Baltimore Ward 14, Baltimore (Independent City), Maryland, United States; citing sheet 12B, NARA microfilm publication T625 (Washington, D.C.: National Archives and Records Administration, n.d.); FHL microfilm 1,820,663; www.zillow.com.
15. Fine, "They Found Her Hidden."
16. Parker, *Who's Who in the Theatre*, p. 618; www.ibdb.com.
17. "Mother of Actress Known Here Dead at Baltimore Home," *Syracuse Herald* (August 14, 1929), p. 3.
18. "Maryland Probate Estate and Guardianship Files, 1796–1940," database with images, *FamilySearch* (https://familysearch.org/ark:/61903/1:1:KX1T-SRY: accessed 16 January 2016), Emma Gombel, 14 Aug 1929; citing Baltimore City, county courts, Maryland.
19. Dan Thomas, "Strange Marriage Pact of Hollywood's 'Happiest Husband and Wife,'" *Ogden Standard-Examiner* (September 16, 1934), n.pag.
20. Thomas, "Strange Marriage Pact."
21. Fine, "They Found Her Hidden."
22. "Their 'Declaration of Trust' a Victory for Matrimony," *San Antonio Light* (August 18, 1935), n.pag.
23. "Minna Gombell and Third Husband in Renewal of Pact," *Syracuse Herald* (May 23, 1935), p. 11.
24. "United States Census, 1940," database with images, *FamilySearch* (https://familysearch.org/ark:/61903/

1:1:K98Q-YBK: accessed 17 January 2016), Mina Gombell Sefton in household of Joseph H Sefton, Councilmanic District 1, San Diego, San Diego Judicial Township, San Diego, California, United States; citing enumeration district (ED) 62–16B, sheet 1B, family 15, NARA digital publication T627 (Washington, D.C.: National Archives and Records Administration, 2012), roll 448; *Los Angeles City Directory 1942* (Los Angeles: Los Angeles Directory, 1942), p. 939.

25. "California Death Index, 1940–1997," database, *FamilySearch* (https://familysearch.org/ark:/61903/1:1:VP4P-Y9R: accessed 17 January 2016), Joseph W Sefton, 03 Mar 1966; Department of Public Health Services, Sacramento; www.findagrave.com. His birth year is sometimes mistakenly given as 1882.

26. http://www.sandiegohistory.org/journal/84winter/trustimages.htm; http://www.sandiegohistory.org/journal/89spring/cityimages.htm.

27. www.findagrave.com; http://www.sandiegohistory.org/journal/89spring/cityimages.htm; http://www.sandiegohistory.org/journal/v53-1/pdf/2007-1_sefton.pdf.

28. "United States Census, 1930," database with images, *FamilySearch* (https://familysearch.org/ark:/61903/1:1:XC6D-VWT: accessed 17 January 2016), Joseph W Sefton, Jr., 1930. The address is now 3850 Narragansett Ave. www.zillow.com indicates that this home has never been sold, so it may still be owned by the Sefton family.

29. Lily Leung, "Point Loma Home that Once Hosted Royalty for Sale," *San Diego Union-Tribune* (June 3, 2011), www.sandiegouniontribune.com; www.zillow.com. This home still stands at 1865 Sefton Place and was listed for sale in 2011 with an asking price of between $9.9 and $12.5 million, before the bank foreclosed on the property.

30. "United States Census, 1930," database with images, *FamilySearch* (https://familysearch.org/ark:/61903/1:1:XC6D-VW5: accessed 17 January 2016), Harriet S Campbell in entry for Erskine J Campbell, 1930.

31. "Miss Gombel a Bride for a Fortnight," *Syracuse Herald* (July 15, 1916), p. 8.

32. "England and Wales Birth Registration Index, 1837–2008," database, *FamilySearch* (https://familysearch.org/ark:/61903/1:1:2XLB-RV4: accessed 16 January 2016), Howard Chesham Rumsey, 1884; from "England & Wales Births, 1837–2006," database, *findmypast* (http://www.findmypast.com: 2012); citing Birth Registration, Gateshead, Durham, England, citing General Register Office, Southport, England; "United States Census, 1900," database with images, *FamilySearch* (https://familysearch.org/ark:/61903/1:1:MSV1-1H2: accessed 16 January 2016), Howard C Rumsy in household of Ellen Rumsy, Borough of Manhattan, Election District 6 New York City Ward 21, New York County, New York, United States; citing sheet 1A, family 3, NARA microfilm publication T623 (Washington, D.C.: National Archives and Records Administration, n.d.); FHL microfilm 1,241,105; "United States World War I Draft Registration Cards, 1917–1918," database with images, *FamilySearch* (https://familysearch.org/ark:/61903/1:1:KXBF-Z76: accessed 16 January 2016), Howard Chesham Rumsey, 1917–1918; citing Syracuse City no 4, New York, United States, NARA microfilm publication M1509 (Washington, D.C.: National Archives and Records Administration, n.d.); FHL microfilm 1,819,045.

33. "New York, New York City Marriage Records, 1829–1940," database, *FamilySearch* (https://familysearch.org/ark:/61903/1:1:24QD-P22: accessed 17 January 2016), Howard Cheshem Rumsey and Minna Marie Gombel, 09 Mar 1916; citing Marriage, Manhattan, New York, New York, United States, New York City Municipal Archives, New York; FHL microfilm 1,614,463.; "Miss Gombel a Bride," *Syracuse Herald*, p. 8.

34. "Howard Rumsey Is Divorced by Minna Gombell," *Syracuse Herald* (March 6, 1921), p. 1.

35. "United States Census, 1940," database with images, *FamilySearch* (https://familysearch.org/ark:/61903/1:1:K797-8P3: accessed 17 January 2016), Howard Rumsey in household of Harry Clark, Assembly District 4, Queens, New York City, Queens, New York, United States; citing enumeration district (ED) 41–1186, sheet 2B, family 37, NARA digital publication T627 (Washington, D.C.: National Archives and Records Administration, 2012), roll 2743.

36. "United States Social Security Death Index," database, *FamilySearch* (https://familysearch.org/ark:/61903/1:1:JYM3-S2R: accessed 17 January 2016), Howard Rumsey, Jun 1968; citing U.S. Social Security Administration, *Death Master File*, database (Alexandria, Virginia: National Technical Information Service, ongoing).

37. "Minna Gombell Seeks to Annul Marital Bond," *Syracuse Herald* (December 12, 1922), p. 10.

38. See, for example, Parker, *Who's Who in the Theatre*, p. 618.

39. "Notes," *The Great Power*, www.tcm.com.

40. https://en.wikipedia.org/wiki/Myron_Coureval_Fagan.

41. "United States World War I Draft Registration Cards, 1917–1918," database with images, *FamilySearch* (https://familysearch.org/ark:/61903/1:1:KXB2-WZ1: accessed 17 January 2016), Myron C Fagin, 1917–1918; citing Westchester County no 6, New York, United States, NARA microfilm publication M1509 (Washington, D.C.: National Archives and Records Administration, n.d.); FHL microfilm 1,819,337; "United States Census, 1930," database with images, *FamilySearch* (https://familysearch.org/ark:/61903/1:1:X4GF-JL3: accessed 17 January 2016), Myron C Fagan, 1930.

42. "California Death Index, 1940–1997," database, *FamilySearch* (https://familysearch.org/ark:/61903/1:1:VGRL-2S7: accessed 17 January 2016), Florence M Fagan, 29 Jan 1966; Department of Public Health Services, Sacramento.

43. "Former Broadway Star Seeks Divorce," *El Paso Herald-Post* (January 1, 1954), n.pag.; "Actress Gets Divorce from Bank President," *Long Beach Press-Telegram* (June 17, 1954), p. A-9.

44. "California Death Index, 1940–1997," Joseph W Sefton, 03 Mar 1966; www.findagrave.com.

45. "California Death Index, 1940–1997," Minna Gombell, 14 Apr 1973; "Former Film Star, 81, Dies," *Redlands Daily Facts* (April 16, 1973), p. 9; www.findagrave.com.

Ethel Griffies

1. William Peper, "Ethel Griffies Keeps Busy at 87," *New York World-Telegram and Sun* (March 23, 1965) (*T-

Clippings, Billy Rose Theatre Division, New York Public Library for the Performing Arts; henceforward abbreviated NYPL).

2. Peper, "Ethel Griffies Keeps Busy at 87"; Louis Calta, "Ethel Griffies, Who at 97 Was Oldest Working Actress, Dies," *New York Times* (September 12, 1975), p. 36; "Ethel Griffies," *Current Biography* 29 (1968), p. 19.

3. Milton Esterow, "Actors in Tribute to Ethel Griffies: Star in 'Write Me a Murder' Cited for 81-Year Career," *New York Times* (March 5, 1962) (NYPL).

4. Calta, "Ethel Griffies," p. 36.

5. Fern Marja, "At 70, She's Latest Toast of Broadway," *New York Post* (July 19, 1949) (NYPL).

6. "Ethel Griffies," *Current Biography*, p. 19.

7. Marja, "At 70."

8. "Ethel Griffies," *Current Biography*, p. 19.

9. Ward Morehouse, "Broadway After Dark: Ageless and Timeless," *New York Sun* [c1949] (NYPL).

10. "Ethel Griffies," *Current Biography*, p. 19.

11. "Ethel Griffies," p. 20.

12. Marja, "At 70."

13. "Ethel Griffies," *Current Biography*, p. 20.

14. Marja, "At 70."

15. Sidney Fields, "Only Human: Retire at 82? Nonsense!," *New York Mirror* (October 27, 1961) (NYPL).

16. www.ibdb.com.

17. Marja, "At 70."

18. "United States Census, 1930," database with images, *FamilySearch* (https://familysearch.org/ark:/61903/1:1:X42L-R4K: accessed 25 July 2015), Ethel G Cooper in household of Edward Cooper, Manhattan (Districts 0501–0750), New York, New York, United States; citing enumeration district (ED) 0563, sheet 8A, family 183, line 7, NARA microfilm publication T626 (Washington, D.C.: National Archives and Records Administration, 2002), roll 1567; FHL microfilm 2,341,302; *Los Angeles City Directory 1932* (Los Angeles: Los Angeles Directory, 1932), p. 874.

19. "United States Census, 1940," database with images, *FamilySearch* (https://familysearch.org/ark:/61903/1:1:K9C2-M62: accessed 25 July 2015), Ethel Cooper in household of Edward Cooper, Councilmanic District 2, Los Angeles, Los Angeles Township, Los Angeles, California, United States; citing enumeration district (ED) 60–174, sheet 6B, family 238, NARA digital publication T627 (Washington, D.C.: National Archives and Records Administration, 2012), roll 404.

20. www.zillow.com.

21. Fred Hift, "Unsentimental Lady," unnamed, undated clipping (NYPL).

22. "United States Census, 1940," Ethel Cooper.

23. "Ethel Griffies," *Current Biography*, p. 20.

24. Hift, "Unsentimental Lady."

25. Marja, "At 70."

26. "The Toast of the Town: Ethel Griffies Has Been Discovered Again," *Cue* (July 30, 1949) (NYPL).

27. Peper, "Ethel Griffies Keeps Busy at 87."

28. Helen Ormsbee, "Old Lady With Acid Tongue Enlivens 'The Druid Circle,'" unnamed, undated clipping [c1947] (NYPL).

29. Ormsbee, "Old Lady."

30. Helen Ormsbee, "Ethel Griffies Started Early on Musicals," *New York Herald Tribune* (July 31, 1949) (NYPL).

31. "The Toast of the Town," *Cue*.

32. "The Toast of the Town." Another sources says 1902 to 1907 (see Ormsbee, "Ethel Griffies").

33. Ormsbee, "Ethel Griffies."

34. "The Toast of the Town," *Cue*.

35. "Actress to Celebrate Seventy Years on Stage," unnamed clipping (February 26, 1951) (NYPL); Hift, "Unsentimental Lady"; "Ethel Griffies on Stage 81 Years Next Feb. 28," unnamed, undated clipping [c1962] (NYPL).

36. "Ethel Griffies," *Current Biography*, p. 20.

37. Carol Taylor, "Retired Trouper Returns," unnamed clipping (February 26, 1962) (NYPL).

38. www.ibdb.com.

39. "Ethel Griffies," *Current Biography*, p. 21; Audrey Smith, "Ethel Griffies," *Films and Filming* (April 1976) (NYPL).

40. Marja, "At 70."

41. Peper, "Ethel Griffies Keeps Busy at 87."

42. "Ethel Griffies, 97," *New York Post* (September 12, 1975), p. 57.

Sara Haden

1. "United States Census, 1900," index and images, *FamilySearch* (https://familysearch.org/pal:/MM9.1.1/M3GC-4C7: accessed 3 February 2015), Catherine Haden in household of John B Haden, Galveston city Ward 9, Galveston, Texas, United States; citing sheet 11B, family 228, NARA microfilm publication T623 (Washington, D.C.: National Archives and Records Administration, n.d.); FHL microfilm 1,241,637; "California, Death Index, 1940–1997," index, *FamilySearch* (https://familysearch.org/pal:/MM9.1.1/VGG2-PH5: accessed 3 February 2015), Sara Haden, 15 Sep 1981; Department of Public Health Services, Sacramento; "Veteran Character Actress Visiting in Hill Country," *San Antonio Press and News* (February 6, 1955), p. 8A.

2. Robin Coons, "Hollywood Sights and Sounds," *Salamanca Republican-Press* (September 26, 1936), p. 6.

3. "United States Census, 1900," Catherine Haden.

4. "United States Census, 1880," index and images, *FamilySearch* (https://familysearch.org/pal:/MM9.1.1/MFN8-84X: accessed 3 February 2015), Charlotte Walker in household of Edwin Walker, Galveston, Galveston, Texas, United States; citing enumeration district 70, sheet 175D, NARA microfilm publication T9 (Washington, D.C.: National Archives and Records Administration, n.d.), roll 1305; FHL microfilm 1,255,305.

5. "Ex-First Lady of Stage Dies," *Kerrville Daily Times* (March 25, 1958), p. 1.

6. www.imdb.com.

7. Paul Harrison, "The Gals You Love to Hate," *Laredo Times* (October 4, 1936), n.pag.

8. "United States Census, 1880," index and images, *FamilySearch* (https://familysearch.org/pal:/MM9.1.1/MFNZ-LM4: accessed 5 February 2015), John B Haden in household of John M Haden, Galveston, Galveston, Texas, United States; citing enumeration district 64, sheet 39B, NARA microfilm publication T9 (Washington, D.C.: National Archives and Records Administration, n.d.), roll 1305; FHL microfilm 1,255,305.

9. www.findagrave.com.

10. www.findagrave.com.

11. www.findagrave.com.

12. "Texas, Deaths, 1890–1976," index and images, *FamilySearch* (https://familysearch.org/pal:/MM9.1.1/K3Q5-NHP: accessed 3 February 2015), Henry C Haden, 24 Apr 1956; citing certificate number 20005, State Registrar Office, Austin; FHL microfilm 2,114,668.

13. www.findagrave.com.

14. "United States Census, 1870," index and images, *FamilySearch* (https://familysearch.org/pal:/MM9.1.1/MXG9-L5Y: accessed 3 February 2015), Charlice Ganahl in household of Charles Ganahl, Texas, United States; citing p. 3, family 20, NARA microfilm publication M593 (Washington, D.C.: National Archives and Records Administration, n.d.); FHL microfilm 553,093.

15. "Texas Reunion on Hardy Set," *San Antonio Light* (May 9, 1939), p. 6A.

16. "United States Census, 1880," index and images, *FamilySearch* (https://familysearch.org/pal:/MM9.1.1/MFN8-84X: accessed 3 February 2015), Charlotte Walker in household of Edwin Walker, Galveston, Galveston, Texas, United States; citing enumeration district 70, sheet 175D, NARA microfilm publication T9 (Washington, D.C.: National Archives and Records Administration, n.d.), roll 1305; FHL microfilm 1,255,305; www.findagrave.com.

17. "Glittering Star of 1900's Still Makes Home in Small Texas Town," *Lubbock Evening Journal* (November 5, 1954), p. 10; www.findagrave.com.

18. www.findagrave.com.

19. The following brief survey of Walker's career is based on information from www.ibdb.com, www.imdb.com, and http://en.wikipedia.org/wiki/Charlotte_Walker_(actress).

20. "Ohio, County Marriages, 1789–1997," index and images, *FamilySearch* (https://familysearch.org/pal:/MM9.1.1/XZ1F-Z9S: accessed 5 February 2015), Eugene Walter and Charlotte W. Haden, 01 Dec 1908; citing Hamilton, Ohio, United States, reference cn 51; county courthouses, Ohio; FHL microfilm 355,091.

21. "United States Census, 1910," index and images, *FamilySearch* (https://familysearch.org/pal:/MM9.1.1/M5S6-75F: accessed 3 February 2015), Charlotte Walter in household of Eugene Walter, Manhattan Ward 22, New York, New York, United States; citing enumeration district (ED) 1305, sheet 4A, family 65, NARA microfilm publication T624 (Washington, D.C.: National Archives and Records Administration, n.d.); FHL microfilm 1,375,059.

22. "California, Death Index, 1940–1997," index, *FamilySearch* (https://familysearch.org/pal:/MM9.1.1/VPQ9-52Y: accessed 3 February 2015), Eugene Walter, 26 Sep 1941; Department of Public Health Services, Sacramento; www.imdb.com.

23. www.findagrave.com. Sara Haden and her sister's visits were duly recorded in the *Kerrville Times*'s "Center Point News" column. See, for example, *Kerrville Times* (May 30, 1951), p. 6 and *Kerrville Times* (August 13, 1952), p. 6.

24. "United States Census, 1940," database with images, *FamilySearch* (https://familysearch.org/ark:/61903/1:1:K9CL-41R: accessed 31 January 2016), Charlott [sic] Walker in household of Seamon Vandenburg, Councilmanic District 3, Los Angeles, Los Angeles Township, Los Angeles, California, United States; citing enumeration district (ED) 60–204, sheet 2A, family 38, NARA digital publication T627 (Washington, D.C.: National Archives and Records Administration, 2012), roll 405.

25. "Sara Haden, Native Galvestonian, Wins Motion Picture Fame for Portrayal of Character Roles," *Galveston Daily News* (February 6, 1938), p. 12; "Texas Reunion on Hardy Set," *San Antonio Light*, p. 6A.

26. "Andy Hardy's Aunt Millie Will Star at Stockbridge," *Berkshire Evening Eagle* (July 1, 1950), p. 14.

27. "Texas Reunion on Hardy Set," *San Antonio Light*, p. 6A.

28. *Galveston Tribune* (March 9, 1934), p. 7.

29. "Actress Praised," *Galveston Tribune* (September 21, 1934), p. 6.

30. *San Mateo Times* (March 28, 1936), p. 5.

31. www.ibdb.com.

32. "United States Social Security Death Index," index, *FamilySearch* (https://familysearch.org/pal:/MM9.1.1/V3G7-TP6: accessed 5 February 2015), Richard Abbott, Jun 1986; citing U.S. Social Security Administration, *Death Master File*, database (Alexandria, Virginia: National Technical Information Service, ongoing); www.imdb.com.

33. In the 1930 U.S. Census, Abbott claims to have immigrated in 1902. See "United States Census, 1930," index and images, *FamilySearch* (https://familysearch.org/pal:/MM9.1.1/X4KR-R74: accessed 5 February 2015), Richard Abbott in household of Harry E Cook, Manhattan (Districts 0251–0500), New York, New York, United States; citing enumeration district (ED) 0424, sheet 16B, family 258, line 63, NARA microfilm publication T626 (Washington, D.C.: National Archives and Records Administration, 2002), roll 1554; FHL microfilm 2,341,289.

34. "Sara Haden," *Variety* (September 23, 1981), p. 94.

35. See Coons, "Hollywood Sights and Sounds," p. 6; "Andy Hardy's Aunt Millie," *Berkshire Evening Eagle*, p. 14.

36. www.ibdb.com.

37. "United States Census, 1930," Richard Abbott in household of Harry E Cook.

38. "United States Census, 1930," index and images, *FamilySearch* (https://familysearch.org/pal:/MM9.1.1/X424-K5J: accessed 5 February 2015), Beatrice Haden in household of Rachel Ruedan, Manhattan (Districts 0501–0750), New York, New York, United States; citing enumeration district (ED) 0517, sheet 14A, family 2, line 24, NARA microfilm publication T626 (Washington, D.C.: National Archives and Records Administration, 2002), roll 1560; FHL microfilm 2,341,295.

39. "United States Census, 1930," index and images, *FamilySearch* (https://familysearch.org/pal:/MM9.1.1/XMG8-1PB: accessed 5 February 2015), John B Haden, Hill, Pulaski, Arkansas, United States; citing enumeration district (ED) 0077, sheet 1A, family, line 46, NARA microfilm publication T626 (Washington, D.C.: National Archives and Records Administration, 2002), roll 92; FHL microfilm 2,339,827.

40. Harrison, "The Gals You Love to Hate."

41. Parish and Bowers, *The MGM Stock Company*, p. 305.

42. Theresa Loeb, "Creeps Fill Double Bill at Esquire," *Oakland Tribune* (August 21, 1946), p. C9.

43. Tom Weaver, "Interview: June Lockhart on 'She-Wolf of London,'" http://classic-horror.com/newsreel/interview_june_lockhart_on_she_wolf_of_london.

44. Weaver, "Interview: June Lockhart."

45. Alexander Kahn, "Bits of Gossip About Hollywood Film Folk," *Valparaiso Vidette-Messenger* (November 20, 1939), p. 4.

46. Kahn, p. 4.

47. "Sara Haden," *Variety*, p. 94.

48. "Veteran Character Actress," *San Antonio Press and News*, p. 8A.

49. "United States Social Security Death Index," Richard Abbott, Jun 1986; www.findagrave.com.

50. "California, Death Index, 1940–1997," Sara Haden, 15 Sep 1981; "Sara Haden, Actress Played Crabby Roles in Long Film Career," *New York Times* (September 22, 1981), p. A29.

Margaret Hamilton

1. Gregory J. Catsos, "Margaret Hamilton," *American Classic Screen* (1984), p. 34.

2. Burt Berliner, "Mean Witch of 'Oz' Goes Straight," *Philadelphia Inquirer* (December 11, 1977) (*T-Clippings, Billy Rose Theatre Division, New York Public Library for the Performing Arts; henceforward abbreviated NYPL).

3. "New Career for Hamilton," *Morning Telegraph* (June 17, 1959) (NYPL).

4. "If It's a Maid, Miss Hamilton Gets the Part," *New York Herald Tribune* (December 30, 1934) (NYPL).

5. James Bacon, "She Won't Change Faces with Anyone," *Chicago Sunday Tribune* (February 21, [1960?]) (NYPL).

6. Karl Kohrs, "'I'm Glad I'm Homely,'" *Parade* (October 7, 1951) (NYPL).

7. Kohrs, "'I'm Glad I'm Homely.'"

8. www.ibdb.com.

9. www.tcm.com. I discuss *Another Language* at length in my profile of Louise Closser Hale in *Mothers, Mammies and Old Maids.*

10. William Peper, "Actress Still on Broom," *New York World-Telegram and Sun* (May 18, 1963) (NYPL).

11. "If It's a Maid," *New York Herald Tribune.*

12. Sidney Fields, "Only Human: The Gentle Witch," *New York Daily News* (October 22, 1964) (NYPL).

13. "Ohio, County Marriages, 1789–2013," database with images, *FamilySearch* (https://familysearch.org/ark:/61903/1:1:2Q75-YZ8: accessed 28 January 2016), Paul B Meserve and Margaret B Hamilton, 13 Jun 1931; citing Cuyahoga, Ohio, United States, reference; county courthouses, Ohio; FHL microfilm 1,901,663; "California Birth Index, 1905–1995," database, *FamilySearch* (https://familysearch.org/ark:/61903/1:1:VLBV-VSH: accessed 28 January 2016), Hamilton Wadsworth Meserve, 12 Jun 1936; citing Los Angeles, California, United States, Department of Health Services, Vital Statistics Department, Sacramento.

14. Kohrs, "'I'm Glad I'm Homely."

15. Berliner, "Mean Witch of 'Oz' Goes Straight."

16. "Ohio, County Births, 1841–2003," database with images, *FamilySearch* (https://familysearch.org/ark:/61903/1:1:X6MB-WJM: accessed 28 January 2016), Margaret Brainard Hamilton, 09 Dec 1902; citing Birth, Cleveland, Cuyahoga, Ohio, reference, county courthouses, Ohio; FHL microfilm 1,852,605. After the Cleveland streets were reorganized in 1906, with a new four-numeral system and many streets being renamed, 64 Tilden Ave. became 1926 E. 24th St. Hamilton's birthplace in downtown Cleveland is long gone and the site is now part of the campus of Cleveland State University.

17. www.findagrave.com.

18. "Ohio Deaths, 1908–1953," database with images, *FamilySearch* (https://familysearch.org/ark:/61903/1:1:X6WJ-ZDZ: accessed 28 January 2016), Walter J Hamilton, 22 Aug 1935; citing Cleveland, Cuyahoga, Ohio, reference fn 47676; FHL microfilm 2,022,524; *Cleveland Blue Book* (Cleveland, OH: Helen deKay Townsend, 1899), p. 57.

19. The 1900 U.S. Census, her death certificate, and her grave marker all say Jennie Adams Hamilton was born in 1865, but the 1880 U.S. Census taken on June 8, 1880 says she was 16 on her last birthday (i.e., in 1879), indicating that she was actually born in 1863. Maybe she took two years off her real age so as not to be older than her husband. See "United States Census, 1880," database with images, *FamilySearch* (https://familysearch.org/ark:/61903/1:1:MZ1T-P8N: accessed 28 January 2016), Mary J Adams in household of Edgar Adams, Cleveland, Cuyahoga, Ohio, United States; citing enumeration district ED 10, sheet 238D, NARA microfilm publication T9 (Washington, D.C.: National Archives and Records Administration, n.d.), roll 1004; FHL microfilm 1,255,004; "United States Census, 1900," database with images, *FamilySearch* (https://familysearch.org/ark:/61903/1:1:MMZV-54Y: accessed 28 January 2016), Jennie M Hamilton in household of Walter J Hamilton, Precinct G Cleveland City Ward 19, Cuyahoga, Ohio, United States; citing sheet 4B, family 85, NARA microfilm publication T623 (Washington, D.C.: National Archives and Records Administration, n.d.); FHL microfilm 1,241,255; "Ohio Deaths, 1908–1953," database with images, *FamilySearch* (https://familysearch.org/ark:/61903/1:1:X8VG-88Q: accessed 28 January 2016), Jennie A Hamilton, 01 Jul 1926; citing Cleveland, Cuyahoga, Ohio, reference fn 42958; FHL microfilm 1,984,35; www.findagrave.com.

20. The 1910 U.S. Census states that Walter and Jennie Hamilton had been married 17 years. See "United States Census, 1910," database with images, *FamilySearch* (https://familysearch.org/ark:/61903/1:1:ML85-1GN: accessed 28 January 2016), Walter Hamilton, Cleveland Ward 21, Cuyahoga, Ohio, United States; citing enumeration district (ED) ED 318, sheet 6B, NARA microfilm publication T624 (Washington, D.C.: National Archives and Records Administration, n.d.); FHL microfilm 1,375,187. For the birth dates of Hamilton's siblings, see "United States Social Security Death Index," database, *FamilySearch* (https://familysearch.org/ark:/61903/1:1:JP7B-TNY: accessed 28 January 2016), Dorothy Walmsley, Jun 1968; citing U.S. Social Security Administration, Death Master File, database (Alexandria, Virginia: National Technical Information Service, ongoing); "United States Social Security Death Index," database, *FamilySearch* (https://familysearch.org/ark:/61903/1:1:J2JB-JJM: accessed 28 January 2016), Gladys Mohler, Jul 1977; citing U.S. Social Security Administration, *Death Master File*, database (Alexandria, Virginia: National Technical Information Service, ongoing); and "United States Census, 1900," Edwin T Hamilton in household of Walter J Hamilton.

21. *Cleveland Blue Book* (Cleveland, OH: Helen deKay Townsend, 1907), p. 88.

22. *Cleveland Blue Book* (Cleveland, OH: Helen deKay Townsend, 1907), p. 22; *Cleveland Blue Book* (Cleveland, OH: Helen deKay Townsend, 1911), p. 22; *Cleveland Blue Book* (Cleveland, OH: Helen deKay Townsend, 1915), p. 24; www.findagrave.com.

23. *Cleveland Blue Book* (Cleveland, OH: Helen deKay Townsend, 1907), p. 88; *Cleveland Blue Book* (Cleveland, OH: Helen deKay Townsend, 1911), p. 80; *Cleveland Blue Book* (Cleveland, OH: Helen deKay Townsend, 1915), p. 84; *Cleveland Blue Book* (Cleveland, OH: Helen deKay Townsend, 1922), p. 66; *Cleveland Blue Book* (Cleveland, OH: Helen deKay Townsend, 1929), p. 65.

24. "Ohio Death Index, 1908–1932, 1938–1944, and 1958–2007," database, *FamilySearch* (https://familysearch.org/ark:/61903/1:1:VK1Q-HNF: accessed 28 January 2016), Mary J Adams, 07 Jan 1916; from "Ohio, Deaths, 1908–1932, 1938–2007," database and images, *Ancestry* (http://www.ancestry.com: 2010); citing vol., certificate number, Ohio Historical Society, Columbus; Ohio Department of Health, State Vital Statistics Unit, Columbus; "Ohio Deaths, 1908–1953," database with images, *FamilySearch* (https://familysearch.org/ark:/61903/1:1:X8PR-CPV: accessed 28 January 2016), Mary E Hamilton, 23 Jun 1929; citing Cleveland, Cuyahoga, Ohio, reference fn 40227; FHL microfilm 1,991,874.

25. www.findagrave.com.

26. For the home addresses and other information about Hamilton's maternal uncles and aunts, see the *Cleveland Blue Book* for 1911, 1915, 1922, and 1929.

27. "Ohio, County Births, 1841–2003," database with images, *FamilySearch* (https://familysearch.org/ark:/61903/1:1:X6X5-8D4: accessed 28 January 2016), Bessie Jennie Adams, 28 May 1885; citing Birth, Cleveland, Cuyahoga, Ohio, reference v 6 p 314, county courthouses, Ohio; FHL microfilm 877,903.

28. www.findagrave.com.

29. "Ohio Marriages, 1800–1958," database, *FamilySearch* (https://familysearch.org/ark:/61903/1:1:XD7P-YZK: accessed 28 January 2016), Charles F. Brush, Jr., and Dorothy A. Hamilton, 28 Jul 1917; citing Cuyahoga County, Ohio, reference 120566 pg 392; FHL microfilm 1,888,792; https://en.wikipedia.org/wiki/Dorothy_Hamilton_Brush.

30. Jan Cigliano, *Showplace of America: Cleveland's Euclid Avenue, 1850–1910* (Kent, OH and London: Kent State University Press, 1991), p. 167–74; http://www.lafavre.us/brush/mansion.htm.

31. *Cleveland Blue Book* (Cleveland, OH: Helen deKay Townsend, 1922), p. 21; "Ohio Deaths, 1908–1953," database with images, *FamilySearch* (https://familysearch.org/ark:/61903/1:1:X8LQ-7LN: accessed 28 January 2016), Charles Francis Brush, Jr., 29 May 1927; citing Cleveland Heights, Cuyahoga, Ohio, reference fn 27428; FHL microfilm 1,984,848.

32. "Ohio, County Marriages, 1789–2013," database with images, *FamilySearch* (https://familysearch.org/ark:/61903/1:1:XZFN-T5R: accessed 28 January 2016), John G Mohler and Gladys E Hamilton, 02 Oct 1922; citing Cuyahoga, Ohio, United States, reference P500 RN 172499; county courthouses, Ohio; FHL microfilm 1,889,008; "United States Census, 1930," database with images, *FamilySearch* (https://familysearch.org/ark:/61903/1:1:X4Q1-8TY: accessed 28 January 2016), Gladys H Mohler in entry for Giles Mohler, 1930; www.findagrave.com.

33. www.zillow.com.

34. "United States Social Security Death Index," database, *FamilySearch* (https://familysearch.org/ark:/61903/1:1:J22G-SYM: accessed 28 January 2016), John Mohler, Sep 1971; citing U.S. Social Security Administration, *Death Master File*, database (Alexandria, Virginia: National Technical Information Service, ongoing); "United States Social Security Death Index," Gladys Mohler, Jul 1977; www.findagrave.com.

35. "Margaret Hamilton," *Current Biography* 4.4 (April 1979), p. 21.

36. Burr Van Atta, "Margaret Hamilton, 82, Portrayed the Wicked Witch in 'Wizard of Oz,'" *Philadelphia Inquirer* (May 17, 1985), p. 6B.

37. Jim McPherson, "The Wicked Witch of the West," *Toronto Telegram* (January 23, 1959), p. 2.

38. Van Atta, "Margaret Hamilton," p. 6B.

39. "Margaret Hamilton," *Current Biography*, p. 21.

40. "Ohio Deaths, 1908–1953," Jennie A Hamilton, 01 Jul 1926.

41. "Ohio Deaths, 1908–1953," database with images, *FamilySearch* (https://familysearch.org/ark:/61903/1:1:X8LQ-ZTY: accessed 28 January 2016), Jane Hamilton Brush, 23 May 1927; citing Cleveland, Cuyahoga, Ohio, reference fn 27970; FHL microfilm 1,984,848.

42. "Ohio Deaths, 1908–1953," Charles Francis Brush, Jr., 29 May 1927.

43. https://en.wikipedia.org/wiki/Dorothy_Hamilton_Brush.

44. https://en.wikipedia.org/wiki/Dorothy_Hamilton_Brush; "Dorothy Adams Hamilton Brush," The Encyclopedia of Cleveland History, http://ech.case.edu/.

45. https://en.wikipedia.org/wiki/Dorothy_Hamilton_Brush.

46. "United States Social Security Death Index," Dorothy Walmsley, Jun 1968; www.findagrave.com.

47. "United States Census, 1930," database with images, *FamilySearch* (https://familysearch.org/ark:/61903/1:1:X43X-MPT: accessed 28 January 2016), Marguret Hamilton in entry for Walter Hamilton, 1930; "United States Census, 1930," database with images, *FamilySearch* (https://familysearch.org/ark:/61903/1:1:X4GQ-Y73: accessed 28 January 2016), Paul B Meserve, 1930.

48. "Ohio, County Marriages, 1789–2013," Paul B Meserve and Margaret B Hamilton, 13 Jun 1931.

49. "United States Census, 1910," database with images, *FamilySearch* (https://familysearch.org/ark:/61903/1:1:M2V8-DGY: accessed 28 January 2016), Paul B Meserve in household of Frank W Meserve, Framingham, Middlesex, Massachusetts, United States; citing enumeration district (ED) ED 821, sheet 1A, NARA microfilm publication T624 (Washington, D.C.: National Archives and Records Administration, n.d.); FHL microfilm 1,374,611.

50. McPherson, "The Wicked Witch of the West," p. 2.

51. "Ohio Deaths, 1908–1953," Walter J Hamilton, 22 Aug 1935.

52. www.findagrave.com.

53. Cigliano, *Showplace of America*, pp. 173–74; http://www.lafavre.us/brush/mansion.htm.

54. movielanddirectory.com, www.www.zillow.com.

55. "United States Census, 1940," database with images, *FamilySearch* (https://familysearch.org/ark:/61903/1:1:K974-CPK: accessed 28 January 2016), Margret Meserve, Tract 381, Beverly Hills, Beverly Hills Judicial Township, Los Angeles, California, United States; citing enumeration district (ED) 19–38A, sheet 10A, family 175, NARA digital publication T627 (Washington, D.C.: National Archives and Records Administration, 2012), roll 220.

56. movielanddirectory.com, www.www.zillow.com.

57. http://rightherenyc.com/THEYLIVEDHERE_actors.html.

58. Fields, "Only Human"; Beverly Solocheck, "At Home with Margaret Hamilton," *New York Post* (February 13, 1971), p. 37. On Hamilton's increasing senility, see Arthur Bell, "Bell Tells," *Village Voice* (October 18, 1983), p. 44.

59. Joseph Berger, "Margaret Hamilton, 82, Dies; Played Wicked Witch in 'Oz,'" *New York Times* (May 17, 1985), p. D20; "'Wicked Witch' Margaret Hamilton Dies," *Galveston Daily News* (May 17, 1985), p. 4-A.

60. http://friendsofthepoughkeepsieruralcemetery.org/reflections/margaret_hamilton.htm; www.findagrave.com.

61. Peper, "Actress Still on Broom."

Rosalind Ivan

1. "United States Census, 1940," index and images, *FamilySearch* (https://familysearch.org/pal:/MM9.1.1/KQSG-914: accessed 8 February 2015), Rosalind Ivan, Assembly District 15, Manhattan, New York City, New York, New York, United States; citing enumeration district (ED) 31–1388, sheet 88A, family, NARA digital publication T627 (Washington, D.C.: National Archives and Records Administration, 2012), roll 2657.

2. Burns Mantle, "The Season in New York," *The Best Plays of 1940–41*, ed. Burns Mantle (New York: Dodd Mead, 1949), p. 8.

3. Emlyn Williams, *The Corn Is Green* (New York: Dramatists Play Service, 1945), p. 17.

4. *The Corn Is Green* review, *Terre Haute Saturday Spectator* (August 11, 1945), p. 12.

5. Margot Peters, *The House of Barrymore* (New York: A.A. Knopf, 1990), p. 436; www.ibdb.com.

6. Peters, p. 436.

7. www.tcm.com.

8. Williams, *The Corn Is Green*, p. 15.

9. Margarita Landazuri, "*The Corn Is Green* (1945)," www.tcm.com.

10. Quoted in Doug McClelland, "The Unsung Heroes: Rosiland [sic] Ivan," *Film Fan Monthly* no. 80 (February 1968), p. 17.

11. Bosley Crowther, *The Corn Is Green* review, *New York Times* (March 30, 1945), www.nytimes.com.

12. McClelland, "The Unsung Heroes," p. 17.

13. "California, Los Angeles Passenger Lists, 1907–1948," index and images, *FamilySearch* (https://familysearch.org/pal:/MM9.1.1/KZQ7-VQF: accessed 8 February 2015), Rosalind Ivan, 1935; citing Immigration, ship name California, NARA microfilm publication M1764 (Washington, D.C.: National Archives and Records Administration, n.d.), roll 59; FHL microfilm 1,734,663.

14. "New York, Passenger Arrival Lists (Ellis Island), 1892–1924," index, *FamilySearch* (https://familysearch.org/pal:/MM9.1.1/JFQF-BJ3: accessed 8 February 2015), ROSALIND IVAN, 16 May 1905; citing departure port Tilbury Docks, London, England, arrival port NEW YORK, NEW YORK, NEW YORK, ship name Minnehaha, NARA microfilm publication T715 and M237 (Washington, D.C.: National Archives and Records Administration, n.d.); www.imdb.com.

15. "England, Middlesex, Westminster, Parish Registers, 1538–1912," index and images, *FamilySearch* (https://familysearch.org/pal:/MM9.1.1/KCCJ-X3V: accessed 7 February 2015), Rosalind Muriel Johnson, 1885, Baptism; from "Parish registers 1539–1945," index and images, *findmypast* (www.findmypast.com: n.d.); citing St Martin In The Fields, Middlesex, England, City of Westminster Archives Centre, London; FHL microfilm 561,149; "England and Wales Census, 1891," database with images, *FamilySearch* (https://familysearch.org/ark:/61903/1:1:35JX-46Z: accessed 7 February 2016), Rosalind M Johnson in household of Charles Johnson, Hampstead, London, England; from "1891 England, Scotland and Wales census," database and images, *findmypast* (http://www.findmypast.com: n.d.); citing PRO RG 12, London county, subdistrict, The National Archives of the UK, Kew, Surrey.

16. McClelland, "The Unsung Heroes," p. 18.

17. "Rosalind Ivan, 75, Actress, Is Dead," *New York Times* (April 7, 1959) (*T-Clippings, Billy Rose Theatre Division, New York Public Library for the Performing Arts; henceforward abbreviated NYPL).

18. "Miss Rosalind Ivan," *London Mainly About People* (August 3, 1901), p. 114.

19. "Miss Rosalind Ivan," p. 114. In the 1930 U.S. Census, Ivan gives 1901 as her "Year of immigration to the United States." See "United States Census, 1930," index and images, *FamilySearch* (https://familysearch.org/pal:/MM9.1.1/X42Q-X86: accessed 8 February 2015), Rosalind Ivan, Manhattan (Districts 0251–0500), New York, New York, United States; citing enumeration district (ED) 0270, sheet 4B, family 26, line 82, NARA microfilm publication T626 (Washington, D.C.: National Archives and Records Administration, 2002), roll 1558; FHL microfilm 2,341,293.

20. "California, Southern District Court (Central) Naturalization Index, 1915–1976," index and images, *FamilySearch* (https://familysearch.org/pal:/MM9.1.1/KXQQ-NRY: accessed 8 February 2015), Rosalind Or Rosalind Muriel Ivan Or Johnson, 1948; citing Los Angeles, Los Angeles, California, United States, National Archives and Records Service, Los Angeles Branch, Laguna Niguel; FHL microfilm 1,570,128.

21. "Rosalind Ivan, 75, Actress, Is Dead," *New York Times*.

22. *London Standard* (November 22, 1911), p. 10; www.ibdb.com.

23. "Nazimova Engaging as 'Hilda Wangel,'" *New York Times* (September 24, 1907), p. 11.

24. "Personnel of the Ben Greet Woodland Players," *New Harmony Times* (June 18, 1915), p. 1.

25. *Boston Sunday Post* (September 9, 1917), p. 28.

26. "Rosalind Ivan, 75, Actress, Is Dead," *New York Times*.

27. "New York, New York Passenger and Crew Lists, 1909, 1925–1957," index and images, *FamilySearch*

(https://familysearch.org/pal:/MM9.1.1/24F9-K6Z: accessed 7 February 2015), Rosalind M Johnson, 1929; citing Immigration, New York, New York, United States, NARA microfilm publication T715 (Washington, D.C.: National Archives and Records Administration, n.d.); FHL microfilm 1,756,325.

28. "United States Census, 1930," Rosalind Ivan.

29. Burns Mantle, *The Best Plays of 1938–39* (New York: Dodd, Mead, 1939), p. 441.

30. McClelland, "The Unsung Heroes," p. 18.

31. Quoted in Axel Nissen, *The Films of Agnes Moorehead* (Lanham: Scarecrow Press, 2013), p. 103.

32. McClelland, "The Unsung Heroes," p. 18.

33. "California, Southern District Court (Central) Naturalization Index, 1915–1976," Rosalind Or Rosalind Muriel Ivan Or Johnson, 1948; "Rosalind Ivan, 75, Actress, Is Dead," *New York Times*.

34. "Rosalind Ivan, 75, Actress, Is Dead." This large, imposing brick and stone building on the corner of Madison Ave. still exists and is now the Jolly Hotel Madison Towers.

Isabel Jewell

1. http://en.wikipedia.org/wiki/Shoshoni,_Wyoming.

2. "United States Census, 1910," index and images, *FamilySearch* (https://familysearch.org/pal:/MM9.1.1/MPJJ-K31: accessed 31 January 2015), Isabel Jewell in household of Emery L Jewell, Shoshone, Fremont, Wyoming, United States; citing enumeration district (ED) 57, sheet 7B, family 165, NARA microfilm publication T624 (Washington, D.C.: National Archives and Records Administration, n.d.); FHL microfilm 1,375,758; William D. Eppes, "A Chapter from the Life of Isabel Jewell," *Shoshoni Pioneer* 5.6 (April 26, 1984) (*T-Clippings, Billy Rose Theatre Division, New York Public Library for the Performing Arts; henceforward abbreviated NYPL). Eppes relates that after Jewell's father died and her mother joined her in Los Angeles, the home was vandalized and ultimately torn down. Jewell visited the sad remains of her childhood home for the last time in 1967, five years before her death.

3. "United States Census, 1930," index and images, *FamilySearch* (https://familysearch.org/pal:/MM9.1.1/X7WS-M1V: accessed 31 January 2015), Emory L Jewell, Shoshoni, Fremont, Wyoming, United States; citing enumeration district (ED) 0004, sheet 1B, family 30, line 94, NARA microfilm publication T626 (Washington, D.C.: National Archives and Records Administration, 2002), roll 2622; FHL microfilm 2,342,356; "United States Census, 1940," index and images, *FamilySearch* (https://familysearch.org/pal:/MM9.1.1/VT4P-3P2: accessed 31 January 2015), E L Jewell, Shoshoni, Election District 4, Fremont, Wyoming, United States; citing enumeration district (ED) 7–4, sheet 2A, family 30, NARA digital publication T627 (Washington, D.C.: National Archives and Records Administration, 2012), roll 4570.

4. According to the 1910 U.S. Census, the Jewells had been married five years. See "United States Census, 1910," Emery L Jewell; William D. Eppes, "Second in a Series: A Chapter from the Life of Isabel Jewell; The Early Years," *Shoshoni Pioneer* (1984) (NYPL).

5. "Minnesota, Births and Christenings, 1840–1980," index, *FamilySearch* (https://familysearch.org/pal:/MM9.1.1/FDSQ-6NL: accessed 31 January 2015), Lee Jewell, 09 Jul 1875; citing Pine Island, Goodhue, Minnesota, reference v 1 p 118; FHL microfilm 1,379,164.

6. "Minnesota, State Census, 1895," index and images, *FamilySearch* (https://familysearch.org/pal:/MM9.1.1/MQ8R-K14: accessed 31 January 2015), Wallace W Jewell, Pine Island village, Goodhue, Minnesota; citing p. 20, line 15, State Library and Records Service, St. Paul; FHL microfilm 565,773; "United States Census, 1900," index and images, *FamilySearch* (https://familysearch.org/pal:/MM9.1.1/M9SC-GXM: accessed 31 January 2015), W W Jewell, Pine Island Township Pine Island village, Goodhue, Minnesota, United States; citing sheet 2B, family 41, NARA microfilm publication T623 (Washington, D.C.: National Archives and Records Administration, n.d.); FHL microfilm 1,240,764; www.findagrave.com.

7. www.findagrave.com.

8. www.findagrave.com.

9. "United States Census, 1900," Scott W Jewell in household of W W Jewell; www.findagrave.com.

10. www.findagrave.com.

11. "Famed Doctor Taken by Death," *Kalispell Daily Inter Lake* (October 22, 1949), p. 2; www.findagrave.com.

12. www.findagrave.com.

13. Eppes, "Second in a Series."

14. *Ogden Standard Examiner* (May 16, 1930), p. 2; *Pinedale Roundup* (June 5, 1930), n.pag.; http://en.wikipedia.org/wiki/Order_of_the_Eastern_Star.

15. "United States Census, 1930," Emory L Jewell.

16. "California, Death Index, 1940–1997," index, *FamilySearch* (https://familysearch.org/pal:/MM9.1.1/VP6R-H9B: accessed 31 January 2015), Livia A Jewell, 08 Aug 1971; Department of Public Health Services, Sacramento.

17. "United States Census, 1900," index and images, *FamilySearch* (https://familysearch.org/pal:/MM9.1.1/M3VR-6ZJ: accessed 31 January 2015), Liva A Willoughby in household of Sidney Willoughby, Lost Cabin, Thermopolis, Muskrat Thermopolis town, Fremont, Wyoming, United States; citing sheet 2A, family 42, NARA microfilm publication T623 (Washington, D.C.: National Archives and Records Administration, n.d.); FHL microfilm 1,241,826.

18. "United States Census, 1940," index and images, *FamilySearch* (https://familysearch.org/pal:/MM9.1.1/K9W3-346: accessed 31 January 2015), Sidney Willoughby in household of Eliza K Johnson, Tract 419, Pasadena, Pasadena Judicial Township, Los Angeles, California, United States; citing enumeration district (ED) 19–453, sheet 1A, family 11, NARA digital publication T627 (Washington, D.C.: National Archives and Records Administration, 2012), roll 240.

19. "California, Death Index, 1940–1997," index, *FamilySearch* (https://familysearch.org/pal:/MM9.1.1/VPWV-HKT: accessed 31 January 2015), Sidney Willoughby, 18 May 1958; Department of Public Health Services, Sacramento.

20. "United States Social Security Death Index," index, *FamilySearch* (https://familysearch.org/pal:/MM9.1.1/V9T5-1X3: accessed 31 January 2015), Isabel Jewell, Apr 1972; citing U.S. Social Security Administration,

Death Master File, database (Alexandria, Virginia: National Technical Information Service, ongoing). The California Death Index indicates that Jewell was born in 1909, but that is not possible, as the 1910 U.S. Census for Shoshone, Wyoming, taken on April 20, 1910, clearly states that she was two years old at her last birthday. See "California, Death Index, 1940–1997," index, *FamilySearch* (https://familysearch.org/pal:/MM9.1.1/VGTG-SY9: accessed 31 January 2015), Isabel Jewell, 05 Apr 1972; Department of Public Health Services, Sacramento and "United States Census, 1910," Isabel Jewell.

21. Eppes, "Second in a Series."

22. Eppes, "Second in a Series"; William D. Eppes, "Third in a Series: A Chapter from the Life of Isabel Jewell; The College Years," *Shoshoni Pioneer* (1984) (NYPL).

23. Eppes, "Third in a Series."

24. Eppes, "Third in a Series," including quotes from Underwood.

25. "United States Social Security Death Index," index, *FamilySearch* (https://familysearch.org/pal:/MM9.1.1/JG3M-QYS: accessed 31 January 2015), Lovell T Underwood, 13 Jul 1997; citing U.S. Social Security Administration, *Death Master File*, database (Alexandria, Virginia: National Technical Information Service, ongoing).

26. "United States Census, 1910," index and images, *FamilySearch* (https://familysearch.org/pal:/MM9.1.1/M282-8CH: accessed 31 January 2015), Lovell Underwood in household of Susan Hignite, Iron Hill, Carter, Kentucky, United States; citing enumeration district (ED) 49, sheet 11B, family 199, NARA microfilm publication T624 (Washington, D.C.: National Archives and Records Administration, n.d.); FHL microfilm 1,374,482; "United States Census, 1920," index and images, *FamilySearch* (https://familysearch.org/pal:/MM9.1.1/MH2B-TMW: accessed 31 January 2015), Lovel T Underwood in household of William H Lewis, Charlotte Furnace, Carter, Kentucky, United States; citing sheet 1B, family 10, NARA microfilm publication T625 (Washington, D.C.: National Archives and Records Administration, n.d.); FHL microfilm 1,820,565; Eppes, "Third in a Series."

27. "United States Census, 1940," index and images, *FamilySearch* (https://familysearch.org/pal:/MM9.1.1/K9SR-9NX: accessed 31 January 2015), Lovell T Underwood, Yakima, Election Precinct 13, Yakima, Washington, United States; citing enumeration district (ED) 39–13, sheet 5B, family 115, NARA digital publication T627 (Washington, D.C.: National Archives and Records Administration, 2012), roll 4371.

28. "California, Death Index, 1940–1997," index, *FamilySearch* (https://familysearch.org/pal:/MM9.1.1/VGRT-4DS: accessed 30 January 2015), William L Tracy, 18 Oct 1968; Department of Public Health Services, Sacramento; "United States Census, 1910," index and images, *FamilySearch* (https://familysearch.org/pal:/MM9.1.1/M2YN-7XL: accessed 30 January 2015), William L Tracy, Jr., in household of William L Tracy, Sr., Kansas Ward 4, Jackson, Missouri, United States; citing enumeration district (ED) 164, sheet 3A, family 65, NARA microfilm publication T624 (Washington, D.C.: National Archives and Records Administration, n.d.); FHL microfilm 1,374,801; "United States Census, 1920," index and images, *FamilySearch* (https://familysearch.org/pal:/MM9.1.1/MX9F-PY7: accessed 30 January 2015), William Lee Tracy in household of William L Tracy, Sayre, Bradford, Pennsylvania, United States; citing sheet 19B, family 519, NARA microfilm publication T625 (Washington, D.C.: National Archives and Records Administration, n.d.); FHL microfilm 1,821,541.

29. George Johnstone, "Lee Tracy's Double," *Oakland Tribune* (December 9, 1934), p. 5; "A New Hollywood Triumph (on the Wreck of a Shattered Love)," *Portsmouth Times* (August 9, 1936), n.pag.

30. Johnstone, p. 5.

31. Robin Coons, "Hollywood Sights and Sounds," *Corsicana Daily Sun* (November 22, 1933), n.pag.; "Hard Work: That's Miss Jewell's Story, and She Has Stuck to It," *New York Post* (July 16, 1934) (NYPL).

32. Johnstone, "Lee Tracy's Double," p. 5.

33. Johnstone, p. 5; *New York Times* (June 17, 1934) (NYPL).

34. Johnstone, p. 5.

35. Johnstone, p. 5; "Isabel Jewell, 62, '30s Film Actress," *New York Times* (April 7, 1972), p. 38.

36. "Isabel Jewell, Film Star, Dead at 62," *Redlands Daily Facts* (April 6, 1972), p. 6.

37. Rick DuBrow, "Ex-Film Star Pleads for Applause," *Lubbock Evening Journal* (January 20, 1959), n.pag.; "A New Hollywood Triumph," *Portsmouth Times*.

38. www.imdb.com.

39. "'Why I Love Mexico,' Says Tracy, Subdued After Window Ledge Scene," *Port Arthur News* (November 24, 1933), p. 11. See also the photographs of Jewell and Tracy at the station in "Conqueror's(?) Return," *San Antonio Light* (November 27, 1933), p. 2A and *Syracuse Herald* (November 27, 1933), n.pag.

40. Louella O. Parsons, "Marriage of Film Actress, Tracy Denied," *San Antonio Light* (December 24, 1933), p. 7.

41. Robin Coons, "Nicknames of Movie Stars Are Varied," *Danville Bee* (February 16, 1934), p. 2.

42. Louella O. Parsons, "Columbia's Next Picture an Old-Fashioned Story," *San Antonio Light* (December 26, 1933), p. 6A.

43. Louella O. Parsons, "1934 to See Many Film Events," *San Antonio Light* (December 31, 1933), p. 4.

44. Louella O. Parsons, "Corinne Griffith Is Sought by Independent Producer," *Charleston Gazette* (May 5, 1934), p. 12.

45. Harrison Carroll, "Behind the Scenes in Hollywood," *Tyrone Herald* (July 20, 1934), p. 4; Louella O. Parsons, "Loretta, Polly Ann Young Are Booked for New Film," *Charleston Gazette* (September 2, 1934), p. 10.

46. Louella O. Parsons, "Movie Go Round," *San Antonio Light* (January 27, 1935), p. 8.

47. Louella O. Parsons, "Lucien Hubbard Will Direct Noted Stage Hit for M-G-M," *Charleston Gazette* (February 5, 1935), p. 7.

48. Dan Thomas, "Hollywood Gossip," *Edwardsville Intelligencer* (March 4, 1935), p. 8.

49. Louella O. Parsons, "Pitts Subject of Movie Yarn," *Charleston Gazette* (July 22, 1935), p. 3.

50. Hubbard Keavy, "Screen Life in Hollywood," *Sandusky Register* (December 22, 1935), p. 19.

51. www.imdb.com.

52. DuBrow, "Ex-Film Star Pleads."

53. Keavy, "Screen Life in Hollywood," p. 19.

54. Keavy, p. 19.

55. "Famed Doctor Taken by Death," *Kalispell Daily Inter Lake*, p. 2.

56. www.findagrave.com.

57. "A New Hollywood Triumph," *Portsmouth Times.*

58. "United States Census, 1910," index and images, *FamilySearch* (https://familysearch.org/pal:/MM9.1.1/MLQK-XXY: accessed 31 January 2015), Owen Crump in household of William J Crump, Muskogee Ward 4, Muskogee, Oklahoma, United States; citing enumeration district (ED) 119, sheet 14A, family 79, NARA microfilm publication T624 (Washington, D.C.: National Archives and Records Administration, n.d.); FHL microfilm 1,375,277; "United States Census, 1920," index and images, *FamilySearch* (https://familysearch.org/pal:/MM9.1.1/MN1G-HRQ: accessed 31 January 2015), Owen E Crump in household of William J Crump, Muskogee Ward 4, Muskogee, Oklahoma, United States; citing sheet 10B, family 243, NARA microfilm publication T625 (Washington, D.C.: National Archives and Records Administration, n.d.); FHL microfilm 1,821,478.

59. "United States Census, 1930," index and images, *FamilySearch* (https://familysearch.org/pal:/MM9.1.1/XMT1-6XK: accessed 31 January 2015), Owen Crump, Shreveport, Caddo, Louisiana, United States; citing enumeration district (ED) 0059, sheet 13B, family 313, line 58, NARA microfilm publication T626 (Washington, D.C.: National Archives and Records Administration, 2002), roll 787; FHL microfilm 2,340,522.

60. "Screen Love Scene Inspires Engagement," *El Paso Herald-Post* (July 6, 1936), p. 12; "Isabel Jewell Engaged," *San Antonio Light* (July 6, 1936), p. 7A. See also Wood Soanes, "Curtain Calls," *Oakland Tribune* (July 15, 1936), p. B19.

61. See Henry Sutherland, "Arline Judge Has Pluperfect Figure, Marriott Gushes," *Nevada State Journal* (August 14, 1936), p. 8; "Cupid Must Wait," *Cumberland Times* (August 23, 1936), p. 10.

62. Wood Soanes, "Curtain Calls," *Oakland Tribune* (November 6, 1936), p. 27.

63. "Women in the News," *Raleigh Register* (November 6, 1936), p. 5.

64. "Behind the Scenes in Hollywood," *Bonham Daily Favorite* (January 4, 1937), n.pag.

65. Walter Winchell, "Walter Winchell on Broadway," *Logansport Pharos-Tribune* (March 3, 1937), p. 6.

66. Louella O. Parsons, "Kay Francis to Talk Films," *San Antonio Light* (August 22, 1939), p. 10B.

67. www.imdb.com.

68. *Los Angeles City Directory 1939* (Los Angeles: Los Angeles Directory, 1939), p. 1078.

69. I discuss *Born to Kill* at length in my chapter on Esther Howard in *Mothers, Mammies and Old Maids.*

70. "Actress Married," *Berkeley Gazette* (October 11, 1941), p. 2; "Movie Actress Weds Selectee at Camp," *Oakland Tribune* (October 12, 1941), p. A5.

71. "United States Social Security Death Index," index, *FamilySearch* (https://familysearch.org/pal:/MM9.1.1/VHCQ-K91: accessed 31 January 2015), PAUL MARION, 08 Sep 2011; citing U.S. Social Security Administration, *Death Master File*, database (Alexandria, Virginia: National Technical Information Service, ongoing); "United States World War II Army Enlistment Records, 1938–1946," index, *FamilySearch* (https://familysearch.org/pal:/MM9.1.1/K8RH-LYW: accessed 31 January 2015), Paul Marion, enlisted 29 Aug 1941, Cp Upton, Yaphank, New York, United States; citing "Electronic Army Serial Number Merged File, ca. 1938–1946," database, *The National Archives: Access to Archival Databases (AAD)* (http://aad.archives.gov: National Archives and Records Administration, 2002); NARA NAID 126323, National Archives and Records Administration, Washington, D.C.; www.ibdb.com.

72. www.imdb.com.

73. "United States Census, 1940," index and images, *FamilySearch* (https://familysearch.org/pal:/MM9.1.1/K9C6-SVM: accessed 31 January 2015), Paul Marion in household of Laila Gulbransen, Councilmanic District 2, Los Angeles, Los Angeles Township, Los Angeles, California, United States; citing enumeration district (ED) 60–129, sheet 3A, family 58, NARA digital publication T627 (Washington, D.C.: National Archives and Records Administration, 2012), roll 398.

74. movielanddirectory.com.

75. Harrison Carroll, "Behind the Scenes in Hollywood," *Massillon Evening Independent* (August 13, 1943), p. 4; William D. Eppes, "Fifth in a Series: A Chapter from the Life of Isabel Jewell; A Star Is Recognized," *Shoshoni Pioneer* (1984) (NYPL); www.imdb.com.

76. movielanddirectory.com.

77. www.imdb.com.

78. www.imdb.com.

79. "A New Hollywood Triumph," *Portsmouth Times.*

80. Bob Musel, "Only a Pinch Hitter—Yet Superb," unnamed, undated clipping [c1940] (NYPL).

81. "United States Social Security Death Index," Isabel Jewell, Apr 1972; "California, Death Index, 1940–1997," Isabel Jewell, 05 Apr 1972; "Isabel Jewell," *Variety* (April 12, 1972) (NYPL); Eppes, "A Chapter from the Life of Isabel Jewell."

82. "California, Death Index, 1940–1997," Livia A Jewell, 08 Aug 1971.

83. "United States Social Security Death Index," Lovell T Underwood, 13 Jul 1997.

84. "United States Social Security Death Index," index, *FamilySearch* (https://familysearch.org/pal:/MM9.1.1/JTZ7-WJW: accessed 30 January 2015), Owen E Crump, 13 Feb 1998; citing U.S. Social Security Administration, *Death Master File*, database (Alexandria, Virginia: National Technical Information Service, ongoing).

85. "United States Social Security Death Index," PAUL MARION, 08 Sep 2011.

Violet Kemble-Cooper

1. Parker, *Who's Who in the Theatre*, p. 415; www.ibdb.com.

2. "Violet Kemble Cooper Is Dead; Actress on Stage and Screen," *New York Times* (August 19, 1961) (*T-Clippings, Billy Rose Theatre Division, New York Public Library for the Performing Arts; henceforward abbreviated NYPL). See also Enid Hart, "Theatrical Chit-Chat," *San Marino Tribune* (September 7, 1934), p. 10.

3. Stuart C. Ferris, "Walter L. Ferris: Some Facts, Some Recollections, Some Thoughts, 1878–1965," unpublished ms., p. 4. I am grateful to Stuart Ferris's daughter, Angeline Ferris, for sharing a copy of this interesting biographical sketch of her grandfather with me.

4. "Portrait Painter by Choice, an Actress Through Heritage," *New York American* (September 11, 1921) (NYPL).

5. "Portrait Painter."

6. Mordaunt Hall, *Our Betters* review, *New York Times* (February 24, 1933) (NYPL).

7. Zilch, "Cinema View and Reviews," *La Crosse Tribune and Leader-Press* (March 30, 1933), p. 9.

8. Ferris, "Walter L. Ferris," p. 4.

9. "United States World War I Draft Registration Cards, 1917–1918," database with images, *FamilySearch* (https://familysearch.org/ark:/61903/1:1:KZFN-BP9: accessed 31 January 2016), Walter Lewis Ferris, 1917–1918; citing New Haven County no 6, Connecticut, United States, NARA microfilm publication M1509 (Washington, D.C.: National Archives and Records Administration, n.d.); FHL microfilm 1,562,004.

10. Walter's granddaughter, Angeline Ferris, kindly shared family photographs with me. One of these may be seen on Walter Ferris's page at www.findagrave.com.

11. Ferris, "Walter L. Ferris," p. 1.

12. Ferris, p. 1.

13. Ferris, p. 1.

14. Ferris, p. 2.

15. Ferris, p. 1; "United States Social Security Death Index," index, *FamilySearch* (https://familysearch.org/pal:/MM9.1.1/VMJ9-X29: accessed 6 January 2015), Alice Ferris, Oct 1971; citing U.S. Social Security Administration, *Death Master File*, database (Alexandria, Virginia: National Technical Information Service, ongoing). In the 1940 census, though, it says Alice Ferris only had two years of high school and no college education. See "United States Census, 1940," index and images, *FamilySearch* (https://familysearch.org/pal:/MM9.1.1/KWM1-54G: accessed 6 January 2015), Alice C Ferris, Ward 15, New Haven, New Haven Town, New Haven, Connecticut, United States; citing enumeration district (ED) 11–96, sheet 6B, family 129, NARA digital publication of T627, roll 541, NARA digital publication of T627, National Archives and Records Administration, Washington, D.C.

16. Ferris, p. 2.

17. Ferris, p. 3.

18. Ferris, p. 3.

19. Ferris, pp. 3–4.

20. Ferris, p. 4.

21. *Oak Park Leaves* (October 31, 1930), p. 87.

22. "United States Census, 1930," index and images, *FamilySearch* (https://familysearch.org/pal:/MM9.1.1/X42V-188: accessed 6 January 2015), Cooper Violet Kemble, Manhattan (Districts 0501–0750), New York, New York, United States; citing enumeration district (ED) 0697, sheet 15B, family 409, line 78, NARA microfilm publication T626 (Washington, D.C.: National Archives and Records Administration, 2002), roll 1565; FHL microfilm 2,341,300.

23. "New York, New York Passenger and Crew Lists, 1909, 1925–1957," index and images, *FamilySearch* (https://familysearch.org/pal:/MM9.1.1/24XG-3WQ: accessed 6 January 2015), Walter Ferris, 1929; citing Immigration, New York, New York, United States, NARA microfilm publication T715, National Archives and Records Administration, Washington, D.C.; FHL microfilm 1,756,246.

24. Parker, *Who's Who in the Theatre*, p. 415; "United States Census, 1940," index and images, *FamilySearch* (https://familysearch.org/pal:/MM9.1.1/K9C5-DPM: accessed 6 January 2015), Violet C Ferris in household of Walter Ferris, Councilmanic District 3, Los Angeles, Los Angeles Township, Los Angeles, California, United States; citing enumeration district (ED) 60–230, sheet 63B, family 302, NARA digital publication of T627, roll 408, NARA digital publication of T627, National Archives and Records Administration, Washington, D.C.

25. "United States Census, 1940," Alice C Ferris.

26. Quoted in Ferris, "Walter L. Ferris," p. 6.

27. Ferris, p. 7; "Violet Kemble Cooper Dies; Was an Actress 40 Years," *New York Herald Tribune* (August 19, 1962) (NYPL).

28. "Violet Kemble Cooper Is Dead," *New York Times*.

29. www.findagrave.com.

30. Ferris, "Walter L. Ferris," p. 8; www.findagrave.com.

31. His son's memoir makes it abundantly clear that Ferris provided practically no financial support to his ex-wife and children after the divorce.

32. Quoted in Joseph Van Raalte, "Bo-Broadway," *Chester Times* (August 11, 1930), n.pag. The columnist takes her to task for "yipping publicly about love and marriage."

33. Alice Cheney Ferris survived both her ex-husband and his second wife and died in her native New Haven in 1971 at the age of 92. She never remarried. See "United States Social Security Death Index," Alice Ferris, Oct 1971.

Doris Lloyd

1. Springer and Hamilton, *They Had Faces Then*, p. 162.

2. "Stage More Appreciative of Doris Lloyd Than Pictures," unnamed, undated clipping (*T-Clippings, Billy Rose Theatre Division, New York Public Library for the Performing Arts; henceforward abbreviated NYPL).

3. "Stage More Appreciative."

4. She gave her age as 27 when she and her mother traveled to the United States in 1923. She was in fact 32 at the time. See "New York, Passenger Arrival Lists (Ellis Island), 1892–1924," index, *FamilySearch* (https://familysearch.org/pal:/MM9.1.1/JN63-TY6: accessed 20 January 2015), Hessy Doris Lloyd, 25 Sep 1923; citing departure port Southampton, arrival port New York, ship name Pittsburgh, NARA microfilm publication T715 and M237 (Washington, D.C.: National Archives and Records Administration, n.d.).

5. "England and Wales, Birth Registration Index, 1837–2008," index, *FamilySearch* (https://familysearch.org/pal:/MM9.1.1/2X19-BR2: accessed 20 January 2015), Hessy Doris Lloyd, 1891; from "England & Wales Births, 1837–2006," index, *findmypast* (http://www.findmypast.com: 2012); citing Birth Registration, Toxteth Park, Lancashire, England, citing General Register Office, Southport, England; "England Births and Christenings, 1538–1975," index, *FamilySearch* (https://familysearch.org/pal:/MM9.1.1/NTV4-FLF: accessed 20 January 2015), Hessy Doris Lloyd, 02 Aug 1891; citing, reference item 4 rn 507; FHL microfilm 1,656,677.

6. "England and Wales, Birth Registration Index, 1837–2008," index, *FamilySearch* (https://familysearch.org/pal:/MM9.1.1/2X3Q-XNZ: accessed 21 January

2015), Edward Franklin Lloyd, 1855; from "England & Wales Births, 1837–2006," index, *findmypast* (http://www.findmypast.com: 2012); citing Birth Registration, Holywell, Flintshire, Wales, citing General Register Office, Southport, England; "California, Death Index, 1940–1997," index, *FamilySearch* (https://familysearch.org/pal:/MM9.1.1/VP72-7RM: accessed 21 January 2015), Hessy Jane Lloyd, 23 May 1953; Department of Public Health Services, Sacramento.

7. Helen Ormsbee, "Broadway Debut by Long-Distance Phone," unnamed clipping (December 1947) (NYPL).

8. "England and Wales, Marriage Registration Index, 1837–2005," index, *FamilySearch* (https://familysearch.org/pal:/MM9.1.1/2D81-49G: accessed 21 January 2015), Edward Franklin Lloyd, 1886; from "England & Wales Marriages, 1837–2005," index, *findmypast* (http://www.findmypast.com: 2012); citing Marriage, Toxteth Park, Lancashire, England, General Register Office, Southport, England; "England and Wales, Birth Registration Index, 1837–2008," index, *FamilySearch* (https://familysearch.org/pal:/MM9.1.1/2XTC-GNQ: accessed 21 January 2015), Edward Vernon F Lloyd, 1888; from "England & Wales Births, 1837–2006," index, *findmypast* (http://www.findmypast.com: 2012); citing Birth Registration, Toxteth Park, Lancashire, England, citing General Register Office, Southport, England; "England Births and Christenings, 1538–1975," index, *FamilySearch* (https://familysearch.org/pal:/MM9.1.1/J7L3-3LR: accessed 21 January 2015), William Norman Lloyd, 28 Oct 1889; citing, reference item 4 rn 483; FHL microfilm 1,656,677; "California, Death Index, 1940–1997," index, *FamilySearch* (https://familysearch.org/pal:/MM9.1.1/VGG1-XV6: accessed 21 January 2015), Milba Katleen [sic] Lloyd, 27 May 1984; Department of Public Health Services, Sacramento.

9. "England and Wales Census, 1911," index, *FamilySearch* (https://familysearch.org/pal:/MM9.1.1/XWTW-4HK: accessed 22 January 2015), Hessy Doris Lloyd, 1911.

10. Parker, *Who's Who in the Theatre*, p. 890.

11. Parker, p. 890; Ormsbee, "Broadway Debut."

12. Parker, p. 890.

13. www.imdb.com.

14. See "England and Wales, Death Registration Index 1837–2007," index, *FamilySearch* (https://familysearch.org/pal:/MM9.1.1/2JWW-KQV: accessed 22 January 2015), Edward J Lloyd, 1915; from "England & Wales Deaths, 1837–2006," index, *findmypast* (http://www.findmypast.com: 2012); citing Death, West Derby, Lancashire, England, General Register Office, Southport, England. The "J" may be a misprint for "F."

15. "England and Wales, Birth Registration Index, 1837–2008," index, *FamilySearch* (https://familysearch.org/pal:/MM9.1.1/2F41-136: accessed 21 January 2015), Arthur George Brest, 1899; from "England & Wales Births, 1837–2006," index, *findmypast* (http://www.findmypast.com: 2012); citing Birth Registration, Brentford, Middlesex, England, citing General Register Office, Southport, England.

16. "New York, Passenger Arrival Lists (Ellis Island), 1892–1924," index, *FamilySearch* (https://familysearch.org/pal:/MM9.1.1/JN2L-YMR: accessed 22 January 2015), Arthur George Brest, 20 Dec 1922; citing departure port Southampton, arrival port New York, ship name Olympic, NARA microfilm publication T715 and M237 (Washington, D.C.: National Archives and Records Administration, n.d.).

17. "New York, Passenger Arrival Lists (Ellis Island), 1892–1924," index, *FamilySearch* (https://familysearch.org/pal:/MM9.1.1/JNJF-VZ8: accessed 22 January 2015), Milba Kathleen Brest, 26 Feb 1923; citing departure port Southampton, arrival port New York, ship name Pittsburgh, NARA microfilm publication T715 and M237 (Washington, D.C.: National Archives and Records Administration, n.d.).

18. See "The Youngest Sculptress in England," *Medicine Hat News* (October 21, 1921), p. 1.

19. "Duplicate Museum Is Rushed," *Oakland Tribune* (September 9, 1923), n.pag.; "Hang Bluebeard's Seven Wives? Nix; Wax Models Used," *Woodland Daily Democrat* (February 24, 1924), p. 6.

20. Howard Dietz, "Husbands and Wives of Celebrities Shine In Their Own Spheres," *Syracuse Herald* (April 25, 1926), p. 3.

21. "New York, Passenger Arrival Lists (Ellis Island), 1892–1924," Hessy Doris Lloyd, 25 Sep 1923; "New York, Passenger Arrival Lists (Ellis Island), 1892–1924," index, *FamilySearch* (https://familysearch.org/pal:/MM9.1.1/JN63-TYD: accessed 22 January 2015), Hessy Jane Lloyd, 25 Sep 1923; citing departure port Southampton, arrival port New York, ship name Pittsburgh, NARA microfilm publication T715 and M237 (Washington, D.C.: National Archives and Records Administration, n.d.). They claimed to be 27 and 58.

22. "United States Census, 1930," index and images, *FamilySearch* (https://familysearch.org/pal:/MM9.1.1/XCFF-TF8: accessed 22 January 2015), Doris Lloyd, Beverly Hills, Los Angeles, California, United States; citing enumeration district (ED) 0839, sheet 7A, family 217, line 33, NARA microfilm publication T626 (Washington, D.C.: National Archives and Records Administration, 2002), roll 124; FHL microfilm 2,339,859; "United States Census, 1930," index and images, *Family Search* (https://familysearch.org/pal:/MM9.1.1/XCFF-B6F: accessed 22 January 2015), Arthur Brest, Beverly Hills, Los Angeles, California, United States; citing enumeration district (ED) 0839, sheet 8B, family 263, line 78, NARA microfilm publication T626 (Washington, D.C.: National Archives and Records Administration, 2002), roll 124; FHL microfilm 2,339,859; "California, Birth Index, 1905–1995," index, *FamilySearch* (https://familysearch.org/pal:/MM9.1.1/VGHD-RWG: accessed 22 January 2015), Jeane [sic] Milba Brest, 18 Feb 1925; citing Los Angeles, California, United States, Department of Health Services, Vital Statistics Department, Sacramento.

23. Myrtle Gebhardt, "Shady Lady at Home," unnamed, undated clipping [c1930] (NYPL).

24. "United States Census, 1940," index and images, *FamilySearch* (https://familysearch.org/pal:/MM9.1.1/K9H2-KVX: accessed 22 January 2015), Hessy Doris Lloyd in household of Hessy J Lloyd, Councilmanic District 1, Los Angeles, Los Angeles Township, Los Angeles, California, United States; citing enumeration district (ED) 60–53, sheet 18A, family 514, NARA digital publication T627 (Washington, D.C.: National Archives and Records Administration, 2012), roll 376; www.zillow.com.

25. "California, County Marriages, 1850–1952," index and images, *FamilySearch* (https://familysearch.org/

pal:/MM9.1.1/K82W-86X: accessed 22 January 2015), Charles Robert Gray and Mllba [sic] Jeanne Brest, 01 Apr 1950; citing Los Angeles, California, United States, county courthouses, California; FHL microfilm 2,117,733.

26. "California, Death Index, 1940–1997," Hessy Jane Lloyd, 23 May 1953.

27. "California, Death Index, 1940–1997," Milba Katleen [sic] Lloyd, 27 May 1984.

28. Clipping on Lloyd from the program of *An Inspector Calls* (October 21, 1947) (NYPL).

29. Undated press release from Phyllis Perlman and Miriam Byram (NYPL); www.ibdb.com. All the other shows currently listed under Doris Lloyd's name in the Internet Broadway Database (IBDb) belong to another Doris Lloyd.

30. "California, Death Index, 1940–1997," index, *FamilySearch* (https://familysearch.org/pal:/MM9.1.1/VPHS-CDX: accessed 22 January 2015), Hessy D Lloyd, 21 May 1968; Department of Public Health Services, Sacramento; "Doris Lloyd," *Variety* (May 29, 1968) (NYPL).

31. Dorothy Manners, "Joni, Mate Make Sweet Musical Deal," *San Antonio Light* (May 28, 1968), p. 6; www.findagrave.com.

Helen Lowell

1. "Ontario Census, 1861," index, *FamilySearch* (https://familysearch.org/pal:/MM9.1.1/MQ7L-MZY: accessed 23 January 2015), William Robb, East Oxford, Oxford, Ontario, Canada; citing p., line; Library and Archives Canada film number, Public Archives, Toronto; FHL microfilm; "United States Census, 1870," index and images, *FamilySearch* (https://familysearch.org/pal:/MM9.1.1/M8D1-MXT: accessed 23 January 2015), Mary K Robb in household of William L Robb, New York, United States; citing p. 11, family 103, NARA microfilm publication M593 (Washington, D.C.: National Archives and Records Administration, n.d.); FHL microfilm 552,507.

2. "United States Census, 1870," Helen L Robb; Parker, *Who's Who in the Theatre*, p. 906; "Miss Lowell, Film and Stage Actress," *New York Times* (June 30, 1937), p. 24. Most sources give Lowell's year of birth as 1866, but the 1870 U.S. Census makes it clear she must have been born in 1865.

3. "United States Census, 1870," Helen L Robb.

4. www.findagrave.com.

5. Parker, *Who's Who in the Theatre*, p. 906.

6. www.findagrave.com.

7. Parker, *Who's Who in the Theatre*, p. 906; Alanson Edwards, "Hollywood Film Shop," *Florence Morning News* (July 3, 1934), p. 3.

8. *New York Sun* (January 3, 1934) (*T-Clippings, Billy Rose Theatre Division, New York Public Library for the Performing Arts; henceforward abbreviated NYPL).

9. *Boston Daily Globe* (March 8, 1904), p. 11.

10. Charles Stumpf, *Zasu Pitts: The Life and Career* (Jefferson, NC: McFarland, 2010), p. 65.

11. "Mrs. Wiggs Company Has Future Stars," *La Crosse Tribune* (October 21, 1905), n.pag.

12. "Helen Lowell Given 'Break,'" *Los Angeles Times* (January 20, 1934) (NYPL).

13. "'The Torch-Bearers' Is Screamingly Funny,'" *Toledo Blade* (March 2, 1923) (NYPL).

14. "Warners Signs Helen Lowell," *New York Herald Tribune* (January 3, 1934) (NYPL).

15. *New York Times* (January 3, 1934) (NYPL).

16. *New York Times* (January 4, 1934) (NYPL).

17. "Helen Lowell Given 'Break,'" *Los Angeles Times*.

18. www.tcm.com.

19. "Attractions of the Week at the Sosna Theater," *Moberly Monitor-Index and Democrat* (July 11, 1936), p. 3.

20. I also discuss *Side Streets* in my chapter on Aline MacMahon in *Mothers, Mammies and Old Maids*.

21. www.tcm.com.

22. "At the Theatres," *Monessen Daily Independent* (July 3, 1934), p. 2.

23. "At the Theatres," p. 2.

24. "Miss Lowell, Film and Stage Actress," *New York Times* (June 30, 1937), p. 24.

25. George Ross, "In New York," *Fitchburg Sentinel* (August 4, 1937), p. 6.

26. "Forms Meal Club for Actors," *New York Herald Tribune* (February 28, 1934) (NYPL).

Eily Malyon

1. "Eily Malyon, 82," *Variety* (Oct. 4, 1961) (*T-Clippings, Billy Rose Theatre Division, New York Public Library for the Performing Arts; henceforward abbreviated NYPL).

2. "England Births and Christenings, 1538–1975," index, *FamilySearch* (https://familysearch.org/pal:/MM9.1.1/NYGC-R4D: accessed 18 January 2015), Harry Craston, 20 Dec 1856; citing CATHEDRAL, MANCHESTER, LANCASHIRE, ENGLAND, reference; FHL microfilm 438,179.

3. "England and Wales Census, 1871," index and images, *FamilySearch* (https://familysearch.org/pal:/MM9.1.1/KD84-V5F: accessed 18 January 2015), Harry Craston in household of Thomas Craston, Broadwater, Sussex, England; from "1871 England, Scotland and Wales census," index and images, *findmypast* (www.findmypast.com: n.d.); citing PRO RG 10, folio 93, p. 36, East Preston registration district, Worthing subdistrict, ED 4g, household 213, The National Archives, Kew, Surrey; FHL microfilm 827,511.

4. "England and Wales Census, 1881," index, *FamilySearch* (https://familysearch.org/pal:/MM9.1.1/X322-XX8: accessed 18 January 2015), Lily S L Craston in household of Harry Craston, Islington, Middlesex, England; from "1881 England, Scotland and Wales census," index and images, *findmypast* (www.findmypast.com: n.d.); citing p., PRO RG 11/, The National Archives, Kew, Surrey; FHL microfilm.

5. "California, Death Index, 1940–1997," index, *FamilySearch* (https://familysearch.org/pal:/MM9.1.1/VGR6-WNG: accessed 18 January 2015), Eily S Craston, 26 Sep 1961; Department of Public Health Services, Sacramento.

6. See *London Daily News* (October 22, 1878), p. 4; *London Daily News* (October 30, 1878), p. 4.

7. See *Lloyd's Weekly* (August 17, 1879), p. 5.

8. "An Interview with Miss Agnes Thomas," *South Australian Advertiser* (November 24, 1886), p. 6 (http://trove.nla.gov.au/ndp/del/article/37163004).

9. "Law Intelligence: Probate and Divorce Division," *London Standard* (October 28, 1887), p. 6.

10. "Law Intelligence."

11. *New York Times* (April 9, 1885), p. 5; *New York Times* (April 14, 1885), p. 5; *New York Times* (April 17, 1885), p. 5.

12. "England and Wales, Death Registration Index 1837–2007," index, *FamilySearch* (https://familysearch.org/pal:/MM9.1.1/2J63-WQG: accessed 18 January 2015), Harry Craston, 1885; from "England & Wales Deaths, 1837–2006," index, *findmypast* (http://www.findmypast.com: 2012); citing Death, Camberwell, London, England, General Register Office, Southport, England.

13. "An Interview with Miss Agnes Thomas."

14. "Takes Role of Nun," *Oakland Tribune* (September 7, 1935), p. 4B; Rose Pelswick, "When They Hate Her, Eily's Really Happy," unnamed, undated clipping (NYPL).

15. *St. James's Gazette* (February 28, 1890), p. 5.

16. *London Standard* (January 31, 1899), p. 3.

17. *St. James's Gazette* (January 31, 1899), p. 11.

18. "Obituary," *London Standard* (May 24, 1902), p. 5.

19. See *Black and White* (August 8, 1903), p. 180.

20. *New York Times* (December 6, 1912), p. 15; *New York Times* (December 22, 1912), p. 7; www.ibdb.com.

21. See the cast list in Bernard Shaw, *Man and Superman: A Comedy and a Philosophy* (Harmondsworth: Penguin, 1971), p. 6.

22. See Michael Egan, ed., *The Critical Heritage: Henrik Ibsen* (London: Routledge, 1999), p. 431.

23. *London Evening News* (March 6, 1918), p. 4; *London Evening News* (April 18, 1918), p. 4.

24. "Actress Gets 'Mean' Roles," *Arizona Independent* (July 23, 1939), p. 9.

25. "England and Wales Census, 1911," index, *FamilySearch* (https://familysearch.org/pal:/MM9.1.1/XWL6-7WR: accessed 18 January 2015), Eily Craston, St George Hanover Square, Sw, London, England; from "1911 England and Wales census," index and images, *findmypast* (www.findmypast.com: n.d.); citing PRO RG 14, county, registration district, subdistrict, The National Archives of the UK, Kew, Surrey.

26. *London Standard* (January 31, 1911), p. 4.

27. Desley Deacon, "Cosmopolitans at Home: Judith Anderson and the American Aspirations of J.C. Williamson Stock Company Members, 1897–1918," *Impact of the Modern: Vernacular Modernities in Australia 1870s to 1960s*, ed. Robert Dixon and Veronica Kelly (Sydney: Sydney University Press, 2008), p. 221n58. According the author of this article, "Malyon was a rival for Anderson's iconic role as Mrs. Danvers in *Rebecca*."

28. "Australia, Victoria, Index to Probate Registers, 1841–1989," index and images, *FamilySearch* (https://familysearch.org/pal:/MM9.1.1/JVJL-HM6: accessed 18 January 2015), Eily Malyon, 20 Jul 1977; citing Melbourne, Victoria, Australia, series 825, record 700, Public Record Office, Victoria.

29. "Actress Gets 'Mean' Roles," *Arizona Independent*, p. 9.

30. "Stage, Film Jobs Keep Player Hustling," unnamed, undated clipping (NYPL).

31. Frank S. Nugent, *On Borrowed Time* review (July 7, 1939), www.nyt.com.

32. Pelswick, "When They Hate Her." A slightly different version of this interview, probably based on the same press release, is found as "'Meanest Woman' Yearns For Fans' Angry Letters," *Syracuse Herald* (July 9, 1939), p. 8D.

33. *On Borrowed Time* review, *Ogden Standard-Examiner* (November 12, 1939), p. 12A.

34. "She's Screen's No. 1 'Meanie': Eily Malyon Continues Career in 'Tom Edison,'" *Syracuse Herald* (January 4, 1940), p. 28.

35. "Actress Gets 'Mean' Roles," *Arizona Independent*, p. 9.

36. *Los Angeles City Directory 1936* (Los Angeles: Los Angeles Directory, 1936), p. 1162; "United States Census, 1940," index and images, *FamilySearch* (https://familysearch.org/pal:/MM9.1.1/K9H2-KVJ: accessed 18 January 2015), Eily Malyon, Councilmanic District 1, Los Angeles, Los Angeles Township, Los Angeles, California, United States; citing enumeration district (ED) 60–53, sheet 18A, family 515, NARA digital publication T627 (Washington, D.C.: National Archives and Records Administration, 2012), roll 376. Malyon lived in this home from at least 1936. The house has been replaced by a modern monster house from 2004, while Lloyd's modest, Spanish style bungalow is still standing covered in heliotrope and with its shabby, bohemian charm intact.

37. "California, Death Index, 1940–1997," Eily S Malyon, 26 Sep 1961; Quinlan, *Quinlan's Character Stars*, p. 286.

Una Merkel

1. My account of Bessie Merkel's suicide is based on the following sources: "Una Merkel Is Saved, Mother Dies from Gas," *Berkeley Evening Gazette* (March 5, 1945), p. 1; "Una Merkel Near Death After Mother Suicides," *Coshocton Tribune* (March 5, 1945), p. 1, 6; "Mother of Screen Star Found Dead; Actress Una Merkel Burla Revived by an Inhalator," *Hagerstown Morning Herald* (March 6, 1945), p. 5.

2. "Una Merkel Is Saved," p. 1.

3. "Una Merkel Near Death," p. 1.

4. "Una Merkel Is Saved," p. 1.

5. Carl Merkel (1884–1977) was Arno Merkel's younger brother and had moved from Cincinnati to Los Angeles with his family by 1940. Una Merkel's father-in-law Given F. Burla had been dead for nearly 9 years at this point, which makes Bessie Merkel's request even more curious. William Thayer was actually called Willis M. Thayer (1874–1947) and was married to Arno Merkel's older sister Lenore L. Merkel Thayer (1874–1958).

6. "New York, New York City Municipal Deaths, 1795–1949," database, *FamilySearch* (https://familysearch.org/ark:/61903/1:1:2WPP-SW3: accessed 24 January 2016), Bessie Phares Merkel, 05 Mar 1945; citing Death, Manhattan, New York, New York, United States, New York Municipal Archives, New York; FHL microfilm 2,132,195; www.findagrave.com.

7. "United States Census, 1900," database with images, *FamilySearch* (https://familysearch.org/ark:/61903/1:1:M9H2-B9F: accessed 25 January 2016), James C Phares, Precinct B Covington city Ward 6, Ken-

ton, Kentucky, United States; citing sheet 2A, family 28, NARA microfilm publication T623 (Washington, D.C.: National Archives and Records Administration, n.d.); FHL microfilm 1,240,535.

8. "United States Census, 1900," James C Phares.

9. "Kentucky Marriages, 1785–1979," database, *FamilySearch* (https://familysearch.org/ark:/61903/1:1:FW1C-4YC: accessed 24 January 2016), John A. Hanks and Josephine A. Phares, 18 Jan 1905; citing Covington, Kenton, Kentucky, reference cn 1905 p325; FHL microfilm 551,107.

10. "Kentucky Marriages, 1785–1979," database, *FamilySearch* (https://familysearch.org/ark:/61903/1:1:FWBJ-64B: accessed 24 January 2016), Arno Merkel and Bessie Phares, 01 Jan 1903; citing Covington, Kenton, Kentucky, reference 11; FHL microfilm 551,106.

11. See, for example: "New York, New York Passenger and Crew Lists, 1909, 1925–1957," database with images, *FamilySearch* (https://familysearch.org/ark:/61903/1:1:24FW-S1F: accessed 25 January 2016), Arno Merkel, 1929; citing Immigration, New York, New York, United States, NARA microfilm publication T715 (Washington, D.C.: National Archives and Records Administration, n.d.); "New York, New York Passenger and Crew Lists, 1909, 1925–1957," database with images, *FamilySearch* (https://familysearch.org/ark:/61903/1:1:24NS-N8Q: accessed 25 January 2016), Arno Merkel, 1930; citing Immigration, New York, New York, United States, NARA microfilm publication T715 (Washington, D.C.: National Archives and Records Administration, n.d.). The "California Death Index" claims Arno Merkel was born in 1883, while 1882 is the year of birth on his grave marker and in SSDI. See "California Death Index, 1940–1997," database, *FamilySearch* (https://familysearch.org/ark:/61903/1:1:VPH4-1QN: accessed 25 January 2016), Arno Merkel, 23 Dec 1969; Department of Public Health Services, Sacramento; "United States Social Security Death Index," database, *FamilySearch* (https://familysearch.org/ark:/61903/1:1:VMV4-X3J: accessed 25 January 2016), Arno Merkel, Dec 1969; citing U.S. Social Security Administration, *Death Master File*, database (Alexandria, Virginia: National Technical Information Service, ongoing); www.findagrave.com.

12. "United States Census, 1880," database with images, *FamilySearch* (https://familysearch.org/ark:/61903/1:1:M8MR-1KT: accessed 24 January 2016), Albert Merkel, Cincinnati, Hamilton, Ohio, United States; citing enumeration district ED 136, sheet 221A, NARA microfilm publication T9 (Washington, D.C.: National Archives and Records Administration, n.d.), roll 1025; FHL microfilm 1,255,025. It appears that Arno Merkel's father died in 1886, when he was only four or five years old (The Church of Jesus Christ of Latter-day Saints, "Pedigree Resource File," database, *FamilySearch* (https://familysearch.org/ark:/61903/2:2:SBNS-X46: accessed 2016-01-24), entry for Adelbert (Albert) Hans / Merkel/). His mother may have remarried or died young herself, as I have found no record of her as Amelia Merkel after 1880.

13. "United States Census, 1880," Albert Merkel; "United States Census, 1880," database with images, *FamilySearch* (https://familysearch.org/ark:/61903/1:1:M89M-PZJ: accessed 24 January 2016), James Phares, Cincinnati, Hamilton, Ohio, United States; citing enumeration district ED 178, sheet 339B, NARA microfilm publication T9 (Washington, D.C.: National Archives and Records Administration, n.d.), roll 1028; FHL microfilm 1,255,028.

14. "California Death Index, 1940–1997," database, *FamilySearch* (https://familysearch.org/ark:/61903/1:1:VPVM-QML: accessed 25 January 2016), Una Merkel, 02 Jan 1986; Department of Public Health Services, Sacramento; "United States Social Security Death Index," database, *FamilySearch* (https://familysearch.org/ark:/61903/1:1:JG4W-WZQ: accessed 25 January 2016), Una Merkel, Jan 1986; citing U.S. Social Security Administration, *Death Master File*, database (Alexandria, Virginia: National Technical Information Service, ongoing).

15. Burton Rascoe, "Theater: Una Merkel Succeeds in Three Is a Family," *New York World-Telegram* (March 29, 1944), p. 18.

16. May Mann, "Una Forgets Inhibitions After Face Slapping Role," *Ogden Standard-Examiner* (April 20, 1941), p. 13A.

17. www.findagrave.com.

18. "Kentucky Deaths and Burials, 1843–1970," database, *FamilySearch* (https://familysearch.org/ark:/61903/1:1:FWP9-SPX: accessed 24 January 2016), Josephine Hanks, 19 Oct 1910; citing reference; FHL microfilm 1,844,129; www.findagrave.com.

19. "New York, New York City Municipal Deaths, 1795–1949," database, *FamilySearch* (https://familysearch.org/ark:/61903/1:1:2WBP-HYN: accessed 24 January 2016), Mary Elizabeth Phares, 13 Oct 1920; citing Death, Manhattan, New York, New York, United States, New York Municipal Archives, New York; FHL microfilm 2,026,456.

20. "United States Census, 1920," database with images, *FamilySearch* (https://familysearch.org/ark:/61903/1:1:MJ1J-PKC: accessed 24 January 2016), Mary E Phares in household of Arno Merkel, Manhattan Assembly District 21, New York, New York, United States; citing sheet 7B, NARA microfilm publication T625 (Washington, D.C.: National Archives and Records Administration, n.d.); FHL microfilm 1,821,224.

21. "New York, New York City Municipal Deaths, 1795–1949," database, *FamilySearch* (https://familysearch.org/ark:/61903/1:1:2WLR-2FR: accessed 25 January 2016), Hazel Phares, 20 Feb 1926; citing Death, Manhattan, New York, New York, United States, New York Municipal Archives, New York; FHL microfilm 2,047,591.

22. www.findagrave.com.

23. "United States World War I Draft Registration Cards, 1917–1918," database with images, *FamilySearch* (https://familysearch.org/ark:/61903/1:1:K6JQ-4C5: accessed 25 January 2016), Arno Merkel, 1917–1918; citing New York City no 139, New York, United States, NARA microfilm publication M1509 (Washington, D.C.: National Archives and Records Administration, n.d.); FHL microfilm 1,786,671.

24. "United States Census, 1920," Una Merkel in household of Arno Merkel.

25. "United States Census, 1930," database with images, *FamilySearch* (https://familysearch.org/ark:/61903/1:1:X4GB-M9J: accessed 25 January 2016), Una Merkel, 1930.

26. Parker, *Who's Who in the Theatre*, p. 980; www.ibdb.com.

27. "New York, New York Passenger and Crew Lists, 1909, 1925–1957," Arno Merkel, 1930; *Los Angeles City Directory 1932* (Los Angeles: Los Angeles Directory, 1932), p. 1450; Parker, *Who's Who in the Theatre*, p. 981.

28. "Una Merkel Is Wed in Mexico," *Oakland Tribune* (January 4, 1932), p. 4B.

29. "At the Forsythe Theatre," *Hammond Times* (October 17, 1934), p. 16.

30. "California Death Index, 1905–1939," database with images, *FamilySearch* (https://familysearch.org/ark:/61903/1:1:QKSM-R8GM: accessed 25 January 2016), Gwan [sic] F Burla, 18 Jul 1936; citing 44176, Department of Health Services, Vital Statistics Department, Sacramento; "California Death Index, 1940–1997," database, *FamilySearch* (https://familysearch.org/ark:/61903/1:1:VPDR-J4V: accessed 25 January 2016), Elizabeth Cedergren Burla, 15 Jul 1958; Department of Public Health Services, Sacramento.

31. "New York, New York Passenger and Crew Lists, 1909, 1925–1957," database with images, *FamilySearch* (https://familysearch.org/ark:/61903/1:1:24JY-7GC: accessed 25 January 2016), Ronald L Burla, 1932; citing Immigration, New York, New York, United States, NARA microfilm publication T715 (Washington, D.C.: National Archives and Records Administration, n.d.); "Week in Billings Society," *Billing Daily Gazette* (September 20, 1908), p. 7; "Former Local Man Marries Film Actress," *Billings Gazette* (January 24, 1932), p. 2; "As It Was in Billings ... 35 Years Ago," *Billings Gazette* (June 24, 1953), p. 4. SSDI says Burla was born on February 10th. See "United States Social Security Death Index," database, *FamilySearch* (https://familysearch.org/ark:/61903/1:1:JGWK-WPF: accessed 25 January 2016), Ronald L Burla, 14 Oct 1991; citing U.S. Social Security Administration, *Death Master File*, database (Alexandria, Virginia: National Technical Information Service, ongoing).

32. "United States Census, 1920," database with images, *FamilySearch* (https://familysearch.org/ark:/61903/1:1:MH74-G5R: accessed 25 January 2016), Ronald Burla in household of Grew F Burla, Los Angeles Assembly District 75, Los Angeles, California, United States; citing sheet 20B, NARA microfilm publication T625 (Washington, D.C.: National Archives and Records Administration, n.d.); FHL microfilm 1,820,116.

33. "United States Census, 1940," database with images, *FamilySearch* (https://familysearch.org/ark:/61903/1:1:K97C-SKQ: accessed 25 January 2016), Ronald L Burla in household of Arno Merkel, Tract 381, Beverly Hills, Beverly Hills Judicial Township, Los Angeles, California, United States; citing enumeration district (ED) 19–39, sheet 11A, family 303, NARA digital publication T627 (Washington, D.C.: National Archives and Records Administration, 2012), roll 221; Kyle Crichton, "Something to Fight About," unnamed, undated clipping (NYPL); "Movie Bride," *Nevada State Journal* (January 10, 1932), p. 7; "Weds First in '32," *Oakland Tribune* (January 4, 1932), p. B4; Paul Harrison, "Una Merkel, Fired by Metro, Won New Fame as Free-Lancer," *Lowell Sun* (June 20, 1939), p. 14; Harrison Carroll, "Slapstick Comedy Returns," *Winnipeg Free Press* (November 6, 1939), p. 10; Mann, "Una Forgets Inhibitions," p. 13A.

34. "United States Census, 1930," database with images, *FamilySearch* (https://familysearch.org/ark:/61903/1:1:XCVH-83T: accessed 25 January 2016), L Ronald Burla in entry for F Given Burla, 1930; "United States Census, 1940," Ronald L Burla.

35. "New York, New York Passenger and Crew Lists, 1909, 1925–1957," Ronald L Burla, 1932.

36. "New York, New York Passenger and Crew Lists, 1909, 1925–1957," Ronald L Burla, 1932; *Los Angeles City Directory 1936* (Los Angeles: Los Angeles Directory, 1936), p. 323; *Los Angeles City Directory 1938* (Los Angeles: Los Angeles Directory, 1938), p. 355, 1408.

37. Hollis Wood, "Una Merkel in Private Life Very Different from Her Role in Latest Picture," unnamed, undated clipping (NYPL).

38. Dan Thomas, "Hollywood Close-Ups," *Monroe News-Star* (March 1, 1934), p. 4.

39. Crichton, "Something to Fight About."

40. "United States Census, 1940," Una Burla in household of Arno Merkel; www.zillow.com.

41. Harrison, "Una Merkel, Fired by Metro," p. 14.

42. Mann, "Una Forgets Inhibitions," p. 13A.

43. "Una Merkel Now Fully Recovered," *Neosho Daily Democrat* (July 23, 1946), p. 2.

44. "Files Divorce Suit," *Walla Walla Union-Bulletin* (December 3, 1946), p. 3; "Florida Divorce Index, 1927–2001," database, *FamilySearch* (https://familysearch.org/ark:/61903/1:1:VK76-LLS: accessed 25 January 2016), Ronald L Burla and Una Burla, 1947; from "Florida Divorce Index, 1927–2001," database and images, *Ancestry* (http://www.ancestry.com: 2005); citing Dade, Florida, certificate 4136, volume 388, Florida Department of Health, Jacksonville. Ronald L. Burla died in 1991. See "United States Social Security Death Index," Ronald L Burla, 14 Oct 1991.

45. See "Actress Una Merkel in Critical Condition," *Joplin Globe* (March 4, 1952), p. 7; "Una Merkel Is Found in Coma: Overdose of Sleeping Pills Suspected," *Lubbock Evening Journal* (March 4, 1952), n.pag.; "Una Merkel Faces Battle for Life," *Charleston Gazette* (March 5, 1952), p. 8.

46. "Behind the Scenes in Hollywood," *Greenville Delta Democrat-Times* (March 26, 1952), n.pag.

47. "California Death Index, 1940–1997," Arno Merkel, 23 Dec 1969; "United States Social Security Death Index," Arno Merkel, Dec 1969.

48. "California Death Index, 1940–1997," Una Merkel, 02 Jan 1986; "United States Social Security Death Index," Una Merkel, Jan 1986; "Una Merkel Dies at Age of 82; From Silent Films to a Tony," *New York Times* (January 5, 1986), p. 24.

49. www.findagrave.com.

Greta Meyer

1. Ragan, *Who's Who in Hollywood*, p. 358. No other standard reference work on supporting players in Hollywood I have consulted, except the *All Movie Guide*, so much as mentions Meyer.

2. Ragan, p. 352.

3. "United States Social Security Death Index," index, *FamilySearch* (https://familysearch.org/pal:/MM9.1.1/V9TM-BZ4: accessed 25 January 2015), Greta Meyer, Oct 1965; citing U.S. Social Security Administration, *Death Master File*, database (Alexandria, Virginia: National Technical Information Service, on-

going). The Social Security Death Index gives only the month and year and that Meyer died in California. Her exact date and place of death is taken from www.imdb.com.

4. "Actress Evicted, Will Quit U.S. for Germany," *Long Beach Press-Telegram* (July 11, 1963), p. A22.

5. Her address is given in Wikipedia: http://en.wikipedia.org/wiki/Greta_Meyer.

6. "Hollywood Chatter," *Lowell Sun* (December 16, 1933), p. 11.

7. www.imdb.com, www.ibdb.com, http://en.wikipedia.org/wiki/Greta_Meyer.

8. "United States Social Security Death Index," index, Greta Meyer, Oct 1965.

9. "New York, Passenger Arrival Lists (Ellis Island), 1892–1924," index, *FamilySearch* (https://familysearch.org/pal:/MM9.1.1/JF9Y-HJH: accessed 25 January 2015), Greta Meyer, 29 Apr 1909; citing departure port Hamburg via Cuxhaven, arrival port New York, ship name President Lincoln, NARA microfilm publication T715 and M237 (Washington, D.C.: National Archives and Records Administration, n.d.).

10. "Matters of Interest to Playgoers: Best Sellers on the Stage," *New York Times* (December 24, 1911), www.nyt.com.

11. www.ibdb.com.

12. www.ibdb.com.

13. *New York Times* (October 17, 1915), www.nyt.com.

14. http://www.museumoffamilyhistory.com/yt/lex/M/meyer-greta.htm.

15. www.imdb.com.

16. Burns Mantle, *The Best Plays of 1930–31* (New York: Dodd, Mead, 1931), p. 456.

17. "'Laddie' Runs Two More Days at the Liberty," *Cumberland Sunday Times* (April 21, 1935), p. 10.

18. www.allmovie.com.

19. "50 Years Ago: Yiddish Theater Actress Evicted," *Jewish Daily Forward* (July 12, 2013), http://forward.com/articles/179931/moyshe-the-shtarker-jewish-gangster-stabbed-and-sh/.

20. "Actress Evicted," *Long Beach Press-Telegram*, p. A22; "Nothing So Terrible: Evicted Aging Star Dreads Loneliness," *Lubbock Avalanche-Journal* (July 16, 1963), p. 8A.

Dennie Moore

1. Mark Barron, "A Play of Coney Island," *Kansas City Star* (December 11, 1932), p. 11D.

2. "From a Champion Family," *Oakland Tribune* (November 15, 1935), p. E31.

3. https://en.wikipedia.org/wiki/Joe_Moore_(speed_skater). Confirmed by the Social Security Death Index: "United States Social Security Death Index," database, *FamilySearch* (https://familysearch.org/ark:/61903/1:1:JTTN-3T1: accessed 30 July 2015), Joseph Moore, Apr 1982; citing U.S. Social Security Administration, *Death Master File*, database (Alexandria, Virginia: National Technical Information Service, ongoing).

4. New York, State Census, 1905, database with images, *FamilySearch* (https://familysearch.org/ark:/61903/1:1:SPXP-BY4: accessed 30 July 2015), Joseph Moore in household of Philip Moore, Manhattan, A.D. 15, E.D. 18, New York, New York; citing p. 9, line 31, county offices, New York.; FHL microfilm 1,433,090. This traditional, weather-beaten red brick row house is still standing on the north side of 47th St. between 8th and 9th Ave. in Hell's Kitchen.

5. "United States Census, 1910," database with images, *FamilySearch* (https://familysearch.org/ark:/61903/1:1:M53G-JYL: accessed 31 July 2015), Florence Moore in household of Philip Moore, Manhattan Ward 22, New York, New York, United States; citing enumeration district (ED) 1348, sheet 8B, family 374, NARA microfilm publication T624 (Washington, D.C.: National Archives and Records Administration, n.d.); FHL microfilm 1,375,060. This building has been razed to make way for the Intercontinental Hotel.

6. "United States Census, 1920," database with images, *FamilySearch* (https://familysearch.org/ark:/61903/1:1:MJY2-1S3: accessed 30 July 2015), Florence Moore in household of Phillip Moore, Manhattan Assembly District 7, New York, New York, United States; citing sheet 3A, family 43, NARA microfilm publication T625 (Washington, D.C.: National Archives and Records Administration, n.d.); FHL microfilm 1,821,197.

7. www.ibdb.com.

8. See https://en.wikipedia.org/wiki/Stage_name and https://www.actorsequity.org/docs/about/About Equity_web.pdf, p. 6.

9. "United States Census, 1930," database with images, *FamilySearch* (https://familysearch.org/ark:/61903/1:1:X42G-4CL: accessed 31 July 2015), Florence Moore, Manhattan (Districts 0501–0750), New York, New York, United States; citing enumeration district (ED) 0570, sheet 2B, family 101, line 62, NARA microfilm publication T626 (Washington, D.C.: National Archives and Records Administration, 2002), roll 1567; FHL microfilm 2,341,302.

10. www.ibdb.com.

11. "New York, New York Passenger and Crew Lists, 1909, 1925–1957," database with images, *FamilySearch* (https://familysearch.org/ark:/61903/1:1:24J9-HNY: accessed 30 July 2015), Florence Rita Deny Moore, 1934; citing Immigration, New York, New York, United States, NARA microfilm publication T715 (Washington, D.C.: National Archives and Records Administration, n.d.); FHL microfilm 1,757,257.

12. "Play Will Go to England: 'The Pursuit of Happiness' May Open There in June," *New York Times* (March 27, 1934), www.nytimes.com.

13. "Pals Reunited," *Oakland Tribune* (September 9, 1935), p. D27.

14. "United States Social Security Death Index," database, *FamilySearch* (https://familysearch.org/ark:/61903/1:1:JBGM-BNG: accessed 30 July 2015), Dennie Moore, Feb 1978; citing U.S. Social Security Administration, *Death Master File*, database (Alexandria, Virginia: National Technical Information Service, ongoing).

15. "United States Census, 1940," database with images, *FamilySearch* (https://familysearch.org/ark:/61903/1:1:K7MZ-TGR: accessed 31 July 2015), Florence D Moore, Assembly District 10, Manhattan, New York City, New York, New York, United States; citing enumeration district (ED) 31–813, sheet 82A, family, NARA digital publication T627 (Washington, D.C.: National Archives and Records Administration, 2012), roll 2643.

16. "New York, New York Passenger and Crew Lists, 1909, 1925–1957," Florence Rita Deny Moore, 1934.
17. Walter Winchell, "On Broadway," *Wisconsin State Journal* (March 2, 1935), n.pag.
18. "United States Census, 1940," Florence D Moore.
19. "Screen Notes," *New York Times* (August 24, 1935), www.nytimes.com.
20. Ragan, *Who's Who in Hollywood*, p. 308.
21. "United States Social Security Death Index," Dennie Moore.
22. Brooks Atkinson, *Say When* review, *New York Times* (November 9, 1934), www.nytimes.com.

Ona Munson

1. Barris, *Hollywood's Other Women*, p. 185.
2. "Michigan, Marriages, 1822–1995," index, *FamilySearch* (https://familysearch.org/pal:/MM9.1.1/FCX4-YW1: accessed 19 February 2015), Edgar Wolcott and Christina Carrion, 28 Feb 1867; citing reference Vol 5 pg 272; FHL microfilm 1,009,295.
3. "United States Census, 1870," index and images, *FamilySearch* (https://familysearch.org/pal:/MM9.1.1/MHD3-KFR: accessed 19 February 2015), Owen Wolcott in household of Edgar Wolcott, Nebraska, United States; citing p. 11, family 85, NARA microfilm publication M593 (Washington, D.C.: National Archives and Records Administration, n.d.); FHL microfilm 552,329.
4. "United States Census, 1880," index and images, *FamilySearch* (https://familysearch.org/pal:/MM9.1.1/MDL3-FGX: accessed 19 February 2015), Owen Wolcott in household of Edgar Wolcott, Marshalltown, Marshall, Iowa, United States; citing enumeration district 293, sheet 181D, NARA microfilm publication T9 (Washington, D.C.: National Archives and Records Administration, n.d.), roll 0355; FHL microfilm 1,254,355.
5. "Iowa State Census, 1885," index and images, *FamilySearch* (https://familysearch.org/pal:/MM9.1.1/HD8X-Z6Z: accessed 19 February 2015), Owen Wolcott in household of Edgar Wolcott, Marshalltown, Marshall, Marshall, Iowa; citing p.,, State Historical Society, Des Moines; FHL microfilm.
6. "Iowa, County Marriages, 1838–1934," index, *FamilySearch* (https://familysearch.org/pal:/MM9.1.1/XJH2-FSC: accessed 19 February 2015), Edgar Wolcott and Josie Andrews, 26 Jun 1889; citing Marshalltown, Marshall, Iowa, United States, county courthouses, Iowa; www.findagrave.com.
7. "California, Great Registers, 1866–1910," index, *FamilySearch* (https://familysearch.org/pal:/MM9.1.1/VNFT-RGK: accessed 19 February 2015), Owen P Wolcott, 01 Aug 1892; citing Voter Registration, 416 Bernard, Los Angeles, California, United States, county clerk offices, California; FHL microfilm 976,929.
8. The 1900 U.S. Census states that the Wolcotts have been married seven years. See "United States Census, 1900," index and images, *FamilySearch* (https://familysearch.org/pal:/MM9.1.1/M9PJ-DGV: accessed 19 February 2015), Owen P Wolcott, Precinct 37 Los Angeles city Ward 5, Los Angeles, California, United States; citing sheet 5A, family 95, NARA microfilm publication T623 (Washington, D.C.: National Archives and Records Administration, n.d.); FHL microfilm 1,240,089.
9. "California, Death Index, 1940–1997," index, *FamilySearch* (https://familysearch.org/pal:/MM9.1.1/VPFY-W62: accessed 19 February 2015), Sally E Wolcott, 21 Dec 1955; Department of Public Health Services, Sacramento.
10. "California, Great Registers, 1866–1910," index, *FamilySearch* (https://familysearch.org/pal:/MM9.1.1/VNFB-NXH: accessed 19 February 2015), Owen Parrett Wolcott, 13 Jul 1896; citing Voter Registration, 167 N Spring, Los Angeles, California, United States, county clerk offices, California; FHL microfilm 976,930.
11. "United States Census, 1900," index and images, *FamilySearch* (https://familysearch.org/pal:/MM9.1.1/M9PJ-DGV: accessed 19 February 2015), Owen P Wolcott, Precinct 37 Los Angeles city Ward 5, Los Angeles, California, United States; citing sheet 5A, family 95, NARA microfilm publication T623 (Washington, D.C.: National Archives and Records Administration, n.d.); FHL microfilm 1,240,089.
12. "United States Census, 1910," index and images, *FamilySearch* (https://familysearch.org/pal:/MM9.1.1/MLYV-RSP: accessed 19 February 2015), Owena Wolcott in household of Owen P Wolcott, Portland Ward 4, Multnomah, Oregon, United States; citing enumeration district (ED) 144, sheet 1A, family 13, NARA microfilm publication T624 (Washington, D.C.: National Archives and Records Administration, n.d.); FHL microfilm 1,375,299.
13. "New York, New York Passenger and Crew Lists, 1909, 1925–1957," index and images, *FamilySearch* (https://familysearch.org/pal:/MM9.1.1/24KQ-WQC: accessed 19 February 2015), Owena Wolcott, 1936; citing Immigration, New York, New York, United States, NARA microfilm publication T715 (Washington, D.C.: National Archives and Records Administration, n.d.); FHL microfilm 1,757,594.
14. "United States Census, 1910," Owena Wolcott in the household of Owen P Wolcott.
15. "United States Census, 1920," index and images, *FamilySearch* (https://familysearch.org/pal:/MM9.1.1/M4ZL-S42: accessed 19 February 2015), Owena Walcott in household of Owen P Walcott, Portland, Multnomah, Oregon, United States; citing sheet 3A, family 63, NARA microfilm publication T625 (Washington, D.C.: National Archives and Records Administration, n.d.); FHL microfilm 1,821,499.
16. *New York Times* (November 28, 1926) (*T-Clippings, Billy Rose Theatre Division, New York Public Library for the Performing Arts; henceforward abbreviated NYPL).
17. "Ona Munson in 'Wind' After Twenty-Six Others Had Tests," unnamed, undated clipping (NYPL).
18. "United States Census, 1930," index and images, *FamilySearch* (https://familysearch.org/pal:/MM9.1.1/XCSC-M6K: accessed 19 February 2015), Owen P Wolcott, Portland (Districts 271–553), Multnomah, Oregon, United States; citing enumeration district (ED) 0540, sheet 2B, family 53, line 88, NARA microfilm publication T626 (Washington, D.C.: National Archives and Records Administration, 2002), roll 1954; FHL microfilm 2,341,688.
19. "Oregon, Death Index, 1903–1998," index, *FamilySearch* (https://familysearch.org/pal:/MM9.1.1/VZWL-4T4: accessed 19 February 2015), Owen Wolcott, 1937; from "Oregon, Death Index, 1898–2008," *Ancestry*; citing

Multnomah, Oregon, certificate number 378, Oregon State Archives and Records Center, Salem.

20. Parker, *Who's Who in the Theatre*, p. 1022.

21. Parker, p. 1022.

22. Parker, p. 1022.

23. Parker, p. 1022; www.imdb.com.

24. Gavin Lambert, *Nazimova: A Biography* (New York: Alfred A. Knopf, 1997), p. 340.

25. "New York, New York Passenger and Crew Lists, 1909, 1925–1957," database with images, *FamilySearch* (https://familysearch.org/ark:/61903/1:1:24KQ-WQC: accessed 7 February 2016), Owena Wolcott, 1936; citing Immigration, New York, New York, United States, NARA microfilm publication T715 (Washington, D.C.: National Archives and Records Administration, n.d.).

26. movielanddirectory.com.

27. "United States Census, 1940," index and images, *FamilySearch* (https://familysearch.org/pal:/MM9.1.1/K9CD-NR3: accessed 19 February 2015), Ona Munson in household of Sally Munson, Councilmanic District 2, Los Angeles, Los Angeles Township, Los Angeles, California, United States; citing enumeration district (ED) 60–119, sheet 21A, family 483, NARA digital publication T627 (Washington, D.C.: National Archives and Records Administration, 2012), roll 398.

28. "New York, New York Passenger and Crew Lists, 1909, 1925–1957," database with images, *FamilySearch* (https://familysearch.org/ark:/61903/1:1:24Y9-ZCF: accessed 1 February 2016), Owena Or Ona Wolcott-Berman Or Munson, 1951; citing Immigration, New York City, New York, United States, NARA microfilm publication T715 (Washington, D.C.: National Archives and Records Administration, n.d.); movielanddirectory.com.

29. www.imdb.com.

30. "United States World War I Draft Registration Cards, 1917–1918," index and images, *FamilySearch* (https://familysearch.org/pal:/MM9.1.1/KXYV-NHS: accessed 19 February 2015), Edward N Buzzell, 1917–1918; citing New York City no 63, New York, United States, NARA microfilm publication M1509 (Washington, D.C.: National Archives and Records Administration, n.d.); FHL microfilm 1,754,590.

31. www.imdb.com.

32. Ed Johnson, "Believes Boys in Hollywood Spoiled," unnamed, undated clipping (NYPL).

33. Lambert, *Nazimova*, p. 340.

34. Lambert, p. 347, including the quote.

35. Axel Madsen, *The Sewing Circle: Sappho's Leading Ladies* (New York: Kensington Books, 2002), p. 66.

36. Acosta's memoir *Here Lies My Heart* quoted in Lambert, *Nazimova*, p. 347.

37. "United States Census, 1940," index and images, *FamilySearch* (https://familysearch.org/pal:/MM9.1.1/K9CG-RRV: accessed 19 February 2015), Mercedes De Acosta, Councilmanic District 3, Los Angeles, Los Angeles Township, Los Angeles, California, United States; citing enumeration district (ED) 60–217, sheet 20B, family 567, NARA digital publication T627 (Washington, D.C.: National Archives and Records Administration, 2012), roll 407; movielanddirectory.com.

38. Munson's letters to Acosta quoted in Madsen, *The Sewing Circle*, p. 66.

39. "Actress Reveals Engagement," unnamed, undated clipping [Sept. 1941] (NYPL).

40. Unnamed, undated clipping (NYPL), including description of engagement ring.

41. Frederick C. Othman, "The Hollywood Reporter," *Middlesboro Daily News* (September 30, 1941), p. 3.

42. Dorothy Kilgallen, "Broadway," *Mansfield News Journal* (February 26, 1942), p. 13.

43. "Ona Munson Wed to Artist," *New York Times* (January 30, 1950) (NYPL).

44. "Eugene Berman, Painter and Set Designer for the Met, Dies at 73," *New York Times* (December 15, 1972) (NYPL); "United States Social Security Death Index," index, *FamilySearch* (https://familysearch.org/pal:/MM9.1.1/V95G-W4F: accessed 19 February 2015), Eugene Berman, Dec 1972; citing U.S. Social Security Administration, *Death Master File*, database (Alexandria, Virginia: National Technical Information Service, ongoing).

45. "California, Southern District Court (Central) Naturalization Index, 1915–1976," index and images, *FamilySearch* (https://familysearch.org/pal:/MM9.1.1/KX3B-LS2: accessed 19 February 2015), Eugene Berman Or Bermann, 1944; citing Los Angeles, Los Angeles, California, United States, National Archives and Records Service, Los Angeles Branch, Laguna Niguel; FHL microfilm 1,561,838.

46. This account builds on Josephine Di Lorenzo, "Ona Munson Is Killed by Overdose of Pills," *New York Daily News* (February 12, 1955), p. 3; "Ona Munson Dies After Taking Pills," *New York World* (February 11, 1955) (NYPL).

47. Di Lorenzo, "Ona Munson Is Killed," p. 3.

48. www.findagrave.com.

49. "Eugene Berman, Painter and Set Designer," *New York Times*; "United States Social Security Death Index," Eugene Berman, Dec 1972.

50. "California, Death Index, 1940–1997," Sally E Wolcott, 21 Dec 1955.

51. "Ona Munson's Set to Turn Over a New Movie Leaf," unnamed, undated clipping (NYPL). See also Frederick C. Othman, "Ona Munson Fed Up with Belle," unnamed, undated clipping (NYPL).

52. Lambert, *Nazimova*, p. 374.

53. Louis Raymond, "Good Bad Girl," unnamed, undated clipping [c1941] (NYPL).

54. Sidney Carroll, "Any Odd Role Like a Glove to Versatile Ona Munson," unnamed, undated clipping [c1941] (NYPL).

55. "Halts Cycle of Type Roles," unnamed, undated clipping [1941] (NYPL).

56. "Ona Munson Does an About Face!" unnamed clipping [1942] (NYPL).

Mary Nash

1. Parker, *Who's Who in the Theatre*, p. 1029; "California, Death Index, 1940–1997," index, *FamilySearch* (https://familysearch.org/pal:/MM9.1.1/VGT7-Q79: accessed 13 February 2015), Mary Nash, 03 Dec 1976; Department of Public Health Services, Sacramento; "United States Social Security Death Index," index, *FamilySearch* (https://familysearch.org/pal:/MM9.1.1/J5D3-VT5: accessed 13 February 2015), Mary Nash, Dec 1976; citing U.S. Social Security Administration,

Death Master File, database (Alexandria, Virginia: National Technical Information Service, ongoing).

2. "California, Death Index, 1940–1997," index, *FamilySearch* (https://familysearch.org/pal:/MM9.1.1/VPQ2-8V4: accessed 13 February 2015), Ellen Frances Nash, 06 Dec 1946; Department of Public Health Services, Sacramento; "United States Census, 1900," index and images, *FamilySearch* (https://familysearch.org/pal:/MM9.1.1/MS6M-C34: accessed 13 February 2015), Ellen F Nast [sic] in household of Philip F Nast, Albany city Ward 14, Albany, New York, United States; citing sheet 10A, family 215, NARA microfilm publication T623 (Washington, D.C.: National Archives and Records Administration, n.d.); FHL microfilm 1,241,005.

3. "Mary Nash Dead; Character Actress of Stage and Film," *New York Times* (December 8, 1976), p. D22.

4. "Has Had Her Share of Stage Adventures," *Philadelphia Inquirer* (September 4, 1927) (*T-Clippings, Billy Rose Theatre Division, New York Public Library for the Performing Arts; henceforward abbreviated NYPL).

5. "United States Census, 1900," Philip F Nast [sic].

6. "California, Death Index, 1940–1997," index, *FamilySearch* (https://familysearch.org/pal:/MM9.1.1/VP74-QMN: accessed 13 February 2015), Florence Nash, 02 Apr 1950; Department of Public Health Services, Sacramento; "Famed Actress, Troy Native Dies Suddenly," *Troy Record* (April 4, 1950), p. 3.

7. "United States Census, 1920," index and images, *FamilySearch* (https://familysearch.org/pal:/MM9.1.1/MJYG-2NM: accessed 13 February 2015), Mary Nash in household of Ellen Nash, Manhattan Assembly District 7, New York, New York, United States; citing sheet 1A, family 8, NARA microfilm publication T625 (Washington, D.C.: National Archives and Records Administration, n.d.); FHL microfilm 1,821,198.

8. "United States Census, 1930," index and images, *FamilySearch* (https://familysearch.org/pal:/MM9.1.1/X4K5-MRL: accessed 13 February 2015), Mary Nash in household of Ellen Nash, Manhattan (Districts 0251–0500), New York, New York, United States; citing enumeration district (ED) 0406, sheet 7A, family 190, line 46, NARA microfilm publication T626 (Washington, D.C.: National Archives and Records Administration, 2002), roll 1554; FHL microfilm 2,341,289.

9. Parker, *Who's Who in the Theatre*, p. 1029.

10. "Philip Nash," *New York Times* (October 5, 1914), www.nytimes.com.

11. "United States Census, 1910," database with images, *FamilySearch* (https://familysearch.org/ark:/61903/1:1:M593-NNH: accessed 7 February 2016), Mary H Nash in household of Philip F Nash, Manhattan Ward 22, New York, New York, United States; citing enumeration district (ED) ED 1282, sheet 7A, NARA microfilm publication T624 (Washington, D.C.: National Archives and Records Administration, n.d.); FHL microfilm 1,375,058.

12. "Philip Nash," *New York Times*.

13. Edward Harold Crosby, "Under the Spotlight," *Boston Sunday Post* (December 17, 1922), p. A5. See also "Hair Not Bobbed Because She Needs It," *Kansas City Star* (November 25, 1924), p. 22.

14. "Famed Actress," *Troy Record*, p. 3.

15. "Bequest to Florence Nash," *New York Times* (April 18, 1916), p. 11.

16. Parker, *Who's Who in the Theatre*, p. 1029; Crosby, "Under the Spotlight," p. A5; www.ibdb.com.

17. Crosby, "Under the Spotlight," p. A5; www.ibdb.com.

18. Crosby, p. A5; Parker, *Who's Who in the Theatre*, p. 1029.

19. "Mary Nash and Jose Ruben Marry," *New York Times* (October 24, 1918), www.nytimes.com.

20. "New York, Passenger Arrival Lists (Ellis Island), 1892–1924," index, *FamilySearch* (https://familysearch.org/pal:/MM9.1.1/JJDL-VYM: accessed 13 February 2015), Jose Rubens, 29 Oct 1910; citing departure port Havre, arrival port New York, ship name La Provence, NARA microfilm publication T715 and M237 (Washington, D.C.: National Archives and Records Administration, n.d.).

21. I base this description on a photograph in the article "Actors—All Married and Happy," *Appleton Post Crescent* (December 28, 1921), p. 11.

22. "United States World War II Draft Registration Cards, 1942," index and images, *FamilySearch* (https://familysearch.org/pal:/MM9.1.1/F3HD-FJM: accessed 13 February 2015), Jose Ruben, 1942; citing NAID identifier 2555973, NARA microfilm publication M1936, M1937, M1939, M1951, M1962, M1964, M1986, M2090, and M2097 (Washington, D.C.: National Archives and Records Administration, n.d.); FHL microfilm 2,368,854.

23. "New York, New York Passenger and Crew Lists, 1909, 1925–1957," index and images, *FamilySearch* (https://familysearch.org/pal:/MM9.1.1/24NT-QZS: accessed 13 February 2015), Jose Ruben, 1934; citing Immigration, New York, New York, United States, NARA microfilm publication T715 (Washington, D.C.: National Archives and Records Administration, n.d.); FHL microfilm 1,757,200.

24. "Thanksgiving Week Brings Three New York Premieres," *Indianapolis Star* (November 28, 1920), p. 1.

25. "Actors," *Appleton Post*, p. 11.

26. "New York, New York Passenger and Crew Lists, 1909, 1925–1957," index and images, *FamilySearch* (https://familysearch.org/pal:/MM9.1.1/KXMD-1SS: accessed 13 February 2015), Jose Ruben, 1926; citing Immigration, New York, New York, United States, NARA microfilm publication T715 (Washington, D.C.: National Archives and Records Administration, n.d.); FHL microfilm 1,755,645.

27. "United States Census, 1920," Mary Nash in household of Ellen Nash.

28. "United States Social Security Death Index," index, *FamilySearch* (https://familysearch.org/pal:/MM9.1.1/J5T8-Y4S: accessed 13 February 2015), Jose Ruben, Apr 1969; citing U.S. Social Security Administration, *Death Master File*, database (Alexandria, Virginia: National Technical Information Service, ongoing). Ruben and his second wife, Victoria Wehrum Ruben (1909–90), are buried in Amityville, New York (www.findagrave.com).

29. Robert Garland, "'A Woman Denied,'" unnamed clipping (February 26, 1931) (NYPL).

30. Garland, "'A Woman Denied.'"

31. Garland, "'A Woman Denied.'"

32. Alexander Woollcott, *The Lady* review, *New York Herald* (December 7, 1923) (NYPL).

33. www.tcm.com.

34. "United States Census, 1940," index and images,

FamilySearch (https://familysearch.org/pal:/MM9.1.1/K9CP-Q2J: accessed 13 February 2015), Mary Nash in household of Ellen F Nash, Councilmanic District 3, Los Angeles, Los Angeles Township, Los Angeles, California, United States; citing enumeration district (ED) 60–218, sheet 21A, family 126, NARA digital publication T627 (Washington, D.C.: National Archives and Records Administration, 2012), roll 407; movielanddirectory.com; www.zillow.com.

35. Paul Roen, *High Camp: A Guide to Camp and Cult Films, Vol. 1* (San Francisco: Leyland, 1994), p. 49.

36. "California, Death Index, 1940–1997," Ellen Frances Nash, 06 Dec 1946.

37. "California, Death Index, 1940–1997," Florence Nash, 02 Apr 1950; "Florence Nash Dies," *Newport News* (April 4, 1950), p. 9.

38. "Mary Nash Dead," *New York Times*, p. D22.

Barbara O'Neil

1. Barris, *Hollywood's Other Women*, p. 22.

2. Gavin Lambert, *GWTW: The Making of Gone with the Wind* (Boston: Little Brown, 1973), p. 49.

3. Davis, *The Lonely Life*, p. 200; Charlotte Chandler, *The Girl Who Walked Home Alone: Bette Davis—A Personal Biography* (New York: Simon and Schuster, 2006), p. 145.

4. "United States Social Security Death Index," database, *FamilySearch* (https://familysearch.org/ark:/61903/1:1:JG7G-46Y: accessed 2 February 2016), Barbara Oneil, Sep 1980; citing U.S. Social Security Administration, *Death Master File*, database (Alexandria, Virginia: National Technical Information Service, ongoing).

5. "Society: Come West to Make Their Home," *Oakland Tribune* (April 6, 1920), p. 10; "United States Census, 1920," database with images, *FamilySearch* (https://familysearch.org/ark:/61903/1:1:MH38-HHY: accessed 13 January 2016), Barbara O'Neil in household of David N O'Neil, Oakland, Alameda, California, United States; citing sheet 6B, NARA microfilm publication T625 (Washington, D.C.: National Archives and Records Administration, n.d.); FHL microfilm 1,820,092.

6. "A Nurse's Aid, She's Playing Nazi Nurse," unnamed, undated clipping (*T-Clippings, Billy Rose Theatre Division, New York Public Library for the Performing Arts; henceforward abbreviated NYPL).

7. "United States Census, 1880," database with images, *FamilySearch* (https://familysearch.org/ark:/61903/1:1:M6FP-V29: accessed 13 January 2016), Geo Blackman, St Louis, St Louis, Missouri, United States; citing enumeration district ED 137, sheet 129C, NARA microfilm publication T9 (Washington, D.C.: National Archives and Records Administration, n.d.), roll 0723; FHL microfilm 1,254,723; "United States Census, 1900," database with images, *FamilySearch* (https://familysearch.org/ark:/61903/1:1:M3DD-YCD: accessed 13 January 2016), Barbara Blackman in household of George Blackman, Precinct 14 St. Louis city Ward 28, St. Louis, Missouri, United States; citing sheet 10A, family 168, NARA microfilm publication T623 (Washington, D.C.: National Archives and Records Administration, n.d.); FHL microfilm 1,240,901.

8. The 1910 census states that the couple has been married for six years. See "United States Census, 1910," database with images, *FamilySearch* (https://familysearch.org/ark:/61903/1:1:M21S-61K: accessed 13 January 2016), David N Oneil, Central, St Louis, Missouri, United States; citing enumeration district (ED) ED 116, sheet 13B, NARA microfilm publication T624 (Washington, D.C.: National Archives and Records Administration, n.d.); FHL microfilm 1,374,823; https://en.wikipedia.org/wiki/David_O%27Neil.

9. www.findagrave.com.

10. "United States Census, 1900," database with images, *FamilySearch*(https://familysearch.org/ark:/61903/1:1:M3DD-FF3: accessed 13 January 2016), Katharine Oneil, Precinct 4 St. Louis city Ward 28, St. Louis, Missouri, United States; citing sheet 15A, family 203, NARA microfilm publication T623 (Washington, D.C.: National Archives and Records Administration, n.d.); FHL microfilm 1,240,901; "United States Census, 1920," database with images, *FamilySearch*(https://familysearch.org/ark:/61903/1:1:M884-FLN: accessed 13 January 2016), Catherine A O'Neil, St Louis Ward 25, St Louis (Independent City), Missouri, United States; citing sheet 2A, NARA microfilm publication T625 (Washington, D.C.: National Archives and Records Administration, n.d.); FHL microfilm 1,820,961; www.zillow.com; www.findagrave.com.

11. Program note, *Doctors Disagree* (December 28, 1943) (NYPL). See also "A Nurse's Aid."

12. "Barbara O'Neil Is Known on Stage and in Films," unnamed, undated clipping (NYPL).

13. "Horton O'Neil '30," *Princeton Alumni Weekly* (September 10, 1997), https://paw.princeton.edu.

14. The couple decided the marriage was a mistake on the third day of their honeymoon in Cuba, but did not divorce until 1942. Logan was a manic depressive and claimed in his autobiography that O'Neil did not want to have any children by him, because she didn't want to, in her own words, "bring insane children into this world." O'Neil herself never made any public statement on her brief marriage to Logan. See Joshua Logan, *Josh: My Up and Down, In and Out Life* (New York: Delacorte Press, 1976), pp. 120–21, 125 (incl. quote) and Ragan, *Who's Who in Hollywood 1900–1976*, p. 339.

15. Springer and Hamilton, *They Had Faces Then*, p. 321, www.ibdb.com.

16. Springer and Hamilton, p. 321.

17. www.allmovie.com, www.ibdb.com.

18. "United States Social Security Death Index," Barbara Oneil, Sep 1980; "People," *Winnipeg Fress Press* (September 5, 1980), p. 37.

19. www.findagrave.com.

Rafaela Ottiano

1. There were five villagers from Viggiano aboard the Kaiser Wilhelm II on that journey. My claim that the girls were in the care of Pasquale Sammartino is based on the admittedly circumstantial evidence that he was living only a few blocks from the Ottianos in North Boston in 1897 and that he was a fellow musician and roughly the same age as the girls' father Antonio. See "United States Italians to America Index, 1855–1900," index, *FamilySearch* (https://familysearch.org/pal:/MM9.1.1/KD4T-JVV: accessed 28 January 2015), Pasquale

Sammartino, 30 Apr 1899; citing Italians to America Passenger Data File, 1855–1900, Ship Kaiser Wilhelm Ii, departed from Genoa, arrived in New York, New York, New York, United States, NAID identifier 1746097, National Archives and Records Administration, Washington, D.C.; "Massachusetts, Births, 1841–1915," index and images, *FamilySearch* (https://familysearch.org/pal:/MM9.1.1/FXX2-ZBG: accessed 27 January 2015), Pasquale Sammartino in entry for Mary Sammartino, 03 Jan 1897; citing Boston, Suffolk, Massachusetts, reference v 468 p 304, Massachusetts Archives, Boston; FHL microfilm 1,843,700. For documentation of the girls' Transatlantic journey and immigration, see "United States Italians to America Index, 1855–1900," index, *FamilySearch* (https://familysearch.org/pal:/MM9.1.1/KD4K-G21: accessed 27 January 2015), Raffaela Ottaviano, 30 Apr 1899; citing Italians to America Passenger Data File, 1855–1900, Ship Kaiser Wilhelm Ii, departed from Genoa, arrived in New York, New York, New York, United States, NAID identifier 1746097, National Archives and Records Administration, Washington, D.C; "United States Italians to America Index, 1855–1900," index, *FamilySearch* (https://familysearch.org/pal:/MM9.1.1/KD4K-GBK: accessed 27 January 2015), Ma. Francesca Ottaiano, 30 Apr 1899; citing Italians to America Passenger Data File, 1855–1900, Ship Kaiser Wilhelm Ii, departed from Genoa, arrived in New York, New York, New York, United States, NAID identifier 1746097, National Archives and Records Administration, Washington, D.C.

2. "Massachusetts, Births, 1841–1915," index and images, *FamilySearch* (https://familysearch.org/pal:/MM9.1.1/FX69-D1B: accessed 27 January 2015), Raffaella Ottiano, 01 Aug 1886; citing Boston, Massachusetts, reference, Massachusetts Archives, Boston; FHL microfilm 1,428,239.

3. "United States Census, 1900," index and images, *FamilySearch* (https://familysearch.org/pal:/MM9.1.1/M9YS-6KW: accessed 27 January 2015), Loti Oltiano [sic] in household of Antonio Oltiano, Precinct 7 Boston city Ward 2, Suffolk, Massachusetts, United States; citing sheet 3B, family 62, NARA microfilm publication T623 (Washington, D.C.: National Archives and Records Administration, n.d.); FHL microfilm 1,240,676.

4. In the 1900 U.S. census, Maddalena Ottiano is listed as the mother of six children, five of whom are living. See "United States Census, 1900," Madolina Oltiano [sic] in household of Antonio Oltiano. Antonio Ottiano's mother's full name is given in his death record. See "Massachusetts, Deaths, 1841–1915," index and images, *FamilySearch* (https://familysearch.org/pal:/MM9.1.1/N4X9-ZQ7: accessed 27 January 2015), Antonio Ottaiano, 12 Nov 1915; citing Boston, Massachusetts, 10219, State Archives, Boston; FHL microfilm 2,408,969. The name Ottiano as often is spelled Ottaiano or even Otteano, but for reasons of simplicity, I will use Ottiano consistently here.

5. "United States Census, 1900," Frances Oltiano [sic] in household of Antonio Oltiano.

6. "Massachusetts, Births, 1841–1915," index and images, *FamilySearch* (https://familysearch.org/pal:/MM9.1.1/FXWM-7VP: accessed 27 January 2015), Pasquale Ottaiano, 23 Oct 1892; citing Boston, Suffolk, Massachusetts, reference p 86, Massachusetts Archives, Boston; FHL microfilm 1,651,220.

7. "Massachusetts, Births and Christenings, 1639–1915," index, *FamilySearch* (https://familysearch.org/pal:/MM9.1.1/FHX2-KFS: accessed 27 January 2015), James Ottaiano, 03 Mar 1896; citing Boston, Suffolk, Massachusetts, 17221; FHL microfilm 740,448.

8. "Massachusetts, Births, 1841–1915," index and images, *FamilySearch* (https://familysearch.org/pal:/MM9.1.1/FXNX-F4M: accessed 27 January 2015), August Ottaiano, 30 Aug 1898; citing Boston, Suffolk, Massachusetts, reference 165, Massachusetts Archives, Boston; FHL microfilm 1,843,706.

9. "United States, New England Petitions for Naturalization Index, 1791–1906," index and images, *Family Search* (https://familysearch.org/pal:/MM9.1.1/VXRH-24W: accessed 28 January 2015), Antonio Ottaiano, 1896; citing Massachusetts, NARA microfilm publication M1299 (Washington, D.C.: National Archives and Records Administration, n.d.), roll 99; FHL microfilm 1,429,769.

10. "Massachusetts, Deaths, 1841–1915," index and images, *FamilySearch* (https://familysearch.org/pal:/MM9.1.1/NW5R-DYB: accessed 27 January 2015), Maddalena Ottaiano, 15 Oct 1914; citing Boston, Massachusetts, 519, State Archives, Boston; FHL microfilm 2,404,056. The year 1868 or 1870 is also indicated in some sources, but 1869 is the year given on her gravestone.

11. "United States Census, 1910," index and images, *FamilySearch* (https://familysearch.org/pal:/MM9.1.1/M2KN-7ZR: accessed 28 January 2015), Antonio Otteano, Boston Ward 2, Suffolk, Massachusetts, United States; citing enumeration district (ED) 1281, sheet 1B, family 14, NARA microfilm publication T624 (Washington, D.C.: National Archives and Records Administration, n.d.); FHL microfilm 1,374,627.

12. "United States Census, 1900," Antonio Oltiano; "United States Census, 1910," Antonio Otteano.

13. "United States, New England Petitions for Naturalization Index, 1791–1906," Antonio Ottaiano, 1896.

14. "United States Census, 1910," Antonio Otteano.

15. "Massachusetts, Marriages, 1841–1915," index and images, *FamilySearch* (https://familysearch.org/pal:/MM9.1.1/N462-8LW: accessed 28 January 2015), Carmeno De Stefano and Frances Ottiano, 02 Jan 1913; citing p 9 no 203, Boston,, Massachusetts, State Archives, Boston; FHL microfilm 2,409,946.

16. "Massachusetts, Deaths, 1841–1915," Maddalena Ottaiano, 15 Oct 1914.

17. http://www.stmichaelcemetery.com/history.html.

18. "Massachusetts, Deaths, 1841–1915," Antonio Ottaiano, 12 Nov 1915.

19. "United States Census, 1920," index and images, *FamilySearch* (https://familysearch.org/pal:/MM9.1.1/MFM4-PMM: accessed 27 January 2015), Francis Destefano in household of Carmine Destefano, Boston Ward 1, Suffolk, Massachusetts, United States; citing sheet 4A, family 70, NARA microfilm publication T625 (Washington, D.C.: National Archives and Records Administration, n.d.); FHL microfilm 1,820,728; "United States Census, 1930," index and images, *FamilySearch* (https://familysearch.org/pal:/MM9.1.1/XQ5L-DX3: accessed 28 January 2015), Frances Distefano in household of Carmine Distefano, Boston (Districts 1–250), Suffolk, Massachusetts, United States; citing enumeration district (ED) 0010, sheet 8B, family 144, line 87, NARA

microfilm publication T626 (Washington, D.C.: National Archives and Records Administration, 2002), roll 941; FHL microfilm 2,340,676.

20. "United States Census, 1920," index and images, *FamilySearch* (https://familysearch.org/pal:/MM9.1.1/MJBQ-QJ1: accessed 27 January 2015), Raphaella Ottiano in household of Catherine Pfeiffer, Manhattan Assembly District 10, New York, New York, United States; citing sheet 2A, family 22, NARA microfilm publication T625 (Washington, D.C.: National Archives and Records Administration, n.d.); FHL microfilm 1,821,203.

21. *Bondage* review, *Bedford Gazette* (May 19, 1933), p. 2.

22. Alexander Kahn, "Screen's Top Villainess, But Hates It," *Salt Lake Tribune* (December 12, 1940), p. 18, including quote from Ottiano.

23. Charles G. Sampas, "N.Y.—Hollywood," *Lowell Sun* (January 24, 1941), p. 2.

24. Springer and Hamilton, *They Had Faces Then*, p. 194.

25. Emily Wortis Leider, *Becoming Mae West* (N.p.: Da Capo Press, 2000), p. 199; www.ibdb.com. Leider says there were 323 performances on Broadway.

26. www.tcm.com, www.imdb.com.

27. Ottiano had acted in two silent films produced on the East coast prior to *Grand Hotel*.

28. www.ibdb.com.

29. www.tcm.com.

30. *Los Angeles City Directory 1936* (Los Angeles: Los Angeles Directory, 1936), p. 1388; *Los Angeles City Directory 1938* (Los Angeles: Los Angeles Directory, 1938), p. 1568; *Los Angeles City Directory 1939* (Los Angeles: Los Angeles Directory, 1939), p. 1537.

31. Quoted in her entry at www.allmovie.com.

32. *The Devil-Doll* review, *Kansas City Star* (July 19, 1936), n.pag.

33. *Monroe News-Star* (September 8, 1932), p. 3.

34. Leider, *Becoming Mae West*, p. 247.

35. Leider, p. 248.

36. Dee Lowrance, "From 'Wind' to 'Bell,'" *Salt Lake Tribune* (November 1, 1942), n.pag.

37. "Rafaela Ottiano, Actress, Is Dead," *New York Times* (August 18, 1942), p. 22; Quinlan, *Quinlan's Character Stars*, p. 330.

38. "Rafaela Ottiano," p. 22.

39. "United States Census, 1940," database with images, *FamilySearch* (https://familysearch.org/ark:/61903/1:1:K4JD-X1G: accessed 2 February 2016), Frances Destefano in household of Carmen Destefano, Ward 1, Boston, Boston City, Suffolk, Massachusetts, United States; citing enumeration district (ED) 15–13, sheet 5B, family 87, NARA digital publication T627 (Washington, D.C.: National Archives and Records Administration, 2012), roll 1657.

40. "United States Census, 1940," index and images, *FamilySearch* (https://familysearch.org/pal:/MM9.1.1/K4N3-MSV: accessed 27 January 2015), Augustine Ottiano, Winchester Town, Middlesex, Massachusetts, United States; citing enumeration district (ED) 9–637, sheet 5A, family 99, NARA digital publication T627 (Washington, D.C.: National Archives and Records Administration, 2012), roll 1622. Augustine Ottiano survived his sister by 45 years, dying on April 6, 1987 in Winchester, Massachusetts, as the last of the five Ottiano siblings. His wife Angeline died in 1982 and his son John in 1995. I have not been able to locate his daughter Jacqueline, born in about 1924, who may have married and changed her name.

41. I am grateful to Michael D. Sheehan, General Manager, St. Michael Cemetery Corp. for confirming that Rafaela Ottiano, her parents and brother Pasquale are buried in St. Michael Cemetery and for sending me photographs of the Ottiano family grave.

Tempe Pigott

1. Ragan, *Who's Who in Hollywood*, p. 751.

2. www.allmovie.guide.

3. www.allmovie.com, www.imdb.com.

4. More than 20 years later, Pigott and her screen son Gowland were "reunited" in *Kitty* (M. Leisen, Paramount, 1945) in which Pigott was uncredited as "woman in the window" and Gowland played a prison guard, also uncredited. It was his final film role and he died in London six years later.

5. "In Lima Theatres: Pirates Remain at Lyric," *Lima News* (November 15, 1926), p. 10.

6. *Terre Haute Saturday Spectator* (August 2, 1930), p. 22.

7. The house has made way for a parking lot, but two old-time apartment buildings are still standing next door. We have two earlier addresses for Pigott in Los Angeles: 529 W. 3rd St. in 1926 and 1447½ N. Fuller Ave. in 1936. Both these buildings have also been torn down, in fact the location of her 3rd St. home is now in a tunnel under Bunker Hill. See *Los Angeles City Directory 1936* (Los Angeles: Los Angeles Directory, 1936), p. 1446; movielanddirectory.com.

8. "United States Census, 1940," index and images, *FamilySearch* (https://familysearch.org/pal:/MM9.1.1/K9C6-Z4T: accessed 8 January 2015), Tempa Pigott in household of Mary T Tracy, Councilmanic District 2, Los Angeles, Los Angeles Township, Los Angeles, California, United States; citing enumeration district (ED) 60–133, sheet 4A, family 100, NARA digital publication T627 (Washington, D.C.: National Archives and Records Administration, 2012), roll 398.

9. "California, Los Angeles Passenger Lists, 1907–1948," index and images, *FamilySearch* (https://familysearch.org/pal:/MM9.1.1/KZQ4-VMR: accessed 8 January 2015), Tempe Pigott, 1937.

10. The show was *Perkins*, a new play by Douglass Murray, which ran for 23 performances at the Henry Miller's Theatre in October and November 1918. Violet Kemble-Cooper's father Frank and sister Lillian Kemble-Cooper, Ruth Chatterton, and actor-producer Henry Miller were also in the cast. See www.ibdb.com.

11. "California, Death Index, 1940–1997," index, *FamilySearch* (https://familysearch.org/pal:/MM9.1.1/VP47-D5G: accessed 7 January 2015), Tempe Pigott, 06 Oct 1962; Department of Public Health Services, Sacramento; www.imdb.com.

12. "California, Death Index, 1940–1997," Tempe Pigott, 06 Oct 1962.

Anita Sharp-Bolster

1. "Change of Cast," *Bridgeport Post* (August 22, 1951), p. 45; Alma R. Lockwood, "Acting is 100 Proof in

Case of Scotch at Westport," *Bridgeport Post* (August 28, 1951), p. 22.

2. "Wizard of Oz Opens Aug. 4," *Paris News* (July 31, 1952), p. 4.

3. "United States Social Security Death Index," index, *FamilySearch* (https://familysearch.org/pal:/MM9.1.1/VM27-3PF: accessed 13 March 2015), Anita Bolster, Jun 1985; citing U.S. Social Security Administration, *Death Master File*, database (Alexandria, Virginia: National Technical Information Service, ongoing); "Summer Visitor to Appear in Movie at Criterion Sun.," *Bar Harbor Times* (May 29, 1947), p. 1; Program notes, *Pygmalion*, Ethel Barrymore Theatre [1945] (*T-Clippings, Billy Rose Theatre Division, New York Public Library for the Performing Arts; henceforward abbreviated NYPL).

4. "Summer Visitor," *Bar Harbor Times*, p. 1.

5. "Summer Visitor," p. 1.

6. "Summer Visitor," p. 1; Program notes, *Where There's a Will*, John Golden Theatre [1939] (NYPL); Program notes, *Lady in Waiting*, Martin Beck Theatre [1940] (NYPL); Program notes, *Pygmalion*.

7. "Summer Visitor," p. 1; Program notes, *Where There's a Will*.

8. Program notes, *Where There's a Will*; Program notes, *Lady in Waiting*.

9. "Summer Visitor," p. 1.

10. "Summer Visitor," p. 1.

11. "Summer Visitor," p. 1.

12. Burns Mantle, *The Best Plays of 1938–39* (New York: Dodd, Mead, 1939), p. 451.

13. Mantle, p. 450.

14. Burns Mantle, *The Best Plays of 1939–40* (New York: Dodd, Mead, 1966), p. 450.

15. Mantle, p. 449.

16. Brooks Atkinson, *Lady in Waiting* review, *New York Times* (March 28, 1940), www.nytimes.com.

17. "On the Air Waves," *News-Palladium* (April 8, 1940), p. 10.

18. Louise Liebhardt, "Theatrical Chit-Chat," *San Marino Tribune* (August 14, 1941), p. 5.

19. www.tcm.com, www.imdb.com.

20. "'Saboteur' Calls for Bearded Lady," *Oakland Tribune* (September 24, 1942), p. C21.

21. Nissen, *The Films of Agnes Moorehead*, p. 112.

22. "Summer Visitor," *Bar Harbor Times*, p. 1.

23. www.ibdb.com.

24. www.ibdb.com.

25. See "Summer Visitor," *Bar Harbor Times*, p. 1; "About Town," *Bar Harbor Times* (June 26, 1947), p. 5; "In Comedy," *Bar Harbor Times* (February 5, 1948), p. 4; "About Town," *Bar Harbor Times* (April 1, 1948), p. 5.

26. www.tcm.com.

27. Bob MacKenzie, "On Television: He Should Have Ate and Run," *Oakland Tribune* (November 30, 1972), p. 18E.

28. MacKenzie, p. 18E.

29. "Florida, Death Index, 1877–1998," index, *FamilySearch* (https://familysearch.org/pal:/MM9.1.1/VV8Y-W8H: accessed 13 March 2015), Anita Bolster, 01 Jun 1985; from "Florida Death Index, 1877–1998," index, *Ancestry* (www.ancestry.com: 2004); citing vol., certificate number 56961, Florida Department of Health, Office of Vital Records, Jacksonville; "United States Social Security Death Index," Anita Bolster, Jun 1985.

Libby Taylor

1. "United States Social Security Death Index," index, *FamilySearch* (https://familysearch.org/pal:/MM9.1.1/V3GV-NTP: accessed 1 March 2015), Elizabeth A Taylor, 01 Jan 1990; citing U.S. Social Security Administration, *Death Master File*, database (Alexandria, Virginia: National Technical Information Service, ongoing).

2. "United States Census, 1940," index and images, *FamilySearch* (https://familysearch.org/pal:/MM9.1.1/K9WS-J6G: accessed 28 February 2015), Elizabeth Taylor, Tract 417, Pasadena, Pasadena Judicial Township, Los Angeles, California, United States; citing enumeration district (ED) 19–446, sheet 64B, family 529, NARA digital publication T627 (Washington, D.C.: National Archives and Records Administration, 2012), roll 240. Taylor's house in North Central Pasadena, like almost all her other homes that I have uncovered, is gone now. It stood where the playing fields of Robinson Park are currently to be found.

3. "United States Census, 1930," index and images, *FamilySearch* (https://familysearch.org/pal:/MM9.1.1/X4L7-SFN: accessed 28 February 2015), Elizabeth Taylor, Manhattan (Districts 0751–1000), New York, New York, United States; citing enumeration district (ED) 0917, sheet 24B, family 51, line 81, NARA microfilm publication T626 (Washington, D.C.: National Archives and Records Administration, 2002), roll 1573; FHL microfilm 2,341,308.

4. "United States Census, 1910," database with images, *FamilySearch* (https://familysearch.org/ark:/61903/1:1:MK8D-PLG: accessed 7 February 2016), Elizabeth A Taylor in household of Mattie Taylor, Chicago Ward 32, Cook, Illinois, United States; citing enumeration district (ED) ED 1386, sheet 10A, NARA microfilm publication T624 (Washington, D.C.: National Archives and Records Administration, n.d.); FHL microfilm 1,374,291.

5. "United States Census, 1920," database with images, *FamilySearch* (https://familysearch.org/ark:/61903/1:1:MJ34-TQV: accessed 7 February 2016), Mattie Taylor in household of William Bradley, Chicago Ward 7, Cook (Chicago), Illinois, United States; citing sheet 11A, NARA microfilm publication T625 (Washington, D.C.: National Archives and Records Administration, n.d.); FHL microfilm 1,820,316.

6. "United States World War I Draft Registration Cards, 1917–1918," index and images, *FamilySearch* (https://familysearch.org/pal:/MM9.1.1/K6ZS-LV7: accessed 1 March 2015), William Bradley, 1917–1918; citing Lynchburg County, Virginia, United States, NARA microfilm publication M1509 (Washington, D.C.: National Archives and Records Administration, n.d.); FHL microfilm 1,984,809.

7. "Illinois, Cook County Birth Certificates, 1878–1938," index, *FamilySearch* (https://familysearch.org/pal:/MM9.1.1/N73M-6RX: accessed 28 February 2015), William Ollie Bradley, 04 Jul 1918; citing Chicago, Cook, Illinois, United States, reference/certificate 22302, Cook County Courthouse, Chicago; FHL microfilm 1,308,835.

8. "United States Census, 1930," index and images, *FamilySearch* (https://familysearch.org/pal:/MM9.1.1/XST7-S6Q: accessed 28 February 2015), William Bradley, Chicago (Districts 0001–0250), Cook, Illinois, United States; citing enumeration district (ED) 0142,

sheet 13A, family 250, line 42, NARA microfilm publication T626 (Washington, D.C.: National Archives and Records Administration, 2002), roll 420; FHL microfilm 2,340,155.

9. "United States Census, 1930," index and images, *FamilySearch* (https://familysearch.org/pal:/MM9.1.1/XSLK-NS5: accessed 1 March 2015), Mattie Taylor, Chicago (Districts 0501–0750), Cook, Illinois, United States; citing enumeration district (ED) 0611, sheet 2B, family 43, line 57, NARA microfilm publication T626 (Washington, D.C.: National Archives and Records Administration, 2002), roll 442; FHL microfilm 2,340,177.

10. "Illinois Deaths and Stillbirths, 1916–1947," index, *FamilySearch* (https://familysearch.org/pal:/MM9.1.1/N3C8-M5M: accessed 28 February 2015), Mattie Taylor, 09 Jun 1934; Public Board of Health, Archives, Springfield; FHL microfilm 1,907,319.

11. George Eels and Stanley Musgrove, *Mae West: A Biography* (New York: William Morrow, 1982), p. 123; Jill Watts, *Mae West: An Icon in Black and White* (Oxford: Oxford University Press, 2001), p. 155, 168.

12. Watts, p. 168.

13. Roscoe Fawcett, "Screen Oddities," *Manitowoc Herald-Times* (August 30, 1933), p. 12.

14. www.tcm.com.

15. "Servants Rule Lives of Film Celebrities," *Uniontown News Standard* (November 5, 1933), p. 2.

16. www.tcm.com.

17. "In Hollywood You'd Find," *Sandusky Register* (April 22, 1934), p. 2.

18. Hubbard Keavy, "Hollywood Has Star Servants, Too," *Moberley Monitor-Index and Democrat* (April 27, 1934), p. 10.

19. Walter R. Clausen, "Heart [sic] Meals Are Favored by Greta Garbo and Other Notables of Hollywood," *Reno Evening Gazette* (September 8, 1934), p. 8.

20. movielanddirectory.com.

21. Thomas Cripps, *Slow Fade to Black: The Negro in American Film, 1900–1942* (New York: Oxford University Press, 1977), p. 109.

22. Cripps, p. 109.

23. "Gossip of the Movie Lots," *Galveston Guide* (April 17, 1937), p. 2.

24. Violet LeVoit, "Belle of the Nineties (1934)," www.tcm.com.

25. "Negro Songs in Mae West Film," *Mason City Globe-Gazette* (September 21, 1934), p. 12.

26. "Hollywood Chatter," *Lowell Sun* (June 30, 1934), p. 5.

27. For interesting discussions of racial representation and politics in Mae West's films in general and *Belle of the Nineties* in particular, see Ramona Curry, *Too Much of a Good Thing: Mae West as Cultural Icon* (Minneapolis and London: University of Minnesota Press, 1996), pp. 12–17, 84–90; and Watts, *Mae West.*

28. Watts, p. 186.

29. *New York Herald Tribune* (December 13, 1934) (*T-Clippings, Billy Rose Theatre Division, New York Public Library for the Performing Arts).

30. "Mae's Maid Scores," *Salt Lake Tribune* (January 20, 1935), p. C11.

31. Leicester Wagner, "Hollywood Film Shop," *Nevada State Journal* (December 28, 1934), p. 5.

32. "News and Comment of Stage and Screen," *Fitchburg Sentinel* (May 25, 1935), p. 10.

33. *Chester Times* (June 7, 1935), p. 21.

34. Emily Wortis Leider, *Becoming Mae West* (N.p.: Da Capo Press, 2000), p. 306.

35. Quoted in Leider, p. 306.

36. Willa Okker, "The Hollywood Parade," *San Mateo Times* (November 11, 1935), p. 6.

37. Douglas W. Churchill, "Screen News Here and in Hollywood," *New York Times* (June 30, 1939), www.nytimes.com.

38. Sam Woolford, "Luise Rainer Pulls One Out of the Coals," *San Antonio Light* (July 4, 1938), p. 11A.

Zeffie Tilbury

1. Frank Capra, *The Name Above the Title* (New York: Vintage, 1985), p. 149.

2. Springer and Hamilton, *They Had Faces Then*, p. 245.

3. Ragan, *Who's Who in Hollywood*, p. 807.

4. www.allmovie.com.

5. Marlene Dietrich, *Marlene*, trans. Salvator Attanasio (New York: Avon Books, 1990), p. 174.

6. Steven Bach, *Marlene Dietrich: Life and Legend* (New York: William Morrow, 1992), p. 208; Jeffrey Meyers, *Gary Cooper: American Hero* (New York: William Morrow, 1998), p. 113.

7. www.allmovie.com.

8. It is worth remembering that 19th-century burlesque was a form of theater which might involve a certain degree of undress, but which was not the same thing as the later burlesque of the Gypsy Rose Lee variety.

9. Olive Cooper, who was the screenwriter on both *Rhythm in the Clouds* and *Sheriff of Tombstone*, specialized in westerns for Roy Rogers and Gene Autry. George Stevens directed his great-aunt Zeffie in *Bachelor Bait* (RKO, 1934), *Alice Adams* (RKO, 1935), and the short film *Ocean Swells* (RKO, 1934). He was probably the one who got her work at RKO.

10. "England and Wales, Birth Registration Index, 1837–2008," index, *FamilySearch* (https://familysearch.org/pal:/MM9.1.1/2XM9-XWY: accessed 17 February 2015), James Robert Zeffie Agnes Tilburn [sic], 1863; from "England & Wales Births, 1837–2006," index, *findmypast* (http://www.findmypast.com: 2012); citing Birth Registration, Marylebone, London, England, citing General Register Office, Southport, England; "England Births and Christenings, 1538–1975," index, *FamilySearch* (https://familysearch.org/pal:/MM9.1.1/NPYY-R7H: accessed 17 February 2015), Ziffie Agnes Lydia Tilbury, 22 Feb 1864; citing HOLY TRINITY, PADDINGTON, LONDON, ENGLAND, reference; FHL microfilm 804,224; "California, Death Index, 1940–1997," index, *FamilySearch* (https://familysearch.org/pal:/MM9.1.1/VPD6-GWF: accessed 17 February 2015), Zeffie Tilbury, 22 Jul 1950; Department of Public Health Services, Sacramento; Parker, *Who's Who in the Theatre*, p. 1325.

11. Kurt Gänzl, *Lydia Thompson: Queen of Burlesque* (New York and London: Routledge, 2002), p. 7, 10.

12. Gänzl, pp. 53–54, 59–60.

13. Gänzl, p. 196, 219.

14. Gänzl, pp. 219–20, 221, www.findagrave.com.

15. www.ibdb.com.

16. "England and Wales, Marriage Registration Index,

1837–2005," index, *FamilySearch* (https://familysearch.org/pal:/MM9.1.1/2DYF-DLF: accessed 17 February 2015), Zeffie Agnes L Tilbury, 1887; from "England & Wales Marriages, 1837–2005," index, *findmypast* (http://www.findmypast.com: 2012); citing Marriage, West Derby, Lancashire, England, General Register Office, Southport, England; Parker, *Who's Who in the Theatre*, p. 1325.

17. www.ibdb.com.

18. "United States Census, 1870," index and images, *FamilySearch* (https://familysearch.org/pal:/MM9.1.1/MN6Y-Q75: accessed 17 February 2015), Louis Woodthorpe in household of John Woodthorpe, California, United States; citing p. 169, family 1339, NARA microfilm publication M593 (Washington, D.C.: National Archives and Records Administration, n.d.); FHL microfilm 545,583.

19. "United States Census, 1880," index and images, *FamilySearch* (https://familysearch.org/pal:/MM9.1.1/M6PX-GGH: accessed 17 February 2015), Louis Woodthorpe in household of John W Woodthorpe, San Francisco, San Francisco, California, United States; citing enumeration district 213, sheet 256B, NARA microfilm publication T9 (Washington, D.C.: National Archives and Records Administration, n.d.), roll 0079; FHL microfilm 1,254,079; "United States Census, 1900," index and images, *FamilySearch* (https://familysearch.org/pal:/MM9.1.1/MMPJ-4VS: accessed 17 February 2015), L E Woodthorpe in household of Eliza Waterhouse, Precinct 2 Seattle city Ward 4, King, Washington, United States; citing sheet 10A, family 151, NARA microfilm publication T623 (Washington, D.C.: National Archives and Records Administration, n.d.); FHL microfilm 1,241,745.

20. The 1910 U.S. Census makes it clear they have been married five years. See "United States Census, 1910," index and images, *FamilySearch* (https://familysearch.org/pal:/MM9.1.1/MVLZ-HB9: accessed 17 February 2015), Bud Woodthorpe in household of Nathaniel Goodwin, Santa Monica Ward 2, Los Angeles, California, United States; citing enumeration district (ED) 343, sheet 20A, family 533, NARA microfilm publication T624 (Washington, D.C.: National Archives and Records Administration, n.d.); FHL microfilm 1,374,100.

21. "United States Census, 1910," Bud Woodthorpe in the household of Nathaniel Goodwin.

22. Parker, *Who's Who in the Theatre*, p. 1325; www.ibdb.com.

23. "Michigan, Deaths and Burials, 1800–1995," index, *FamilySearch* (https://familysearch.org/pal:/MM9.1.1/FHLG-8JD: accessed 17 February 2015), Louis E. Woodthrope, 08 Apr 1915; citing Saginaw, Saginaw, Michigan, reference v 1908–1917 p 211; FHL microfilm 967,177.

24. www.ibdb.com.

25. movielanddirectory.com.

26. www.ibdb.com.

27. Parker, *Who's Who in the Theatre*, p. 1325.

28. *Los Angeles City Directory 1932* (Los Angeles: Los Angeles Directory, 1932), p. 2110; movielanddirectory.com.

29. Parker, *Who's Who in the Theatre*, p. 1326.

30. *Los Angeles City Directory 1936* (Los Angeles: Los Angeles Directory, 1936), p. 2057; *Los Angeles City Directory 1942* (Los Angeles: Los Angeles Directory, 1942), p. 2395.

31. "United States Census, 1940," index and images, *FamilySearch* (https://familysearch.org/pal:/MM9.1.1/K9C6-XJG: accessed 17 February 2015), Zeffie Tilbury, Councilmanic District 2, Los Angeles, Los Angeles Township, Los Angeles, California, United States; citing enumeration district (ED) 60–137, sheet 81B, family, NARA digital publication T627 (Washington, D.C.: National Archives and Records Administration, 2012), roll 399. The entry for Elizabeth Patterson is on the same sheet of the census.

32. "California, Death Index, 1940–1997," Zeffie Tilbury, 22 Jul 1950; "Zeffie Tilbury," unnamed, undated obituary [*Variety*?] (*T-Clippings, Billy Rose Theatre Division, New York Public Library for the Performing Arts).

33. www.findagrave.com.

Norma Varden

1. "California, Southern District Court (Central) Naturalization Index, 1915–1976," database with images, *FamilySearch* (https://familysearch.org/ark:/61903/1:1:KX3B-W28: accessed 25 July 2015), Norma Or Norma Varden Varden Or Shackleton, 1949; citing Los Angeles, Los Angeles, California, United States, National Archives and Records Service, Los Angeles Branch, Laguna Niguel; FHL microfilm 1,558,694; www.zillow.com.

2. Her address there was 6941 Camrose Dr. See *Los Angeles City Directory 1942* (Los Angeles: Los Angeles Directory, 1942), p. 2453.

3. *Los Angeles City Directory 1936* (Los Angeles: Los Angeles Directory, 1936), p. 1676.

4. "United States Census, 1940," database with images, *FamilySearch* (https://familysearch.org/ark:/61903/1:1:K97Z-TMG: accessed 25 July 2015), Harold Minjir, Beverly Hills Judicial Township, Los Angeles, California, United States; citing enumeration district (ED) 19–67, sheet 6B, family 169, NARA digital publication T627 (Washington, D.C.: National Archives and Records Administration, 2012), roll 222; movielanddirectory.com.

5. Boze Hadleigh, *Conversations with My Elders* (New York: St. Martin's Press, 1986), p. 24.

6. Jim Bigwood, "Norma Varden," *Film Fan Monthly* no. 165 (March 1975), p. 21.

7. "England and Wales Birth Registration Index, 1837–2008," database, *FamilySearch* (https://familysearch.org/ark:/61903/1:1:2F49-3KL: accessed 30 July 2015), Norma Varden Shackleton, 1898; from "England & Wales Births, 1837–2006," database, *findmypast* (http://www.findmypast.com: 2012); citing Birth Registration, Wandsworth, London, England, citing General Register Office, Southport, England; "California Death Index, 1940–1997," database, *FamilySearch* (https://familysearch.org/ark:/61903/1:1:VPXL-DKS: accessed 30 July 2015), Norma Varden, 19 Jan 1989; Department of Public Health Services, Sacramento; "United States Social Security Death Index," database, *FamilySearch* (https://familysearch.org/ark:/61903/1:1:V3KV-H4W: accessed 30 July 2015), Norma Varden, 19 Jan 1989; citing U.S. Social Security Administration, *Death Master File*, database (Alexandria, Virginia: National Technical Information Service, ongoing).

8. "England and Wales Birth Registration Index, 1837–2008," database, *FamilySearch* (https://familysearch.org/ark:/61903/1:1:2XDC-RMN: accessed 30 July 2015), Julia Maria Shackleton, 1876; from "England & Wales Births, 1837–2006," database, *findmypast* (http://www.findmypast.com: 2012); citing Birth Registration, Lambeth, London, England, citing General Register Office, Southport, England; "California Death Index, 1940–1997," database, *FamilySearch* (https://familysearch.org/ark:/61903/1:1:VPKT-59G: accessed 30 July 2015), Julia M Shackleton, 14 Sep 1969; Department of Public Health Services, Sacramento.

9. "England and Wales Census, 1901," database, *FamilySearch* (https://familysearch.org/ark:/61903/1:1:X9CD-4F6: accessed 30 July 2015), Z Shackleton, Streatham, London, Middlesex, England; from "1901 England, Scotland and Wales census," database and images, *findmypast* (http://www.findmypast.com: n.d.); citing county, registration district, Streatham subdistrict, PRO RG 13, The National Archives, Kew, Surrey; "England and Wales Census, 1901," database, *FamilySearch* (https://familysearch.org/ark:/61903/1:1:X9CD-4FX: accessed 30 July 2015), Julia Shackleton, Streatham, London, Middlesex, England; from "1901 England, Scotland and Wales census," database and images, *findmypast* (http://www.findmypast.com: n.d.); citing county, registration district, Streatham subdistrict, PRO RG 13, The National Archives, Kew, Surrey; "England and Wales Census, 1901," database, *FamilySearch* (https://familysearch.org/ark:/61903/1:1:X9CD-4FF: accessed 30 July 2015), Norman [sic] Shackleton, Streatham, London, Middlesex, England; from "1901 England, Scotland and Wales census," database and images, *findmypast* (http://www.findmypast.com: n.d.); citing county, registration district, Streatham subdistrict, PRO RG 13, The National Archives, Kew, Surrey.

10. "California, Los Angeles Passenger Lists, 1907–1948," database with images, *FamilySearch* (https://familysearch.org/ark:/61903/1:1:KZQZ-DJ8: accessed 30 July 2015), Julia Marie Shackleton, 1939; citing Immigration, ship name Pacific President, NARA microfilm publication M1764 (Washington, D.C.: National Archives and Records Administration, n.d.), roll 98; FHL microfilm 1,734,702; "United States Census, 1940," database with images, *FamilySearch* (https://familysearch.org/ark:/61903/1:1:K97C-K5V: accessed 30 July 2015), Julia Shackelton [sic] in household of Noma [sic] Varden, Tract 387, West Hollywood, Beverly Hills Judicial Township, Los Angeles, California, United States; citing enumeration district (ED) 19–63, sheet 6A, family 147, NARA digital publication T627 (Washington, D.C.: National Archives and Records Administration, 2012), roll 222.

11. Bigwood, "Norma Varden," pp. 21–24. See also "English Actress Makes Debut at the Curran," *Oakland Tribune* (November 8, 1942), p. B9 for a brief survey of Varden's career in England.

12. "New York, New York Passenger and Crew Lists, 1909, 1925–1957," database with images, *FamilySearch* (https://familysearch.org/ark:/61903/1:1:246G-44L: accessed 30 July 2015), Norma Varden, 1928; citing Immigration, New York, New York, United States, NARA microfilm publication T715 (Washington, D.C.: National Archives and Records Administration, n.d.); FHL microfilm 1,755,976.

13. "Michigan, Detroit Manifests of Arrivals at the Port of Detroit, 1906–1954," database with images, *FamilySearch* (https://familysearch.org/ark:/61903/1:1:K8MZ-M68: accessed 30 July 2015), Norma V Shackleton, 01 Jul 1939; citing NARA microfilm publication M1478 (Washington, D.C.: National Archives and Records Administration, n.d.); FHL microfilm 1,490,541.

14. "California, Los Angeles Passenger Lists, 1907–1948," Julia Marie Shackleton, 1939; www.tcm.com.

15. "United States Census, 1940," Julia Shackelton [sic] in household of Noma [sic] Varden.

16. Bigwood, "Norma Varden," p. 24.

17. Quoted in Bigwood, p. 28.

18. Bracken quoted in Bigwood, p. 26.

19. "California Death Index, 1940–1997," Julia M Shackleton, 14 Sep 1969; "Norma Varden, 90, TV and Film Actress," *New York Times* (January 22, 1989), p. 26.

20. Ragan, *Who's Who in Hollywood*, p. 488.

21. Bigwood, "Norma Varden," p. 28.

22. "California Death Index, 1940–1997," Norma Varden, 19 Jan 1989; "United States Social Security Death Index," Norma Varden, 19 Jan 1989; "Norma Varden," *New York Times*, p. 26.

23. www.findagrave.com.

Nydia Westman

1. Jack O'Brian, "On Broadway," *Mansfield News Journal* (September 12, 1970), p. 17.

2. Springer and Hamilton, *They Had Faces Then*, p. 252.

3. Ragan, *Who's Who in Hollywood*, p. 828.

4. Quinlan, *Quinlan's Character Stars*, p. 453.

5. www.allmovie.com.

6. Vic Wilmot, "On the Town with Vic Wilmot," *Arizona Republic* (January 27, 1965), p. 22.

7. Jimmie Fidler, "Movieland," *Appleton Post-Crescent* (March 1, 1940), p. 4.

8. "California, Death Index, 1940–1997," index, *FamilySearch* (https://familysearch.org/pal:/MM9.1.1/VPHD-QXV: accessed 15 January 2015), Nydia E Westman, 23 May 1970; Department of Public Health Services, Sacramento; "Notice to Creditors," *Van Nuys News* (June 30, 1979): n.pag. Some sources mistakenly give her year of birth as 1907.

9. Whitney Williams, "She Doesn't Need Beauty to Succeed," *Oakland Tribune Screen and Radio Weekly* (December 30, 1934), p. 10.

10. Williams, "She Doesn't Need Beauty," p. 10; "Pennsylvania, County Marriages, 1885–1950," index and images, *FamilySearch* (https://familysearch.org/pal:/MM9.1.1/VF92-6S9: accessed 15 January 2015), Theodore Westman and Lillie Wren, 15 Jan 1900; citing Marriage, Pennsylvania, county courthouses, Pennsylvania; FHL microfilm 878,593.

11. See the news item in the *Boston Sunday Globe* (June 24, 1900), p. 16 about their first Boston appearance, in the "rural playlet" "In Hayin' Time" at Keith's Theatre ("said to be a gem of its kind"); and a similar item in the *Syracuse Post Standard* (March 12, 1901), p. 5, calling it "a charming sketch ... that breathes romance from end to end."

12. Williams, "She Doesn't Need Beauty," p. 10.

13. "United States Census, 1910," index and images,

FamilySearch (https://familysearch.org/pal:/MM9.1.1/M5C5-RQK: accessed 15 January 2015), Nydia E Westman in household of Theodore Westman, Brooklyn Ward 24, Kings, New York, United States; citing enumeration district (ED) 657, sheet 10A, family 249, NARA microfilm publication T624, National Archives and Records Administration, Washington, D.C.; FHL microfilm 1,374,988.

14. Parker, *Who's Who in the Theatre*, p. 1410; Williams, "She Doesn't Need Beauty," p. 10.

15. Parker, p. 1410; Williams, p. 10.

16. "United States Census, 1920," index and images, *FamilySearch* (https://familysearch.org/pal:/MM9.1.1/MV3W-BGV: accessed 15 January 2015), Neville Westman in household of William Johnson, Mount Pleasant, Westchester, New York, United States; citing sheet 8A, family 159, NARA microfilm publication T625, National Archives and Records Administration, Washington, D.C.; FHL microfilm 1,821,276.

17. www.imdb.com.

18. www.ibdb.com, www.imdb.com.

19. "Whole Westman Family Theatrical So Nydia Does Her Part In Films," *Hattiesburg American* (October 27, 1934), p. 4.

20. Parker, *Who's Who in the Theatre*, p. 1410; www.ibdb.com.

21. "Nydia Westman, Star of 'Pigs,'" *Escabana Daily Press* (June 3, 1926), p. 3.

22. www.imdb.com.

23. "United States Census, 1900," index and images, *FamilySearch* (https://familysearch.org/pal:/MM9.1.1/MM62-9VH: accessed 15 January 2015), Salathiel Sparks in household of John Sparks, Seal Township Piketon village, Pike, Ohio, United States; citing sheet 3A, family 60, NARA microfilm publication T623 (Washington, D.C.: National Archives and Records Administration, n.d.); FHL microfilm 1,241,314; "United States Census, 1910," index and images, *FamilySearch* (https://familysearch.org/pal:/MM9.1.1/ML8N-1FV: accessed 15 January 2015), Salathiel W Sparks in household of John H Sparks, Tiffin, Adams, Ohio, United States; citing enumeration district (ED) 21, sheet 10B, family 290, NARA microfilm publication T624, National Archives and Records Administration, Washington, D.C.; FHL microfilm 1,375,163.

24. www.imdb.com.

25. *Bar Harbor Times* (November 14, 1928), p. 6.

26. "North Carolina Marriages, 1759–1979," database, *FamilySearch* (https://familysearch.org/ark:/61903/1:1:F867-RYP: accessed 3 February 2016), Sam A. Burton and Lolita A. Westman, 12 Oct 1925; citing Winston-Salem, Forsyth, NC, reference; FHL microfilm 899,633; "United States Census, 1930," index and images, *FamilySearch* (https://familysearch.org/pal:/MM9.1.1/XCJB-43B: accessed 15 January 2015), Lolita W Burton in household of Sam A Burton, Los Angeles (Districts 0001–0250), Los Angeles, California, United States; citing enumeration district (ED) 0044, sheet 1B, family 17, line 56, NARA microfilm publication T626 (Washington, D.C.: National Archives and Records Administration, 2002), roll 133; FHL microfilm 2,339,868.

27. Williams, "She Doesn't Need Beauty," p. 10.

28. Edna Silverton, "They Don't Want To Be Stars," *Oakland Tribune Screen and Radio Weekly* (September 13, 1936), p. 9.

29. Springer and Hamilton, *They Had Faces Then*, p. 337.

30. "United States Census, 1940," index and images, *FamilySearch* (https://familysearch.org/pal:/MM9.1.1/KWDX-5NS: accessed 15 January 2015), Robyna J Sparks in household of Merwin Dean Fields, Seaman Village, Scott Township, Adams, Ohio, United States; citing enumeration district (ED) 1–15, sheet 61A, family 73, NARA digital publication T627 (Washington, D.C.: National Archives and Records Administration, 2012), roll 3019.

31. "United States Census, 1940," index and images, *FamilySearch* (https://familysearch.org/pal:/MM9.1.1/K9CD-NRJ: accessed 15 January 2015), Nydia Westman, Councilmanic District 2, Los Angeles, Los Angeles Township, Los Angeles, California, United States; citing enumeration district (ED) 60–119, sheet 21B, family 494, NARA digital publication T627 (Washington, D.C.: National Archives and Records Administration, 2012), roll 398.

32. www.imdb.com.

33. www.imdb.com.

34. See "Ex-Hoofer Kelly Plays TV's Gene-ial Priest," *Appleton Sunday Post-Crescent* (October 28, 1962), p. 16, which includes a caricature of Kelly, Carroll, and Westman.

35. *Portland Sunday Telegram and Sunday Press Herald* (July 30, 1950), p. 18; *Portland Sunday Telegram* (August 6, 1950), p. 18.

36. Quoted in "Beauty after Forty," *Lubbock Evening Journal* (February 28, 1952), n.pag.

37. "California, Death Index, 1940–1997," Nydia E Westman, 23 May 1970; "United States Social Security Death Index," index, *FamilySearch* (https://familysearch.org/pal:/MM9.1.1/JTZZ-4Y9: accessed 15 January 2015), Nydia Westman, May 1970; citing U.S. Social Security Administration, *Death Master File*, database (Alexandria, Virginia: National Technical Information Service, ongoing); *Sheboygan Press* (May 25, 1970), p. 4; "Nydia Westman, 62, Dies from Cancer," *Pasadena Star-News* (May 25 1970), p. 19; www.findagrave.com.

Margaret Wycherly

1. "England and Wales Census, 1881," index, *FamilySearch* (https://familysearch.org/pal:/MM9.1.1/XQW9-SLD: accessed 10 February 2015), Margaret L De Wolfe in household of Caroline De Wolfe, Wendover, Buckinghamshire, England; from "1881 England, Scotland and Wales census," index and images, *findmypast* (www.findmypast.com: n.d.); citing p., PRO RG 11/, The National Archives, Kew, Surrey; FHL microfilm; Parker, *Who's Who in the Theatre*, p. 1454.

2. "England and Wales Census, 1881," Margaret L De Wolfe.

3. Parker, *Who's Who in the Theatre*, p. 1454.

4. "England and Wales Census, 1891," index, *FamilySearch* (https://familysearch.org/pal:/MM9.1.1/WBNT-XT2: accessed 10 February 2015), Caroline M De Wolfe; "United States Census, 1900," Caroline M De Wolfe; "United States Census, 1910," index and images, *FamilySearch* (https://familysearch.org/pal:/MM9.1.1/M53N-HMM: accessed 10 February 2015), Margaret Veiller in household of Elizabeth D Veiller, Manhattan Ward 12,

New York, New York, United States; citing enumeration district (ED) 481, sheet 16B, family 324, NARA microfilm publication T624 (Washington, D.C.: National Archives and Records Administration, n.d.); FHL microfilm 1,375,033.

5. "England and Wales Census, 1881," Caroline De Wolfe.

6. "United States Census, 1900," index and images, *FamilySearch* (https://familysearch.org/pal:/MM9.1.1/MSVG-C74: accessed 10 February 2015), Caroline M De Wolfe in household of William M Evarts, Borough of Manhattan, Election District 2 New York City Ward 18, New York County, New York, United States; citing sheet 8A, family 82, NARA microfilm publication T623 (Washington, D.C.: National Archives and Records Administration, n.d.); FHL microfilm 1,241,101.

7. "United States Census, 1920," index and images, *FamilySearch* (https://familysearch.org/pal:/MM9.1.1/MJBS-WJB: accessed 10 February 2015), Caroline M De Wolfe in household of John Harris, Manhattan Assembly District 10, New York, New York, United States; citing sheet 4A, family 76, NARA microfilm publication T625 (Washington, D.C.: National Archives and Records Administration, n.d.); FHL microfilm 1,821,202.

8. www.findagrave.com.

9. "United States Census, 1910," Margaret Veiller in the household of Elizabeth D Veiller.

10. The address of this apartment building today is 26 91st St. and the only entrance is on 91st St.

11. "Philip Bayard Veiller," *New York Times* (September 4, 1906), p. 9.

12. Parker, *Who's Who in the Theatre*, p. 1454. Bayard Veiller's *New York Times* obituary states that they were married in 1901. See "Bayard Veiller, Writer of Plays," *New York Times* (January 17, 1943), p. 21.

13. Walter Prichard Eaton, "Margaret Wycherly: In Remembrance," *Berkshire Eagle* (June 13, 1956), p. 27.

14. See Franklin Fyles, "New York's Only New Offering Has Even Chance to Win or Fail," *Washington Post* (May 5, 1907), p. 2; www.ibdb.com.

15. "A Detective Play by Bayard Veiller," *New York Times* (November 21, 1916), www.nytimes.com.

16. *Syracuse Herald* (July 21, 1918), p. 3; www.ibdb.com, www.findagrave.com.

17. "California, San Francisco Passenger Lists, 1893–1953," index and images, *FamilySearch* (https://familysearch.org/pal:/MM9.1.1/KX4N-HTP: accessed 10 February 2015), Margaret Bayard Veiller, 1918; citing San Francisco, California, United States, NARA microfilm publication M1410 (Washington, D.C.: National Archives and Records Administration, n.d.); FHL microfilm 1,465,684.

18. Alexander Woollcott, *Jane Clegg* review, *New York Times* (February 25, 1920), p. 14.

19. Alexander Woollcott, *The Verge* review, *New York Times* (November 15, 1921), p. 27.

20. www.ibdb.com.

21. "Miss Wycherly, Actress, Was 74," *New York Times* (June 7, 1956), p. 31.

22. "New York, New York Passenger and Crew Lists, 1909, 1925–1957," index and images, *FamilySearch* (https://familysearch.org/pal:/MM9.1.1/KXMF-CV7: accessed 10 February 2015), Margaret Wycherly Veiller, 1926; citing Immigration, New York, New York, United States, NARA microfilm publication T715 (Washington, D.C.: National Archives and Records Administration, n.d.); FHL microfilm 1,755,659; "New York, New York Passenger and Crew Lists, 1909, 1925–1957," index and images, *FamilySearch* (https://familysearch.org/pal:/MM9.1.1/KXLT-P84: accessed 10 February 2015), Margaret Veiller, 1927; citing Immigration, New York, New York, United States, NARA microfilm publication T715 (Washington, D.C.: National Archives and Records Administration, n.d.); FHL microfilm 1,755,856.

23. "New York, New York Passenger and Crew Lists, 1909, 1925–1957," index and images, *FamilySearch* (https://familysearch.org/pal:/MM9.1.1/246Y-J1T: accessed 10 February 2015), Margaret Wycherly, 1928; citing Immigration, New York, New York, United States, NARA microfilm publication T715 (Washington, D.C.: National Archives and Records Administration, n.d.); FHL microfilm 1,756,029.

24. Wycherly gives this address in several passenger lists between 1930 and 1953. See, for example, "New York, New York Passenger and Crew Lists, 1909, 1925–1957," index and images, *FamilySearch* (https://familysearch.org/pal:/MM9.1.1/24FB-2CJ: accessed 10 February 2015), Margaret Veiller, 1930; citing Immigration, New York, New York, United States, NARA microfilm publication T715 (Washington, D.C.: National Archives and Records Administration, n.d.); FHL microfilm 1,756,575; and "New York, New York Passenger and Crew Lists, 1909, 1925–1957," index and images, *FamilySearch* (https://familysearch.org/pal:/MM9.1.1/2H7J-2GP: accessed 10 February 2015), Margaret Wycherly, 1953; citing Immigration, New York City, New York, United States, NARA microfilm publication T715 (Washington, D.C.: National Archives and Records Administration, n.d.); FHL microfilm 2,321,805. Her obituary in the *New York Times*, gives her final home address. See "Miss Wycherly," *New York Times*, p. 31. This appears also to have been a row house, but it has been razed to make way for the entrance courtyard of the modern apartment complex "Stonehenge Gardens."

25. "United States Census, 1940," index and images, *FamilySearch* (https://familysearch.org/pal:/MM9.1.1/KQT6-4BS: accessed 10 February 2015), Margaret Wycherly, Assembly District 10, Manhattan, New York City, New York, New York, United States; citing enumeration district (ED) 31–888, sheet 65B, family 299, NARA digital publication T627 (Washington, D.C.: National Archives and Records Administration, 2012), roll 2645.

26. "United States Census, 1940," index and images, *FamilySearch* (https://familysearch.org/pal:/MM9.1.1/K974-TKK: accessed 10 February 2015), Anthony De W Veiller, Tract 381, Beverly Hills, Beverly Hills Judicial Township, Los Angeles, California, United States; citing enumeration district (ED) 19–39, sheet 1B, family 13, NARA digital publication T627 (Washington, D.C.: National Archives and Records Administration, 2012), roll 221; "California, County Marriages, 1850–1952," index and images, *FamilySearch* (https://familysearch.org/pal:/MM9.1.1/K8K2-CWC: accessed 10 February 2015), Anthony De Wolfe Veiller and Grace Dorothy Hornburg, 10 Jan 1948; citing Los Angeles, California, United States, county courthouses, California; FHL microfilm 2,116,126.

27. www.imdb.com; "California, Birth Index, 1905–1995," index, *FamilySearch* (https://familysearch.org/

pal:/MM9.1.1/V2Q8-8LB: accessed 10 February 2015), Caroline Margaret Veiller, 17 Mar 1936; citing Los Angeles, California, United States, Department of Health Services, Vital Statistics Department, Sacramento.

28. www.imdb.com.

29. "California, County Marriages, 1850–1952," Anthony De Wolfe Veiller and Grace Dorothy Hornburg, 10 Jan 1948; "California, Birth Index, 1905–1995," index, *FamilySearch* (https://familysearch.org/pal:/MM9.1.1/VG81-BKX: accessed 10 February 2015), Philip Bayard Veiller, 22 Nov 1948; citing Los Angeles, California, United States, Department of Health Services, Vital Statistics Department, Sacramento.

30. Quoted in "Margaret Wycherly Dies; On Stage Half a Century," *New York Herald Tribune* (June 7, 1956) (*T-Clippings, Billy Rose Theatre Division, New York Public Library for the Performing Arts).

31. "Margaret Wycherly Dies."

32. www.ibdb.com.

33. Sam Zolotov, "Two Plays Tonight Involve the Bard; Lead for a Month," *New York Times* (June 3, 1946), p. 34.

34. Eaton, "Margaret Wycherly: In Remembrance," p. 27.

35. Tennessee Williams, *The Selected Letters of Tennessee Williams: Vol. II, 1945–1957*, ed. Albert J. Devlin (New York: New Directions, 2004), p. 54.

36. www.ibdb.com.

37. "Miss Wycherly," *New York Times*, p. 31. The *Times* was mistaken in claiming Wycherly was 74, but that was the common belief at the time. The former St. Clare's Hospital also has a facade facing 51st St. The hospital was taken over and renamed St. Vincent's Midtown Hospital in 2003 and was closed by the Berger Commission on August 31, 2007. It has since been converted into apartments, so someone is living in the room where Margaret Wycherly died.

38. www.findagrave.com.

39. Hedda Hopper, "In Hollywood," *Newark Advocate and American Tribune* (May 14, 1949), p. 4.

Blanche Yurka

1. "United States Census, 1900," index and images, *FamilySearch* (https://familysearch.org/pal:/MM9.1.1/M93X-1Y7: accessed 11 January 2015), Caroline Jurka in household of Anton Jurka, Election District 6 St. Paul city Ward 5, Ramsey, Minnesota, United States; citing sheet 3A, family 52, NARA microfilm publication T623, National Archives and Records Administration, Washington, D.C.; FHL microfilm 1,240,784; Blanche Yurka, *Bohemian Girl: Blanche Yurka's Theatrical Life*. Athens: Ohio University Press, 1970, p. 3.

2. Yurka, p. 3.

3. *Cedar Rapids Evening Gazette* (August 26, 1910), p. 8.

4. "United States Census, 1900," index and images, *FamilySearch* (https://familysearch.org/pal:/MM9.1.1/MSKX-TJR: accessed 10 January 2015), Anton Jurka in household of Peter Larkin, Borough of Manhattan, Election District 19 New York City Ward 26, New York County, New York, United States; citing sheet 3B, family 57, NARA microfilm publication T623, National Archives and Records Administration, Washington, D.C.; FHL microfilm 1,241,113; Yurka, *Bohemian Girl*, pp. 25–26.

5. "United States Civil War Soldiers Index, 1861–1865," index, *FamilySearch* (https://familysearch.org/pal:/MM9.1.1/FSWV-Q3T: accessed 11 January 2015), Alois Uher, 1861–1865; citing military unit 24th Regiment, Illinois Infantry, Soldier Union, NARA microfilm publication M539, roll 92, multiple microfilm publications, National Archives and Records Administration, Washington, D.C.; FHL microfilm 881,712; "United States Census, 1870," index and images, *FamilySearch* (https://familysearch.org/pal:/MM9.1.1/M645-MTK: accessed 11 January 2015), Charlotte Uher in household of Hlaise [sic] Uher, Illinois, United States; citing p. 82, family 680, NARA microfilm publication M593, National Archives and Records Administration, Washington, D.C.; FHL microfilm 545,703; Yurka, *Bohemian Girl*, pp. 25–26. Yurka does not name her mother's first husband, but I have been able to identify him using U.S. census information.

6. "United States Census, 1900," Mildred Jurka in household of Anton Jurka.

7. Yurka, *Bohemian Girl*, p. 26.

8. "United States Census, 1880," database with images, *FamilySearch* (https://familysearch.org/ark:/61903/1:1:MXNL-2KH: accessed 3 February 2016), Charlotte Uher in household of Joseph Nowak, Chicago, Cook, Illinois, United States; citing enumeration district ED 68, sheet 103B, NARA microfilm publication T9 (Washington, D.C.: National Archives and Records Administration, n.d.), roll 0190; FHL microfilm 1,254,190.

9. "Illinois, Cook County Deaths, 1878–1994," database, *FamilySearch* (https://familysearch.org/ark:/61903/1:1:N7N4-453: accessed 3 February 2016), Alois Uher, 02 Jan 1883; citing, Cook, Illinois, United States, source reference 15151, record number 39, Cook County Courthouse, Chicago; FHL microfilm 1,031,445; Yurka, *Bohemian Girl*, p. 26. Alois Uher is buried in the Bohemian National Cemetery in Chicago, IL (www.findagrave.com). Yurka only learned of her mother's first marriage and divorce when she was in her late teens. Growing up, she had no idea that Mila was only her half-sister. See Yurka, *Bohemian Girl*, p. 6, 25–26.

10. "United States Census, 1880," index and images, *FamilySearch* (https://familysearch.org/pal:/MM9.1.1/MZ9K-Y3V: accessed 11 January 2015), Anthony Jurka in household of Peter Mclean, St. Paul, Ramsey, Minnesota, United States; citing enumeration district 10, sheet 221D, NARA microfilm publication T9 (Washington, D.C.: National Archives and Records Administration, n.d.), roll 0630; FHL microfilm 1,254,630.

11. "Minnesota, Marriages, 1849–1950," index, *Family Search* (https://familysearch.org/pal:/MM9.1.1/FDF9-L3P: accessed 11 January 2015), Anthony Jurka and Carolina Uher, 10 Apr 1882; citing FHL microfilm 1,314,550.

12. There is a picture of the house facing p. 84 of Yurka's autobiography and the address is given. "United States Census, 1900," Blanch [sic] Jurka in household of Anton Jurka; Yurka, *Bohemian Girl*, p. 6.

13. "New York, New York Passenger and Crew Lists, 1909, 1925–1957," index and images, *FamilySearch* (https://familysearch.org/pal:/MM9.1.1/KXLB-9D6: accessed 11 January 2015), Rose A Jurka, 1927; citing Immigration, New York, New York, United States, NARA microfilm publication T715, National Archives and Records

Administration, Washington, D.C.; FHL microfilm 1,755,862.

14. "Minnesota, Death Records, 1866–1916," index, *FamilySearch* (https://familysearch.org/pal:/MM9.1.1/XP6B-X2N: accessed 11 January 2015), Charles Jurka, 30 Jul 1884; citing Saint Paul, Ramsey, Minnesota, United States, Public Health Center, St. Paul; FHL microfilm 1,309,042. This is actually a birth record.

15. "United States Social Security Death Index," index, *FamilySearch* (https://familysearch.org/pal:/MM9.1.1/VSNV-J22: accessed 11 January 2015), Blanche Yurka, Jun 1974; citing U.S. Social Security Administration, *Death Master File*, database (Alexandria, Virginia: National Technical Information Service, ongoing). Yurka herself pretended during most of her career to have been born in 1893. Some sources mistakenly claim she was born in Bohemia.

16. "Minnesota, Births and Christenings, 1840–1980," index, *FamilySearch* (https://familysearch.org/pal:/MM9.1.1/FD9J-2ZP: accessed 11 January 2015), Anton Jurka in entry for Jurka, 30 Jul 1891; citing Saint Paul, Ramsey, Minnesota, reference; FHL microfilm 1,309,124.

17. Yurka, *Bohemian Girl*, p. 27. She appears as part of the Jurka family in the 1885 Minnesota State Census though. See "Minnesota, State Census, 1885," index and images, *FamilySearch* (https://familysearch.org/pal:/MM9.1.1/MQFZ-CDC: accessed 10 January 2015), Melida Jurka in household of Anthony Jurka, St Paul Ward 04, Ramsey, Minnesota; citing p. 7, volume 4 Ward, State Library and Records Service, St. Paul; FHL microfilm 565,751.

18. Yurka, p. 8.

19. New York, State Census, 1905, index and images, *FamilySearch* (https://familysearch.org/pal:/MM9.1.1/SPN9-9ZJ: accessed 10 January 2015), Blanche J Jurka in household of Anton Jurka, Manhattan, A.D. 28, E.D. 17, New York, New York; citing p., line, county offices, New York.; FHL microfilm; Yurka, *Bohemian Girl*, p. 10.

20. Yurka, *Bohemian Girl*, pp. 10–14; Walter J. Meserve, "Blanche Yurka," *Notable American Women: A Biographical Dictionary* (Cambridge, MA: Belknap Press of Harvard University Press, 1971), Vol. 3, p. 755.

21. Yurka, pp. 15–21; Meserve, p. 755.

22. Yurka, pp. 21–24, 31–32; Meserve, p. 755.

23. Yurka, p. 4, 11, 24.

24. Parker, *Who's Who in the Theatre*, p. 1464; Yurka, p. 49.

25. Parker, p. 1464; Yurka, p. 54; www.ibdb.com.

26. Beyond *Bohemian Girl*, I would recommend the following briefer accounts of Yurka's life and career: Meserve, "Blanche Yurka," pp. 755–56; and Fran Hassencahl, "Blanche Yurka," *Notable Women in the American Theatre: A Biographical Dictionary*, ed. Alice M. Robinson et al. (New York: Greenwood, 1989), pp. 944–47. Mel Schuster, "Blanche Yurka," *Film Fan Monthly* no. 102 (December 1969), pp. 14–18 contains some more of Yurka's memories of her film career.

27. Davis, *The Lonely Life*, pp. 81–82; Yurka, *Bohemian Girl*, pp. 148–49.

28. Ruth Gordon, *Myself Among Others* (New York: Atheneum, 1971), p. 190.

29. Yurka, *Bohemian Girl*, pp. 48–49.

30. This building was replaced long ago by a large, Neo-Romanesque apartment building, but we can guess at its appearance from the surviving row houses next door.

31. Yurka, *Bohemian Girl*, p. 73.

32. Yurka, p. 104.

33. *New York Times* (December 2, 1926), www.nyt.com; Yurka, pp. 116–18.

34. Yurka, pp. 128–29.

35. "United States Census, 1930," index and images, *FamilySearch* (https://familysearch.org/pal:/MM9.1.1/X4GH-N51: accessed 11 January 2015), Charles A Jurka, Pleasantville, Westchester, New York, United States; citing enumeration district (ED) 0188, sheet 6A, family 126, line 33, NARA microfilm publication T626 (Washington, D.C.: National Archives and Records Administration, 2002), roll 1661; FHL microfilm 2,341,395.

36. Yurka, *Bohemian Girl*, pp. 95–96, 105.

37. Yurka, pp. 106–10. Yurka does not name Rambeau in her autobiography, which was published the year Rambeau died, but she is easily identifiable.

38. "Blanche Yurka, Actress, Dead; Rose to Stardom in 'Wild Duck,'" *New York Times* (June 7, 1974), p. 38.

39. Yurka, *Bohemian Girl*, pp. 284–86.

40. Yurka, p. 130.

41. "United States Census, 1930," index and images, *FamilySearch* (https://familysearch.org/pal:/MM9.1.1/X42N-T9M: accessed 12 January 2015), Blanche Jurka in household of Rosa A Jurka, Manhattan (Districts 0501–0750), New York, New York, United States; citing enumeration district (ED) 0672, sheet 5B, family 149, line 88, NARA microfilm publication T626 (Washington, D.C.: National Archives and Records Administration, 2002), roll 1565; FHL microfilm 2,341,300; Yurka, p. 130, 137.

42. Yurka, p. 220.

43. Yurka, p. 226.

44. Yurka, pp. 261–62.

45. "United States Census, 1940," index and images, *FamilySearch* (https://familysearch.org/pal:/MM9.1.1/K9C2-9W9: accessed 12 January 2015), Blanche Yurka, Councilmanic District 2, Los Angeles, Los Angeles Township, Los Angeles, California, United States; citing enumeration district (ED) 60–174, sheet 10B, family 416, NARA digital publication T627 (Washington, D.C.: National Archives and Records Administration, 2012), roll 404; *Los Angeles City Directory 1942* (Los Angeles: Los Angeles Directory, 1942), p. 2645.

46. Yurka, *Bohemian Girl*, pp. 264–67; movieland directory.com. There is a modern apartment building called North Harper House on the site now. Yurka's house on Hayworth Ave. has also been razed.

47. Yurka, p. 270.

48. Brooks Atkinson, "Afterword," *Bohemian Girl: Blanche Yurka's Theatrical Life* by Blanche Yurka (Athens: Ohio University Press, 1970), p. 301.

49. Quoted in Schuster, "Blanche Yurka," p. 14.

50. Yurka, *Bohemian Girl*, p. 226.

51. Quoted in Schuster, "Blanche Yurka," p. 16.

52. Yurka, *Bohemian Girl*, p. 295.

53. *New York Times* (October 11, 1930), www.nyt.com; Yurka, pp. 130–31, 154, 177.

54. "United States Census, 1930," Charles A Jurka.

55. "United States Social Security Death Index," Blanche Yurka, Jun 1974; "Blanche Yurka," *New York Times*, p. 38.

56. www.findagrave.com.

Bibliography

Atkinson, Brooks. "Afterword." *Bohemian Girl: Blanche Yurka's Theatrical Life*. By Blanche Yurka. Athens: Ohio University Press, 1970. 301–2.

Bach, Steven. *Marlene Dietrich: Life and Legend*. New York: William Morrow, 1992.

Barrios, Richard. *Screened Out: Playing Gay in Hollywood from Edison to Stonewall*. New York and London: Routledge, 2003.

Barris, Alex. *Hollywood's Other Women*. South Brunswick: A.S. Barnes, 1975.

Bigwood, Jim. "Norma Varden." *Film Fan Monthly* 165 (1975): 21–30.

Blum, Daniel. *Great Stars of the American Stage: A Pictorial Record*. New York: Greenburg, 1952.

Bodeen, DeWitt. *From Hollywood*. South Brunswick: A.S. Barnes, 1976.

Capra, Frank. *The Name Above the Title*. New York: Vintage, 1985.

Chandler, Charlotte. *The Girl Who Walked Home Alone: Bette Davis—A Personal Biography*. New York: Simon & Schuster, 2006.

Cigliano, Jan. *Showplace of America: Cleveland's Euclid Avenue, 1850–1910*. Kent: Kent State University Press, 1991.

Clinch, Minty. *Cagney: The Story of His Film Career*. London: Proteus Books, 1982.

Cripps, Thomas. *Slow Fade to Black: The Negro in American Film, 1900–1942*. New York: Oxford University Press, 1977.

Crothers, Rachel. *Expressing Willie/Nice People/39 East: Three Plays by Rachel Crothers*. New York: Brentano's, n.d.

Curry, Ramona. *Too Much of a Good Thing: Mae West as Cultural Icon*. Minneapolis: University of Minnesota Press, 1996.

Davis, Bette. *The Lonely Life: An Autobiography*. London: Macdonald, 1963.

Dayton, Katharine, and George S. Kaufman. *First Lady*. New York: Random House, 1935.

Deacon, Desley. "Cosmopolitans at Home: Judith Anderson and the American Aspirations of J.C. Williamson Stock Company Members, 1897–1918." *Impact of the Modern: Vernacular Modernities in Australia 1870s to 1960s*. Ed. Robert Dixon and Veronica Kelly. Sydney: Sydney University Press, 2008. 202–22.

Dickens, Homer. *The Films of James Cagney*. Secaucus: The Citadel Press, 1972.

Dietrich, Marlene. *Marlene*. Trans. Salvator Attanasio. New York: Avon Books, 1990.

Dunning, John. *On the Air: The Encyclopedia of Old-Time Radio*. New York: Oxford University Press, 1998.

Eels, George, and Stanley Musgrove. *Mae West: A Biography*. New York: William Morrow, 1982.

Egan, Michael, ed. *The Critical Heritage: Henrik Ibsen*. London: Routledge, 1999.

Gänzl, Kurt. *Lydia Thompson: Queen of Burlesque*. New York: Routledge, 2002.

Gill, Brendan. *Tallulah*. New York: Holt, Rinehart, and Winston, 1972.

Gordon, Ruth. *Myself Among Others*. New York: Atheneum, 1971.

Granger, Farley, with Robert Calhoun. *Include Me Out: My Life from Goldwyn to Broadway*. New York: St. Martin's Press, 2007.

Grossman, Barbara Wallace. *A Spectacle of Suffering: Clara Morris on the American Stage*. Carbondale: Southern Illinois University Press, 2009.

Hadleigh, Boze. *Conversations with My Elders*. New York: St. Martin's Press, 1986.

Harris, Robert A,. and Michael S. Lasky. *The Films of Alfred Hitchcock*. Secaucus: The Citadel Press, 1976.

Hassencahl, Fran. "Blanche Yurka." *Notable Women in the American Theatre: A Biographical Dictionary*. Ed. Alice M. Robinson et al. New York: Greenwood, 1989. 944–47.

Howard, Sidney. "Alien Corn." *The Best Plays of 1932–33*. Ed. Burns Mantle. New York: Dodd, Mead, 1933. 205–37.

Hoxie, Elizabeth F. "Effie Ellsler." *Notable American Women: A Biographical Dictionary, 1607–1950*. Ed. Edward T. James. Cambridge: Belknap Press of Harvard University Press, 1971. Vol. 1. 579–80.

Hughes, Langston. "Mulatto." *Three Negro Plays*. Harmondsworth: Penguin, 1969. 19–61.

Jacobs, Diane. *Christmas in July: The Life and Art of Preston Sturges*. Berkeley: University of California Press, 1992.

Lambert, Gavin. *GWTW: The Making of Gone with the Wind*. Boston: Little, Brown, 1973.

______. *Nazimova: A Biography*. New York: Alfred A. Knopf, 1997.

Laurents, Arthur. *Original Story By: A Memoir of Broadway and Hollywood*. New York: Applause, 2000.

Leaming, Barbara. *Bette Davis*. London: Orion, 1992.

Leider, Emily Wortis. *Becoming Mae West*. New York: Da Capo Press, 2000.

Lobenthal, Joel. *Tallulah: The Life and Times of a Leading Lady*. New York: HarperCollins, 2004.

Logan, Joshua. *Josh: My Up and Down, In and Out Life*. New York: Delacorte Press, 1976.

McClelland, Doug. "The Unsung Heroes: Rosiland [sic] Ivan." *Film Fan Monthly* 80 (1968): 17–19.

MacKaye, Steele. "Hazel Kirke." *Representative American Plays from 1767 to the Present Day*. Ed. Arthur Hobson Quinn. New York: Appleton-Century-Crofts, 1953. 433–71.

Madsen, Axel. *The Sewing Circle: Sappho's Leading Ladies*. New York: Kensington Books, 2002.

Mantle, Burns. *The Best Plays of 1929–30*. New York: Dodd, Mead, 1969.

______. *The Best Plays of 1930–31*. New York: Dodd, Mead, 1931.

______. *The Best Plays of 1935–36*. New York: Dodd, Mead, 1936.

______. *The Best Plays of 1936–37*. New York: Dodd, Mead, 1937.

______. *The Best Plays of 1937–38*. New York: Dodd, Mead, 1938.

______. *The Best Plays of 1938–39*. New York: Dodd, Mead, 1939.

______. *The Best Plays of 1939–40*. New York: Dodd, Mead, 1966.

______. *The Best Plays of 1940–41*. New York: Dodd Mead, 1949.

Meserve, Walter J. "Blanche Yurka." *Notable American Women: A Biographical Dictionary*. Cambridge: Belknap Press of Harvard University Press, 1971. Vol. 3. 754–56.

Meyers, Jeffrey. *Gary Cooper: American Hero*. New York: William Morrow, 1998.

Nissen, Axel. *Actresses of a Certain Character: Forty Familiar Hollywood Faces from the Thirties to the Fifties*. Jefferson, NC: McFarland, 2007.

______. *The Films of Agnes Moorehead*. Lanham, MD: Scarecrow Press, 2013.

______. *Mothers, Mammies and Old Maids: Twenty-Five Character Actresses of Golden Age Hollywood*. Jefferson, NC: McFarland, 2012.

Nye, Peter Joffre. *The Fast Times of Albert Champion*. Amherst: Prometheus Books, 2014.

Parish, James Robert. *Hollywood Character Actors*. New Rochelle: Arlington House, 1978.

Parish, James Robert, and Ronald L. Bowers. *The MGM Stock Company: The Golden Era*. New York: Bonanza Books, 1972.

Parker, John. *Who's Who in the Theatre: A Biographical Record of the Contemporary Stage*. 7th ed. London: Pitman, 1933.

Peters, Margot. *The House of Barrymore*. New York: Alfred A. Knopf, 1990.

Quinlan, David. *Quinlan's Character Stars*. London: Reynolds and Hearn, 2004.

Ragan, David. *Who's Who in Hollywood, 1900–1976*. New Rochelle: Arlington House, 1977.

Roen, Paul. *High Camp: A Guide to Camp and Cult Films, Vol. 1*. San Francisco: Leyland, 1994.

Schuster, Mel. "Blanche Yurka." *Film Fan Monthly* 102 (1969): 14–18.

Shaw, Bernard. *Man and Superman: A Comedy and a Philosophy*. Harmondsworth: Penguin, 1971.

Sikov, Ed. *Dark Victory: The Life of Bette Davis*. New York: Henry Holt, 2007.

Springer, John, and Jack Hamilton. *They Had Faces Then: Super Stars, Stars and Starlets of the 1930's*. N.p.: Castle, 1974.

Stanke, Don. "Connie Gilchrist: A Lady of Many Parts." *Films in Review* 3 (1974): 151–64.

Strang, Lewis C. *Famous Actresses of the Day in America: Second Series*. Boston: L.C. Page, 1902.

Stumpf, Charles. *Zasu Pitts: The Life and Career*. Jefferson, NC: McFarland, 2010.

Sturges, Preston. *Preston Sturges by Preston Sturges*. New York: Simon & Schuster, 1990.

Watts, Jill. *Mae West: An Icon in Black and White*. Oxford: Oxford University Press, 2001.

Williams, Emlyn. *The Corn Is Green*. New York: Dramatists Play Service, 1945.

Williams, Tennessee. *The Selected Letters of Tennessee Williams: Vol. II, 1945–1957*. Ed. Albert J. Devlin. New York: New Directions, 2004.

Wolfson, Victor. "Excursion." *The Best Plays of 1936–37*. Ed. Burns Mantle. New York: Dodd, Mead, 1937. 328–56.

Yurka, Blanche. *Bohemian Girl: Blanche Yurka's Theatrical Life*. Athens: Ohio University Press, 1970.

Index

Page numbers in ***bold italics*** indicate pages with illustrations.

www.ingramcontent.com/pod-product-compliance
Ingram Content Group UK Ltd.
Pitfield, Milton Keynes, MK11 3LW, UK
UKHW060611180726
13836UKWH00012B/2511